Northrop Frye

Northrop Frye is one of the great critics of the twentieth century. *Anatomy of Criticism* (1957) transformed literary theory, and his contributions to Blake studies, theories of aesthetics, theology and social criticism have ensured his place at the centre of cultural studies. His belief that ideology is pervasive, and that mythology is related to ideology and can also oppose it, has placed Frye's work at the centre of what is one of the most important contemporary theoretical debates: the relation between myth and ideology, between narrative and imagination.

This book looks at the sweep of Frye's career, incorporating archival material as well as his published work, and will be invaluable both as an introduction to Frye as well as for more advanced studies of his work.

Jonathan Hart is Associate Professor of English and Adjunct Professor of Comparative Literature at the University of Alberta. He is Contributing Editor of the *Canadian Review of Comparative Literature* and author of *Theater and the World: the Problematics of Shakespeare's Histories*.

CRITICS OF THE TWENTIETH CENTURY
General Editor: Christopher Norris,
University of Wales, College of Cardiff

A. J. GREIMAS AND THE NATURE OF MEANING
Ronald Schleifer

CHRISTOPHER CAUDWELL
Robert Sullivan

FIGURING LACAN
Criticism and the Cultural Unconscious
Juliet Flower MacCannell

HAROLD BLOOM
Towards Historical Rhetorics
Peter de Bolla

JULIA KRISTEVA
John Lechte

GEOFFREY HARTMAN
Criticism as Answerable Style
G. Douglas Atkins

INTRODUCING LYOTARD
Art and Politics
Bill Reading

EZRA POUND AS LITERARY CRITIC
K. K. Ruthven

F. R. LEAVIS
Michael Bell

DELEUZE AND GUATTARI
Ronald Bogue

POSTMODERN BRECHT
A Re-Presentation
Elizabeth Wright

THE ECSTACIES OF ROLAND BARTHES
Mary Bittner Wiseman

PAUL RICŒUR
S. H. Clark

JÜRGEN HABERMAS
Critic in the Public Sphere
Robert C. Holub

WILLIAM EMPSON
Prophet Against Sacrifice
Paul H. Fry

ANTONIO GRAMSCI
Beyond Marxism and Postmodernism
Renate Holub

KENNETH BURKE
Rhetoric and Ideology
Stephen Bygrave

ROMAN JAKOBSON
Life, Language, Art
Richard Bradford

Northrop Frye

The theoretical imagination

Jonathan Hart

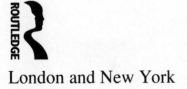

London and New York

First published 1994
by Routledge
11 New Fetter Lane, London EC4P 4EE

Simultaneously published in the USA and Canada
by Routledge
29 West 35th Street, New York, NY 10001

© 1994 Jonathan Hart

Typeset in Times by
Ponting–Green Publishing Services, Chesham, Bucks

Printed and bound in Great Britain by
T.J. Press (Padstow) Ltd, Padstow, Cornwall

British Library Cataloguing in Publication Data
A catalogue record for this book is available from the
British Library.

Library of Congress Cataloging in Publication Data
Hart, Jonathan Locke, 1956–
    Northrop Frye: the theoretical imagination/Jonathan Hart.
    p. cm. – (Critics of the twentieth century)
    Includes bibliographical references and index.
    1. Frye, Northrop. 2. Literature–History and
    criticism–Theory, etc. 3. Criticism–Canada–History–20th
    century. I. Title. II. Series: Critics of the twentieth century
    (London, England)
    PN75.F7H37   1994
    801.95'092–dc20
                                                    93–28764
                                                    CIP
ISBN 0–415–07536–X (hbk)   0–415–07537–8 (pbk)

For George Edward Hart and
Jean MacLean Jackman Hart

Besides, there must have been times when even the noble and pure-hearted Sir Galahad said, 'Bugger the grail'.

(Northrop Frye, Criticism and Society, 1987)

Contents

Editor's foreword   viii
Preface   xii

1 **The theoretical imagination**   1
2 **Reconstructing Blake**   25
3 **Reconstructing criticism**   56
4 ***The Great Code***   109
5 **History**   143
6 **On education**   164
7 **Mythology and ideology**   191
8 **A visionary criticism**   243
9 **The critic as writer**   266
10 **The power of words**   296

Appendix   306
References   307
Index   324

Editor's foreword

The twentieth century has produced a remarkable number of gifted and innovative literary critics. Indeed it could be argued that some of the finest literary minds of the age have turned to criticism as the medium best adapted to their complex and speculative range of interests. This has sometimes given rise to regret among those who insist on a clear demarcation between 'creative' (primary) writing on the one hand, and 'critical' (secondary) texts on the other. Yet this distinction is far from self-evident. It is coming under strain at the moment as novelists and poets grow increasingly aware of the conventions that govern their writing and the challenge of consciously exploiting and subverting those conventions. And the critics for their part – some of them at least – are beginning to question their traditional role as humble servants of the literary text with no further claim upon the reader's interest or attention. Quite simply, there are texts of literary criticism and theory that, for various reasons – stylistic complexity, historical influence, range of intellectual command – cannot be counted a mere appendage to those other 'primary' texts.

Of course, there is a logical puzzle here since (it will be argued) 'literary criticism' would never have come into being, and could hardly exist as such, were it not for the body of creative writings that provide its *raison d'être*. But this is not quite the kind of knock-down argument that it might appear at first glance. For one thing, it conflates some very different orders of priority, assuming that literature always comes first (in the sense that Greek tragedy had to exist before Aristotle could formulate its rules), so that literary texts are for that very reason possessed of superior value. And this argument would seem to find commonsense support in the difficulty of thinking what 'literary criticism' could *be* if it seriously renounced all sense of the distinction between literary and critical texts. Would it not then find itself in the unfortunate position of a discipline that had willed its own demise by declaring its subject non-existent?

But these objections would only hit their mark if there were indeed a special kind of writing called 'literature' whose difference from other kinds of writing was enough to put criticism firmly in its place. Otherwise there is nothing in the least self-defeating or paradoxical about a discourse, nominally that of literary criticism, that accrues such interest on its own account as to force some fairly drastic rethinking of its proper powers and limits. The act of crossing over from commentary to literature – or of simply denying the difference between them – becomes quite explicit in the writing of a critic like Geoffrey Hartman. But the signs are already there in such classics as William Empson's *Seven Types of Ambiguity* (1928), a text whose transformative influence on our habits of reading must surely be ranked with the great creative moments of literary modernism. Only on the most dogmatic view of the difference between 'literature' and 'criticism' could a work like *Seven Types* be counted generically an inferior, sub-literary species of production. And the same can be said for many of the critics (including Northrop Frye, subject of the present volume) whose writings and influence this series sets out to explore.

Some, like Empson, are conspicuous individuals who belong to no particular school or larger movement. Others, like the Russian Formalists, were part of a communal enterprise and are therefore best understood as representative figures in a complex and evolving dialogue. Then again there are cases of collective identity (like the so-called 'Yale deconstructors') where a mythical group image is invented for largely polemical purposes. (The volumes in this series on Hartman and Bloom should help to dispel the idea that 'Yale deconstruction' is anything more than a handy device for collapsing differences and avoiding serious debate.) So there is no question of a series format or house-style that would seek to reduce these differences to a blandly homogeneous treatment. One consequence of recent critical theory is the realization that literary texts have no self-sufficient or autonomous meaning, no existence apart from their after-life of changing interpretations and values. And the same applies to those *critical* texts whose meaning and significance are subject to constant shifts and realignments of interest. This is not to say that trends in criticism are just a matter of intellectual fashion or the merry-go-round of rising and falling reputations. But it is important to grasp how complex are the forces – the conjunctions of historical and cultural motive – that affect the first reception and the subsequent fortunes of a critical text. This point has been raised into a systematic programme by critics like Hans-Robert

Jauss, practitioners of so-called 'reception theory' as a form of historical hermeneutics. The volumes in this series will therefore be concerned not only to expound what is of lasting significance but also to set these critics in the context of present-day argument and debate. In some cases (as with Walter Benjamin) this debate takes the form of a struggle for interpretative power among disciplines with sharply opposed ideological viewpoints. Such controversies cannot simply be ignored in the interests of achieving a clear and balanced account. They point to unresolved tensions and problems which are there in the critic's work as well as in the rival appropriative readings. In the end there is no way of drawing a neat methodological line between 'intrinsic' questions (what the critic really thought) and those other, supposedly 'extrinsic' concerns that have to do with influence and reception history.

The volumes will vary accordingly in their focus and range of coverage. They will also reflect the ways in which a speculative approach to questions of literary theory has proved to have striking consequences for the human sciences at large. This breaking-down of disciplinary bounds is among the most significant developments in recent critical thinking. As philosophers and historians, among others, come to recognize the rhetorical complexity of the texts they deal with, so literary theory takes on a new dimension of interest and relevance. It is scarcely appropriate to think of a writer like Derrida as practising 'literary criticism' in any conventional sense of the term. For one thing, he is as much concerned with 'philosophical' as with 'literary' texts, and has indeed actively sought to subvert (or deconstruct) such tidy distinctions. A principal object in planning this series was to take full stock of these shifts in the wider intellectual terrain (including the frequent boundary disputes) brought about by critical theory. And, of course, such changes are by no means confined to literary studies, philosophy and the so-called 'sciences of man'. It is equally the case in (say) nuclear physics and molecular biology that advances in the one field have decisive implications for the other, so that specialized research often tends (paradoxically) to break down existing divisions of intellectual labour. Such work is typically many years ahead of the academic disciplines and teaching institutions that have obvious reasons of their own for adopting a business-as-usual attitude. One important aspect of modern critical theory is the challenge it presents to these traditional ideas. And lest it be thought that this is merely a one-sided takeover bid by literary critics, the series will include a number of volumes by authors in those other disciplines, including, for instance, a study of Roland Barthes by an American 'post-analytic' philosopher.

We shall not, however, cleave to theory as a matter of polemical or principled stance. The series will extend to figures like F. R. Leavis, whose widespread influence went along with an express aversion to literary theory; scholars like Erich Auerbach in the mainstream European tradition; and others who resist assimilation to any clear-cut line of descent. Then again there are volumes, like this on Frye, which remind us how great has been the achievement and the influence of thinkers whose work is too often consigned to some convenient slot (e.g. 'mythological criticism') in the history of quick-change cultural fashion. It is hard to imagine that work better served than by Jonathan Hart's eloquently argued and impressively wide-ranging study. Above all his book – like others in the series – strives to resist that current polarization of attitudes that sees no common ground of interest between 'literary criticism' and 'critical theory'.

Christopher Norris

Preface

Although writing a book is in one sense a solitary matter, it is in another a shared experience, not simply for readers but for the people who ask about it, who offer a forgotten book or article or take interest in what seems to have become a fascinating but private wall of words. Above all, I thank Christopher Norris, the editor of the series, who on one of our walks turned my attention from the book on Michel Foucault we had in mind to a study of my former teacher, Northrop Frye. Christopher Norris has shown personal and intellectual generosity: his dedication to ideas and to their reaching as wide an audience as possible, without compromise, is well known. Frye's life as a critic and a writer served as an example, to remind me of the reason I chose to begin writing long ago and, later, to train as a critic and teacher, to bring before me once again how easy it is to get lost on the way, to listen to the cacophony of fascinating voices beckoning in all directions at once. In writing this book, without making an allegory of it, I am not implying that I was lost in the Slough of Despond and have seen the grail or the light, but that the book helped me to understand one of my teachers and a critic who has helped to shape criticism in English, and consequently, to reconsider the role of teacher, critic and writer. By writing the book, I remembered why I came to literature. What strikes me as unfortunate among some theorists today is that they have turned their backs on literature, are ashamed that it isn't politics or something else, and show no joy or terror before literary texts. It seems to me that literature is critical and criticism is literary, that the two read each other, so that Frye's declaration of independence for criticism in 1957 has, as he said a few years ago, been taken too far. There will be a swing back to literature in its ever-shifting configurations. I hope this swing is informed by the vigorous theoretical work of the past few decades and does not appear as muzzy-headed, quasi-religious intuitions, the return of the 'gentleman's' taste or the public censor's hardline pronouncements about morality or the ins and outs.

My hope is that this book is a fitting response to Frye's work. Although I was one of his many students, I was an admirer but never a disciple. The more I worked on the study, the more I admired Frye, but admiration should not be hagiography. I hope that I have neither praised nor criticized Frye too much but have responded to his work according to its merit. My one regret is that I never had the chance to interview Northrop Frye, to ask him questions, especially about the places I cannot quite follow him, to see how much in those areas I have misunderstood him, or simply have to admit difference and even dissent. He died a few months after I agreed to write this book. If I wish to avoid hagiography, I also hope to avoid carpography. It is too easy to debunk.

The goal of my book, realizing the evanescent nature of the telos, is to be fair and just to Frye, to explore his work, especially in the late phase (the past decade or so), so that he can be understood in all his variety. To know Northrop Frye simply as the author of *Anatomy of Criticism* is to know a good deal about a great work, but it is not to know the Frye who did so much for our understanding of William Blake while formulating his own critical theory; who expanded our understanding of Shakespeare, particularly of his comedies and romances; who influenced Spenser studies; who wrote accomplished criticism on the moderns; who helped so much to develop a criticism and theory of Canadian literature; who embraced and practised Comparative Literature; who dedicated much of his writing to teaching, the humanities and the theory of education; who was fascinated with ideology and vision; who returned to the Bible as a cultural document over and over again. Even those who fasten on *Anatomy* often neglect the polemical nature of the work, the fluid, sliding scale of Frye's schemata, and the historical nature of the book, particularly of its 'Tentative Conclusion'. The more one reads Frye, the more one realizes that he has produced a varied body of work, the way Aristotle or Shakespeare has. In his incarnation as a genre critic, he has produced work in many genres, including the fable, the short story, the sermon, the parable, the anatomy, the essay, the lecture and the metaphysical system (full of metaphorical language and aphorisms). Frye is one of those writers we can return to and find more than we found the first time. If value judgements can be pardoned (Frye did not want to abolish them but only to make them secondary and to point out their tendency to embarrass us before posterity), this capacity to accommodate repeated readings is the mark, putting the constructedness of human reality aside for the moment, of a great writer. This is a personal statement, but, like Frye, I think that we pass from the subjective and personal through the objective and impersonal only to find that we are in a new or renewed state of subjectivity and person-ality. Here, I have substituted the word 'writer' for 'critic' or 'theorist' not because I wish to exclude his contributions to criticism and theory but because I want to recognize that Frye has created or constructed a metaphorical and mythical world about fictions that possesses a certain identity with fictional worlds. Frye is a stylist who writes about style, who writes poetically about poetics. As a writer, a term that includes 'critic' and 'theorist', Frye creates his own cosmology, his own imaginative terrain.

Rather than make this study into another explication of *Anatomy*, I have tried to present the many Northrop Fryes. I have also emphasized the last works on the Bible, not because I have any interest in fundamentalism, evangelism and theocracy (but neither, as far as I can see, did Frye), but because it is parochial for many of the critics and theorists today, some of whom are arguing against the Enlightenment, to embrace the anti-clerical attitudes of the Enlightenment and displace them on the literary and cultural document of the Bible, which also happens to be a sacred book. To neglect the Bible is to neglect a large part of our history. Frye may have overstated his argument for the centrality of the Bible because of the intellectual climate in which he found himself. He obviously knew his Plato, Aristotle, Sophocles, Plautus and Cicero, and *Anatomy* is quite classical and secular. It is equally foolish to forget the classical contributions to genre and to our philosophical and literary educations, especially where we are seeking different or divergent ways from our classical antecedents. Since the Renaissance, there have been various debates over the status of ancients and moderns, even as what was once modernity recedes repeatedly from the next generation, and few would argue that the Greeks and Romans thought and wrote all that we need for today and tomorrow. Frye does not negate classicism and modernity but only places them beside the biblical tradition. He implies that although many of us, myself included, would consciously deny the wide-spread influence that he attributes to the Bible in our time, we cannot unconsciously and historically help being influenced by the Christian scriptures, and we inhabit institutions that grew out of the churches that interpreted it. He reminds us of the very structures it gave to our vernacular languages, to discourse, to literary allusions and forms, and to Western societies themselves. Frye thinks, and I agree with him here, that it is folly to forget our literary history in a period where many of us are proclaiming the importance of history to literary and cultural studies.

Why read Frye? If I haven't already given enough reasons, I hope this book will provide more. Frye said he did not want disciples. No matter how much we are within a system, I think that we should attempt to be free and independent. It is not self-evident to me that being a subject and being an individual are mutually exclusive, just as we are biologically unique, as our genetic fingerprints attest, and are also part of the species *homo sapiens*. I'm afraid that no one has convinced me that the old debate on free will and determinism, now displaced in a different historical context into the debate on agency and the human subject, has been resolved in favour of either term. In keeping with my general theory of literature and criticism I think that the energy, disjunction and tension between freedom and necessity is where we read, act and live, even if for a moment in the identities of metaphor and fiction we erase those identities in our imaginations. *Au fait*, which Voltaire took for his motto: Frye is a good antidote to many students and younger scholars who find themselves in the gripping excitement of the critical turmoil of the past two or three decades, which seems to be ever more intensified. There is such a thing as fashion, which can show wit or elegance and gives pleasure, and anxiety (its extreme form being hysteria), which can never come to any good.

It does little good to be in a 'school' and follow leaders. This strategy may bring gratification and promotion, but it rarely brings achievement. To admire and to learn from someone is one thing; to mime and flatter is another. Frye is not on the lips of most of my students, but his work is too substantial to be left to neglect. The dead have a way of 'haunting' the present. I have no more interest in the stock market of reputations among critics than Frye had in a similar market for writers. The ranking that Leavis and Eliot liked is something we do and can study in terms of history, politics, philosophy and sociology, but it is not my particular interest. Canonization cannot be neglected, but it is the writers people want to leave off the lists but who cannot be ignored for long who make such canon-formation interesting yet not absolutely contingent or controlled by intention. I don't think that a crash in someone's stock, which seems inevitable for a time for most 'writers', tells us much about why good writers are neglected. Derrida will deserve to be read after the current excitement over his work has abated. To neglect Frye is to neglect one's education.

A study of poetics is returning and will return. Frye is the great modern theorist of poetics. He wants integrity for literature and for criticism as a discipline. Like Sidney, Shelley and others, his criticism is a declaration of independence for poetry. Like them, he realizes that poetry, or literature, is of and for this world, but that just because it isn't as readily distinguishable from another discourse doesn't mean that one cannot differentiate it from philosophy. Frye argues for an integrity for literature that goes far beyond Sidney's public statements in *Apologie for Poetrie*. Perhaps we have swung too far in taking the commonplace that it is notoriously difficult to say what literature is and making that difficulty or impossibility into an excuse to make literature secondary to history, politics, psychology, ideology or something else, or, conversely, to swallow all these disciplines whole in the imperial discipline, rhetoric or semiotic of critical theory or what used to be known in English as criticism.

In the current debate over ideology, we need to imagine possible or fictional worlds beyond or detached from the ideological, not because it is actually possible to get beyond it and not because we want a reactionary or pastoral neglect or ignorance of our politics or the suffering of others, but because we need to think more clearly about ideology precisely to face our situation. If ideology is everything and everywhere, then how do we make distinctions? The same may be true if God, or whatever term, is made to be all things. Frye may also have something to tell us about the return of the repressed – of the Bible in literary studies. I still think that although recent theories have helped to correct too great a faith in language and its ability to communicate, it is possible, with difficulty, to attempt to understand another writer or person and to communicate that understanding to others. I have tried to understand Frye's work and to communicate his ideas to others. That is the primary goal of this book. I have subtitled the book *The Theoretical Imagination* because in *Anatomy* Frye built his theory, one of the greatest metacritical accomplishments in literary criticism in English, on the imagination of William Blake and because Frye is a cosmologist and unites theory and imagination at the centre of his work. Frye's great code is based on Blake's, which is based on the Bible's.

My thanks to Jane Widdicombe, who, for years, was Northrop Frye's secretary. As usual she has been generous. Most recently, she has shared her knowledge of Frye and of his papers, of which she is the literary executor. I also thank Robert D. Denham, who has done so much to make writing on Frye easier, for his advice on the Frye papers in the E. J. Pratt Library at Victoria University in the University of Toronto. Eva Kushner, President of Victoria University (Toronto), has been generous in her interest in and support of this project. My thanks also to Robert Brandeis, chief librarian, and Ann Black and Delores Signori at that library for their concern and gracious assistance and to Eugene Olson at Rutherford Library, University of Alberta, for his interest in and help with bibliographical matters; to Margaret Drummond for her help, especially for discussing her work on Attis with me. I thank friends and colleagues who have taken a particular interest in this book and in Northrop Frye more generally: Ross Chambers, Harry Levin, Brian Parker and Robert Rawdon Wilson, all of whom will recognize their guiding spirits in different chapters. Once again, I would like to express gratitude to the Department of English and American Literature and Language at Harvard for giving me the opportunity to be a visitor, and especially to Barbara Johnson. Thanks are also due to David Gay and Garry Sherbert, whose work is imbued with Frye's theory and criticism and who suffered my conversations on Frye in hallways and offices. My thanks to those who, in addition to those I have mentioned above, have generally encouraged and supported my work with generosity: Catherine Belsey, Milan Dimić, G. Blakemore Evans and Margaret Ferguson. My research assistants, Len Falkenstein and Sharon Howe, have given me the kind of assistance that is too often unnamed in our profession: to them, my thanks. To Lynda Schultz and Adele Fors and the administration and general office of the Department of English, I extend my thanks for their help with computers and with the styling of the typescript. The hospitality of Alfred and Sally Alcorn made it more pleasurable to put the finishing touches on the typescript. Above all, I thank my family for their support. My parents, to whom this book is dedicated in the year of their fiftieth anniversary, have been inspiring teachers from the very start. My wife, Mary, and our children, James and Julia, are part of a silent dedication. My present gratitude to them is also deferred for future thanks. There is not space enough to thank many others for their support.

To more institutional matters: I thank the Faculty of Arts at the University of Alberta for course relief, the Social Science and Humanities Council of Canada (SSHRCC) for a grant that helped me to complete this book and go back to the next one, the Department of English and the Department of Comparative Literature for supporting my work, my co-editors at the *Canadian Review of Comparative Literature/Revue Canadienne de Littérature Comparée*, who have been generous and helpful in administrative and intellectual matters, the Canadian Association of Comparative Literature and the Association of Canadian University and College Teachers of English for having me speak to their joint session in May 1991, and to Alvin Lee and the organizers of 'The Legacy of Northrop Frye', a conference held at Victoria College in October 1992, for inviting me to speak there (where I gave the paper 'The Enduring Frye: Why a Theorist Need Not Pass into Literary History'). I also thank the following publishers and journals and their editors for giving me permission to include work that appears in other versions or is related to work in the book. Thanks, in chronological order, to the following editors and journals for inviting essays and for publishing them: Eva-Marie Kröller, for 'Northrop Frye and the 1960s', published by the University of Toronto Press; the *Canadian Review of Comparative Literature*, for 'Frye's Anatomizing and Anatomizing Frye'; Robert Snyder, editor of *Christianity and Literature*, for 'The Mystical-Visionary Criticism of Northrop Frye'; and Rajnath, editor of the *Journal of Literary Criticism*, for 'Educating the Imagination: The General Principles of Northrop Frye's Criticism'. Finally, it is my pleasure to thank Janice Price, Managing Director at Routledge, for taking a personal as well as a professional interest in this and other projects.

Edmonton, Alberta
Belmont, Massachusetts

1 The theoretical imagination

Northrop Frye is one of the greatest critics to have written in English. His work has been translated into many languages round the world. It is no exaggeration to say that he has made an enduring contribution to Western criticism, to an understanding of theory and literature, and to readings of individual authors and texts. Frye is best known for his argument that literature and criticism are each autonomous, by which he means that they are disciplines like any other and should not play secondary and subordinate roles in ideological systems by deferring to science, history, politics, psychology, anthropology, or any other discipline. He wants literary criticism to be scientific, to approach social science, to constitute a method and a body of knowledge. Frye builds his system on the structural principles of mythology but is not simply a myth critic who would subordinate literature to an ur-literature – mythology. He thinks that literature is the most complex and interesting manifestation or translation of mythology and that without literature a study of mythology would become sterile. Conversely, he considers a literary criticism without an understanding of mythology to be, given mythology's historical priority, ahistorical if not anti-historical. Frye admits that ideology is everywhere, but he thinks that mythology is prior to it. Literature and criticism, according to Frye, use myth and metaphor to create an imaginative language that complicates and creates problems for those who think that all discourse is dialectic or argument and that literature and criticism are entirely ideological constructs or historical documents. His understanding of convention and genre has made this blurring of all distinctions, this homogenization of all types or kinds of writing into Writing, difficult to accept. Like Sidney, Milton, Blake, Shelley, he belongs to the radical Protestant tradition that defends poetry but shows social and political concern. Frye resembles Sidney and Shelley in making overt defences of poetry. Even though Frye has been sympathetic to the Commonwealth

Confederation Party (CCF) and to its successor, the New Democratic Party (NDP), which are socially progressive and 'socialist' political parties, and, from about 1948 to 1950, was managing editor of Canada's progressive magazine *Canadian Forum*, he is less enthusiastic about political revolution than Blake and Shelley were ('Ideas' 1990: 12, Cayley: 1991: 29).

Like that of many great writers, Frye's work is various and difficult: to call him a myth critic, or a New Critic, a structuralist or proto-structuralist, or anything else may be helpful to some, but to me they are partial insights. Like Frye, I am not much interested in arguments or labels, although argument and classification are what many of Frye's readers will think about when they think about his work. But Frye's schema in his work on Blake, *Anatomy of Criticism*, and the Bible, the major projects of his life, are fluid and heuristic. He puts into play a dance between theory and imagination, literature and criticism, the Bible and literature, the literary and the social world. He does not retreat from the pressing issues of our time – ideology and language, literary production and politics – but he has his own point of view that may not be that popular among theorists during the 1980s and 1990s, though he shares with them more misgivings, ambivalences and social concerns than younger theorists might like to admit. Although Frye died in Toronto on 23 January 1991 at the age of 78, he will continue to play a role in the theoretical and critical debates for years to come. To think otherwise is to have been blinded by fashion, a myth of progress, or a political agenda. The world has changed and will always change. To embrace change does not mean that we have to forget our cultural past.

We need, as Albert Einstein said, a new way of thinking to survive in an atomic age. While remaking ourselves, we should not throw out all history. Instead, to transform the world and our understanding of literature and criticism, we need to take what is helpful from the past to that end. Frye admits the historical and social roots of black studies, feminism and the ecology movement, all of which he thinks legitimate. They will help in the transformation. Although he initially sympathized with the student movement of the 1960s, particularly in the students' desire to be treated in a more humane way, he came to see it as a movement without deep social roots and disliked what he took to be the fascist tactics of sit-ins and the occupation of buildings as well as a totalitarian and anti-intellectual stance behind these actions ('Ideas' 1990: 12). For Frye, who found so much in the university to transform his life and to free him intellectually, to be anti-intellectual in the only intellectual place in society was inexcusable. It is precisely the ability of the university to transform our thought to meet the changes in the world and in ourselves that prompted Frye to become a leading defender of the university. He admits that the university he envisages is an ideal university, but he uses that ideal as a means of representing the ways we could aspire intellectually and as a society. This is the utopian Frye of the liberal imagination.

Frye always fought fascism. He wrote against it repeatedly from the 1930s and never flagged in his attack on totalitarianism and his advocacy of liberalism and democracy. In 1936, when he was in Cheltenham on his way to Oxford, he had a long conversation with Jackson Knight, who taught classics at Exeter College and was the brother of G. Wilson Knight. Although Frye wrote to his fiancé, Helen Kemp, that 'the Knights are the only people I have met who really speak my language', that is they understood mythology, he admits in a letter to her that he was uneasy about a pro-fascist British poet to whom Jackson Knight had introduced him. In the same letter, Frye says that this poet showed the exaggerated respect for nature, which Frye thinks is part of fascism, that occurs in D. H. Lawrence's *The Plumed Serpent*, and that no matter how clever the pro-fascist poet, 'he represents everything in this world I detest and fear ... when civilization approaches a precipice, there is always a group seized with an instant desire for suicide. That's what the Fascists represent and what he represents' (Ayre 1989: 127). In the August 1940 issue of *Canadian Forum*, Frye contributes an article, 'War on the Cultural Front', in which he defends democracy and attacks fascism:

> A world-state would be therefore a handful of dictators backed up by huge armies of Praetorian guards ready to supply more when they die, ruling over vast slave populations. After criticism has been clubbed, reform machine-gunned, art degraded to the poster and circus, religion to caesar-worship, science to engineering, the surviving slaves would be well-fed and clothed, and nothing could overthrow such a state but an invasion from Mars . . . . In the present war it is our business to disintegrate and disorganize the world state *whatever else happens.*
>
> (Frye 1940; see also Ayre 1989: 170)

Frye also criticizes fascism and Communism as religious or synthetic modes of thought that represent 'efforts of an organized social will to compel human life and science to fit a certain pattern of ideas' (1940; see also Ayre 1989: 169). Frye exhibits something akin to the reforming spirit of Voltaire and something that is and is not a latter-day version of the Whig history. It is possible to be grateful to the men and women who have uncovered the darker side, hidden tyrannies and propaganda of liberalism, but still interested in its possibilities.

The radical and revolutionary tradition in England, New England and, more generally, British North America are part of Frye's heritage as they are of mine. Part of the reason I feel close to Frye is that we share a heritage derived from the English radical tradition and the New England myth of religious freedom and political experiment. Frye also complicates Canadian literature and experience by contrasting them with those in Britain and the United States and by emphasizing the regionalism in Canada and the great changes the country has undergone ('Ideas' 1990: 14–17, Cayley 1991: 28–30). This political liberalism in Frye is coupled with an understanding of textual instabilities and the human construction of meaning. But Frye's view does not abide a disintegration of the text and a shift of authority (not authoritarianism) from the author to the reader. His radicalism has, as well as gets to, roots: it conserves as well as controverts. In his youth Northrop Frye was less leery of anarchy and revolution than he came to be. Perhaps, like Frye, I think that liberalism and social democracy, which includes democratic socialism, are quiet revolutions. There is no excuse for tyranny, especially in the name of liberal democracy. In its language and organization literature is multiple, pluralistic, ambivalent and ambiguous and offers a critique of ideology, tyranny and single-mindedness. That is not to deny the existence, pervasiveness or ubiquity of the ideological, the tyrannical and the single-minded. Nor am I saying that in the world anything that is not Western liberalism has to display these traits. Literature can act as a critique of bourgeois liberal humanism, which is the place Frye claims for himself whenever he characterizes himself (Cayley 1991: 26). Although, like Frye, I am not a member of any political party, am suspicious of the goals of political interests and can see the flaws of liberalism and democracy, I prefer liberal democracy to other political systems. It has been criticized by those within its bounds, which is the very life of the system. I am suspicious of illiberalism, from the left and the right, which are old and inadequate terms but recognizable shorthand. Frye appeals to me partly because he would not cast off liberalism, which has become an unfashionable garment. The term 'liberalism' is probably not adequate to define Frye's critical path and social criticism. The danger with liberalism is that it can subsume and appropriate other options in a society. While stating my situation in relation to Frye's, which is *de rigueur* in today's theoretical climate, I do so with some irony because the assumptions we set out are often less telling than those we repress or of which we are unaware. On the other hand, however uncomfortable I am talking about my 'position' when Northrop Frye is the subject of the book, I do not want to appear to hide when a central part of my concern is with social vision and ideology. Like Frye, I hope not to solidify into a 'position' but to work towards an expansion and transformation.

Before I proceed, I want to say what my book is not attempting and then what it is. It is not an extended explication of Frye's most famous book, *Anatomy of Criticism* (1957). Others have covered that ground very well indeed, especially Robert Denham (1978) and A. C. Hamilton (1990). Although I look at *Anatomy* closely, I have tried not to reproduce good critical work that has already been done. *Anatomy* is a great work, but *Fearful Symmetry* (1947), Frye's commentary on William Blake, prefigures it. Frye's best-known book is an important part of his achievement but not all of it. I am glad that in a recent book on Frye, Ian Balfour has also emphasized the importance of *Fearful Symmetry*. Even though I share some of Balfour's concerns, I am writing a different kind of book and have avoided repeating material in detail on Northrop Frye's role in Canadian literature, which Balfour and others have looked at so well (Balfour 1988: ix–x, 78–88). Nor am I writing a study of Frye's liberal social vision from the point of view of social science as David Cook (1985) has done, though the terms 'liberal', 'social' and 'vision' recur in this study. Cook also includes a discussion of Frye and the Canadian identity, a subject that I shall not address, except incidentally and tangentially. Jan Ulrik Dyrkjob (1979) has published a book on Frye in Danish that examines the relation between the vision in poetry with that of utopian politics. Dyrkjob also thinks that Frye's ideological assumptions derive from the left-wing Protestant tradition in England, the romantic celebration of creativity and nineteenth-century liberalism. Dyrkjob's study uses a Marxist critique to examine Frye's theory of literature (see Denham 1987: 190). Denham, Balfour and Hamilton dismiss or ignore the first book on Frye, Pauline Kogan's (1969), which is a polemic against him because she sees Frye as a clerical obscurantist and reactionary critic (see Denham 1978: 204). While her method may not be sophisticated and her rhetoric forceful and unsubtle, which may have caused embarrassment among those who preceded me in the field, Kogan's claims will be answered by the very existence of my book. Others within the university have hinted that Frye is trying to recuperate literature for the dominant ideology and have suggested that he is conservative and religious, so that he is not a critic for our times. Frye is not a reactionary. His views on literature and the Bible are liberal and sometimes radical. Since so few books have been written on Frye, I also want to mention Ronald Bates' early book. This brief study (1971), the tenth book in McClelland and Stewart's

Canadian Writers Series, was part of an effort to establish in the minds of Canadians that they too have a literature, as strange as that might sound to someone from outside the country. Bates' book examines Frye's criticism of Blake, Shakespeare, Milton, and Canadian literature, as well as discussing *Anatomy*. Bates sees the influence of the public lecture on Frye's production and stresses his aphoristic style, which he thinks is more important than Frye's systematic approach. Robert Denham's annotated bibliography (1987) and John Ayre's biography (1989) are both indispensable but are not the kinds of book I am writing. I shall also refer to some of the essays in the two collections on Frye edited by Murray Krieger (1966) and by Eleanor Cook and others (1983). Unfortunately, because of time and space, my study will not examine other aspects of Frye's work. Frye is one of the great Shakespearian critics of this century. He has many influential things to say about Milton, the modernists (Joyce, Eliot, Yeats), Romanticism, romance, comedy and other topics. Although in addition to critical theory my training is primarily in the Renaissance and the twentieth century, I have decided that in rediscovering the scope of Frye's work, I have had to lay aside his practical criticism and some of the areas where others have preceded me (see my bibliography). In addition to the few books that have been written on Frye, Denham's large bibliography will testify to the large number of essays and articles on these and the other aspects of Frye's œuvre that I have chosen not to discuss in detail. My study will suggest ways in which Frye is a writer and storyteller and touch on his relation to literary history, but not as exhaustively as I would like.

This study will examine what I consider the most important aspects of Frye's work. It often focuses on his later works because of their concentration on history, ideology and society. These are topics at the heart of contemporary theory and criticism. No study has focused on this phase of his work. *Words with Power* is significant for this study because it faces the contemporary context of critical theory. It was published after all the books on Frye except Hamilton's, which came out the same year. One of the major goals of my argument is to complicate the common version, that Frye is the author of a great book, *Anatomy*, of which the other books and essays are paler versions. There is no denying the critical and rhetorical power of *Anatomy*, but Frye built on it as he built it on his early articles on genre and education and on *Fearful Symmetry*. In no work is Frye a critic who turns from the world. This is an understandable but common misconception of his work. To value literature and criticism for themselves is difficult, and to create a schema – no matter how fluid – as Frye does is to read against the grain in society, if not now in the academy, because (in North America at least) literature and literary studies are not considered central to economic and political power. The fascination with what's difficult might please Yeats but not the instant society, and the schematic approach to literature is associated in the minds of many humanists with the dread science, with a reduction of individuality and individualism because such schemata do not consider the uniqueness of a literary work. This book is one of the steps some critics have taken in attempting to enable a better understanding of Frye's work.

In successive chapters my book will attempt to give a general overview of Frye's theory; will set out the grounds of his theoretical and critical work, particularly as they were established in *Fearful Symmetry*, *Anatomy of Criticism* and *The Critical Path* and developed in relation to the Bible in *The Great Code*; discuss Frye's notion of history, especially in regard to the 'Tentative Conclusion' of *Anatomy*; examine Frye's ideas about education and their relation to his work in the 1960s and the student unrest in that decade; place Frye's view of mythology and ideology in the theoretical context of the past two decades and comment more specifically on his view of the ideological in *Words with Power* (1990); elaborate Frye's visionary criticism, which begins with Blake and ends with the vision at the end of *The Double Vision* (1991); and conclude with suggestions on how Frye is a writer and how his work constitutes a defence and celebration of the imagination and of writing in a community. In reading Frye's work for this book my view of him was transformed: I hope that this study will do the same for those coming to Frye or returning to him. My basic method is to accept Frye's basic theoretical assumptions and then see where he goes with them. It is not always possible, except in an alternative idealized world, to suspend disbelief or to stop reading against the grain from occurring while one reads with it. My differences from Frye, which must by definition occur, will arise in the course of the book, but it is my wish to read with him, to see where he will lead us. My reading of Frye should be sympathetic but not uncritical.

To give a general view of Frye's thought, let me begin with illustrations that come from the Introduction of *Words with Power* (1990), from interviews with Imre Salusinszky in 1985 and with David Cayley about thirteen months before Frye's death (pub. 1991), and from the Canadian Broadcasting Corporation (CBC) radio programme, *The Ideas of Northrop Frye* (1990), which involved Frye, Cayley and others and is a longer and more intricate version of Cayley's interview (see Appendix for notice of Cayley's *Northrop Frye in Conversation* (1992)). In conversations or public lectures Frye often reiterates in a simpler way the main points he elaborates in the arguments of his books. This is a teaching technique and mnemonic device. But Frye is also like the piano player in one of the epigraphs to this book: he practises the right note over and over where freedom meets necessity. Since Frye often claimed that all his books were teaching books, it seems fair to return to his oral and public voice, which informs the books but appears here in a more basic form. I encountered Frye as a teacher at about the same time I encountered him as a critic. I soon realized that I was hearing his books in his lectures and later learned that I would hear his lectures in his books. The interview in a displaced form is a conversation overheard (with some editing). Later in the book, his lectures will be overheard in public lectures, his favourite mode of production, as essays or parts of books.

Frye's general views on criticism are my first concern. In *Words with Power* Frye defines the nature of criticism: it 'has the paradoxical task of both defining and opening the boundaries of literature, but there still has to be a continuous dialogue between criticism and what it criticizes' (1990e: xviii). Frye is taking aim at the division between theory and practical criticism. He does not think that metacriticism, which debates the abstract principles of theory, should be cut off from the literature to which it is related. Unity is one of the fundamental principles of Frye's criticism. Beneath the surface squabbles of contemporary criticism, by which Frye means theory and criticism, Frye sees a potential unity among the major critics:

> There remains however a genuinely 'productive' group, who, though operating in a variety of 'schools,' seem to me to have, for all their surface disagreements, an underlying consensus of attitude, out of which a progress toward some unified comprehension of the subject could emerge, and lead to a construction far more significant than any deconstruction of it could possibly be. This corresponds to the situation of literature itself, where 'original' writers form a core within a larger group that follows fashionable conventions and *idées reçues*.
> (1990e: xviii; see Cayley 1991: 26 for a similar passage)

Frye has sought and thinks that we should seek a field theory. He sees much wisdom in some of the criticism on historical periods and single authors and says that many humanists feel threatened by the possibility of a coherent criticism (xviii–xix). He thinks that 'the pluralistic tendency' must work itself out until effective 'unifying movements' will be able to replace it (xix). My own tendencies are towards pluralism, but the pluralism of pluralisms, which I have discussed in relation to comparative literature and possible world theory, may be such a unity out of pluralities (Hart 1988). The danger, however, with unifying schemes is that they can be used as forms of domination or totalitarian tools rather than the consensus in scientific method that Frye has had in mind at least since *Anatomy*. Perhaps he is suggesting that a paradigm shift, with Karl Popper and Thomas Kuhn in mind, is now occurring in critical theory before the next consensus or consolidation is reached. The abuse of pluralism can be a cacophony of voices without sense. The difference that determines the plurality of peoples, literatures, societies and groups within societies means that distinctions are a celebration of difference. The problem is where distinctions end. Are we left with the individual or an individual subject whose selves are 'infinitely' different? Frye admits uniqueness in experience but not in literature, which tends towards unity and coherence, a symbolic order of words that structures the chaotic flow of experience. By implication, Frye might accept pluralism in experience but think that the genres and conventions of a symbolic order like literature do not afford pluralism to criticism. How the unique personality of the reader enters into the impersonality of literature becomes one of the most important questions in Frye's work. As Robert Denham suggests, Frye is a syncretist (or an eclectic critic) who would take partially valid critical schemas and extract the best from each to create a metacriticism to look at any literary text, whereas a pluralist, true to the spirit of the Chicago school, thinks that the critical method depends on the problem at hand (Denham 1978: 27–30). It seems that many of us – but I shall speak for myself – are caught between unity and plurality, syncretism and pluralism.

Frye wants his criticism to be public and democratic. As he says, he has been practising the criticism of 'public address' for over twenty years (1990e: xix). Education is at the centre of this work. This is an independent stance in North America, where less in Frye's generation but certainly now, there is a split between the academic and public audience, between professional and public criticism. Scholarly books are often written for two expert readers selected by publishers or a dozen or a hundred specialists in the area. Frye chooses the mode of public address for two reasons. First, he believes that the only way to find radically new directions in the humanities is to be aware of 'the cultural needs' of the public and 'not from any one version of critical theory, including my own so far as I have one' (xix). Second, books appear saying that educators have betrayed society by allowing the young to grow up ignorant of its cultural traditions, but these works get nothing done because they recommend that we prod the educational bureaucracy. Instead, Frye recommends that we turn the question around and make scholarship in the humanities available to as many people as possible, so that education can begin (xix–xx).

Frye assumes that his interest in the relation between the Bible and literature arises from his 'view of critical theory as a comprehensive *theoria*' (1990e: xx). By studying Blake, Frye found that the Bible was central to an understanding of his poetry and also of most of English poetry. From these insights, Frye proceeded to seek a unified theory of literature, a kind of secular scripture, in *Anatomy*. Here is Frye's explanation of the relation between *Anatomy* and the books on the Bible, *The Great Code* (1982) and *Words with Power* (1990), which does not mention the debt of *Anatomy* to his book on Blake, *Fearful Symmetry*:

> The theory of genres in *Anatomy of Criticism* led me up to the sacred book, along with secular analogies or parodies of it, as the most comprehensive form that could reasonably be examined within a literary orbit. It then occurred to me that the perspective could be reversed, starting with the sacred book and working outwards to secular literature.
>
> (1990e: xx)

He was interested in the comprehensive form of the Bible. In this post-*Anatomy* project Frye realizes that classical literature is often as old as the Bible and developed its own genres independently of biblical influence. By alluding to other literatures and traditions, especially in *The Great Code*, Frye recognizes that together the Jewish, Christian, Greek and Latin influences, not to mention the Celtic or Viking influences in parts of Europe, help to define the forms of European literature. Still, Frye's focus at the end was the Bible. For much of Europe, the Bible was an import, a latecomer to their different cultures. A reader should keep in mind at once Frye's secular *Anatomy* and his two major books on the Bible, perhaps with the study of Blake acting as a balance or fulcrum. Frye's project in *Words with Power* is to explore 'the extent to which the canonical unity of the Bible indicates or symbolizes a much wider imaginative unity in secular European literature' (xx). With his usual brilliance, Frye uses the criticism of Edgar Allan Poe's story 'The Purloined Letter' to suggest his own view of letters and the letter, that it is an allegory of what he is talking about in discussing the relation between the Bible and literature, a 'story about a verbal message that various people want to kidnap, can't kidnap because they can't see it, and can't see it precisely because it is staring them in the face' (xxi). The purloined letter for literary critics is the

Bible, and for biblical scholars it is the language of myth and metaphor in which the Bible is written (xxi).

In *Words with Power* Frye returns to his earlier questions about what is the distinctive social function of literature and what, if anything, is the basis of the poet's authority. Frye does and does not apologize for this 'old-hat Romanticism' but wonders whether the shift from poet to reader can make readers heroic unless something in literature gives it to them, although he admits that this throws us back to the question of 'what gives this something to literature' (1990e: xxi). He thinks that the poet's authority is bound up with the authority of poetic language, an aspect common to poetry and the Bible. Another characteristic that *Words with Power* shares with Frye's other book is that it focuses on imagery, in this case the image of the *axis mundi*, or the 'vertical dimension of the cosmos' (xxi). The *axis mundi* has no objective existence, but only exists in the verbal world. It occurs frequently and centrally in secular literature as in the Bible, so that 'it illustrates my "great code" principle that the organizing structures of the Bible and the corresponding structures of "secular" literature reflect each other' (xxii). What Frye hopes to achieve in *Words with Power* is characteristic of his critical goals elsewhere. First, he wants to illuminate difficult literary works by suggesting one of the contexts that helps to make up their meaning. Second, he suggests why the poets we consider to be most worth while are those who have used the kind of imagery to which he calls our attention. Third, he hopes to provide 'glimpses of interconnecting structural principles of literature that are actually connected with literature and the experience of studying it' (xxii).

From his student days onwards, Frye was interested in cosmology and its relation to the imagination. Besides his study of Blake's cosmology from about 1934–47, Frye was exposed to C. S. Lewis' lectures at Oxford in 1936, which often related literature and cosmology. The influence of Lewis' *The Allegory of Love* (1936) and *The Discarded Image* (1964), the published version of Lewis' lectures, on Frye's theory is something that Ayre alludes to and that deserves further attention. In Ayre's view, Lewis foreshadows Frye in the following ways: Lewis finds examples from all kinds of poems, good and bad, to support his thesis; he uses a wide range of cultural evidence to discuss the structure of the cosmos and suggests that this shape worked its way into literature; he suggests that poets and artists are interested in the imaginative possibilities of patterns; he thinks that cosmological criticism was foreign to evaluative criticism because it sifted and classified fundamental elements; he insists that scholarship move towards the symbolic centre of literature and not centre on historicism (Ayre 1989:

131–2). These similarities between Lewis and Frye are general and might apply almost as well to the works of James Frazer, Oswald Spengler and Arnold Toynbee, who either represented grand historical narratives or great cosmological patterns, if not both. But Lewis was talking about literature, not mythology or history, so that his comments are less refracted and perhaps helped provide a more direct model for Frye. In the cosmology of the first half of this century, there is a certain sense of *Zeitgeist*. But Frye centres his cosmology – his mythology – on myth. He uses the 'principle of coherence as a critical hypothesis' (1990e: xxii). He relates imagination and metaphor:

> The poetic imagination constructs a cosmos of its own, a cosmos to be studied not simply as a map but as a world of powerful conflicting forces. This imaginative cosmos is neither the objective environment studied by natural science nor a subjective inner space to be studied by psychology. It is an intermediate world in which the images of higher and lower, the categories of beauty and ugliness, the feelings of love and hatred, the associations of sense experience, can be expressed by metaphor and yet cannot be either dismissed or reduced to projections of something else.
>
> (1990e: xxii)

In the very nature of metaphor, Frye implies, we find the core of imagination, the integration of mythological language, which is translated most powerfully into the integrity of literature. The re-creation of primitive metaphorical language in literature gives it power, but that so-called literary language is shared by other aspects of life, including religion:

> Ordinary consciousness is so possessed by the either–or contrast of subject and object that it finds difficulty in taking in the notion of an order of words that is neither subjective nor objective, though it interpenetrates both. But its presence gives a very different appearance to many elements of human life, including religion, which depend on metaphor but do not become less 'real' or 'true' by doing so.
>
> (xxii–xxiii)

Frye says he developed his idea of interpenetration from Malraux's reading in *Voices of Silence* (1951) of Spengler's *Decline of the West* (1918–22) and later found the notion in Alfred North Whitehead's *Science and the Modern World* (1925). Interpenetration is 'the notion that things don't get reconciled, but everything is everywhere at once. Wherever you are is the centre of everything' (Cayley 1991: 25). Literature and the Bible share metaphorical language, so that the literary is not entirely distinct. Frye recognizes that the 'metaphorical' is as 'treacherous a conception as "reality" and "truth" could ever be' (1990e: xxiii). Metaphor may be, as Frye says, good or bad, but it occupies the centre of social and individual awareness. 'It is a primitive form of awareness, established long before the distinction of subject and object became normal, but when we try to outgrow it we find that all we can really do is rehabilitate it' (xxiii).

Literature and criticism depend on vision and recognition. Frye wants criticism to set the 'immeasurable goals, far beyond the hope of achievement' that Italo Calvino envisaged for literature in his Norton Lectures at Harvard. The critic should, Frye says, perhaps with some irony, look into the far distance and see some axiom like 'Criticism can and should make sense of literature' and not settle for less (xxiii). Frye reminds us that much of his critical thought has revolved round the double meaning of Aristotle's *anagnorisis*, discovery and recognition. We always return to something, to paraphrase Eliot, as if it were for the first time. In Frye's version of tradition and the individual talent, he concludes that 'of course every true discovery must in some sense relate to what has always been true, and so all genuine knowledge includes recognition' (xxiii).

From the Introduction to *Words with Power*, this small summa or summing up of many of his theoretical principles, I want to turn to the interviews to move to a more popular expression of his general critical assumptions. As a teacher, Frye believes in incremental repetition or variations on a theme. He repeats himself throughout his writing. This amplification is designed to ensure a refinement of his ideas. It may also have to do with Frye's 'oral poetry', his use of lecture in class and in public as a means of organizing his work, his need or inclination to speak without notes. I have always suspected that *Anatomy* was Frye's memory system. The interview translates the lecture, and the interviewer often seems to prompt Frye's ready-made response, as if extracted from a lecture or subsequent essay or book.

From *Anatomy* onwards, Frye claims to have built his theory on his study of Blake. In 1957 he says that the book on Blake 'forced itself' on him while he was trying 'to apply the principles of literary symbolism and Biblical typology which I had learned from Blake to another poet, preferably one who had taken these principles from the critical theories of his own day, instead of working them out by himself as Blake did' (1957: vii). Frye selected Spenser's *Faerie Queene* as a suitable work. He explains that the book on Spenser became a theory of allegory, which was part of a larger theoretical structure, until the argument became more discursive and less Spenserian and historical.

'Myth', 'symbol', 'ritual' and 'archetype' were the terms of which Frye now had to make sense, and early in the project the theory separated from the practical criticism. In a groundbreaking statement, even though it appears in a context in which he states the need to supplement *Anatomy* with a volume of practical criticism, Frye announces: 'What is here offered is pure critical theory, and the omission of all specific criticism, even, in three of the four essays, of quotation, is deliberate' (vii). *Fearful Symmetry* leads to *Anatomy*. In the interviews Frye remembers his discovery of Blake and repeats that *Anatomy* 'grew directly out of my work on Blake' (Salusinszky 1987: 41). Frye's theoretical epiphany or moment of illumination, he says, occurred when he was a student at Emmanuel College at the University of Toronto, when he was writing a paper on Blake's *Milton*. At about three in the morning, in what appears to have been an all-nighter, Frye says, all of a sudden 'the universe broke open and I've never, as they say, been the same since' (Cayley 1991: 24). The realization was that Milton and Blake both entered into the mythological framework of the Bible (Cayley 1991: 24, Salusinszky 1987: 31; see also 'Ideas' 1990: 2). In the late 1960s Frye discovered something else in his reading of Blake:

> When I was forced to re-read *Fearful Symmetry*, in order to write a preface to a reprint of it, I discovered what I hadn't realized before: how very troubled a book it was and how much the rise of Nazism was on my mind and how terrified I was by the clarity with which Blake saw things like Druidism coming, whereby human sacrifices, as he says, would have depopulated the earth.
>
> (Cayley 1991: 25–6)

Frye was able to avoid the temptations of fascism or the reactionary positions that lured literary figures like W. B. Yeats, Ezra Pound, T. S. Eliot, Paul de Man and many others. He credits Blake with helping him to avoid the lure of mythography and the visions of organic societies that led many modernists astray:

> Well, it was Blake who helped me keep my head. One of the books I picked up was Rosenberg's *Myth of the Twentieth Century*, which was a big Nazi polemic claiming that the racially pure come from Atlantis and so forth. Having been concentrating on Blake so heavily, I could see that this was the devil's parody of Blake. I think Yeats plunged into something rather similar without realizing that it was the devil's parody of Blake.
>
> (Cayley 1991: 26; see also 'Ideas' 1990: 2–3, Salusinszky 1987: 41)

Like Blake, Frye is interested in the vision of Job, and the visionary and prophetic aspect of the Bible. Blake's spiritual world is his world of painting and poetry just as, I suspect, Frye's is his world of criticism because creation organizes and articulates the spiritual world beyond anything the physical world can produce. Frye says: 'Vision, for him, was, as I say, the ability to hear and see in the world' ('Ideas' 1990: 19; see also 23).

By reconstructing Blake, Frye came to reconstruct criticism. He valued metaphorical thinking in criticism as well as in poetry ('Ideas' 1990: 1, Cayley 1991: 32). Frye tells a story about the state of criticism and why he felt compelled to write *Anatomy*:

> The world of criticism was inhabited by a lot of people who were pretty confused about what they were doing, and didn't particularly mind that they were confused about it. I was impatient with all the semi-literate productions which I'd been compelled to read in the way of secondary sources. I was tired of a historical approach to literature that didn't know any literary history, that simply dealt with ordinary history plus a few dates of writers. It was just a matter of just being fed up with a field that seemed to me to have no discipline in it.
>
> ('Ideas' 1990: 5)

Frye wanted autonomy for literary criticism, that is discipline, rules for writing good work as there are in history and philosophy: integrity. Frye later recognized that some of his readers had fastened on to the word 'autonomy' and interpreted his theory to mean that criticism is a retreat from the world. All Frye claims he wanted to do was to show that criticism was a discipline and not a parasitic approach to literature ('Ideas' 1990: 4–5). In 1957 Frye was also tired of value judgements, which are moral judgements of a given historical period that can seem ridiculous at a later time, and which set up the individual critic as a judge. Instead, Frye wanted scholars to read the good, the bad and the indifferent in their fields rather than to let the taste of the 'gentleman' guide them ('Ideas' 1990: 6–7, see also Salusinszky 1987: 32). Frye wished to democratize criticism, which meant placing little value on value judgements, which he calls moral judgements in disguise, which in turn reflect 'the ideological conditioning of a certain age' ('Ideas' 1990: 7). He does not mean that value judgements, like what is a classic or masterpiece, can ever go away, but that they are not of central interest to criticism. But, paradoxically, those who speak of the classic or masterpiece, terms that are value judgements, mean 'works of literature that refuse to go away' ('Ideas' 1990: 7). Frye shows his wit: the ideological judgement coincides in this one place with what criticism reveals about a great work: it refuses to go away (or perhaps to be called, like Hotspur's parody of Glendower's spirits, from the vasty deep) no matter what the change in ideological fashion.

Although Frye is not strictly a historical critic, he thinks that literary history is important. He also discusses the social value of literature. Much of his view of history relates to his discussion of ideology. Frye keeps the historical before him even if that is not his primary emphasis. For instance, when discussing value judgements, which he takes to be disguised ideology, he says: 'I'm not trying to eliminate value judgements from critical practice; I'm merely pointing out their grave limitations and the fact that so many judgements have been thought of as transcending the age in which they're made. Of course, they never do' (Cayley 1991: 27; see also 'Ideas' 1990: 6). Frye has written in an engaged way in and against his times. He insists that literature has a history of its own and should not be a colony of other disciplines or, by implication, they of it. The first essay of *Anatomy* is entitled, 'Historical Criticism: Theory of Modes', and the 'Tentative Conclusion' has historical implications as well as implications for literary history.

Since the early 1940s, Frye has written about education. During the 1960s in particular, education was one of his central preoccupations. His university is a place in and against society. His optimism is, he says, reflected in the period of hope between 1945 and 1950, which 'came out more in my articles on education and the universities' (Salusinszky 1987: 41). Frye thinks that scholarship, which the present conditions in the university often work against, is 'the pursuit of a structure, or of knowledge, so that it gets clearer in the mind' (37). He admits that much of what he has written on education 'has been an attempt to recapture his own pastoral myth' (37). Frye considers culture as the only power that will allow humanity to survive its folly ('Ideas' 1990: 9). The teaching of undergraduates, as opposed to graduate students, who now engage in cutthroat competition and pursue pluralistic and specialized studies, is where he can best open minds to education and culture (9). The educational contract between teacher and students, according to Frye, leads to 'a community of searchers' (10). He wishes to be a 'transparent medium' for his students, so that they can be in the 'full presence of what I'm teaching, Milton or whatever' (10). Frye's most difficult period as a teacher was in the late 1960s:

> The student activism of the '60s was something I had really very little sympathy with. It started out with a group of students in Berkeley feeling that they were not being paid attention to as students, something I could profoundly sympathize with. As it went on, they

became more and more attracted by the clichés of revolutionary ideology and then they turned into something which was an anti-intellectual movement in the one place in society where it had no business being, and once a student gets on a self-righteous kick, he becomes utterly impervious to argument because he's still too young and insecure to listen to anything except the applause of his own conscience. And I knew that that movement would fall dead in a very short time because it had no social roots. It wasn't like feminism or black emancipation or anything of that sort, with a real social cause behind it.

('Ideas' 1990: 11; see also Cayley 1991: 30)

The difficulty for Frye's reputation in the short run is that many of those who were of the generation of 68, whether they were protesters or not, think of the student unrest as a liberation movement, and they are increasingly at the centre of power in the university today and will be for at least another decade. This may be their pastoral myth of education. Perhaps in nostalgia for their youth, they will not remember the excesses, any more than Frye would like to take away from the glory of his days as an undergraduate. Those who were attracted to deconstruction and have forged or participated in new historicism, cultural materialism, postmodernism, feminism and other ways of looking at culture and literature might remember the anti-war protests, civil rights marches, the new generation of women fighting for women's rights and the student protests as part of the same social movement. Whereas Frye separates the violence on campus from historical movements he approves of, such as the protest against the Vietnam war as well as the struggle for equal rights for Afro-Americans and women, some of his students and those who form a new generation of critics and theorists may not agree on that separation. Being on the other side of the generation of protesters (Frye was older than they) I, perhaps, am both more ignorant of and more sympathetic to (perhaps the two are related) their cause. It is also possible that our protests were even less informed than those of our elder brothers and sisters, but at the time, it felt like a stand against the penal servitude that Frye felt in his early education. In retrospect, however, the reforms were uneven, and I cannot claim that being moved from Latin to refrigeration class had anything more than a numbing effect on me. There might be some wisdom in Frye's parable of playing the piano as an example of the joining of freedom and necessity ('Ideas' 1990: 11). In Frye's own student days during the 1930s, he rejected extremes and sought recourse in intellectual matters, so that he had practised what he preached to the younger generation.

Once again, Frye's difference has an ideological basis for many, but a mythological foundation for him. In the long term it is difficult to say how the students' movement of the 1960s will be regarded. If I had been able to interview Frye as I had planned, I would have asked him these questions. What did he think of the contribution of students and intellectuals to the Revolutions of 1848, which were at least as widespread and more politically effective than the rebelliousness of 1968–9 (see Gay and Webb 1973: 713–19)? Were those students fighting more authoritarian regimes in the name of democracy? Were they liberals? How did their teachers react, and why? Frye feared that the students of the 1960s were fighting unreality with unreality, slipping towards a neo-fascist direction by using the slogan of 'relevance' because the useful becomes hostage to the dominant ideology and 'relevance' was a favourite word of the Nazis. He applauds the movement now across the world of a 'gradual loss in the belief in the validity of ideology qua ideology' ('Ideas' 1990: 11; see also 12 and Cayley 1991: 34). Frye's response to my concerns and those of others would be characteristically direct, sensible, witty and challenging: his death is a loss, and rather than pursue an elegiac cliché, it is better to suspend the answers and let Frye's voice throughout this book suggest a provisional response.

Myth and metaphor are central to Frye's view of literature as education and are, in his theory, prior to ideology. Frye distances himself from the ideology of the myth critics and their predecessors. As an undergraduate, Frye

> picked up Spengler's *Decline of the West* and was absolutely
> enraptured with it, and ever since I've been wondering why, because
> Spengler had one of these muzzy, right-wing, Teutonic, folkish
> minds. He was the most stupid bastard I ever picked up. But
> nevertheless I found his book an inspired book, and finally I've more
> or less figured out, I think, what I got from Spengler.
>
> (Cayley 1991: 25)

That 'what' is interpenetration, the idea that wherever one is represents the centre, and how that operates in history. James Frazer's *The Golden Bough* (1890–1915) had a similar effect on Frye, who says it 'was written by a rather stupid man' (25). None the less, Frye thought that scholars could attack *The Golden Bough* on just about any ground, 'but mythically it was the Great Pyramid: it was solid' (25).

In studying Blake, Frye realized that the Bible was a mythological framework, cosmos or body of stories, and that societies live within a mythology. Frye observes that 'The Bible to Blake was really the

Magna Carta of the human imagination. It was the book that told man that he was free to create and imagine, and that the power to create and imagine was ultimately the divine in man' ('Ideas' 1990: 2). Here is the genesis of Frye's central critical notion:

> I soon realized the priority of mythology to ideology in a culture, and then I realized that a mythology is an interconnected series of myths, and that the distinguishing characteristic of the myth – as distinct, say, from the folk-tale or the legend – was that myths tended to link together to form a mythology. I felt that there had never been a corresponding term for works of literature. Because, as literature grows out of mythology, and is the most direct product of the mythology, it also has a group of stories interconnected by convention and by these recurring units that I call archetypes.
>
> (Salusinszky 1987: 31)

For Frye, the story, and not the argument, is at the centre of literature and society. The base of society is mythical and narrative and not ideological and dialectical. He also says that there is ideological conflict in a society with a shared mythological structure because humans cannot stay at the mythological level because they cannot argue about whether they think a story is true or false, or, as Sidney observes, a poet affirms nothing. In Frye's view, 'as soon as the secondary ideological development takes place, then you're in the realm of proposition and thesis, where every statement implies its own opposite' (Salusinszky 1987: 31). Why then not write stories, plays and poems rather than criticism, unless the criticism is formulated in myths, is narrated rather than set out in arguments? This is a central question about Frye's theory, a response to which should arise during the course of this book.

In Frye's theory, language and, in particular, metaphor are closely related to mythology. Here is another critical distinction necessary to an understanding of Frye, his differentiation of poetics and ideology:

> I think that the ideologue addresses the public and wants to make a kinetic effect on them. He wants them to get out there and do something. The poet turns his back on his audience. I begin the *Anatomy* with John Stuart Mill's remark that the poet is overheard, not heard, and he doesn't look for kinetic effect on his audience at all. He's creating an absence so that his audience can move into a presence.
>
> (Cayley 1991: 26–7; see also 'Ideas' 1990: 8)

Poetic language, of which metaphor is the core, is not propositional and can only be translated into ideological propositions beyond the fundamental level of story. But other theorists of narrative are not so sure that mythology is the base of storytelling. If Fredric Jameson (1981) and others accuse Frye of not allowing for the priority of ideology over myth, Frye counters that his critics ignore the priority of myth over ideology. Most of them, Frye says,

> do not know that there is such a thing as a poetic language which is not only different from ideological language but puts up a constant fight against it, to liberalize it and individualize it. There is no such thing as a 'pure myth'. There is no immaculate conception in mythology. Myth exists only in incarnations, but it's the ones that are incarnated in works of literature that I'm primarily interested in, and what they create is a cultural counterenvironment to the ones that are, I won't say perverted, but at any rate, twisted or skewed into ideological patterns of authority.

('Ideas' 1990: 8)

Mythical thinking is the earliest form of thought, something that cannot be outgrown and that 'proceeds metaphorically in a world where everything is potentially identifiable with everything else' and is where the use of words ends and is likely to end ('Ideas' 1990: 19–20). If metaphor is a linguistic aspect of a mythological framework or structure, it also leads to a vision beyond ideology and rhetoric, beyond the word of worldly authority and command:

> Now, that is a metaphor, it's an analogy of the kind of command that comes from the other side of the imagination, what has been called the kerygmatic, the proclamation from God. And that is not so much a command as a statement of what your own potentiality is and of the direction in which you have to go to attain it. But it's a command that leaves your free will, whether you follow it or not.

(Cayley 1991: 21–2)

The question of authority, human or divine, whatever the metaphorical and mythical resonance for Frye, is bound to seem ideological for some. It is a matter of first assumptions. Because this is a book on Frye and because I think he has a telling hypothesis about mythology as the basis of literature and society, I shall explore his ideas on myth and metaphor, and the vision they engender, but not without facing ideology.

In fact, in his last two decades or so but especially in the past ten years, Frye has often discussed mythology and ideology together, partly because of the great interest in the ideological over the past twenty-five years. Frye does not turn his back on one of the most pressing questions in contemporary theory. He is part of a double image, the two-way trick drawings he often mentions, mythology on one side, ideology on the other. Frye describes his side of the drawing:

> I think that what gradually dawned on me over the years was that most people start out with a social context as an ideology, and feel that literature fits within the ideology and to some degree reflects it. Well, that is true, but I think that an ideology is always a secondary and derivative thing, and that the primary thing is a mythology. That is, people don't think up a set of assumptions or beliefs; they think up a set of stories, and derive the assumptions and beliefs from the stories. Things like democratic, progressive, revolutionary, Marxist political philosophies: these are comic plots, superimposed on history.
>
> (Salusinszky 1987: 31)

This comic structure is a movement from an old order through chaos or the overcoming of an obstacle to a new order (see Frye 1948). For Frye, a Christian ideology, which differs from the ideology of Judaism, comes from a Christian myth, which is similar to the Judaic myth (Salusinszky 1987: 31–2). Criticism, according to Frye, is still bound up with ideology, and thus with the language of thesis and argument, rather than 'embarked on the empirical study of literature' (32). Criticism is the mediator between literature and society, but Frye says that it must examine the literary context and then the social context and must distinguish between the mythological and the ideological because this distinction alone will account for why Yeats, Pound and Lawrence are great writers but 'ideological fat-heads' (33). Frye is interested in the mythological structure and not the ideological content of literature and the Bible (33). The university is not simply an ideological state apparatus, as Louis Althusser says, because university teachers are too intelligent not to realize that they in part speak for a 'bourgeois hierarchy' (39).

This emphasis on ideology has a long history. Frye's rebellion is against the authority of a Western tradition that subordinates poetry to other disciplines. This defence of poetry, like that of the theatre, has gone on for a long time, so that one can conclude that poets and critics are paranoid or that there is a problem of the undervaluation of poetry, literature and fiction in the West (see Barish 1981). Frye's position makes sense in relation to history and literary history, as half of a trick drawing of a history or literary history that emphasizes the power of the aesthetic ideology, although that begins in the Enlightenment (see Norris 1988, Eagleton 1990).

Plato was the first of all the people who wanted to take over poetry, hitch it on to an ideology, namely his, and all the poets who wouldn't do that leave the Republic. But according to The Laws, there are others who stay around writing hymns and panegyrics to the greatness of the Platonic ideal, and that's still true of all ideologues. Artists have always been told that they have no real authority, that they live in a world of let's pretend and they just play around with fictions, and their function is to delight and instruct, as Horace says, and they can learn from their own art how to delight, but they can't learn how to instruct unless they study philosophy or theology or politics. And as a literary critic, I've been fighting that notion all my life.

('Ideas' 1990: 7)

For Frye, ideology is not an evil but 'something essential to human life' that has to be subordinate to the simple and primary processes of the imagination, what Frye calls from *The Critical Path* onwards myths of concern – life, love, freedom, dignity (Cayley 1991: 34; see also 33 and 'Ideas' 1990: 24). If primary concerns have priority over ideology, they do not, in Frye's view, have to develop structures of enmity. As a liberal, Frye insists on the 'relativity of ideology to human peace and dignity' (34). These are the closely related social and literary pre-occupations in Frye's last years. They combine in the vision of this visionary critic.

It is no accident that mythology and ideology occupy the centre of my book. With a vision of the eternal now, Frye resists the donkey's carrot of the ideologies of today, which are typological and thus pull us into a future where something is to be fulfilled ('Ideas' 1990: 22). Frye is interested in apocalypse, an uncovering or revelation. He is a both/and, not an either/or, theorist. Except he is interested in one either/or – the apocalypse, a separation of life from death. He does not believe in the separation of good and evil. As a critic one must by definition make decisions. When making choices,

you're always moving towards an apocalyptic vision of something that doesn't die and throwing off the body of the death that you want to be delivered from. So that the final separation of life and death has to be in the form of an imaginative vision, which is what literature expresses and what the critic tries to explain.

('Ideas' 1990: 24, Cayley 1991: 34)

Rather than suggest the many ways Frye is a writer as much as a critic, I shall defer this to the end of the book. One of the more obvious ways is that Frye finds stories in the Bible, not doctrine, Christ as a storyteller and not an ideologue. He explains the imaginative vision of the Bible and of secular writers, but does so throughout his career by ending so many of his books and essays with a comic ending, with a vision of his own. His explanations tell a story of their own.

To summarize the argument or movement of my book: Northrop Frye is a writer who places the imagination at the centre of his theory of literature. He argues that literature and criticism should each be a related and separate imaginative field that has the integrity of other disciplines like history and philosophy. Frye takes up the old struggle between philosophy, history and poetry that begins in earnest with Plato and Aristotle and continues in the English tradition with Sidney, Shelley, Wilde and others. Like these last three writers, Frye wants to defend poetry against philosophy and history. Like them, he also thinks that poetry affirms nothing and is not in the language of dialectic or philosophical argument or the descriptive language of history (although it can share qualities with these discourses). With Oscar Wilde, he sees poetry as an elaborate 'lie', a kind of metaphorical language that does not argue for the truth. In *Fearful Symmetry* and *Anatomy* Frye argues for myth and metaphor as the structural and linguistic centres of literature. Both work against argument and the ideologies that go along with argumentative discourses, so that literature becomes its own 'world' that is governed by conventions, by its own modes, symbols, myths and genres. This theory is not anti-historical but only wishes to establish a literary history that does not deny literature a place within it. One place to teach about the countervailing properties of myth, metaphor and imaginative vision is in the university. Although the university is in society, it needs, in Frye's view, to maintain an ideal of a community or process that encourages intellectual activity, so that the society does not become cut off from its tradition and can no longer be innovative and free. Even if the university falls short of this ideal, to attack it, as some did during the 1960s, is to fight against their only hope for freedom. Frye's teaching and writing are designed to elaborate the potential that literature and criticism have for students, how, for instance, these disciplines translate mythology and use metaphor, the primitive structures of our language and stories that are the foundation of our society, in their most intense forms. Frye's vision is not one that denies ideology but one that realizes how difficult and desirable it is to get beyond it. Here is the visionary critic who believes that if we learn to see the world anew in our personal visions we shall be able to build a better society. Literature, for Frye, is a kind of secular and human apocalypse or revelation, a human speaking to humanity, to translate Wordsworth's description of the poet. It is the freedom of humans to imagine their world free of non-human authority. Even in his work on the Bible, Frye insists on the 'and' in the Bible and literature and always defends the autonomy of literature from the ideology of religion. Frye the critic is Frye the writer with his own cosmology, no matter how much he takes from the Bible, Blake and Milton, and with his own story to tell. What follows in the rest of this book is a part of that story.

2   Reconstructing Blake

I do not know who wrote these Prefaces they are very mischievous &
direct contrary to Wordsworths own Practise.
(William Blake, 'Annotations to Wordsworth's *Poems*', 1815)

In conceiving of this chapter and the two subsequent chapters, I was
caught between the desire to set out the basics of Frye's criticism and
theory so that my book could move on to new explorations of important
and sometimes unexplored or underexplored areas of his work and the
desire not to repeat the fine explications of Frye, especially of *Anatomy
of Criticism*, that Denham, Balfour, Hamilton and others have produced. These three chapters represent a compromise since my book
should be self-sufficient, not because it is desirable to read only one
book on Frye but because if the reader has decided to read one study or
mine is the only one available, it should provide the basics of Frye's
criticism before moving on to the subjects of history, education,
mythology, ideology and fiction. Those who know the whole of Frye's
work well may want to proceed to Chapter 5. To set out the foundations
of his work, these three chapters will examine four key books. This
chapter will look at *Fearful Symmetry: A Study of William Blake* (1947)
because it culminates at least twelve years of on-and-off work on Blake,
represents a major contribution to the study of that poet and is a major
statement of Frye's theory of literature and criticism that leads to
Anatomy but that is not read as much because few outside the speciality
of Blake will travel through Blake to cull the remarkable theoretical
insights. *Fearful Symmetry* may be Frye's greatest book, but *Anatomy*,
as difficult as it is, may be more general, accessible and 'universal' in its
accomplishment. Chapter 3 will examine *Anatomy of Criticism: Four
Essays* (1957), Frye's most famous book, which launched him and
haunted him, as it draws together his interest in genre theory and
incorporates, among other things, his brilliant work on satire and

comedy in the 1940s. It will also discuss *The Critical Path* (1971), which brings together ideas on the myth of concern that he worked out in the late 1960s in lectures at universities then in the middle of student revolts and which looks ahead to twenty years of the development of this idea and others on social criticism and the relation between literature and society. Chapter 4 will explain the principles in *The Great Code: Being a Study of the Bible and Literature* (1981). This book culminates a lifelong encounter with the Bible, brings together Frye's training in literary studies and theology and looks ahead to *Words with Power* (1990) and *The Double Vision* (1991), apparently the last two books, the one before he died and the other posthumous, that Frye thought of as his own. These books represent the vision at the end of things and join in a spiral with *Fearful Symmetry*, which discussed Blake as a visionary poet. From vision to vision, the next three chapters set out in basic terms the work of Northrop Frye in order to lead up to a Frye who will surprise those who have made him a man of one book – *Anatomy*.

Frye divides *Fearful Symmetry* into three parts: the argument, the development of the symbolism and the final synthesis. My discussion will focus mainly on the argument because it contains most of Frye's critical observations and principles that he amplifies in the last two parts. The argument moves from the case against John Locke through discussions of the rising god, beyond good and evil and Blake as a literalist of the imagination to a consideration of the word within the Word. In 'The Case against Locke', Frye argues against what he thinks characterized Blake studies until his book: 'Blake, they tell us, is a mystic enraptured with incommunicable visions, standing apart, a lonely and isolated figure, out of touch with his own age and without influence on the following one' (1947a: 3). Frye says that Blake did not want to be neglected but, like all real artists, had 'an intense desire to communicate' and is a precise and careful artist (4–5). His Blake is not a mystic but a poet who writes for those who want to find out 'what the mystery is' (6–7). Frye wants to call Blake and other poets who are called mystics, visionaries, which is a key to Frye's theory and criticism for the rest of his life. In discussing Blake's vision, Frye maintains that a visionary creates a higher spiritual world that transforms and charges the objects of perception in this one, and that includes the visualization vital to the artist. Vision is perceptive rather than contemplative, according to Frye, and most of the greatest mystics, such as St John of the Cross and Plotinus, find the symbolism of visionary experience a hindrance to mystical contemplation. This divergence, Frye says, suggests that mysticism and art are ultimately mutually exclusive and that vision and art are closely related (8, see my Chapter 8). Frye accepts Blake's use of the term 'visionary' over one he does not use, 'mystic', and we shall do the same with Frye's usage of it, but with one caveat: to close off the boundary between the visionary and the mystic, except at the extremes, is as difficult as shutting down the borders between the literary and non-literary, except at the outer limits.

According to Frye, Blake thought that 'the spiritual world was a continuous source of energy' and 'had the complete pragmatism of the artist, who, as artist, believes nothing but is looking for what he can use' (8). Frye, like Blake, is a person of notebooks, sketching 'what his more reverent colleagues are no longer attempting to see' (9). He outlines Blake's definition of poetry: all major poetry is allegorical that can be explained through the data of sense perception and the ideas from them and that is an imaginative whole, a kind of identity of form and content (an idea like Dante's 'anagogy' or the fourth level of interpretation). Frye distinguishes between debased and genuine allegory, which he has just explained by setting out Blake's definition of poetry, although he admits it is confusing because Blake uses 'allegory' in both senses. What Frye is proposing is a revolution in the study of poetry and literature. In 1947 he is reconstructing criticism as well as Blake:

> As ignorance of the methods and techniques of allegorical poetry is still almost universal, the explicitly allegorical writers have for the most part not received in modern times much criticism which is based directly on what they were trying to do. If Blake can be consistently interpreted in terms of his own theory of poetry, however, the interpretation of Blake is only the beginning of a complete revolution in one's reading of all poetry.
>
> (10–11)

The neglect that Frye has in mind is of allegorical writers like Langland, Spenser and Hawthorne. To read Blake, we need to read the Bible, Ovid's *Metamorphoses*, the Prose Edda and other sources and see how he made their symbolism relate to his. This reading is like learning a language, so that an inner logic emerges until 'the symbolism becomes visible' and later 'until the intellectual powers are able to read without translating' (11). Once the readers learn the 'lost art of reading poetry', which is not 'a technique of mystical illumination' but the language of allegory, they will enjoy all poetry more (11). It is the analogues to Blake, not the sources, that are important for Blake, and even his sources like the Bible and Milton are valuable only as sources of analogues (12). For Blake, the 'sources of art are enthusiasm and inspiration: if society mocks and derides these, it is society that is mad, not the artist, no matter what excesses the latter may commit' (13).

As will become clear throughout my book, Frye identifies with Blake on many matters, although his views are not identical to those of the poet. Like Frye after him, 'Blake distinguishes between opinions and principles, saying that everyone changes the former and that no one, not even a hypocrite, can change the latter. . . . His principles he held with bulldog tenacity all his life' (13). In Blake's poetry, Bacon, Newton and Locke become symbols of tyranny, evil and superstition, whereas Blake, like Berkeley, takes an idealist view of knowledge, that reality is mental, that, in Berkeley's phrase, *esse est percipi*, or to be is to be perceived (15). Frye calls attention to a central aspect of Blake's poetics:

> The unit of this mental existence Blake calls indifferently a 'form' or an 'image'. If there is such a thing as a key to Blake's thought, it is the fact that these two words mean the same thing to him. He makes no consistent use of the term 'idea'.
>
> (15)

Another key to Blake's, and to Frye's, views is summarized in Blake's famous phrase in the marginalia to Reynolds, 'To Generalize is to be an Idiot', which, in Frye's interpretation, means 'that the image or form of perception is the content of knowledge' (15). This view leads Frye to a central perception that, because of genre or its medium, literature was formally different from other types of writing and therefore communicated a different content. For Blake, the distinct perception of things is vastly superior to memory's attempt to classify them into general principles: to be is to be perceived is a principle that unites subject and object, whereas Lockian reflection separates them once more (16–17). In Blake 'body' means the entire person as an object of perception, and 'imagination' is the usual term that he uses to indicate a human 'as an acting and perceiving being' (18–19). For Blake, nothing is real beyond the imaginative patterns that people compose of reality (19). The standard of reality for Blake is genius, for Locke, mediocrity. In Frye's view, Blake says that active, conscious imaginative effort represents the freedom of the active mind, whereas Locke considers the mind to be a quiescent and inert blank slate that responds to external impressions (21–3). In opposing Locke, Blake is defending humans as those who form and imagine the material world and are not material that the external world forms: the perceiver has a unified character because the environment may condition it but not alter it (23). Blake, Frye says, thinks that wisdom 'is the central form which gives meaning and position to all the facts which are acquired by knowledge, the digestion and assimilation of whatever in the material world the man comes in contact with' (23–4). The work of art, 'a unified mental vision of experience', is the clearest form of the imagination, 'an imaginative ordering of sense experience' and the way in which people understand the superiority of perception to abstraction (24–5). 'Vision', according to Blake, is the creative power of the artist and is the telos of all energy, freedom and wisdom. The 'visionary' passes through sight to vision and not stock visual memories (25). There are three worlds, of memory, sight and vision, in Blake's cosmology. In the first we see nothing, in the second what we have to and in the third what we want to: the world of vision is that of art, 'is a world of fulfilled desire and unbounded freedom' (26; see also Chapter 8). Frye distances himself and us from Blake, saying that while most people learn that if we imagine something it almost never happens or does so partially, the visionary, like the child, believes that it ought to happen, that imagination creates reality and that the world desired is more real than the world we accept. 'Art', for Blake, means 'culture' or 'civilization', so that, in Frye's view, that includes scientific, religious and philosophical presentations of reality (27). Vision is never far from Blake's view of art, whose universal language is of images and whose grammars are religions, and allows each imagination to play with its accent. In a phrase that Frye will reiterate in a variation in his last two books – 'Seeing is believing, and belief is vision: the *substance* of things hoped for, the *evidence* of things not seen' (28). Through imagination, he is connecting the philosopher or, by implication, the critic with the writer: 'a metaphysical system, again, is a system; that is, an art-form, to be judged in terms of its inner coherence' (28). Blake's history provides material for the imagination to synthesize, not memory to reflect on (29).

In 'The Rising God' Frye explains that Blake identifies God with the imagination, thinks of God as the eternal Self and the worship of Him as self-development, and, while associating the artist with God, identifies 'men' as 'Man' or God (30). Humans tend to restrict themselves by denying God, thereby limiting the identity of God and humanity. We may perceive as God but cannot perceive God: we can only create God in our own image (31–2). Frye's defence of Blake's numerology and designs might also serve as a defence of his own: 'in Blake all recurrent numbers and diagrams must be explained in terms of their context and their relation to the poems, not as indicating in Blake any affinity with mathematical mysticism' (34). Frye's apologia for Blake fights the charge of mysticism, which his own work is subject to.

Blake's attack on Newton is an opposition to an impersonal and abstract God. His Urizen, whom Frye calls 'the god of empty space and blind will', provides prophetic insight into the geological time of theologies like the 'immanent will' of Thomas Hardy's *The Dynasts*, but Blake regards this latter account of God as superstitious (34). Rather, Blake, in Frye's view, would be more apt to agree with Samuel Butler and Bernard Shaw that an organism's 'imagination' alters that being (35). Until the last years of Frye's life, he seems to have agreed with Blake's view of nature – that humans are maladjusted to it, that their superiority over it has evolved civilization and that without humans it is barren (36; see also 39–41 and Frye 1991a). The barrenness of nature without humanity is a view that the young Frye shared with Blake as he read him on the Canadian prairie or Great Plains in the spring and summer of 1934 and seems to appear in the splinter of a novel in his unpublished papers, which I call the Kennedy–Megill fragment, written in part about that experience (see Chapter 9). Blake's God is not perfect in the abstract sense but represents 'the full development of all one's imagination', and there is no chain of being (36–8). Usually in Blake 'spirit' and 'angel' mean 'imagination functioning as inspiration', a thought worth keeping in mind when we look at Frye's story 'Affable Angel' (1940) in Chapter 9. For Blake, no divinity exists in thought, sky or nature that is greater than ourselves (39). Humans, Blake postulates, are capable of folly and cruelty lower than anything in nature. People realize that the world desired and created with imaginations is more real and better than the 'fallen' world in which they dwell. In *A Vision of the Last Judgment* Blake claims that his art is visionary or imaginative and tries to restore the golden age (40). As all reality is mental, according to Blake, the fall of the human mind involved in the physical world a corresponding fall: for him, the fall and the creation of the world were the same event (41). The fallen world is that of *Songs of Experience*, the unfallen that of *Songs of Innocence* – to avoid mediocrity the adult must maintain a childlike imagination (42–3). But imagination also has great visionary power: the body of life is the totality of imagination: God (43). Blake identifies God and humanity, so that there is no abstract good as postulated in natural religion, only revealed religion, the apocalypse or revelation. There, at the end of the Bible, is a return of paradise. Frye paraphrases Blake: vision is the end of religion; the destruction of the physical universe clears our sight; art trains this kind of vision systematically and is the medium that reveals religion; because of the Bible's unified vision of human life, it is the vehicle of revealed religion and is 'the Great Code of Art'; if all art is visionary, it is also apocalyptic and revelatory; before death, the artist can experience the spiritual world, in which John was interested (45; see also Chapter 8). Frye was later to borrow Blake's phrase in *Laocoön Aphorisms* for the name of the first volume of his study of the Bible and literature. Like Blake, Frye begins and ends with vision. They both prefer the imaginative unity of human culture to the facts of nature. Perhaps it is here, as we shall see, that Frye had his most fundamental quarrel with deconstruction. Of course, the poem or culture is 'artificial', to use the word in Milton's positive sense: how could it be otherwise? For Frye, as for Blake, culture is made and does not answer to nature.

The act of imagination is a union of existence and perception, a time-space complex, in which time and space, at least in our conventional notions, disappear: such is the eternal and infinite for Blake (46). In Blake's scheme imaginative victories endure, and unimaginative ones do not: that is salvation and the 'afterlife' (47). Blake represents three ascending levels of imagination. First, there is Ulro or his hell, full of symbols of sterility, like sand and rocks, a level 'of the isolated individual reflecting on his memories of perception and evolving generalizations and abstract ideas' (48; see also 49). Second, there is Generation, our ordinary world, in which no living thing, except the plants, is adjusted. Third, there is the imaginative world, which has a lower and an upper part. In Beulah, or the lower part, with the purging of vision, we proceed up the ladder of love from sex to 'an imaginative awakening, as in the traditional philosophy of love derived from Plato's *Symposium*' (49). In his last two books Frye revives this image from Plato, the movement from love to wonder in an imaginative expansion. Subject and object become lover and beloved in this union. Eden, or the higher part, involves the union of creator and creature or of energy and form and is, in Blake's symbolism, 'a fiery city of the spiritual sun' (49–50). Ulro is the single world of the subject; Generation is the double world of subject and object; Beulah is the triple world of lover, beloved and their mutual creation. In Eden the father, mother and child, which symbolize this triple world, are contained in the unified imagination in the Bible, which Blake symbolizes by the four Zoas, 'living creatures around the throne or chariot of God', that Ezekiel and John describe. Blake's threefold world, like Frye's, is really fourfold. According to Frye, Blake thinks that God cannot be found through the will or the understanding (50). That Blake identifies religion with art is not, in Frye's view, the same as the Romantics identifying the religious and aesthetic experiences, so that Blake's thought makes no room for aesthetics, 'or general theories of abstract beauty', whose ideology will be discussed briefly in my chapter on ideology (51). This distancing of Blake from Romanticism, especially in light of his debt to Renaissance views of allegory, also applies to Frye himself and qualifies the desire to consider him a Romantic thinker. Blake's fourfold symbolism, like Swedenborg's, makes him question the Trinity, and his God is fourfold, 'power, love and wisdom contained within the unity of civilized human imagination' (52). His God is a 'God-man', the final revelation of Christianity being that 'God is Jesus', so that after having outgrown the fatherhood of God, which implies an imaginative infancy, we find our own being (53).

In 'Beyond Good and Evil' Frye looks at Blake's political and ethical ideas, which, like his views of religion, are based on his theory of knowledge. A person is either for imagination or for memory: there is no neutrality. For Blake, evil is negative, which he calls 'jealousy', a frustration of activity, a self-restraint or a restraint on others, so that he relates it to the medieval *accidia*, the Elizabethan 'melancholy' and Baudelaire's *ennui*. Blake writes against the death-impulse (55-6). Thwarting the imagination is the basis of fear and cruelty: 'all the cruel are frightened, and all the fearful are cruel' (57). In humans the principle of life is the imagination, of death is the 'natural man' (58). Moreover, the 'fully imaginative man is . . . a visionary whose imaginative activity is prophecy and whose perception produces art', and it is 'the superior clarity and accuracy of the prophet's vision that makes him an artist, and that makes the great artist prophetic' (59). Just as for Blake, so too it seems for Frye: convention and socially accepted religion are more dangerous than an opiate of the people but are the source of tyranny, the priesthood that props up the king with divinity. Blake calls state religion the source of all cruelty: this false religion says that God is elsewhere, unknown and mysterious and asks for submission, acceptance and unconditional obedience (60). Those who do not read Blake, or Frye, and turn from their Christianity because, as this age would have it, all Christianity is orthodoxy, would do well to consider Frye's paraphrase of Blake: 'It is in the God of official Christianity, however, invented as a homeopathic cure for the teachings of Jesus, that state religion has produced its masterpiece' (61). Here is the demonic parody Blake and Frye fought against. If we accept the physical world, which is not good enough for our imaginations, then we are left with our Selfhoods, fall into 'hysteria and maniacal warfare' and become prey to the historical succession to Deism, which in *Jerusalem* Blake symbolizes as Druidism. In paraphrasing Blake, Frye seems to have the totalitarian tyrannies of the 1930s and 1940s in mind as well as the movement from Bourbon to Bonaparte in the French Revolution: 'Revolution is always an attempt to smash the structure of tyranny and create a better world, even when revolutionaries do not understand what creation implies or what a better world is' (67). This view also affected Frye's response to the student revolt of the 1960s (see Chapter 6). Imagination is the key to the creation of a better world for Blake and Frye. Society is best off when it realizes its defects enough to listen to the prophet scolding it and the 'honest man' saying what he pleases. For Blake, 'the real war in society is the "Mental Fight" between the visionaries and the champions of tyranny' or the visionary renegades – poets, philosophers, painters and theologians who serve Caesar, the conservatives or Angels whom the radicals or Devils, like Blake, combat in an intellectual fight in which contraries lead to progression. The radical and prophetic Blake's Eden is 'an eternal Valhalla of conflicts waged with bows of burning gold and arrows of desire' (68). One of Blake's cardinal principles is the forgiveness of sins, an antidote for what poisons the imagination – 'the accusation of sins' (68).

In the four imaginative states – Eden, Beulah, Generation and Ulro – Devils and Angels are involved in a fight between self-development and Selfhood that arises from the self, so that the Angels may speak the language of self-development and imitate its processes (71). Frye discusses Blake's Eden first: the poet speaks about joy and sorrow, and, in his view, eternity is the plane of existence in which the fulfilment of desire (joy) becomes possible, so that the 'absence of joy in Nietzsche's philosophy would put him on the side of the Angels for Blake' (72). Nietzsche is a primary source for deconstruction, but contributes less to Frye's theory. Then Frye describes Blake's Beulah. The natural man has a possessive attitude to love: 'Mastery over woman produces the same morbidity and imaginative idleness as mastery over man, and Blake uses the word "jealousy" to cover the Selfhood's attitude to both' (73). Blake thinks that the antinomies or binary oppositions of body and soul are pernicious and that prurience and prudery are similar and the autoeroticism of virginity leads to frustration: denying the body is harmful because it is the soul from the perspective of this world and incorporates desires and imaginative needs (74). The maleness of the artist and the relegation of the maternal principle to natural religion in Blake, and reported by Frye, may be understandable when the artist and critic are male, but to speak of the material world or nature as feminine and as receiving the seeds of 'his' imagination has become increasingly problematic. There was once a preponderance of men in art and criticism, but this is less true in the 1990s (74–5). For Blake, female worship is a form of idolatry like nature worship. It is possible that, to some extent, Blake's discussion of the female will, the Madonna smothering the child's imagination and the coy mistress of courtly love being lord to the man, may also be construed as male anxieties and projections about not being in control and lacking sexual power. In other words, the male poet cannot have the child, so that he traditionally has assimilated to himself the power to give birth to a poem, like a woman to a child, and then exiles the woman from his creativity, so that great poets are male. This exclusion is probably not Blake's intent because it smacks of angelic frustration of activity, but it is a danger in his vision, and like versions of the male creation myth. This is Blake's Generation, but it threatens his view of Eden.

In Generation the worldly struggles of the visionary are mainly concerned with money. Blake's economics are equally interesting. Frye explains them:

> A money economy is a continuous partial murder of the victim, a poverty that keeps many imaginative needs out of reach. Money for those who have it, on the other hand, can belong only to the Selfhood, as it assumes the possibility of enjoyment through possession, which we have seen to be impossible; and hence of being passively or externally stimulated into imagination. An equal distribution of money, even if practicable, would therefore not affect its status as the root of all evil.

> (76)

In Ulro the problem is what is a vision and what is hallucinatory. The difference between the two is that whereas the one is an aspect of genius and is divine, universal and communicable, the other lacks communication because it is from reflection and not something imagined. For Blake, all is a double vision, appropriately the title of Frye's last and posthumous book, because the unfallen world, which is eternal and infinite, persists in this world. This persistent reality is the foundation of vision (77; see also Chapter 8). Frye anchors his paraphrase in Blake's poem on double vision in his letter of 22 November 1802 to Butts, which may serve as a key, gloss or epigraph to Frye's thought.

At all four levels of imaginative conflict, the Selfhood parodies the imagination: the hero's physical fight the artist's mental fight; the jealous wife or teasing mistress the emanation; money (as well as morality) the community of minds; the nightmare or ghost the vision (78). The figure of Jesus – the God and Man, the perfect man not without sin but with forgiveness of sins, the revolutionary and the iconoclast – is the type of all prophets (78–9). To attain heaven is to develop the God within: it is the awakened imagination without frustration, restraint and 'holiness' or the spurious kinds of religious observance (81; see also 83). Jesus helps the sick to heal themselves: they choose to give an imaginative response to his imaginative effort (81). The Christian church is the 'free use of the imagination' (82). Jesus releases imagination, which is life, and makes it more abundant by taking away the memory of sin and releasing it (83).

Frye's discussion of Blake hinges on Blake's being an allegorist and 'A Literalist of the Imagination'. In comparing him to Berkeley and Swedenborg, Frye distinguishes Blake from them because he, unlike them, is a practising artist (85). This distinction applies to the close relation between Blake and Frye: by the time *Fearful Symmetry* came out, Frye had not published a story for seven years (see Chapter 9). As much as Frye identifies with Blake, although there are moments when he allies himself with the reader to establish a distance from the poet, and as much as he insists on Blake's broad definition of art, Frye either has to see Berkeley, Swedenborg and himself as artists, like Blake, or he has to admit the difference. While distinguishing criticism from poetry, Frye insists on its creativity: he tries to have it both ways. Blake's role as a painter also complicates his relation to the verbal arts, and to Frye. Both Blake and Frye may believe that art and knowledge are recreation, but how is literary criticism any different from philosophy, theology and science in being a rational synthesis that does 'not create new images or forms' and, instead, establishes 'new relationships among the images we already have' (86)? Is to create a general theory of literature – which requires abstract and rational ideas or at least generations based on an inductive experience of literary texts or deductive principles tested against individual works – as concrete, imaginative and restorative as the art of poetry? This is perhaps the central question in considering the criticism, if not all the writing, of Northrop Frye. To put it another way, if, as Frye says, 'Wisdom is the application of the imaginative vision taught us by art', and if our control over abstract ideas increases as we grow older as 'part of the expanding child's vision', then fine, but if that control replaces vision, we suffer degeneration. Perhaps there are good criticism and bad criticism, the one imaginative and the other in search of a passive meaning. But why does Frye distinguish Blake from Berkeley and Swedenborg while advising that our response to a philosopher should be 'as the imaginative projection of a creative mind' (87)? The reader becomes the artist, but this idea still leaves a contradiction in Frye's account of Blake's theory of art that, I shall argue, remains in his own theory as he expands it during the rest of his life. Unity and organization in wisdom and vision is one of the principles that Frye sees in Blake and himself. Years before *Anatomy*, Frye could write a sentence that is like a gauntlet thrown down to those who would oppose him in the intellectual battle or mental fight: 'The wise man has a pattern or image of reality in his mind into which everything he knows fits, and into which everything he does not know could fit, and therefore his approach to knowledge is something that the dung-beetles of unorganized learning cannot even grasp' (87). In the study of Blake, and in *Anatomy*, Frye is communicating with the public his epistemological framework, a visionary scheme, and not the hallucinations of a crank. Like Blake, Frye does not think that private mythologies are possible, because a mythology has a unity and organization to it, and is not haphazard. It depends then how readers respond to Frye's vision, as to Blake's, whether they accept this view of mythology or knowledge or wisdom.

Frye's weaving of Blake's tapestry is intricate. For instance, Plato's use of the dialogue shows that 'he was the only philosopher who was artist enough to master a visionary form' and thereby suggests infinite responses rather than insisting on one (87). Does Frye find this form? Art reveals, where religion mystifies (88). In the Preface to *Milton* Blake writes that every man or woman should be a poet, painter, musician or architect and leave families and nations who stand in the way of art and that outward ceremony is Antichrist (89). Frye is an artist if we stick to his paraphrase of Blake, 'Everything worth doing and done well is an art', and if we accept Blake's view that the totality of imaginative power is culture or civilization (89). Besides Blake, Matthew Arnold is a source for Frye's ideas on education and society (see Chapter 6). Frye's contrast of these two writers, their views of culture and anarchy, may give some insight into his own radical and conservative sides:

> Blake believed, like Arnold, that culture preserves society: he did not believe, as Arnold apparently did, that society preserves culture. Society to Blake is an eternally unwilling recipient of culture: every genius must fight society no matter what his age. Arnold's view of both culture and society is conservative, traditional and evolutionary; Blake is radical, apocalyptic and revolutionary. Arnold thinks of the prophet not so much as a visionary as a preacher of moral scruples, and in his thought the boundary line between Hebrews and Philistines becomes even more vague and fluctuating than it was in history.
>
> (90–1; see also 148–9)

Blake believes in the divinity of the imagination, that artists from all times are building Golgonooza, the city of God, the New Jerusalem, which is above time and is the whole form of human civilization and culture. In it and at the same time, the artists will dwell together and all that the good person has done will help to build it, where the completion of what he or she has hoped for or intended to do will occur (91).

The basic principle of Blake's theory of painting is that 'Art is the incorporation of the greatest possible imaginative effort in the clearest and most accurate form' (91). Blake's theory stresses genius, someone inspired and skilled at the craft, a worker in a society in which the artist is a worker with a social function who produces goods in response to 'steady social demand' and not someone socially isolated or forced to earn a living from patronage. Outline is the main characteristic of mastery in art (96). The painter, like the composer, should have imaginative integrity or freedom from external stimulus, to work vision, and not perception, into the painting. All art comes from the mind (98). But Blake has his own version of Burke's sublime and beautiful: they are 'the science of wrath', or the 'explosion of energy', and 'the science of pity', the fruit and incorporation of that explosion, the Dionysiac and the Apollonian, or in Blake's terms more than Nietzsche's, Rintrah and Palamabron. The artist seeks 'a unity of varieties' (99). Art does not improve, 'and all talk of "tradition", in the sense of a progressive improvement from one age to another, is only pedantic jargon' (100). Having already written a story, 'The Resurgent' (1940), about the relation between painting and politics, creativity and totalitarianism, Frye himself later works out his position on tradition in relation to Blake, Arnold and Eliot. Blake prefers the living symmetries of the organism for art as opposed to the dead symmetries of the diagram (104). Frye observes that all that Blake hated in life and thought intensified after his death: 'Impressionism in particular, with its breaking down of outline into color, its interest in scientific theories of light, and its laborious photographic detail, is a more complete denial of Blake's doctrines than anything he ever saw' (105). Blake, Frye observes with sympathetic detachment, is partial because of loneliness, and the most enduring aspect of his views on painting is his defence of the importance and dignity of art and the responsibility of the visionary (105–6).

In 'The Word within the Word' Frye argues that most of the meanings of the word 'symbolic' do not apply to Blake's poetry (107). When we create, we do so as part of Jesus, the universal creator, 'the Logos or Word of God, the totality of creative power, the universal visionary in whose mind we perceive the particular' (108; see also Chapter 10). In this view the world of space and time is 'a single creature in eternity and infinity, fallen and redeemed' (108). The greater the work of art, the more fully it reveals the vision of how God sees this world, a gigantic myth of creation, fall, redemption and apocalypse. Because, for Blake, the Bible is the greatest work of art, it is God's Word (108). Blake's poetry relates to a central myth based mostly on the Bible, which, in his 'diabolical interpretation', is one poem consistent in symbolism and imagery (109). The cyclic vision of the Bible is the foundation of that in poetry or the true epic. It is Blake in the Laocoön Aphorisms who says that 'The Old & New Testaments are the Great Code of Art' (110). Like Blake, who cares little about questions of historical accuracy and authorship, Frye's own approach to the Bible in *The Great Code*, *Words with Power* and *The Double Vision* looks at the structure and imagery and not authorial and historical matters. Frye's paraphrase of Blake is instructive for his own view of history: 'The meaning of history, like the meaning of art, is to be found in its relation to the same great archetype of human existence' (111; see also Chapter 5). Inner form and genre concern Frye and Blake: 'The true epic is a cyclic vision of life, and the true drama, including narrative and heroic poetry, is an episode of that cyclic vision' (111). Great art is more conventional than many recognize. Blake thinks that the author's intention is unreliable because it involves many levels of consciousness unknown to the person, such as the subconscious and superconscious (111–12). The poem is completed beyond the poet, which resembles Frye's view in *Anatomy* that Shakespeare's direction of Hamlet would not be a definitive performance (1957: 5–6). Poems show unity of words and images. Blake's view of diction is apparently summarized in his statement that 'Poetry admits not a Letter that is Insignificant' (113). Just as Blake observes that there are good and bad allegory based on the question of the unity of imagery, so too does Frye. They both oppose allegory arising from the similitude of simile to that from the identity of metaphor because the one becomes a correspondence of abstractions whereas the other identifies two real things (116–17). The artist believes his religion because it gives him a body of generally grasped symbols and the visionary masterpieces on which it was founded, such as the Bible for Christian poets. For Blake, the Giant forms dwindle into gods and then disappear into personifications until the connection with the archetypal myth is all but obliterated (118–19; see also Chapter 7). Apparently, for Frye as for Blake, 'religion is raw imaginative material clarified by art' (119). Another important point furthers the claim that Blake read the Bible imaginatively: 'The central form of Christianity is its vision of the humanity of God and the divinity of risen Man, and this, in varying ways, is what all great Christian artists have attempted to recreate' (120). Frye concludes in outlining Blake's view of allegory that if it signifies 'universal significance in the artist's creation of particular things', then all worthwhile art is allegorical (121). The ultimate significance of a work, Frye says, is a dimension beyond but attached to the literal meaning, a notion akin to Dante's anagogy or the deepest

understanding of poetry (121). Blake has a central 'Form' or myth to his
poetry composed of all other 'Forms' that Frye outlines:

> Its boundaries, once more, are creation, fall, redemption and apoca-
> lypse, and it embraces the four imaginative levels of existence, Eden,
> Beulah, Generation and Ulro. It revolves around the four antitheses
> that we have been tracing in the first four chapters, of imagination and
> memory in thought, innocence and experience in religion, liberty and
> tyranny in society, outline and imitation in art. These four antitheses
> are all aspects of one, the antithesis of life and death, and Blake
> assumes that we have this unity in our heads.
>
> (124–5)

Frye himself is given here and in *Anatomy* to fourfold schemes or
visions unified with his imagination. Although Frye gives a detailed
account of Blake's central myth (125–43), he has provided an outline
that, for the purposes of this chapter on Frye's reconstruction of Blake,
should suggest affinities between the poet and his critic. From Frye's
account of Blake in terms of archetypes and comparative mythology,
we proceed as if we were reading the poet in the light of *The Golden
Bough*, and we can already hear the voice of the theorist and the critic
of *Anatomy*. Frye argues that 'Blake was, it is obvious, so conscious
of the shape of his central myth that his characters become almost
diagrammatic' (143). This problem also arises for Frye, or any of us
who write with a central myth, shape or structure of images or ideas in
mind. The circular critical controversy about which comes first, plot or
character – Aristotle favours plot and A. C. Bradley character – may
affect how poets write as much as how critics do. Unlike Blake,
Dickens, for instance, may have character before him as he plots his
fictional course. Frye calls Blake's characters, like Orc and Ololon,
ideographs from a metaphysical poetry that addresses the intellectual
powers of the reader, and he concludes that the response to it will
depend on taste. This critic has a real taste for it: 'One looks in a poet
for what is there, and what is there in Blake is a dialectic, an anatomy
of poetry, a rigorously unified vision of the essential forms of the
creative mind, piercing through its features to its articulate bones'
(143). It was for Frye to give us an anatomy of criticism to complement
Blake's anatomy of poetry. Like Blake, Frye reads literature and the
Bible with an imaginative eye and a corporeal eye, for instance, seeing
the Bible as beginning in chaos and moving towards the city of God
completed in the disappearance of nature but also being able to see it as
a movement from historical recollection and 'barbarous cosmology' to
'the most impenetrably turgid allegory ever devised in language' (144).

Both Blake and Frye are visionary and satirical, which seems more paradoxical than it needs to.

I want to turn, perhaps all too briefly, only to those critical and theoretical ideas in the second and third parts of *Fearful Symmetry*, 'The Development of the Symbolism' and 'The Final Synthesis', that are not set out in the critical framework of the first part, 'The Argument'. In discussing Blake in relation to tradition and experiment Frye sets out Blake's theory of poetry in the perspective of English literature (1947a: 147–86). Frye furthers his attempt to destroy 'the myth that Blake is a literary freak' (147). Blake prefers Hebrew prophecy and the medieval to the classical, and he thinks that the 'priest' represents tyranny, which a belief in mystery produces (148–9). Frye develops the theme here, as he does later in his career, of a visionary company of scholars – a kind of source for Blake, Frye and others who came later – 'the great cosmopolitan humanist culture which arose in Europe between the Renaissance and the Reformation', of a great visionary culture (see my Chapter 8). Blake considers true theology to comprise prophecy and interpretation: he bases interpretation on Dante's four levels of allegory (which derive from Aquinas and occur in Boccaccio) and equates prophecy and vision. For Blake and Frye, as for many of the humanists of Frye's 'golden age', vision, and not doctrine, is the central form of Christianity (150–1). Frye's method in this discussion is to understand Blake's thought historically. To do so, he says that we must take into account his affinities with three Renaissance traditions: 'the imaginative approach to God through love and beauty in Italian Platonism, the doctrine of inner inspiration in the left-wing Protestants, and the theory of creative imagination in occultism' (155). But Frye is careful to distinguish the differences between Blake and these three traditions:

> The Renaissance development of the *Symposium* is Blakean; the Pythagorean tendencies derived from the *Timaeus* and the Cabbala are not. The occult idea that man can create a larger humanity from nature is Blakean: magic, sympathetic healing and evocation of spirits are not. The belief that the Bible is understood only by an initiated imagination is Blakean: the secret traditions of the Rosicrucians and the rest do not lead us to Blake whatever they may be.
>
> (155)

Similarly, this chapter and my book as a whole will suggest the great affinities between Blake and Frye but also the differences. After all, if Frye had not translated Blake's art of poetry into criticism and had not made significant departures, it is highly unlikely that Frye would have gained the stature he did as a theorist and a critic. Frye concludes that all the movements of thought that he has 'been tracing converge on Blake's identification of the artist's genius with the Holy Spirit' (1947a: 157). He discusses Blake's debt to poets like Spenser and Milton, especially the latter's prophetic vision of an imaginative culture and call for a freeing of creative power, a passing from revolution to apocalypse, in *Areopagitica* (159–60). If Blake had been born between 1530 and 1630, Frye speculates, he would have been able to offer the world what in the *Letter to Ralegh* Spenser called 'a continued Allegory, or darke conceit' and would not have had to put up with the frustration of being told that as a poet he should not invent a private symbolism. Blake, Frye says, hated the Augustan view of culture and science partly because this was the first period in English history that would have called him mad. It also advocated a study of the 'natural man', conceived of memory as the source of the themes and forms of poetry, thought of God as a Selfhood spinning a web of abstract ideas, settled for the chain of being and personification and considered art as an imitation of nature that more and more improves nature (161–5). Frye's Blake is neither of the Augustans nor of the Romantics but relates to the poetic age of Gray, Collins, Chatterton and Ossian and to the age of Berkeley and Sterne, a time, Frye argues, that should not be dismissed, as it traditionally has been, as a transition between Pope and Wordsworth (167–8). This age of Blake reacted against the 'Age of Reason' by developing poetry concerned with Blake's archetypal myth (fall, redemption, judgement, immortality); Blake and his contemporaries write apocalyptic prophecies and prefer visionary themes, the sublime and the gigantic vision, to those that sense experience suggests. These poets return to the poet as prophet, as seer or *vates*, like the ancient bards, those who taught truths higher than reason could yield (168–9). This 'poetic primitivism', to use Frye's phrase, arose in the last half of the eighteenth century. It fostered a new mythopoeia and tended to be associated with the views of Whigs rather than, as in the case of the Augustans, a politically conservative attitude (170–2). The Arthurian and Eddic myths were discovered or revived. Blake and his contemporaries rehabilitated romance and myths from far-off lands just as Frye and some of his contemporaries did. Like James Frazer, an important source for Frye, some of Blake's sources, like Jacob Bryant and Edward Davies, helped develop an impressive idea that, in Frye's view, 'has haunted English criticism at least since Elizabethan times' if not the mythopoeic poetry of all times, 'a morphology of symbolism' (173–4). Blake seems to have postulated an ur-civilization that possessed an ur-myth of which even the Bible preserves only a recollection (175). Frye argues that *Poetical Sketches* (1783), Blake's first and only printed volume of poetry, contains much of what occurs in other poets of his age: 'Gothic horror, the charnel house and the graveyard, primitivism, northern antiquities, oligarchic mercantilism, the renewed appreciation of Renaissance poetry' (177). Whereas the young Blake, who wrote 'King Edward the Third', could extol the *pax Britannica*, Blake soon retracts this view in one of his frequent palinodes. His revolutionary poetry requires a protagonist who champions liberty and an antagonist, tyranny. Class conflict becomes a prominent theme. In Blake's first volume Frye observes three major Blakean themes in an embryonic state: 'the cycle of history, the role of the artist in society, and the Fall' (179–82). Blake experimented extensively in versification: his ideas are difficult but his syntax and vocabulary are 'limpidly pure', so that Frye can conclude, 'Not since Donne had so direct a style been able to express such a variety of moods from apocalypse to ribaldry' (185; see also 182–4). In Frye's view Blake desired a dactylic hexameter in which to express the 'thunder of apocalyptic visions' that occurred in the medieval septenarius and was the metre that Chapman used to recreate the rhythm of the *Iliad* (185). Frye contends that Blake's theory of art applies to music and painting as well as to poetry: he also says that the rhythm of Blake's poetry has close affinities to music (186).

In the chapter on the structural principles of Blake's engraved works, 'The Thief of Fire', Frye shows his understanding of the poet while distancing himself from him, for instance, in his observation that Blake was not fair to Bacon, Locke and Newton, none of whom is a Deist, although he concedes that they are contraries who bear the brunt of Blake's satire, which is often anti-philosophical (1947a: 187–91). Blake's Menippean satire, *An Island in the Moon*, is a prose satire with verse interludes that attacks cultural dilettantism (191). Frye wonders whether Blake 'was not of the race of Rabelais and Apuleius, a metaphysical satirist inclined to fantasy rather than symbolism' (193). Frye himself wrote Menippean or Varronian satire in his brief published stories from 1936 to 1940, a satiric form that deals with mental attitudes, folly and evil as intellectual diseases (such as the mad pedantry of the *philosophus gloriosus*), caricature, and a frequent but not necessary combination of morality and intellectual fancy, and that uses loose-jointed narrative with apparent carelessness. The short form of the Menippean satire is what Frye uses in 'Four Dialogues', a colloquy or dialogue that involves a conflict of ideas and not of character and can shade away from the satiric to moral or fanciful discussions (see Frye 1957: 308–12). This vocation for Menippean satire may, as I suggest in Chapter 9, be the road not taken by Frye, which he points to as the path in the fork that Blake did not take. Frye's interest in Chaucer, like Blake's, derives in large part from an interest in satire, and he praises Robert Burton's *Anatomy of Melancholy* and Swift's *Gulliver's Travels* as great examples of the Menippean satire or, using the term Frye favoured, the anatomy. They organize and satirize exhaustive erudition. Frye's short 'anatomies' of his twenties give way to his great anatomy of his forties, so that Frye, who had a penchant for satire and perhaps a vocation for it, understood all too well the 'serious' and 'fantastic' possibilities of *Anatomy of Criticism*. Blake's *The Marriage of Heaven and Hell* explores the idea that the unrest that has produced the American and French Revolutions shows that the apocalypse or end of the world may occur at any moment (194). If Blake is a great satirist, who creates 'Giant forms', as Rabelais does, and in doing so, is an apocalyptic visionary who through caricature reveals the unreliability and consistency of sense experience and brings us into contact with reality, then *Marriage* belongs to the tradition of Swift, Sterne, Fielding and Hogarth even as it contains new material and portends new movements (200–1). Humanity senses its fallenness because of the gap between its desire and its power, and revolution 'is the sign of apocalyptic yearnings, of an impulse to burst loose from this world altogether and get into a better one, a convulsive lunge forward of the imagination' (201). Blake is a great satirist and, therefore, has, for Frye, an apocalyptic imagination, but, as Frye observes, the term '"revolution" itself contains a tragic irony: it is itself a part of the revolving of life and death in a circle of pain' (218). This is a view that is consistent with Frye's attitude to the student revolt of the late 1960s (see my Chapter 6). Blake's Orc, youth as opposed to the age of Urizen, begins as a Promethean rebel and ends as an exiled and execrated serpent, and the vision of life as an Orc cycle is pessimistic (219–25).

The Orc cycle earns Frye's close attention. Orc and Urizen, Frye notes in his chapter 'The Refiner in Fire', are 'two contrary states of the soul' that Blake calls innocence and experience (Frye 1947a: 227). Vision, not reason, helps us to understand *Songs of Innocence* and *Songs of Experience*, each of which satirizes the other's state with a double-edged irony (236–7). Blake's poems, such as *Tiriel*, often explore tyranny and the fallenness of history (241–5). Frye suggests that we must accept the pessimism of the Orc cycle, the 'vision of "Becoming"', or find some vision of life that succeeds where it fails by imposing 'an intelligible form both on Enitharmon's crystal house and on the time in which it persists' (246; see also 245). Enitharmon is queen of the sky and sits in a house unperturbed as she revolves her unreachable stars in time's indefinite night. In Blake's poetry Frye finds the issue of becoming and being, which is common enough to philosophers like Descartes and Heidegger, but also raises issues for poets and readers about human and literary character. In the Orc cycle Blake represents the human awareness of 'a continuum of identity' and 'a certain permanent form or character which makes us equally ourselves in all stages' of life (247). In *Jerusalem* Blake calls this total form of creative acts and visions evolved over life the 'Real Man' (247). The total form of the creative acts of humans or characters or identities constitutes immortality and isolates the eternally humane from the accidents of becoming (248). For Blake, only the creator possesses the divine spirit and, as Frye says, 'The real artist is not the man creating, but the total form of his creation, his art regarded as his vision of life, and as an individual part of the archetypal vision which is the Word of God' (250). The natural cycle, which played a larger role in the original plan of *Anatomy of Criticism* and remains part of Frye's theory of *mythos*, is the foundation of life and the imagination, so that even though art does not imitate nature, the order of nature is the basis for order in art (258). The imaginative vision turns us about to what Blake says in *The Everlasting Gospel* to be the unique aspect of Jesus' teaching: the forgiveness of sins. The eyes of humanity will open when conscious imagination 'perfects the vision of the world of consciousness' (259). Blake's view of history is an opposition, if not quite a dialectic in which a series of crises occurs: sudden imaginative visions lead to the *status quo*'s counteraction and subsides again until the oppositions grow sharper every time and will eventually present a marked alternative between eternal life and extermination (260; see also my Chapter 5). Civilization tries to remove a feeling of external oppression in the small part of nature that it controls. For instance, in discussing Los and his sons, Frye observes the eternal ecology that he returns to with some urgency, and perhaps with some difference, in *Words with Power* and *The Double Vision*: 'there is no age either without some perception that a genuine culture does not pollute nature but tries to transform it into a garden or park inhabited by friendly animals' (263; see also my chapters 7 and 8). From nature, in Blake's scheme, the artist creates a body that has a mental form and does so by imposing a lasting vision on the flux of time and by rendering the familiar intelligible (267). The image, form or reality of art is its continuous pleasure and shape (268).

   In 'The Nightmare with her Ninefold' Frye claims that *The Four Zoas* is 'the greatest abortive masterpiece in English literature' (1947a: 269; see also Chapter 8). Its theme is the fall of Albion and his regaining of Jerusalem in the apocalypse, which involves the loss of the identity of human and divine natures that the fall and creation of the physical universe caused, the struggle to recover this identity in the fallen world that Jesus completed and the apocalypse (270). Blake reiterates the idea that progress derives from forgiveness of sins, which is, in part, 'the transference of the will from the Selfhood to the imagination' (298). The world of eternity, for Blake, is fourfold: Frye explains that the visionary attempts to combine past, present and future in a vision (300). The first four Nights of the poem describe the fall until Adam's time; the next four Nights focus on human history and the sharpening opposition between Los' evolution and the Orc cycle; the ninth Night represents the apocalypse, the days of wrath, in an inimitable and 'colossal explosion of creative power' and makes its way to 'the very headwaters of Western imagination' (305–6; see also Chapter 8). Blake moves beyond Langland's *Vision of Piers the Plowman* (c. 1367–86), which ends with the triumph of Antichrist in the time of the poet, because although he is close to his predecessor spiritually, his complete vision is, in Frye's view, a divine comedy and not a satire or a tragedy (304). As the poet works with concrete images, a vision of existence beyond the concrete or physical has to be a triumph of technical skill (306). Frye is not sure that Blake's experiment, as beautiful and powerful as it is, succeeds: is the ninth Night the real climax of vision or an addition to *The Four Zoas* as an effort of will as a result of conscience? (308). In the poem Frye does not think that Blake has 'achieved a definitive vision', but has instead left in manuscript a great work and returned to the triumph of reason and nature (309). Frye's canon also shows a disjunction or creative tension between satire and comedy.

In the third part of *Fearful Symmetry* Frye explores Blake's final synthesis. What is of interest to my argument is the critical principles that Frye borrows from Blake's final phase, especially those that do not repeat the principles from the earlier periods of Blake's career as a poet. With Blake, as with Frye, repetition, which is a principle of identity and amplification of the total imaginative form, is unavoidable and desirable. Frye shares with Blake a desire to go beyond surfaces and find dark conceits, for instance, in his view of the end of the first book of *Milton*: 'To the corporeal understanding this is a sufficiently absurd farrago, which implies that if we put our intellectual powers to work on it, it will emerge a great imaginative masterpiece' (1947a: 316). In defining the epic in 'Comus Agonistes' Frye mentions in passing that 'no literary critic of any experience will make much effort to define his terms', a comment that may have some truth to it but is curious as this is Frye's first book and, along with *Anatomy* and *The Great Code*, one of his most rigorous works involving detailed comments on and definitions of genre (316). The function of the epic is to teach the nation or the social unit that the poet is addressing its religious and historical traditions, the 'Giant forms' of the gods and heroes respectively (316). Frye thinks that the Bible, which he calls 'the historical product of a visionary tradition', has gone further than the epic in consolidating the culture of a nation (317). The shape of the Bible concerned Frye in his work on Blake and became, in terms Frye often applied to Milton, a lifelong patience waiting for the subject to unfold in its epic form, which finally happened between 1981 and 1990 (see 338). Of the Bible, he says: 'It records a continuous reshaping of the earlier and more primitive visions, and as it goes on it becomes more explicitly prophetic, until the confused legends of an obscure people take the form of the full cyclic vision of fall, redemption and apocalypse' (317). Blake finds the religious imagination of the Bible connected with its resistance to abstract thought, probably because the Hebrew poets and prophets again and again recreated the religious and historical visions with which their tradition provided them (317–18).

Like Arnold and Eliot, Frye makes the tradition of English poetry, including the Hebraic and Hellenic influences it inherits, and the relation of poet to society two of his major critical themes. In discussing John Milton, Frye says 'the later a poet comes in his tradition, the more explicitly he has to deal with the question of his personal relation to the society of his time' (1947a: 319). The theme of Blake's *Jerusalem* is that the poet in the age of Deism visualizes the reversibility of space and time in order to see as a single form the linear sequence of history, and the theme of *Milton* is that Milton envisions as a single imaginative unity the tradition behind him (320). Frye thinks that the most inspired and vivid works of art are often produced by artists who are unaware of or have ignored the larger implications of their work to concentrate their powers and says that Blake's awareness makes his characters more 'ideographic' than is desirable (321). Blake is to Milton as Jesus is to God, so that, for Blake, to imitate Milton is to imitate or recreate Jesus and for Virgil to imitate Homer is to imitate 'nature' (322). Perhaps for Frye as for Blake, although he has been distancing himself from the poet, art does not improve but may lead to a visionary crisis in time as its palace or Golgonooza, the entirety of human life viewed in the poetic framework of fall and redemption (or House of Fame?), becomes more visible to the poets. Here tradition is not linear but is a single archetypal form. Music is never far from Frye's mind when he speaks about literary structure or form – genre – so that *Milton* and *Jerusalem* compose a double epic, a prelude and fugue on the same theme (323).

Frye warns, quite properly, about something that is a danger in writing about imaginative literature, motivation and intention, the relation between the writer as person and the writer *qua* writer, a danger most apparent in my chapter 'The Critic as Writer' (see Chapter 9). In this biographical criticism, life is real and poetry is a by-product. With characteristic irony and wit, Frye observes: 'The result, in the criticism of English literature, is that the process of interpreting an unchangeable and deliberately created body of poetry has come to be regarded as fanciful, and the process of reconstructing a vanished life out of a chaos of documents, legends, allusions, gossip and guesswork a matter of exact research' (326). Historicism and biography are once again ascendant, although in my view, criticism is an archaeology with many sites and has sites of priority that the generation or culture determines. Although in Chapter 5 I shall argue that Frye is more aware of history than many realize and that he has some affinities with new historicists and cultural materialists, that is not to say that he shares the same view of history or of the material world. He is adamant about returning a work of art to its source of past experience: 'to read the work of art as something to be interpreted by past events is the most arrant Philistinism' (326). Like Blake, Frye seems to value this inspirational view of art, where creative imagination, which is the only important part of a writer's personality, has no connection with memory and sense experience, although the critic admits there are other kinds of art. Frye, like Blake, appears to stress the eternal present more than the remembrance of things past (326–7). He assesses Blake's relation to his patron, William Hayley, by speculating that Hayley knew that Blake possessed genius and wanted to direct it into socially acceptable behaviour. Frye himself is postulating or reconstructing something that may be a fiction, like the autobiographical critics he criticizes, that because society tends to be conservative and its members less than brilliant, Blake must restrain his genius so that the mediocre and conservative can approve of it (328). This postulation goes on for several pages and weaves its way throughout Frye's chapter. Society pays little attention to the wise because it is primarily made up of 'normal' people given to common sense (332). Most artists do not isolate themselves and denounce society from without, but rather 'work within it, come to terms with it, and improve its culture without any desire either to accept or to quarrel with its anomalies' (333). The speculation on the relation between Hayley and Blake, as well as the related matter of Blake's trial for treason, occasions Frye to muse on the role of artists: they are caught between duty to two kinds of good – imagination and duty to family and society (Frye casts the artist as a man, like Blake, who has a vision but is also a protector of and provider for his wife and children). For Frye as for Blake, the unconscious basis of the imaginative life is the moral law and that of the conscious vision is the physical law; artists who live and die in society without giving up imaginative honesty are among Blake's 'Redeemed' (333–4).

Frye observes with great insight into the relation between the Bible and literature, which meant so much to Blake and him: 'The redemption of Moses, the emancipation of morality from routine obedience to the inward discipline of wisdom, is the Biblical archetype of the saving of the artist from the bondage of the law' (1947a: 334). In Frye's story 'Affable Angel' (1940), there are affinities to his discussion of the 'Bard's Song' in Blake's *Milton*, which tells the story of the dispute between Satan and Palamabron, which he also relates to the account in Revelation where a conflict occurs between Satan and Michael. This association implies a connection between Michael and Rintrah, although, as Frye says, 'the characters are distinguished by Blake (and perhaps a corresponding one, not mentioned, between Palamabron and the "affable archangel" Raphael)', a dispute that also occurs in *Jerusalem* and perhaps as an allusive background for Frye's wartime allegorical satire or satirical allegory (335; see also Chapter 9). Blake's Milton wants to re-enter the world and achieve a new vision that will allow him to see the physical world as Satanic and thereby to see his 'emanation', or all that he loves, as part of himself and not as an objective and distant 'female will' (336). Milton enters Blake's 'left foot' to proclaim the visionary and not the Deist inheritance of Puritanism (338).

By one religion, Blake 'means the attainment of civilized liberty and the common vision of the divinity and unity of Man which is the life of Jesus', and by one language he does not mean English but the language of imagination (Frye 1947a: 340). Frye is wary of the jingoism of the period in which he is writing and contrasts Blake's imaginative unity with that totalitarian ideology. Blake's epic attempts to recreate dead facts into living truths, and he draws on the Bible because it shows history as the process of past time becoming history as present vision. The more we read the Old Testament as history, the more puzzling it gets because that history is absurd and dreary, 'the annals of an obscure race in a remote land' (341). Frye suspects that this history is in the service of tyranny and law, what he might later call ideology, as a way of having the pious Hebrew accept the centrality of the deliverance from Egypt and see it as part of 'a chain of causality in time stretching back to some original contract or covenant' that he or she is 'powerless to alter and bound to observe' (341). This is the union of history and law in a priestly reason that preserves traditions, 'the clasping of dead hands over a legal contract in a vanished past' (341). Blake, and apparently

Frye, thinks that imagination recreates past events in the eternal present. Each of the Orc cycles of history shows an antithesis between God as conceived through the imagination and through law and history. The 'natural man' always tries to reach eternity by way of a legal contract and historical tradition (343). The artist that Blake honours is the one who passes through religion to become a citizen of the free city, the Word of God or body of Jesus, and whose creative mind recreates the Word in time (345). *Milton* attempts to recreate a central vision of life founded on the Bible (346). The tyranny of the past and the mystery of the future, the golden age and utopia, rely on law and history, but the creative life unites imagination and history only to separate them with the end of time (347). The defect in Blake's Milton is that his emanation, all that the poet loves, often in the form of a bride, is lacking because he never sees beyond the 'sinister "female will"' and does not see the aspect of women that includes a 'vision of the spiritual nature of love' (352). Blake's view of women, although an improvement over Milton's, needs an expansion just as, perhaps, Frye in his last years would come to be more aware of the problems of male representations of women. This poem may be a prologue in more ways than Frye suggests when he says that it announces the building of a city among the Satanic mills in England (352–5).

'The City of God' looks at Blake's *Jerusalem* and asks how the poet interpreted the Bible and placed that interpretation in an English context. Frye says that the imaginative vision of human life consists of a fall, history (the human struggle in a fallen world), redemption of the world (through a divine man where a simultaneous triumph of eternal life and death occurs) and apocalypse (Frye 1947a: 356–7). The symbolism of the poem combines biblical and English imagery. For his allegorical vision of history, Blake uses the cycle of traditional legends from the Trojan settlement of Britain, the rulers like Lear, Cymbeline and Sabrina, the story of Arthur and the prophecies of Merlin, which Blake seems to find in Geoffrey of Monmouth and in Milton's *History of Britain*, as parallels to Hebrew history in the Bible (372–3). Frye focuses on Blake's use of 'analogy', which takes up his view that experience is an inverted form or parody of the imagination and is implicit in his idea that truth consolidates error until it becomes pure negation and vanishes, and on his contrast between 'Identity' and 'Similitude' (382–3). This contrast is worth elaborating on because Frye himself uses it in his theory. Identity is true allegory or the image that means itself because it is itself, whereas Similitude, which Frye calls sameness, is false allegory and means something else because it is something else. In Blake's fables of identity and similitude, for instance, the heroic leader and the priest are analogies of the visionary prophet (383, 395). *Jerusalem* represents two extremes in thought – life as eternal existence in one divine 'Man' and life as a never-ending series of natural cycles – and addresses the latter pole on account of the propensity of Blake's age, and Frye assumes of ours, to Deism (383). For Blake, according to Frye, 'The true Jesus is the present vision of Jesus, the uniting of the divine and the human in our own minds, and it is only the active Jesus, the teacher and healer and storyteller, who can be recreated' (387). Ceremonial and historical tradition recalls the passive Jesus. There is an imaginative moment in each day without Satan, a moment of eternal life without death. Blake is an 'enemy' to mystery: in the moment of absolute imagination that he describes, 'the mystery of the Incarnation, the uniting of God and man, the attaining of eternity in time, the work of Los, the Word becoming flesh, is recreated, and thereby ceases to be a mystery' (387). In some ways in *Fearful Symmetry* Frye has written his book on the Bible via Blake and the tradition of English literature, although he wanted to focus more directly and fully on the Bible and literature and did so in his last books. In sum, Frye says: 'Blake's religion is civilized life, the Christianity of imagination, art and recreation as opposed to the Christianity of memory, magic and repetition' (387–8). Blake and Frye are writers of magnitude, so it is not surprising to find an identity with a difference between them, so that Frye, like Bernard Shaw, who said he began by copying passages from earlier writers but could not help but make the words his own, may be discovering himself in Blake as much as using Blake to develop himself. In Frye as well as Blake the vision reaches for a Jesus just outside the Bible, who can be reached, perhaps with Dante in mind, by crawling through the gap between the end of Revelation and the beginning of Genesis in order to see as a *katascopos* 'the entire vision of the Bible below us as a vast cycle of existence from the creation of a fallen world to the recreation of an unfallen one' (389; see also Hart 1992c: 4, 9–10, 26, 99). To attain a final understanding of the Bible, our imaginations must 'become possessed by the Jesus of the resurrection, the pure community of a divine Man, the absolute civilization of the city of God', and the upper limit of Beulah is as far as any church can take the individual (389). To crawl into eternity, visionaries must become adult creators, and leave the idea of divine sanction of nature, ultimate mystery in the Godhead and division between divine creator and human creature. These visionaries must abandon the view that repeated imaginative habits form the structure of imaginative life when they comprise the basis of it (389–90). Blake faced a civilization that, from Locke's age onwards, was making indefinite recurrence the goal of its natural reason (390). *Jerusalem* recreates the vision of the Jesus of action for the English public at this crucial time (391–2). Once again, as in the episode of Joseph and Mary in Plate 61, Blake attacks the Christian vision that insists that females are never subject to desire. But Blake's representation of Rahab and, more generally, his image of the harlot, although attacking the hypocritical male Pharisaic attempt to kill harlotry by killing harlots, may be problematic because Blake's 'Virgin Eve' replaces 'Rahab, the female body of mystery which interposes itself between man and his divine apotheosis in the body of Jesus'. Thus, the whore is an analogue of Jesus' forgiven harlot: she is released to live under conditions in which her imagination can prosper (393). Sometimes in Blake, who is progressive if not proleptic in his view of women, there seems to be a gap or elision between man and Man that can be interpreted as not leaving enough room for women and in making them symbols in the relations men imagine. Like Blake, Frye emphasizes a social role for the artist: when society, like the artist, can put the social will in the service of vision, it will begin to build Jerusalem and participate in the miraculous powers of Jesus, which is art. Why must imagination see 'an evil female will' that must be stripped and burned even if the Selfhood translates this action into the burning of an individual woman as a 'witch' (see 397)? Selfhood, as we shall see, takes human sacrifice, an expression of the ascendancy of reason and nature, as its symbolic act (see 397–400). Vision is to analogy what art is to dream, as universal imagination is to egocentric meaning. Selfhood parodies genuine vision. This observation returns us to Blake's view of history, which Frye summarizes and often shares: 'As history, the analogy of the Word, deals chiefly with the Selfhood aspect of life, the visionary sees history, and the life of men in time, as a continuous somnambulism' (394–5). The 'natural man' lives in analogy, and anti-Semitism, for example, is a form of persecution that arises from adherence to legal and historical ideas, so that 'those who persecute Jews can only express by doing so the same attitude that Jesus condemned in the Pharisees: belief in a chosen race, a national moral law and a conquering Messiah' (396). In part, Frye seems to have Hitler and the Nazis in mind here. Blake's poem represents Satan as a reactionary who has to be shown and returns to the central notion in the Blakean canon that we become what we behold because 'the image of God is the form of human life, and the reality of ourselves' (401). Perhaps, like Jonah, Blake may achieve what is the goal of the prophet, to discover that his prophecy of disaster at hand fails because it is being heeded (403).

In Chapter 8, where I discuss Frye's visionary criticism, I examine his twelfth chapter, 'The Burden of the Valley of Vision', a numerological apotheosis of Frye's first major work of visionary hermeneutics or commentary, so that I shall not dwell here on vision at the end of *Fearful Symmetry* but touch briefly on its view of art. It is appropriate that a book on vision should end with a concentrated discussion of vision. As Frye finds his identity in Blake, it is also interesting to see that Frye ends his study with a vision; it completes his book as *Jerusalem* nearly does Blake's canon (1947a: 404). Frye speculates that having completed his epic in the prime of life, Blake might have accomplished an even wider vision in drama, but because that genre depends on more public support than Blake could hope for, he turned to painting and wanted to revive its public aspect. Frye asserts that the arts that need social cooperation flourish in the periods of highest civilization and that the arts, especially of music and drama, were in bad shape in Blake's time when this poet and painter was asking England to move through its crisis by recreating itself spiritually (405–8). Blake was not aware he was living in the midst of the Romantic movement. He hoped that an exhibition of his paintings would bring about a Renaissance in English art, but it received only one review, and a hostile one that called him a genial madman. Frye does not concur with the virulence of the review but agrees that Blake was on the wrong track. Blake foreshadows John Ruskin and William Morris in insisting on communal art, that social reform is a revival of art and that the Middle Ages and Renaissance provided a healthier environment for art than does 'capitalist imperialism' (410–11). Frye says that art has a social value and the artist, social significance, but he thinks that Blake was in danger of sacrificing his imagination to his will in order to appeal to the public because 'The only legitimate compulsion on the artist is the compulsion to clarify the form of his work, and in accepting other compulsions he is at once trapped in compromise' (412–13). Public art is a worthy and healthy goal in Frye's view, but Blake was going about it the wrong way. After praising Blake's mental independence, an integrity achieved in part because of isolation, Frye says that he displayed 'Cockney cheek and the Nonconformist conscience, two of the most resolute and persistent saboteurs of the dark Satanic mills in English life' (413). Frye the non-conformist set his only story with an English locale among the Cockneys (see 'Affable Angel'; Chapter 9). Satire is a bond between Blake and Frye. After *Jerusalem*, Blake comments on pictures and ceases to illustrate poems and his interest in writing shifts from 'creation to criticism, and from poetry to prose' (414). A connection between Blake and Frye through criticism emerges: 'Even in the prophecies themselves we can see that the poetic utterance becomes for

Blake increasingly a means of explanation or comment on the central form of the poem, and after *Jerusalem* all his important literary ambitions were concerned with prose criticism' (414–15). In his youth, as a writer and as a critic, Frye had to wrestle with the relation between literature and criticism and apparently found some solace in Blake. An important element in Blake's theory of art is the recreation of the archetype. This process 'unites a sequence of visions' into tradition, then into scripture. Later, Blake decides 'to illustrate other poets' visions so that their readers may more easily understand their archetypal significance' (415). With Blake, Frye demolishes the theories of art that divide instruction and delight, or make art fragile in its beauty, or a set of moral generalizations. Blake's view of art is something that Frye and he repeat: 'The work of art suggests something beyond itself most obviously when it is most complete in itself: its integrity is an image or form of the universal integration which is the body of a divine Man' (418). Perhaps, Frye suggests, Blake does, as some readers feel, concentrate too much on revelation and takes all magic and mystery from his art, thereby producing prophetic poems that are 'too diagrammatic to have the impact of great art' (418–19). But Frye appeals once more to Blake's historical context, in which, unlike the Greek dramatists, he could not assume that his audience would attach archetypal significance to his mythological figures (419). Here is a quintessential point in Frye's criticism that he would reiterate throughout his career:

> Every poet, including Blake, must first be studied in connection with his own age, but there comes a point at which the value of this study becomes exhausted and the conception of 'anachronism' is rendered meaningless. What makes the poet worth studying at all is his ability to communicate beyond his context in time and space: we therefore are the present custodians of his meaning, and the profundity of his appeal is relative to our own outlook.

> (420)

This passage will recur in new contexts as Frye's canon expands. Criticism is historical, but has at least as much to do with the context of the reader or critic as with that of the author. Blake's total vision is a return to the Renaissance and is an effort to round off the humanist revolution in which rhetorical and mythological handbooks, including commentaries on and allegorical interpretations of classical poets, helped to show how the classical and biblical traditions approximated each other. Blake's 'cultural revolution' – Frye's term was to gather controversial overtones in the mid-1960s – would expand culture into 'a single visionary synthesis', enliven public response to art, deliver the artist from the bondage of realism and restore catholicity (420). Like Michel Foucault, Frye seems to look to the late Middle Ages and the early Renaissance as a kind of golden age before the rationalism of the Enlightenment (see Foucault 1961; trans. 1971). Frye distances himself and his age from Romanticism and wants criticism to move beyond it as modern art has. He wishes to leave behind 'the Romantic psychological myth of a subliminal real self conflicting with a censorious rational consciousness' (421–2). A return to allegorical criticism is Frye's chief aim, and it is not coincidence that this is the approach of Aquinas, Dante and Boccaccio as well as the foundation of humanist and Renaissance writers like Spenser. We do not have to wait for the 'Polemical Introduction' of *Anatomy* to find polemics: 'The allegorical approach to literature is often, therefore, spoken of as a fantastic freak of pedantry, though it lasted for centuries, and probably millennia, whereas our modern neglect of it is an ignorant parvenu of two centuries and a half' (422). Here, Frye returns to 'genius', perhaps unable to avoid a myth that the Romantics made popular. Another Frygian statement might apply as much to critics of his own work as to those of Blake: 'Of course those who are incapable of distinguishing between a recognition of archetypes and a Procrustean methodology which forces everything into a prefabricated scheme would be well advised to leave the whole question alone' (422).

But Frye himself could not leave the question alone: he was developing a theory of symbolism in which laws must be established to recognize the real relations, neither dismissing resemblances as coincidence nor reducing them to a single ancestor. He concludes: 'If such laws exist, it will be quite possible to develop an imaginative accuracy in reading the arts which is not, like the accuracy of pedantry, founded purely on inhibitions' (423). Frye values one aspect of the Romantic tradition: it encourages poets to find symbols in their own way. After reviewing the use of myth among great modernists, Frye concludes that 'It is fortunate that art does not have to wait for critical theory to keep pace with it' and proclaims his time 'a great mythopoeic age' (423). His ambivalence to critical theory is apparent here, especially when he also observes the increasingly critical nature of Blake's work. Frye knows what he wants to do and, retrospectively, we can see that he did just that: 'To all the symbols mentioned above there are many suggestive analogues in Blake, and a theory of symbolism broad enough to develop the critical and appreciative side of contemporary culture will almost have to draw heavily on him' (423). Frye prefers to search for the unity of the human mind through a comparative study of works of art, rather than of ritual or mythopoeic dreams. Conscious unity is a more worthy end than unconscious unity is for Frye (424). He is searching for nothing less than a field theory – the study of anagogy – as he calls it to find the missing link and unite the whole pattern of contemporary thought. He finds in Blake forebodings of twentieth-century theories. With confidence, Frye says: 'Now of course the critic's task is to stimulate the understanding of the poet, not belief in what he says' (425–6). Frye has sought to establish Blake as a typical poet and the importance of the imaginative unity of his ideas (426). Blake's archetypal symbolism may help us to understand the symbolism of another poet. In Frye's scheme, in all literary texts the author provides the words and the reader the meaning. Historical context is important in this process and we must move on to genre, the giant tragedy, for instance, which helps us to understand Sophocles better. Blake returns us to the Renaissance, especially to *The Faerie Queene* and *Areopagitica*, to Protestant and humanist tendancies, particularly in regard to the 'word' as 'unit of meaning, the Scripture, and the Son of God and Man' (428). But, Frye says, we are standing outside Blake's gate, and it remains to be opened in a vision. By interpreting Blake's vision of light through Falstaff's tender but comic vision at the end of his life, which the Hostess reports and which involves a textual crux that Theobald amended to the pastoral 'babbling of green fields', Frye shows the identification of the interpreter's vision as well as its mediation (428).

3   Reconstructing criticism

> For my part, I have honourable precedents for this which I have done: I
> will cite one for all, Anthony Zara, *Pap. Episc.*, his Anatomy of Wit, in
> four sections, members, subsections, etc., to be read in our libraries.
>
> (Robert Burton, 'Democritus Junior to the Reader',
> *Anatomy of Melancholy*, 1621)

In the Preface to the reprint of *Fearful Symmetry* in 1969, Frye notes
that the fifth and final complete rewriting of the book 'consisted largely
of cutting out of it a mass of critical principles and observations, some
of which found their way into my next long book, *Anatomy of
Criticism*'. From the critical observations that Frye left in his study of
Blake, this is no idle boast. In discussing *Anatomy* I want to
concentrate most on the 'Polemical Introduction', partly because it sets
out Frye's theory most clearly, partly because this book is much
discussed and partly because I have looked at the 'Tentative Conclusion'
in my fifth chapter, which examines Frye and history. Another genesis
of *Anatomy* is that, as Frye tells us, he wanted to apply the principles of
literary symbolism and biblical typology to a poet who took these
principles from contemporary theory, in this case Edmund Spenser, as
opposed to someone who worked them out, like Blake (1957: vii).
Anatomy of Criticism is a book that changed the debate in critical theory
irrevocably: it will not fade like unwanted age in the dust and can never
remain long in the shadows.

In the 'Polemical Introduction' Frye says his book gives reasons for
'believing in a synoptic view of the scope, theory, principles, and
techniques of literary criticism' and provides 'a tentative version of it
which will make enough sense to convince my readers that *a* view, of
the kind that I outline, is attainable' (1957: 3). Frye then makes a claim
that was often a cause of confusion and resistance in the reception of
Anatomy for a generation:

The gaps in the subject as treated here are too enormous for the book to be regarded as presenting *my* system, or even my theory. It is to be regarded rather as an interconnected group of suggestions which it is hoped will be of some practical use to critics and students of literature. Whatever is of no practical use to anybody is expendable.

(3)

Frye's suggestions were so suggestive that many came to regard his synoptic view as his system and found wide applications to specific literary texts. Some, however, expected Frye to perform the practical application of his theory in *Anatomy*. Frye, the Blake critic, was charged with building a system for others, but, like Blake, he was, perhaps, setting out a framework – a mythology.

Frye identifies himself with Matthew Arnold, who was an educational reformer as well as a poet and who said that the critic should be flexible and without prejudice and should try 'to see the object as in itself it really is'. The approach Frye wants to use is Arnold's 'precept of letting the mind play freely around a subject in which there has been much endeavor and little attempt at perspective' (Frye 1957: 3). Frye is the overviewer, the *katascopos* who brings the strands of criticism into focus. In alluding to Arnold, he is calling to mind one of the great critics of the English tradition, someone who influenced critics as diverse as T. S. Eliot, F. R. Leavis and Raymond Williams, but someone who is part of a 'liberal humanist' line that is more questioned in the 1990s than it was in the 1950s. But in 1957 Frye wanted to define and defend criticism. For him, criticism was 'the whole work of scholarship and taste concerned with literature' that is an 'essential part' of liberal education or culture or the study of the humanities (according to one's preference in terminology) (3). Partly because of the success of Frye and his generation, few critics are questioning the necessity of criticism, although a few more doubts or even a hubris in the subjunctive might now be salutary. The satirical Frye points his polemic against criticism as an art. He wants to guard against all the clichés and anodynes about criticism as 'a second-hand imitation of creative power', as a parasitical activity, as art that could not be art, as impotence and dryness, a kind of wasteland in which the Gerontions of this world criticize the poets. In this satirical portrait, which Frye is using in order to refute it, critics are intellectuals who lack art and money but have a taste for art and who form a class of 'cultural middlemen' who distribute culture to society for profit and who exploit artists and confound the life of their public. With dry wit, Frye says that the 'golden age of anti-critical criticism' was the end of the nineteenth century, although some of its 'prejudices' persist (3). He argues that the fate of art without criticism is not encouraging and that it is a mistake to assume that public taste is natural and that criticism is artificial. Theories that favour natural taste, which can be found in Tolstoy and Romantic theories of a 'creative' folk, have not, Frye says, stood up to the 'facts of literary history and experience' and thus suggest that we move beyond them (4). Frye proposes that we avoid this extreme and the reaction against it – art for art's sake, which glorifies art 'as a mystery, an initiation into an esoterically civilized community' (4). Like Blake (or Frye's Blake), he is not interested in art as occult mystery, which is trivialized in the knowingness of raised eyebrows, masonic gestures and other secret badges of snobbery. Frye shows insight when saying that a fallacy connects the two attitudes – the direct communication of artist and public and art for art's sake – that there is 'a rough correlation between the merit of art and the degree of public response to it', even though for the one the correlation is assumed to be direct and for the other, inverse (4). The critic, Frye says, has to exist to pioneer education and shape cultural tradition. A public without criticism 'brutalizes the arts and loses its cultural memory', a theme of Frye's story 'The Resurgent' (1940), a critique of totalitarian art and of the nightmare of the 'folk' as guardians of the arts (see Chapter 9). In my discussion of the critic as writer I shall raise the issue of whether this defence of criticism is special pleading, or a sign of Frye's own anxiety over abandoning the publication of his fiction in 1940 while still desiring to produce it for a public or a sound position that needed to be taken as a corrective to the Romantic myth of the poet as creator and the critic as analysing literature to death. Was Frye to be like Blake's Newton or Blake himself? In fact, it may not be an either/or situation. The questions I am raising are not meant to trivialize or personalize Frye's criticism and theory, but only to illuminate it. Frye's criticism is too important to reduce to autobiography just as Blake's poetry should not be reduced to history, but the autobiographical and historical can complicate our view.

It is hard to disagree with Frye that 'Whatever popularity Shake-speare and Keats have *now* is equally the result of the publicity of criticism' (1957: 4). Criticism speaks while art (sculpture, painting, music and poetry) cannot. Here is a sentence crucial to an understanding of Frye's poetics: 'Poetry is a *disinterested* use of words: it does not address a reader directly' (4). It is not 'metrical talk' because the artist, 'as John Stuart Mill saw in a wonderful flash of critical insight, is not heard but overheard' (5). The moments of illumination or epiphanies, so important to modern writers like Henry James, James Joyce and

Virginia Woolf, are crucial to Frye as a visionary critic. Just as Sidney and others have tried to declare poetry's difference and independence from philosophy, or more specifically the legacy of Plato, Frye is declaring criticism's from poetry:

> The axiom of criticism must be, not that the poet does not know what he is talking about, but that he cannot talk about what he knows. To defend the right of criticism to exist at all, therefore, is to assume that criticism is a structure of thought and knowledge existing in its own right, with some measure of independence from the art it deals with.
>
> (5)

Frye declares criticism a discipline. Some poets may have an ability to write criticism and to write commentary on their own work, but their criticism is not definitive. Frye is part of a shift in the English-speaking tradition, in which the major critics were often major writers, towards the Continental tradition, in which the critic was often not a 'writer'. In Frye's view, the critic is the final judge of meaning. Criticism says something and is assertive or descriptive writing that comes from the conscious mind and active will, whereas literature affirms nothing and is not of that conscious and willed writing (1957: 5). Frye's declaration of the autonomy of criticism is based on a paradox: the framework of criticism is not of literature or outside it because to be of it is to be parasitical and to be outside it is to be assimilated to another field. This latter view is determinism, whether it is Thomist, Marxist, liberal-humanist, existentialist or whatever, that is the substitution of a critical attitude for criticism or the attachment of criticism to some framework outside it.

Frye proposes to find a conceptual framework from within literature because it has grown out of the art it examines. In summing up the job of literary critics, Frye says that the first thing they should do is read literature, make 'an inductive survey' of their own field and let their 'critical principles shape themselves' only out of their knowledge of that discipline (1957: 6–7). He argues against the taking over of 'ready-made' critical principles from any other field or combination of fields because to subordinate criticism to these external attitudes is to exaggerate whatever external source is being used. The disinterested critic is Frye's ideal. Another of Frye's important questions is 'What if criticism is a science as well as an art?' (7). Frye is interested in scientific, systematic or progressive criticism as a way to guard the integrity of the discipline from 'external invasions' (7–8). Although Frye and Harry Levin agree that literary criticism is not an exact science and that, unlike art, it is progressive, they choose different but complementary critical paths (Levin 1967, rpt. 1972; see also Hart 1989). Frye wants to move from the critic telling us about literature to telling us what literature is, from the public criticism of taste, as exemplified in Lamb, Hazlitt, Arnold and Saint-Beuve, to a 'genuine criticism' that makes intelligible the whole of literature. As much as Frye draws on and likes Arnold's work, he sides with Ruskin as opposed to Arnold, who does not see the genuine criticism in a footnote on Shakespeare's names in *Munera Pulveris* (8–10). Frye will not abide Arnold's universalizing of some 'plain-sense' axioms hardly met in criticism before the age of Dryden and unlikely, in Frye's view, to endure the age of Freud, Jung, Frazer and Cassirer (10). The scholar attempts to make the study of literature possible, whereas the public critic assumes that it exists. Frye is more interested in what follows from the possibility of literature rather than the use of literature. He says that the mental process that occurs in the study of literature is as progressive and coherent as the study of science: both involve a recognition of the unity of the subject. By implication, Frye offers an assumption

> that scholars and public critics are directly related by an intermediate form of criticism, a coherent and comprehensive theory of literature, logically and scientifically organized, some of which the student unconsciously learns as he goes on, but the main principles of which are as yet unknown to us. The development of such a criticism would fulfil the systematic and progressive element in research by assimilating its work into a unified structure of knowledge, as other sciences do. It would at the same time establish an authority within criticism for the public critic and the man of taste.

(11)

Whether Frye's theory of unity, which is analogous to Blake's in poetry, is prophetic in the hope of 'some synthesizing critical Messiah' or whether the rest of *Anatomy* fulfils typologically the messianic wish of the 'Polemical Introduction' has no certain answer and suggests the energetic tensions and ambivalences in Frye's theory.

In this desire for criticism as a science, Frye contends that one learns criticism and not nature just as one learns physics and not nature: literature cannot be taught; the criticism of it is the only thing that can be taught directly (1957: 11). He thinks that criticism has its own 'conceptual universe' that the critic creates and dwells in. Frye says that this universe is one element in Arnold's idea of culture. A comprehensive view of what criticism is doing represents Frye's goal. He is resisting what he perceives to be the hegemony in the 1950s of history, philosophy and other disciplines in literary studies as a result of a 'power vacuum' that 'the absence of systematic criticism has created' (12). The undertow that carries the student away from literature and into history and philosophy would disappear, Frye asserts, 'if the varied interests of critics could be related to a central expanding pattern of systematic comprehension' (12). In setting out his putative handbook to literature, Frye laments that we have no real standards to differentiate literary and non-literary verbal structures, do not know what to do with 'the vast penumbra of books' and do not have a word for literary works in general (though we do for poems and plays). I spoke before of Frye's strategy of distancing himself from Blake as a counterpoise to his identification with him: he says that critics are like 'savages' who have words for specific trees but no word for tree, so that they have not, with all due respect to Blake, generalized enough (13). The undertow of history shows the dark side of anthropology and even the imperialism that Frye so opposed in the differences between the diction – and, let us hope, the social conditions – of the 1950s and the 1990s. It is not clear who these 'savages' were or could be and why they are necessary for this hypothesis. If the Chinese have no word for 'irony', does it mean that they know less about the practice of irony? For that matter, the same question applies to the Greeks before Plato or, more generally, to English speakers whose language, syncretic as it is, lacks words that other languages have (see Yü 1992).

Frye's handbook would attempt to explain the distinction in rhythm between prose and verse, which he calls 'the most far-reaching of literary facts', and to make advances in the theory of genre by complicating the Aristotelian division of drama into comedy and tragedy in order to take into account opera and other forms that occur in subsequent ages and by trying to classify prose forms. 'Novel' will not do to cover prose fiction (Frye 1957: 13). Frye's interest in Menippean satire resurfaces here as he says a knowledge of this genre would enhance our understanding of *Gulliver's Travels*. Critics should know about the Bible and biblical typology, which are crucial to the comprehension of many literary texts (14). Like Frye, I have often wondered why too many instructors and students have resisted the teaching of theory and the elementary principles of criticism to first-year students when in physics they assume that Frye's 'intelligent nineteen-year-old' could learn his or her fundamental theories. Perhaps there have been substantial advances in criticism since 1957, but it is worth while to ask whether Frye's observation still applies: 'What critics now have is a mystery-religion without a gospel, and they are initiates who can communicate, or quarrel, only with one another' (14).

It is possible that a first-year physics student could not understand the communications of advanced physicists, but he or she could learn to: possibly, a similar student in literature would also learn the terms of agreement and disagreement.

But that brings us back to the question of criticism as an inexact science, to the question of evidence. Frye's meaning is clearer when he invokes Aristotle as a positive example, someone who approached poetry as a biologist would a system of organisms, as if there were 'a totally intelligible structure of knowledge attainable about poetry which is not poetry' or the experience of it, that is poetics, a 'theory of criticism whose principles apply to the whole of literature and account for every valid type of critical procedure' (1957: 14). Apparently, Frye hopes to reassess Aristotelian poetics in the light of fresh evidence while following the basic procedure Aristotle set out in his *Poetics* (14–15). In Frye's view, criticism should attempt to move beyond the naive induction of the early stages of a science, when the structure of the object observed is often confused with the structure of the study of that object, to a 'coordinating principle' or 'central hypothesis' that 'will see the phenomena it deals with as parts of a whole' (16). The tropes of perspective and vision recur in Frye's theory. He is suggesting a Baconian inductive leap, which involves 'the assumption of total coherence' for the advancement of science, a development that occurs first in the sciences closest to mathematics, like physics and astronomy, and then in those furthest from it, like the social sciences (16). The one organizing principle of literary study, according to Frye, has been chronology and its corollary tradition, as if sheer sequence could provide the necessary coherence. Instead, he proposes a total literary history, in essence a perspectivist history of genres, a way of seeing literature as complication, or at least a complicated pattern, 'of a relatively restricted and simple group of formulas that can be studied in primitive culture' (17). This visionary critic conceives of literature katascopically: 'We begin to wonder if we cannot see literature, not only as complicating itself in time, but as spread out in conceptual space from some kind of center that criticism could locate' (17).

That centre is that just as science assumes an order of nature, so too does criticism assume an order of words, but neither can ever prove that order completely, and therefore neither can exhaust its subject. In his polemics Frye denounces the intentional fallacy, that a critic should get out of a poem only what the poet put into it, as 'one of the many slovenly illiteracies that the absence of systematic criticism has allowed to grow up' (1957: 17). The first stage in making a 'genuine poetics is to recognize and get rid of meaningless criticism, or talking about literature in a way that cannot help build a systematic structure of knowledge', the 'critical generalities, reflective comments, ideological perorations, and other consequences of taking a large view of an unorganized subject' (18). Frye wants to be rid of what he calls 'leisure-class gossip', the 'casual, sentimental, and prejudiced value-judgments' that are part of a literary stock exchange in which reputations are made and broken by wealthy investors like T. S. Eliot (18). The history of taste is not part of the '*structure* of criticism', although since the late 1960s the notion of structure has come under attack in literary studies (18). On the other hand, Frye thinks that real criticism would show unity, coherence and agreement if taste were left for systematic study. For instance, Frye thinks that Eliot's view in *The Function of Criticism*, where he says that the existing monuments of literature are not collections of the writings of individuals but 'form an ideal among themselves', constitutes real criticism and provides the text that much of *Anatomy* will annotate (18; see also Frye, 1963d). There are then two Eliots, the person of taste and the genuine critic. It is the latter whom Frye admires and builds upon, partly because Eliot's critical principle could, in Frye's view, be found in the better critics of all ages. Although Frye is writing a polemical introduction, he does not think that positions are part of his real or fundamental criticism, because in science there are no positions. In fact, in Frye's scheme one's definite position is one's weakness, given to error and prejudice and gaining adherents that multiply that weakness (18–19). The second stage is to recognize the neighbours of criticism in a way that allows for exploration of these adjacent fields without compromising the critic's independence. The critic can learn about the natural sciences without emulating their methods. Even though a sociologist may study literature exclusively, he or she can disregard literary values. The critic reads religious poems differently from a theologian (19).

The practitioner of literature and the literary theorist interest Frye more than the producer of literature and the consumer of it, although he admits that the two pairs are related. He is not interested in value judgements. He does not think that the elaborate rhetorical analysis of New Criticism, or any other critical fashion, provides a definitive technique for judging the excellence of a work: these fashions are value judgements that are part of the history of taste and are naturalized as if they were facts (Frye 1957: 20). There are, according to Frye, two kinds of value judgements, the comparative and the positive. The comparative divides into two principal parts. First, the work of art as product leads to biographical criticism and relates the work to the person who produced it and to personal authority, as if the poem were the 'heroic' creator's oratory. Second, the work of art as possession leads to tropical criticism, is concerned with the contemporary reader and deals comparatively with craft and style as well as complex figures and meaning. Both are forms of rhetorical criticism that distrust the other's type of rhetoric. Whereas the one treats persuasive speech, the other treats verbal ornament (20–1). Frye considers rhetorical value judgements to be cleared through moral metaphors, from sincerity to simplicity. Because of the undeveloped state of poetics, an 'illegitimate extension of rhetoric into the theory of literature' occurs (21). Arnold's 'touchstone' theory, like those of Eliot and Leavis afterwards, creates a use of one set of literary values as natural and universal, which Frye aptly points out was ridiculed when in *The Frogs* Aristophanes satirized the weighing of lines. This kind of ins and outs, as in politics, is often a fight of elites while the public is left to freeze. Frye also questions Arnold's 'high seriousness' because it favours epic and tragedy, in which ruling-class figures and high style prevail, over comedy and satires, which represent a 'lower' class and style (21–2). It may be surprising to some, who might construe Frye's ends to be like Arnold's in regard to the relation between religion and literature, that Frye does not agree with Arnold's attempt to make a new scriptural canon from poetry to enable a guide for social principles that he would have culture assimilate from religion. For Frye, such efforts are the result of a power vacuum in criticism (22).

What would a systematic study of literature look like? It would alternate between 'inductive experience and deductive principles', so that in 'criticism rhetorical analysis provides some of the induction, and poetics, the theory of criticism, should be the deductive counterpart' (22). Without poetics, one is thrown back into rhetoric to assume that one's inadequate deduction or prejudice from social being is a theory of criticism. Like Marx, Frye prefers a movement away from the relation of the high, middle and low styles to economic, political and social hierarchy. Frye says: 'criticism, if it is not to reject half the facts of literary experience, obviously has to look at art from the standpoint of an ideally classless society' (1957: 22). Like Eliot, Arnold has two sides for Frye because Arnold also wants culture to do away with classes. In every conscious hierarchy of values in literature Frye sees a hidden moral, social or intellectual analogy, whether it is Arnold's conservative and Romantic construction or Bernard Shaw's radical raising up of satire, comedy, prose and reason. These hierarchies constitute a challenge or defence of the views of decorum of the ascendant social or intellectual class. This game, Frye says, is the abstraction of a tradition from the whole of literature that is attached to current social values, which is in turn used to document those values. He even provides an example of the game or the exercise to illustrate his point (23–4). He is consistent in his fight with ideology and will use the same argument against student radicals during the 1960s: the game or exercise that Frye has laid out should immediately make the reader realize that 'the whole procedure involved is an anxiety neurosis prompted by a moral censor, and is totally devoid of content' (24). Not even a conspiracy of moralists, poets who prize like poets, critics who use authors as toy soldiers in political, religious and anti-religious campaigns and students who find 'urgent reasons' for not doing important reading makes criticism (24; see also Chapter 6).

The true dialectics of criticism must combine historical criticism and ethical criticism, which grow out of biographical criticism and tropical criticism respectively, so that historical interpretation can be distanced from contemporary application and vice versa. If the study of history is an attempt to look at the past in and of itself, ethical criticism translates the past into present terms. Each has its dangers and counterbalances the other. In the 1990s Frye might say that the newest historicisms are really forms of ethical criticism without the tools of history for looking at a period in terms of itself. He warns against 'a naive translation of all cultural phenomena into our own terms without regard to their original character', but says that only on the ethical level can we see that every new fashion that increases appreciation for writers has been right, every depreciation wrong (1957: 25). Frye's canon is ever-expanding. The critic will make value judgements, but when he or she soon finds that Milton is a more rewarding and suggestive poet than Blackmore, less time should be spent labouring the point, because 'the difference between redeemable and irredeemable art, being based on the *total* experience of criticism, can never be theoretically formulated' (25). The history of taste is full of poets who, rejected at one time, become important in another age. There are no rules for what the poet should do, only an examination of what they do (26). Aesthetics must follow ethics in doing away with the ought/is opposition, as if the good, the social habit of the critic, is a good enough measure. It is better, in Frye's view, to find positive value in a poem than to rate the greatness of its author. But he qualifies this statement: good taste arises from the knowledge of literature but does not produce knowledge. Before Paul de Man, Frye is using his ironic perspective, even as Aristophanes did, to show the blindness of criticism: 'Honest critics are continually finding blind spots in their taste' (27). The other qualification occurs because 'the positive value-judgement is founded on a direct experience which is central to criticism yet forever excluded from it' (27). But for all of

Frye's paradoxes of present absences and absent presences, he differs from deconstructionists because he is less certain that the rhetoric of reading and the reading of rhetoric, the eschewing of the historical for the ethical (arising out of tropical criticism), gives critics enough to work with. He does not think that the experience of literature and literature itself can speak, whereas criticism can, just as physics explains the vision of colour in a way that, from the experience itself, seems irrelevant. Criticism and the direct experience of literature are separate from each other: whereas one is a specific skill in responding to literature, the other is a mass of personal responses from memory (27–8). A third-rate work may be connected to something that the critic thinks is important enough to justify making it part of his or her work (28–9). In the spirit of the law Frye has swept away the dust from his interpreter's parlour (the name of one of his early stories), raised the dust and wants to 'try it again with whatever unguents of revelation we may possess' (29). Frye confesses that his polemic is as much a confession as a polemic. He says that his deductive method and selective use of examples have to do with tactics, time and possibility. The schematic nature of *Anatomy* is deliberate and used without apology because classification is necessary since criticism 'is more important than an elegant accomplishment of some mandarin caste' (29). For Frye, every experience of literature is unique, but criticism is a body of knowledge that needs classification. He hopes that much of the scaffolding will be knocked away when the house of criticism is in better shape. The book is also, in the spirit of Aristotle, a 'systematic study of the formal causes of art' (29). However much one agrees with Frye's separation of reading from criticism, his theory has changed literary theory for good, even, if not especially, for those who disagree with him.

Like Frye, I must be schematic and deductive when I would rather not be, but time and the endless work of words can lead to commentary without end. Instead, because of the existence of other good discussions of *Anatomy*, the most recent and thorough being A. C. Hamilton's, I shall discuss the rest of *Anatomy* with more brevity than I might have done otherwise. In the first essay, 'Historical Criticism: Theory of Modes', Frye begins with fictional modes and proceeds to the modes of the tragic fictional, the comic fictional and the thematic. In the discussion of fictional modes he moves from Aristotle's differentiation of fiction according to character, which appears to be based on morals, to the conclusion that fictions may be classified according to the hero's power of action, which may be more or less than, or the same as, that of the audience or reader. Stories about divine beings as heroes are myths;

those about heroes superior to people and their environment and who can slightly suspend the laws of nature are romances; those about a hero who are superior to other people but not to their environment are epics and tragedies; those about a hero who is one of us are comedies and realistic fiction; those about a hero inferior to us in power and intelligence are in an ironic mode (Frye 1957: 33–4). In Frye's view, during the past fifteen centuries, European fiction has been moving its centre of gravity down the list, descending in the Frygian diagram, which implies no descent in value: in classical literature this progression also occurs, in a much foreshortened form (34–5). Frye translates Schiller's naive and sentimental into the naive and sophisticated. By 'naive' Frye means primitive or popular, and by 'sophisticated' or 'sentimental', he signifies 'a later recreation of an earlier mode', such as the fairy tale's recreation of the folk tale (35). He uses the word 'tragic' to mean fictions, not simply plays, in which the hero becomes isolated from society and 'comic' when he or she is incorporated into it (35). Frye's classification is subtle and complex, so that I am outlining the barest bones of his argument. Tragic stories are Dionysiac when about divine beings (dying gods) and are associated with images of sunset and autumn. High mimetic tragedy involves 'the fiction of the fall of a leader', raises and casts out pity and terror and mixes the heroic and ironic. Frye associates pathos, which relates closely 'to the sensational reflex of tears', with low or domestic tragedy (35–43). Integration into society, which most often is the incorporation of a central character into it, is the theme of the comic. The Apollonian tale, or the story of how a society of gods accepts a hero, is the mythical comedy corresponding to the death of Dionysius. High mimetic comedy is Aristophanes' Old Comedy, in which there is a comic hero who constructs an alternative society that triumphs and in which a catharsis of sympathy and ridicule occurs. Menander's New Comedy approximates low mimetic comedy. New Comedy usually involves an erotic intrigue that is blocked by a father or a similar opposition and is resolved by a comic 'discovery' or *anagnorisis*, which is more manipulated than its tragic analogue. Ironic comedy begins with society's expulsion of the *pharmakos* or scapegoat. The comedy of manners portrays 'a chatter-monkey society devoted to snobbery and slander'.

Frye says that two poles exist in literature – the mythic and the realistic (43–51). He sums up their cyclic relation: 'Reading forward in history, therefore, we may think of our romantic, high mimetic and low mimetic modes as a series of *displaced* myths, *mythoi* or plot-formulas progressively moving over towards the opposite pole of verisimilitude, and then, with irony, beginning to move back' (52). Frye takes his cue from Aristotle, who classifies the six aspects of poetry as melody, diction, spectacle, *mythos* (plot), *ethos* (which includes setting and characters) and *dianoia* (theme or ideas or poetic thought). Here, Frye concentrates on *dianoia* or the thematic aspect of literature, where themes, like plots, have their recognitions. He reminds us that all literary works have the four ethical elements more or less present: the hero, the hero's society, the poet and the poet's readers. It is a matter of emphasis, then, how fictional (plot-centred) and how thematic (thought-centred) a text is. If in fiction tragic and comic tendencies exist, in thematic literature, the poet can express a personal (episodic) or social (encyclopedic) vision. The sacred scripture is the encyclopedic form in Frye's mythical mode, and in his other modes the encyclopedic forms 'constitute a series of increasingly human *analogies* of mythical or scriptural revelation' (56). Episodic forms are the germs for encyclo-pedic ones, such as, in the mythical mode the central episodic form, the oracle, whose subsidiary forms are the parable, commandment, aphor-ism and prophecy. The episodes of the Book of Isaiah and the Bible itself show how episodes have focus or thematic shape, in this case 'the parable of Israel lost, captive, and redeemed' (56). Frye continues the two parallels in this chapter. Classicism or the neo-classical is mainly 'a sense of poetic *dianoia* as a manifestation of the true form of nature, the true form being assumed to be ideal', whereas the Romantic 'turns away from contemporary forms of fiction and develops its own contrasting kind' (59). The successors of the Romantics, the *symboliste* poets, for example, start with the ironic gesture in order to turn away from the market with all its idols, rhetoric and moral judgement and emphasize the poems and their craft as makers. Whether a poet is 'classical' or 'Romantic', claiming to create or find philosophy, his or her technical problems are the same. In discussing the high and low mimetic, Frye navigates between Aristotle and Longinus and answers Plato along the way. He distinguishes between the fictional and the thematic as a division between the aesthetic and the creative, literature as product and literature as process, the Aristotelian and the Longinian. Whereas Aristotle is interested in *techne*, objective fictional forms and the detachment that his central concept, catharsis, implies, ecstasis or absorption is Longinus' central idea, and his emphasis is thematic and is on the individual. The one critic is more useful for drama and the other for lyric (52–67).

In his second essay, 'Ethical Criticism: Theory of Symbols', Frye discusses the literal and descriptive phases (symbol as motif and as sign), the formal phase (symbol as image), the mythical phase (symbol as archetype) and the anagogic phase (symbol as monad). Poetics lacks a proper word for a work of literary art and a clear meaning for the term 'symbol'. For the former Frye chooses the synecdoche of 'poem' and terms like 'hypothetical verbal structure'. His definition of 'symbol' is 'any unit of any literary structure that can be isolated for critical attention' (Frye 1957: 71). He considers the principle of 'polysemous' meaning (Dante's term) as an established critical fact and says that a student must admit this principle or choose a school and try to make all other criticism subordinate to it. To select this principle is to be on the side of scholarship, but to choose a school 'is the way of pedantry, and gives us a wide choice of goals, the most conspicuous today being fantastical learning, or myth criticism, contentious learning, or historical criticism, and delicate learning, or "new" criticism' (72). Frye does not think of himself as a myth critic or New Critic, as some others have considered him (see Eagleton 1983b, Donaghue 1992). Having accepted polysemous meaning, a student can be a pluralist or can, like Frye, say that there are 'a finite number of valid critical methods' that can be contained in a single theory. Although Frye adapts the medieval four-level scheme, he does not think of the levels as degrees in a hierarchy (71–3). He also thinks that *dianoia* or meaning relates closely to *mythos* or narrative and *ethos* or characterization, so that it is better to think of a sequence of relations or contexts – what he calls phases – 'in which the whole work of literary art can be placed', each context having these three elements that are characteristic to it as opposed to a simple *dianoia* or sequence of meanings (73). When reading, we find our attention moving centrifugally and centripetally, outside our reading or external meaning and the larger verbal pattern of the words or the internal meaning. In an assertion central to his whole theory, Frye says:

> In literature, questions of fact or truth are subordinated to the primary literary aim of producing a structure of words for its own sake, and the sign-values of symbols are subordinated to their importance as a structure of interconnected motifs. Wherever we have an autonomous verbal structure of this kind, we have literature. Wherever this autonomous structure is lacking, we have language, words used instrumentally to help human consciousness do or understand something else. Literature is a specialized form of language, as language is of communication.
>
> (74)

Frye's literature is a self-contained verbal pattern that appeals to a sense of beauty, pleasure and interest (as in curiosity and not special interest): for literary criticism, metaphysics and theology have to be considered assertive because they are outside literature and are part of influences that put centrifugal pressure on the literary. The question of whether creative criticism and critical fiction complicate this division is one that Frye might answer in the affirmative as he sees that the fictional and thematic, the deductive and the inductive complement each other. Like Philip Sidney, Frye thinks that the poet affirms nothing and neither tells the truth nor lies. He quotes Blake to buttress his own view that a reader assumes a hypothetical unity in a poem. Literary works move in time and so are like music; they expand spatially in images like painting. *Mythos* or narrative has to do with listening to a movement; *dianoia* implies a simultaneous seeing. We listen to a poem move and then attempt to see it as a whole, have a vision of *dianoia* or meaning. In its descriptive context literature is a body of hypothetical verbal structures. From the vantage-point of criticism, didactic and descriptive writing, the representation of ideas and of natural objects, are two aspects of centrifugal meaning. Although Frye speaks of different fictional modes that have a pattern in literary history, he says that all literary structures are ironic because they 'say' something different from what they 'mean', whereas discursive writing tends to approximate what is meant or ideally to become 'identified' with it. Both literature and criticism reflect the differentiation between the literal and descriptive elements of symbolism.

Literal criticism (like New Criticism), which treats the poem as a poem, and descriptive criticism, which looks at the poem as a verbal document whose meaning can be separated as it is related to history and ideas, constitute complementary methods that Frye hopes to resolve in the third phase: symbolism (1957: 73–82). Frye's categories overlap: 'The *mythos* is the *dianoia* in movement; the *dianoia* is the *mythos* in stasis' (83). One of the basic principles of criticism, he says, is that events in a literary fiction are hypothetical and not real, imitations of real propositions but not real ones. Formal criticism shares its point of departure with New Criticism, that is it begins by examining the imagery of a poem in order to bring out its distinctive pattern. It differs from New Criticism because it is commentary or the process of translating what is implicit in the poem into explicit or discursive language and does not push the interpretation too far because it draws its evidence from the work as derived from a study of the structure of its imagery. The poet creates a form, an order of words, and not a discursive alignment of words with meanings: the poem does not have an intended meaning. But the literal meaning is ambiguous and variable. In Frye's view, the amount of commentary on a poetic structure that has attained a particular degree of social recognition or concentration is infinite. The two major kinds of 'genuine mystery' in art are the extrinsic and intrinsic. The extrinsic mystery is the mystery of the unknown or unknowable essence when art is an illustration of something else, whereas the intrinsic mystery is the revelation of something unlimited in the art no matter how well we know it. Frye wishes to avoid simplistic psychological images or clichés to describe literature, but in speaking about the arts, he cannot avoid, even with his ironic awareness, a use of the biological image of 'creation'. Frye may not want to avoid creativity because of his own interest in criticism as an imaginative act, and in the writing of literature and his theological habit, and the culture's tradition, in talking about God as a creator (see Chapter 9). Commentary, which attaches ideas to the structure of poetic imagery, is allegorical interpretation. Literature is 'a body of hypo- thetical creations' that is related to truth and fact not simply as an involvement or withdrawal but as a sliding scale of relation from the most to the least explicit. Like mathematics, Frye says, literature is hypothetical and internally consistent and is not descriptive or out- wardly faithful to nature, so that both studies are applied to external facts to verify their applicability and not their truth. Art has a potential relation to reality, not one that is direct or negative, a view Frye thinks resolves the oppositions between instruction and delight, message and style, a point of view that Leibniz could have agreed on and which is a point of departure for much of subsequent possible and fictional world theory (92–4; see also Hart 1988). At the end of Frye's allegorical inter- pretation or commentary, the criticism of art is a mixture of catharsis and recognition, the raising and casting out of an actual emotion on the wave of 'exhilaration or exuberance: the vision of something liberated from experience, the response kindled in the reader by the transmutation of experience into mimesis, of life into art, of routine into play' (93). Frye considers this vision of his visionary criticism to be creative, the ecstasy of birth, a metaphor of women and childbirth displaced or translated into a cliché applied to poetic creation. He has adopted the terms poets have taken from women for themselves and have given its ecstasy (and perhaps pain), even if metaphorically, to the reader. Art, for Frye, produces buoyancy, the release that accompanies discipline, or *sprezzatura*: quoting Blake's phrase 'Exuberance is beauty', Frye suggests that pleasure is not enough to include this buoyancy, so that he can also remind us of Blake's formulation of poetry as 'allegory addressed to the intellectual powers', which implies that exuberance is as much intellectual as emotional (94). With Eliot's idea of tradition in mind, Frye expresses the vision of imagination, which contains truth, morality and beauty but is never subordinate to them, and which rises free of the compulsions on action (law), on thinking (fact) and on feeling: 'The work of imagination presents us with a vision, not of the personal greatness of the poet, but of something impersonal and far greater: the vision of a decisive act of spiritual freedom, the vision of the recreation of man' (94). This is a vision of vision that Frye was to reiterate like recurrent imagery until his death (see Chapter 8).

The mythical phase leads Frye to a discussion that acknowledges the uniqueness of each literary work but that focuses on convention and genre (based on analogies in form), aspects that historical and rhetorical criticism cannot treat (95–115). Poems imitate nature and other poems. The study of genres has to be based on the study of convention, the way symbols connect poems. Frye observes that the underestimation of convention seems to arise out of or help to comprise Romanticism, which makes the individual prior to his or her society, but he thinks that the opposite view, 'that the new baby is conditioned by a hereditary and environmental kinship to a society which already exists', is closer to the facts (1957: 97). Human beings are not original, not aboriginal and created *ex nihilo*. For Frye, the new poem 'manifests something that was already latent in the order of words': poems are made out of other poems, so while the content of literature may have life, nature, truth and so on, its forms, just as the sonata, fugue and rondo can exist only in music, are only in literature (97). Private enterprise, and copyright law more specifically, have, in Frye's view, obscured the facts of criticism, such as the impersonality of poetry and that the original poet is the one who is most profoundly imitative. In the wake of the McCarthy era, Frye appeals to 'the communism of convention' (98). Later, critics would talk about intertextuality. He discusses the birth of a poem, a cliché among male critics and an image that recurs in *Anatomy*, in terms of the poet as midwife or of female genitalia. In this scheme the poet assumes a hypothetical 'feminine, or at least receptive, relation to some god or lord' (98). This seems to be a different Oedipal struggle from the anxiety of influence and the agony that Harold Bloom describes. The mythical phase regards 'poetry as one of the techniques of civilization' and is thus concerned with the social element in poetry (99). The unit of communication or symbol is the archetype, a recurring or typical image that brings poems together and thereby unifies literary experience. Archetypal criticism considers literature as communication and as a social fact and studies conventions and genres in order to locate poems in the body of poetry (95–100). Frye leads us back to criticism as science and as poetry, two sources of prestige from the past and the 'modern' world. By tracing the pastoral, he concludes that 'we have a situation in literature more like that of mathematics or science, where the work of genius is assimilated to the whole subject so quickly that one hardly notices the difference between creative and critical activity' (100). In 1957 Frye is suggesting the possibility of archetypal criticism, which is most effective in studying highly conventionalized literature, such as popular fiction, and which would mean extending to the rest of literature the type of comparative and morphological study made of ballads and folk tales (see Propp 1968). Archetypal criticism foregrounds recurrence and desire: its content is the conflict between desire and reality based in the work of the dream. Narrative in literature is a ritual or recurrent act of symbolic communication. Dream and ritual are, respectively, the significant and narrative content of literature in its archetypal aspect (100–5). In the mythical phase, there is amid this recurrence 'the central recurrent cycle of sleeping and waking life, the daily frustration of the ego, the nightly awakening of a titanic self' (105). Blake's giants have awakened in Frye. Myth is the union of dream and ritual in a form of verbal communication. Frye interprets mimesis 'as an emancipation of externality into image, nature into art', so that art must be its own object. Beauty in art is like happiness in morals: it accompanies the act (113). In Frye's view, when beauty is made the intention of art, it means attractiveness or loveliness and becomes reactionary because it restricts the artist's choice of subject and method (105–15). He says that the anagogic phase is necessary beyond the mythical phase because it allows us to 'pass from civilization, where poetry is still useful and functional, to culture, where it is disinterested and liberal, and stands on its own feet' (115).

Frye tells us what he has been doing in this essay, which is obvious to anyone who has studied medieval criticism, and more specifically, Aquinas, Dante and Boccaccio. We have been ascending the four-level hierarchy as Dante expresses it, but with some differences in terminology. Frye has established a different meaning of 'literal'. His second level (the descriptive) corresponds to the literal or historical one in Dante. Frye's third level (commentary and interpretation) is Dante's second or allegorical level. Frye's fourth level (myth, poetry as social communication) corresponds to the third medieval level (moral and tropological meaning) (115–16). Anagogy or universal meaning is Frye's last phase: here he wants to establish a modern parallel to the medieval conception. A parallelism also exists between Frye's five modes in the first essay and the five phases in this one. In 1957, Jay Macpherson, a poet and scholar who co-taught the Bible and Mythology course with Frye at Victoria College, wrote a poem called 'The Anagogic Man', which can be identified with Frye. Anagogy is at the heart of his critical vision:

When we pass into anagogy, nature becomes, not the container, but the thing contained, and the archetypal universal symbols, the city, the garden, the quest, the marriage, are no longer the desirable forms that man constructs inside nature, but are themselves the forms of nature. Nature is now inside the mind of an infinite man who builds his cities out of the Milky Way. This is not reality, but it is the conceivable or imaginative limit of desire, which is infinite, eternal, and hence apocalyptic. By an apocalypse I mean primarily the imaginative conception of the whole of nature as the content of an infinite and eternal living body which, if not human, is closer to being human than to being inanimate.

(119)

Frye cites Blake and Richard Hooker to support his view. This is the kind of vision Frye describes in his criticism, and by doing so, in a metacritical and metafictional way, he expresses his own inexpressible apocalyptic vision (see Chapter 8). In terms of anagogy, poetry unites unlimited social action (total ritual) with unlimited individual thought (total dream): the poetic universe is a boundless hypothesis. In the anagogic phase the symbol is a monad, an infinite and eternal verbal act or Logos (as *dianoia*) and a total creative act (as *mythos*), a kind of inscaped epiphany or epiphanic inscape. There are, for Frye, no real universals in poetry, only poetic universals. Although poetry tends towards the supernatural, towards the revelation of apocalypse, a kind of creative word, it cannot be religion, which constrains poetry's infinite supposition with its declaration of the truth and the real, so that criticism must detach itself and, as one of the humanities, take a human view of the superhuman. It is one thing for the poet and critic to be aligned with religion; it is another to mistake poetry and criticism for religion. Frye thinks that the social task of the 'intellectual' in contemporary society is to defend the autonomy of culture, which Frye defines 'as the total body of imaginative hypothesis in a society and its tradition' (1957: 127; see also 118–28). Religion and culture should not reduce each other into the other: he cites Coleridge and Arnold as cautionary examples.

Having supposed what archetypal criticism might be, in his third essay Frye develops his views of this proposed method, which involves a theory of myths. He has moved from modes in the first essay and symbols in the second to myths in the third. Within the third chapter, 'Archetypal Criticism: Theory of Myths', he proceeds from a theory of archetypal meaning, which includes imageries of the apocalyptic, the demonic and the analogical, to a theory of *mythoi*, which includes the *mythoi* of spring (comedy), summer (romance), autumn (tragedy) and winter (irony and satire). Frye's fourfold diagram of correspondences, a kind of field theory, is taking shape. He wants to use the symbolism of the Bible, and to a more limited extent classical mythology, 'as a grammar of literary archetypes' (Frye 1957: 135). 'Displacement' is a central concept in Frye's schema: it is devices that solve technical problems for making realistic fiction plausible that arise out of the presence of a mythical structure in it (136). There are two undisplaced myths, like the heaven and hell of contemporary religions, the apocalyptic and the demonic. A romantic tendency exists that suggests implicit mythical patterns in a world closely connected with human experience. The tendency of realism to emphasize content and representation is opposed to the shape of the story. Ironic literature starts with realism and moves towards myth. Frye then proceeds to set out the *dianoia* or structure of imagery in the undisplaced worlds of the apocalyptic and demonic (using examples from the Bible, the main source in our tradition for undisplaced myth), to look at two intermediate structures of imagery and to examine the *mythoi* or generic narratives, the structures of imagery in movement (139–40). The apocalyptic world (the heaven of religion) provides categories of reality in the forms of human desire in the shapes they assume in the making of civilization (141–6). Demonic imagery belongs to the world of nightmare and the scapegoat or *pharmakos*, of confusion, pain and bondage, of perverted or wasted work, of torture and folly, in short the world before the human imagination has begun to work on it. This is the world that desire rejects outright (147–50). Most imagery in poetry deals with intermediate situations, not the unchanging worlds of heaven and hell. Although Frye says there are three intermediate structures – romance, high mimetic and low mimetic modes – he concentrates on the first and the third, romance and realism (151–8). He proceeds to the movement of imagery in a cyclical process in the three intermediate fields. Seven categories of images are also different forms of cyclical movement. First, death and rebirth (disappearance and return, incarnation and withdrawal, of a god) is the central movement in the divine world. Second, three important cyclical rhythms occur in the fire-world of heavenly bodies: the daily journey of the sun-god across the sky, the solstitial cycle of the solar year and the lunar cycle. Third, the human world, half-way between the spiritual and the animal, reflects that duality in its cycles. Fourth, it is rare to live a long and peaceful life and die a natural death. Fifth, the vegetable world has the cycle of the seasons. Sixth, poets, like critics, have been Spenglerians, and have used the cycles of decline and fall. Seventh, water-symbolism has its own cycle like the course of water in nature. These cyclical symbols are often divided into four main phases: the four seasons, four periods of the day, four aspects of the water-cycle (rain, fountains, rivers, sea or snow) and four periods of life (159–60). Frye suggests that the form of cosmology is close to that of poetry and that 'symmetrical cosmology' may be a branch of myth (161).

The *mythoi*, 'narrative categories of literature broader than, or logically prior to, the ordinary literary genres', form two opposing pairs, tragedy versus comedy, romance versus irony. But Frye notes the blurring of opposites, for instance, comedy shading into satire at one extreme and romance at the other; romance may be tragic or comic; tragedy moves from high romance to ironic realism (162).

In discussing the *mythos* of spring (comedy), Frye outlines the plots and characters of comedy, extending the work of Cornford and his own articles from the late 1940s and 1950s (1957: 163–86; see also Frye 1944, 1948, 1951a). Frye's observations on comedy are brilliant and are perhaps the most influential part of his theory on critical practice, especially among students and critics of Shakespeare (see Frye 1952a, 1953a, 1965b, 1986b). Rather than repeat all these well-known principles, I want to mention a few. Frye is drawn to the conventionality of comedy, which is not surprising considering that conventions and the genres they build are at the centre of archetypal criticism. His theory also emphasizes the comic discovery, *anagnorisis* or *cognitio*, for instance, when the heroine and hero find themselves together in a new society as part of the resolution at the end of Greek New Comedy, and this emphasis is in keeping with a critic fascinated with recognition, with a modernism or modern poetic temperament that returns to the Middle Ages for an inscaped epiphany (163; see also Cave 1988). In observing the tendency of comedy to include as many characters in its final society as possible, Frye sees its complexity, the tragic possibilities of the scapegoat as well as the usual practice of reconciling or converting the blocking characters (165–6). He thinks that comedy, like tragedy, has a catharsis in which sympathy and ridicule are raised only to be cast out (177). Shakespeare's romantic comedy, like that of Robert Greene and John Lyly, is what Frye calls 'the drama of the green world, its plot being assimilated to the ritual theme of the triumph of life and love over the waste land' (182). In his observations on Shakespearean comedy, Frye returns to one of his favourite themes. He says this genre is as clear as any *mythos* as an example of 'the archetypal function of literature in visualizing the world of desire, not as an escape from "reality", but as the genuine form of the world that human life tries to imitate' (184). He reminds us that Plautine comedy and the Bible itself have the same kind of comic plot, a son appeasing the wrath of his father and 'redeeming' a society and a bride (185).

Frye also has a subtle view of romance, so that I can only mention a few of his key observations. The *mythos* of summer is romance, which is, according to Frye, closest of all genres to wish-fulfilment and therefore has a paradoxical social role. He says that in each age the reigning 'social or intellectual class tends to project its ideals in some form of romance, where the virtuous heroes and beautiful heroines represent the ideals and the villains the threats to their ascendancy' (Frye 1957: 186). But he notes too that there is also a proletarian aspect in romance, which, despite revolutions, crops up in search of new hopes and desires and is subject to persistent nostalgia for a golden age. The basic element of romance is adventure: its form is sequential and processional. The complete form of romance is the successful quest, which involves three major phases – the perilous journey and minor adventures (*agon*); the crucial struggle, involving the death of the hero or foe or both (*pathos*); and the exaltation of the hero (*anagnorisis*) (186–7). Dragon-killing is the central form of quest-romance (189–90). Two concentric quest-myths occur in the Bible, a Genesis-apocalypse myth, in which Adam is exiled, suffers loss, wanders in history and is restored by the Messiah and the exodus-millennium myth, in which Israel experiences exile, wanders in captivity and is restored to the Promised Land (191). In English literature the first book of *The Faerie Queene* is the nearest following of the biblical theme of the quest-romance (194). Romance uses a parallel characterization to comedy (197). Frye considers the point at which the cyclical world of nature and the undisplaced apocalyptic world become aligned, an epiphany, on mountain-tops, towers, ladders, stairs or lighthouses (203). He notes the typological link between the mountain-top epiphanies in the Bible, the Transfiguration and the mountain vision of Pisgah, the end of the road where, after wandering through the wilderness, Moses saw the Promised Land. Pisgah visions occur in the first book of *The Faerie Queene* and find thematic development in *Paradise Regained*. The point of epiphany persists in modern literature even if the Ptolemaic cosmos has vanished (204–6).

As a fulcrum in Frye's scheme, the four *mythoi* of comedy, romance, tragedy and irony become elements of a central unifying myth. The archetypal theme of comedy is *anagnorisis* (recognition), of romance is *agon* (conflict), of tragedy is *pathos* (catastrophe) and of irony and satire is *sparagmos* (frustration and confusion of heroism and effective action) (Frye 1957: 192).

Tragedy is Frye's *mythos* of autumn. Because of the effectiveness and familiarity of Aristotle's theory of tragedy, Frye looks at tragedy more briefly than the other genres. It lends to literature a disinterested quality and is not, like the other genres, 'expressions of emotional attachments, whether of wish-fulfilment or of repugnance' (206). Frye argues that it is from Greek tragedies that a natural foundation of human character begins in literature: in comedy the happy end twists characters; in romance they are dream characters; in satire they tend towards caricature. Tragedy is about the present (Frye 1957: 206–7). In tragedy's most elementary form, 'the vision of law (*dike*) operates as *lex talionis* or revenge' (208). In looking at the two most common theories of tragedy – that it shows the omnipotence of an external fate or that *hamartia* or a flaw that violates divine or human law sets the tragic process off – Frye says that tragedy 'seems to elude the antithesis of moral responsibility and arbitrary fate, just as it eludes the antithesis of good and evil' (211; see also 209–10). Unlike Aristotle, who begins his theory of tragedy with *Oedipus Tyrannus*, and Hegel, who begins his with *Antigone*, Frye follows Chaucer's monk and begins his with Lucifer and Adam. Frye's appeal to the Bible is a characteristic move in his criticism and theory. In tragedy, the audience, and not the hero, experiences, at an *Augenblick* or crucial moment, the dramatic irony of being able simultaneously to see what might have been and what will be (212–13). In terms of archetypes, tragedy is 'a mimesis of sacrifice' (214). Frye's focus on the Bible, which has a comic structure, may help to explain his emphasis on comedy. He suggests that romance, tragedy, irony and comedy are episodes in a larger quest-myth in which comedy contains a potential tragedy in itself. In his view, the characterization of tragedy reverses that of comedy (215–16). Frye says that the phases of tragedy move from the heroic to the ironic and relates the first three to their counterparts in romance and the last three to the parallel phases in irony (219). At the end of the sixth and final stage of tragedy, Frye suggests that the audience reaches a 'demonic epiphany, where we glimpse the undisplaced demonic vision, the vision of the *Inferno*' (223). Symbols such as the madhouse or prison and instruments of torture and death are found here.

The fourth and last *mythos* is that of winter. It involves irony and satire. Here, we observe the attempt 'to give form to the shifting ambiguities and complexities of unidealized existence' (223). Structurally, the ironic myth is a parody of romance because it applies romantic mythical forms to realistic content in an unexpected manner. Satire is 'militant irony' as it has clearer moral norms and assumes standards against which the absurd and the grotesque can be measured (223; see also Frye 1944, Hart 1992c, esp. 8–11, 164–9, 223–31). Frye elaborates his view:

> Irony is consistent both with complete realism of content and with the suppression of attitude on the part of the author. Satire demands at least a token fantasy, a content which the reader recognizes as grotesque, and at least an implicit moral standard, the latter being essential in a militant attitude to experience. . . . The satirist has to select his absurdities, and the act of selection is a moral act.
>
> (224)

If the traditional view of art as selection and order is correct, all artists and writers, in no matter what genre, will be making moral choices by selecting their material. Selection as a moral act might call into question, or at least complicate, Frye's hypothesis of the possibility of disinterestedness for the tragic writer (or any writer) and for the critic. Satire is irony whose structure resembles comedy because its 'double focus' on fantasy and morality reflects the comic struggle between the absurd and the normal societies. Irony without satire is the puzzled defeat of tragedy without its heroism. The two basic elements of satire are wit (humour) founded on fantasy, absurdity or the grotesque and an object of attack. Both aspects are conventions (224–6). The first three phases of this *mythos* are of satire (corresponding to the first three ironic phases of comedy), and the last three phases are of irony and correspond to the last three phases of tragedy. For instance, the satire of the low norm (the encyclopedic form) corresponds to ironic comedy. The fourth phase is of irony and corresponds to the ironic aspect of tragedy as the satire starts to recede; in the fifth phase, irony corresponds to fatalistic tragedy that emphasizes the natural cycle; the sixth phase shows the mainly 'unrelieved bondage' of human life (225–38). In Frye's journey we now arrive at the 'demonic epiphany . . . the goal of the quest that isn't there' (238–9). But here at the bottom of Dante's heel, we pass through the bottom of the bottom-up Satan, perhaps with Apuleius' ass behind us and Bottom, the weaver, before us as we surface once more into comic spring (238).

Perhaps as some readers are sketching Frye's diagram to see where his sliding scale will take them, they will discover the author claiming that his 'diagrammatic framework' has its precedent in poetics since Plato's time. So begins Frye's fourth essay, 'Rhetorical Criticism: Theory of Genres'. Frye moves from questions of rhythm to specific forms or genres. He examines epos (the rhythm of recurrence), prose (the rhythm of continuity), drama (the rhythm of decorum) and lyric (the rhythm of association). In turn, he looks at specific dramatic forms, thematic forms (lyric and epos), continuous forms (prose fiction) and encyclopedic forms, as well as the rhetoric of non-literary prose. In Frye's expanding diagram, history, art and philosophy (science) correspond to will, feeling and reason, as well as law, beauty and truth. To fill out the diagram, Frye says he has depicted the poetic symbol as between example and precept, event and idea, ritual and dream and has ultimately shown it to be 'Aristotle's *ethos*, human nature and the human situation, between and made up of *mythos* and *dianoia*', respectively, verbal imitations of action and thought (Frye 1957: 243). These constitute Aristotle's first three elements of poetry. Frye says that there is a close association of social action and event, time and process with the ear, of individual thought and idea with the eye. He argues that expressions for thought, like *theoria*, are visual metaphors and that art is central to events and ideas, literature to the arts. Literature combines, although in a less concentrated form, the aural nature of music and the visual nature of the plastic arts, especially painting. The final three of the six elements of poetry that Aristotle sets out are *melos*, an element analogous or connected to music, *lexis*, diction or imagery, and *opsis*, spectacle or an aspect analogous or connected to the visual arts. Frye wants to see how much sense the musical and pictorial make as critical terms. He also wishes to see how rhetoric relates to the other two members of the trivium, grammar and logic. For Frye, grammar is the linguistic aspect of a verbal structure, logic the sense, and rhetoric ornamental speech and persuasive speech. The desire to ornament is disinterested whereas the desire to persuade is the reverse, so that ornamental rhetoric is inseparable from literature, or the hypothetical verbal structure, and persuasive rhetoric is applied literature or literary art in the service of argument. Ornamental rhetoric, according to Frye, is the texture of poetry or *lexis* (243–5). Frye suggests 'a tentative postulate' that is central to his thought: 'if the direct union of grammar and logic is characteristic of non-literary verbal structures, literature may be described as the rhetorical organization of grammar and logic' (245). As a means of distinguishing the literary from the non-literary, Frye tends to emphasize ornamental rhetoric over persuasive rhetoric, although he includes the latter and realizes that it qualifies the autonomy of literature.

In the previous chapter, he looked at the poet's intention in regard to theme and images; here he is doing so in regard to genre and 'the integrating rhythm' (Frye 1957: 246). Frye recalls his complaint in his Introduction that the theory of genres is an undeveloped area of criticism. He sets out to complicate the Aristotelian generic triad of drama, epic and lyric. In Frye's view, presentation, or the rhetorical relation between the poet and his or her public (audience), is the foundation for generic distinctions in literature. Simply put, 'Words may be acted in front of a spectator; they may be spoken in front of a listener; they may be sung or chanted; or they may be written for a reader' (247). In the age of the printing press, the acted, spoken and written word are radicals (roots) or ideals of presentation, for instance, because a Romantic's play may be intended for print and not for the stage while using dramatic conventions. The purpose of generic criticism is, rather than to classify, 'to clarify ... traditions and affinities, thereby bringing out a large number of literary relationships that would not be noticed as long as there were no context established for them' (247–8). Frye chooses 'epos' as a term to describe texts in which the radical of presentation is oral address and that preserve recitation and a listening audience as a convention and 'fiction' for the genre of the printed page. As the connection between speaking poet and listening audience becomes more and more theoretical, *epos* 'passes insensibly into fiction', though the one tends to be episodic and the other continuous (248–9). The written word monopolizes literature, and music and drama suffer when a society, such as Victorian England, becomes individualistic and competitive. In written literature, he says, author and characters are hidden from the reader, whereas in the lyric the poet's audience is concealed from the poet. In the lyric the poet is overheard and overseen in a kind of secular 'I-Thou' relation (249–50). The lyric is an internal mimesis of sound and imagery, whereas the drama is an outward mimesis of them. *Epos* and fiction are at the centre of literature, flanked by drama and lyric. Literature occurs in the form of imitation and not as direct communication, so that *epos* is a mimesis of direct address. Drama is connected with ritual 'and lyric with dream or vision, the individual communing with himself'. The kind of historical overview of genre that Frye suggests may be glimpsed in his summary of the movement at the centre of literature:

> *Epos* and fiction first take the form of scripture and myth, then of traditional tales, then of narrative and didactic poetry, including the epic proper, and of oratorical prose, then of novels and other written forms. As we progress historically through the five modes, fiction increasingly overshadows *epos*, and as it does, the mimesis of direct address changes to a mimesis of assertive writing. This in its turn, with the extremes of documentary or didactic prose, becomes actual assertion, and so passes out of literature.

(250)

Like Plato and Aristotle, Frye thinks of literature as mimetic, so that to imitate an argument is different from engaging in an argument. Frye's penchant for the cycle of history draws him to Vico, Gibbon, Joyce, Yeats and others. In a sense, biblical typology breaks the linearity and irrevocability of history, but if one has a different view of history, even as a postulate, then Frye's schema is more difficult to accept or at least read from within its conventions.

The rhythm of the genres fascinates Frye. A regular metre tends to predominate in *epos* (Frye 1957: 251–63); prose tends to predominate in prose (fiction) (263–8); there is no rhythm specific to drama, except that in earlier modes it is related to *epos* and in later ones to fiction (268–70); and a rhythm that is poetic but not necessarily metrical usually occurs in lyric (270–82). Frye admits that his comments on diction and linguistic elements may only apply to English, although the main principles may be adapted to other languages (250–1). Rather than represent Frye's detailed observations on rhythm, a subject that fascinated him throughout his life, I want to mention a few comments that are especially characteristic of his thinking or that are particularly striking. Frye argues that the dissonant poem by a competent poet demonstrates in poetry 'the tension and the driving accented impetus of music' and that the poem of balanced vowels and consonants and of 'a dreamy sensuous flow of sound' shows that the poet is unmusical (256). While reversing a usual or popular critical judgement, Frye is not using 'musical' and 'unmusical' as value judgements. He is not saying that musical Browning is a better poet than unmusical Tennyson. Whereas the recurrent rhythm organizes the *epos*, the semantic rhythm organizes prose (263). In the past twenty years or so, critics and writers, through the mediation of rhetoric, have consciously set out to break down the boundaries between the literary and the non-literary, so that Frye's certainty about that boundary in prose style is not as self-evident as he says it is in 1957: 'It goes without saying that such neutral clarity is far from dullness, as dullness is invariably opaque. Hence, while there is no *literary* reason why prose should not be as rhetorical as the writer pleases, rhetorical prose often becomes a disadvantage when prose is used for non-literary purposes' (265). Frye is not saying this disadvantage is invariable, and never mentions it in relation to Jacques Derrida's prose, let alone Martin Heidegger's. There has been, as there is wont to be in the history of language and literature, a shift from the Attic to the Ciceronian in the literary theory of the past two decades. Paradoxically, Frye says, the very ornament that makes persuasive prose delightful neutralizes its effect, but, conversely, one may say that persuasion can neutralize ornament (265). Can creativity and criticism co-exist, or do they contradict each other, or do they amplify each other? This is a crucial question in response to Frye's schema and to Frye, the critic who claimed creativity for critics (see Chapter 9). In discussing free verse in the context of the lyric, he argues that this kind of verse rebelled against conventions of *epos* and metre but also articulated a rhythm that is distinct from metre and from prose (272). He identifies experimental writing with the attempt 'to bring words as near as possible to the more repetitive and emphatic rhythm of music or to the more concentrated stasis of painting' (275). He returns to metaphor, which is, along with myth and vision, one of the under-pinnings of Frye's theory (see chapters 7 and 8):

> All poetic imagery seems to be founded on metaphor, but in the lyric, where the associative process is strongest and the ready-made descriptive phrases of ordinary prose furthest away, the unexpected or violent metaphor that is called catechresis has a peculiar import-ance. Much more frequently than any other genre does the lyric depend for its main effect on the fresh or surprising image, a fact which often gives rise to the illusion that such imagery is radically new or unconventional.

> (281)

Frye comes down on the side of convention against originality, of pre-Romantic and post-Romantic notions of creativity: for him, the more a poet knows conventions, the more 'original' he or she will be.

When discussing Frye's elaboration on specific dramatic, thematic, continuous and encyclopedic forms as well as the rhetoric of non-literary forms, I shall also be selective. His wish is to see how much his expansion of perspective over Aristotle's, which suggests the relation of the verbal pattern or *lexis* to music and spectacle, will throw any new light on the traditional classes in the genres. Drama has moved beyond the primitive idea that it was 'to present a powerful sensational focus for a community' (Frye 1957: 282). Frye classifies drama according to a cycle of fictions (293; see also 282–92). His scheme has, like Blake's, its own potent symmetry:

> Just as tragedy is a vision of the supremacy of *mythos* or thing done, and just as irony is a vision of *ethos*, or character individualized against environment, so comedy is a vision of *dianoia*, a significance which is ultimately social significance, the establishing of a desirable society. As an imitation of life, drama is, in terms of *mythos*, conflict; in terms of *ethos*, a representative image; in terms of *dianoia*, the final harmonic chord revealing the tonality under the narrative movement, it is community.

> (285–6)

Frye sees vision, community and recognition in drama, and especially in comedy, something that he will build on in his comments on the social function of literature and something that his own writing exemplifies. When he is speaking about sophisticated drama, he says that its progress is towards *anagnorisis*, or recognition, of the satyr play or an 'emancipated antimasque . . . the most primitive of all dramatic forms' and the source of tragedy (291–2). Frye classifies the lyric according to a cycle of themes. Whereas the drama is conventionalized in relation to its audience and has a 'fixed radical of presentation' in the theatre, the lyric is not. It can be on any subject and in any shape (293; see also 293–303).

Increasingly, critics who study prose fiction have come to agree with Frye's catholic taste in fiction and his refusal to accept the novel and realism as the only worthy exemplars: 'The literary historian who identifies fiction with the novel is greatly embarrassed by the length of time that the world managed to get along without the novel, and until he reaches his great deliverance in Defoe, his perspective is intolerably cramped' (1957: 303; see also 303–15). Frye champions the prose romance and wants to rescue it from a devaluation because critics have misclassified it as a novel and so have judged it as a failed or an inferior novel. Romance is older than the novel and, quite unfairly, has been represented as something to be outgrown. The novel tends to be extroverted, objective, psychological and personal and concentrates on human character in society; the romance is introverted, subjective, heroic and personal (305–8). It is not surprising that the author of *Anatomy of Criticism* would defend the anatomy, one of his favourite forms. The anatomy, or Menippean satire (sometimes called Varronian satire), is an important form that has been too often mistaken for the novel and has suffered accordingly in criticism from a kind of misguided metonymic misapprobation, something that one of its characters might be satirized for but in life goes unnoticed or unpunished among readers, critics, agents and publishers (see 313). Menippean satire treats mental attitudes more than people: 'Pedants, bigots, cranks, parvenus, virtuosi, enthusiasts, rapacious and incompetent professional men of all kinds, are handled in terms of their occupational approach to life as distinct from their social behavior' (309). Perhaps this content, which may be too close to home, becomes built into the value system and its concomitant judgements that devalue this kind of satire as failed fiction. The crux is the ridicule of the *philosophus gloriosus*, the maddened pedant in Menippean satire who symbolizes and defines evil and folly as diseases of the intellect as opposed to social diseases as the novel represents them. Other critics confuse the anatomy with the romance because some of its practitioners, like Petronius, Apuleius, Rabelais, Swift and Voltaire, use a loose-jointed narrative form. There may be a parable in the misreading of the anatomy that Frye is trying to clarify so that it will be avoided in the reading of his own anatomy. The anatomy presents 'a vision of the world in terms of a single intellectual pattern', so that in its 'fictional' form 'The intellectual structure built up from the story makes for violent dislocations in the customary logic of narrative, though the appearance of carelessness that results reflects only the carelessness of the reader or his tendency to judge by a novel-centered conception of fiction' (310). In crafting his own anatomy, Frye seems to be thinking of Robert Burton's *Anatomy of Melancholy*, which Frye calls the greatest Menippean satire in English before *Gulliver's Travels* and the most comprehensive survey of human life in a single book in English literature since Chaucer. Whereas Burton's single intellectual pattern is based on melancholy, Frye's is based on criticism. Frye says: 'The word "anatomy" in Burton's title means a dissection or analysis, and expresses very accurately the intellectualized approach of his form' (311). The same could be said of Frye's *Anatomy*. If the anatomy later merges with the novel, creating in particular forms like the *roman à thèse*, even later the anatomy may be merging with criticism, begetting Frye's creative criticism or criticism of creativity.

In discussing specific encyclopedic forms Frye centres on the Bible as Christian epic and on the Homeric epic. The comments on the structure of the Bible are the germs for *The Great Code* (1982), *Words with Power* (1990) and *The Double Vision* (1991). Frye argues that in every age there tends to be a central encyclopedic form, which is usually a scripture in the mythical mode and an 'analogy of revelation' in the other modes (1957: 315). The Bible is such a central form, and is literary but more than literature. He says that only recently has there been genuine literary criticism of the Bible, which is necessary for an increase in our knowledge of literary criticism. By a genuine criticism, Frye means analytic or typological criticism and not historical criticism: The former 'seems to me to be a purely literary criticism which would see the Bible, not as a scrapbook of corruptions, glosses, redactions, insertions, conflations, misplacings, and misunderstandings revealed by the analytic critic, but as the typological unity which all these things were originally intended to help construct' (315). Frye says that the Bible has had a great cultural influence and defines what he thinks would be a 'genuine higher criticism of the Bible'. It would represent

a synthesizing process which would start with the assumption that the Bible is a definitive myth, a single archetypal structure extending from creation to apocalypse. Its heuristic principle would be St. Augustine's axiom that the Old Testament is revealed in the New and the New concealed in the Old: that the two testaments are not so much allegories of one another as metaphorical identifications of one another. We cannot trace the Bible back, even historically, to a time when its materials were not being shaped into a typological unity, and if the Bible is to be regarded as inspired in any sense, sacred or secular, its editorial and redacting processes must be regarded as inspired too.

(315)

In 1957, and perhaps in 1947 and 1990, Frye sees typology as the centre of the studies of the Bible, literary symbolism and criticism. He says that the Bible can be examined from an Aristotelian or aesthetic point of view as a single form or from a Longinian vantage-point as a series of points of expanding apprehension or ecstatic moments (Frye 1957: 326).

Frye does, however, recognize 'secular' forms of the encyclopedic, such as the epic. Here, he views Homer as the great source of the secular encyclopedic:

It is hardly possible to overestimate the importance for Western literature of the *Iliad's* demonstration that the fall of an enemy, no less than of a friend or leader, is tragic and not comic. With the *Iliad*, once and for all, an objective and disinterested element enters into the poet's vision of human life. Without this element, poetry is merely instrumental to various social aims, to propaganda, to amusement, to devotion, to instruction: with it, it acquires authority that since the *Iliad* it has never lost, an authority based, like the authority of science, on the vision of nature as an impersonal order.

(319)

With this moment of the *Iliad*, we have the birth of Western literature because, for Frye, the literary is the disinterested and non-instrumental. Here, he follows Philip Sidney, John Stuart Mill and many others, such as the critics of Shakespeare, who generation after generation praised him for his objectivity and, beginning with Beaumont and continuing with Milton, as the poet of nature (see Hart 1992c). The tradition, in Eliot's sense, is as much as or is part of the impersonal order of nature. Frye still speaks of an objective vision, perhaps implying that it is intersubjectivity that composes objectivity.

In his discussion of the rhetoric of non-literary prose, Frye says that prose, unlike verse, is used for extra-literary purposes. It extends to the outer worlds of social action (*praxis*) and individual thought (*theoria*) as well as to the literary boundaries of *melos* and *opsis*. Frye asks a question that has been much pursued since he raised it: 'what literary elements are involved in the verbal structures in which the literary or hypothetical intention is not the primary one?' (326). Frye's answer is different from that of many of his successors. He considers non-literary texts, like *Areopagitica*, Johnson's letter to Chesterfield, Lincoln's Gettysburg address and Vanzetti's death speech, which are now also considered for their literary qualities because of their rhetorical properties such as anaphora and emphatic patterns of repetition. Literature, in Frye's schema, faces social action on one side, individual thought on the other. The rhetoric of non-literary prose would, through the ear, stress emotion and the appeal to action in the world of social action and would, founded mainly on visual metaphors, emphasize the appeal to contemplation in the realm of individual thought (326–7). Social action becomes Frye's focus in the last two decades of his life, especially in the late sixties and early seventies, and foremost in *The Critical Path* (1971) (see Chapters 6 and 7). He is also interested in what he calls 'benign jargon', which may be found in writing like government reports, military instructions and inter-office memoranda. The writers of this jargon wish to be impersonal but utter 'the voice of the lonely crowd, the anxiety of the outward-directed conformist' (331). This jargon can also be found in journalism and informs a great deal of professional writing, including that of humanists. He observes:

We are not surprised to find that the further we depart from literature, or the use of language to express the completely integrated state of emotional consciousness we call imagination, the nearer we come to the use of language as the expression of reflex. Whether we go in the emotional or in the intellectual direction, we arrive at much the same point, a point antipodal to literature in which language is a running commentary on the unconscious, like a squirrel's chatter.

(331)

The only way, Frye suggests, from grammar to logic is through the intermediary of rhetoric. He returns to the spatial and the diagrammatic, both of which are important parts of Frye's style and thought. For instance, he says, 'We cannot go far in any argument without realizing that there is some kind of graphic formula involved' and 'As soon as one starts to think of the role of association and diagram in argument, one begins to realize how extraordinarily pervasive they are' (336). And they pervade *Anatomy*. But Frye also defends metaphor generally and spatial metaphors in particular as important aspects of literary and non-literary prose. He advocates that we become more aware of the role of metaphor in argument rather than debunk an argument because of it, something that has been going on from Thomas Sprat through Bertrand Russell and beyond. Because of the place of honour that Western culture has given to discursive reason, in religion the authority of the theologian's propositions, as opposed to poetry (except for that of the Bible), is given authority; in philosophy and science reason has the greatest authority. The arts, Frye says, have been given the role of accommodating reason to what is below in the culture like emotions and the senses. Rhetoric has, in its verbal structures, provided that accommodation by rousing emotions and working towards 'kinetic persuasion' in the service of dialectic. Frye's conclusion is suggestive for the work done since the late 1960s: 'The notion of a *conceptual* rhetoric raises new problems, as it suggests that nothing built out of words can transcend the nature and conditions of words, and that nature and conditions of *ratio*, so far as *ratio* is verbal, are contained by *oratio*' (337). This is an assertion that deconstructionists will develop, that all texts, philosophical ones included, are rhetorical. The work of Derrida and de Man on philosophers like Rousseau, Heidegger, Husserl and others is a case in point. Whereas Frye wants to see the literary in the non-literary but thinks that reason is not necessarily all verbal and that genres are useful in the study of writing and of the literary, the deconstructionists balk at the law of genre and tend to place all writing on one level as 'Writing'.

In the 'Tentative Conclusion', which I discuss in relation to history in Chapter 5, Frye says that he wants to present a 'comprehensive view' of criticism in which the various types of criticism – those dealing with archetype or myth, form, history, four levels of interpretation and text and texture – would be included (1957: 341). He notes that he attacks the barriers between these types of criticism and not the methods themselves. A critic, in Frye's view, should not have one method or focus because that will take him or her to a discipline outside literature. He admits that he has stressed the central role of archetypal criticism and the importance of allegory to it. Frye wants to supplement the brilliant, ingenious and futile tradition of commentary (an allegorical form) on literary texts by supplementing it with archetypal criticism that gives a shape to literature. There is a *mythos*, or structural organizing principle of literary form, for criticism as well. Frye writes in terms of hope and teleology. Criticism must find hope in the fact that it 'has an end in the structure of literature as a total form, as well as a beginning in the text studied' (342). Archetypal criticism distributes the commentary over various texts as part of a conventional structure of imagery (archetypes) and the conventions of genre, thereby preventing scholars from isolating their scholarship on a single poem. Frye wants to break down barriers between methods in criticism, so that the critic will be more aware of its relation to other disciplines (342–3). On education, Frye reiterates his views that we can teach criticism and not literature directly and that art does not improve, but that our comprehension of it does (342–4). Works of art have a social function in their time, and whether they are considered so then or later depends on convention, social acceptance and cultural criticism, whether the culture thinks of art as existing for pleasure. Criticism recreates the original function of the work of art in a new context. Frye advocates a recreation of the past in a kind of self-resurrection, in our vision that gives flesh and blood to the vision of the valley of the dry bones (345). History is the memory of humankind and our own buried life, so that a 'study of it leads to a recognition scene, a discovery in which we see, not our past lives, but the total cultural form of our present life' (see my Chapter 5) (346). Having criticized historical criticism for focusing only on the past, Frye turns from ethical criticism, especially the notion of a tradition – be it that of Eliot or of revolution, such as Marxism – because it involves ins and outs, the selected and the purged. This indoctrination is part of class struggle. Revolution destroys culture and reinforces, in Arnold's terms, the barbarity of the ruling class, the philistinism of the middle class and the populism of the working class. Frye prefers the spiritual to the material, Hegel to Marx (346–7). By choosing Arnold's society without classes, Frye leaves himself open to attacks by Marxists, who have a different view of classless society. Imagination frees people to consider this society in their imaginations, which also preserve works of art, which participate 'in the vision of the goal of social effort, the idea of complete and classless civilization', an ideal (347–8). For Frye, 'Culture is a present social ideal which we educate and free ourselves by trying to attain, and never do attain' (348). The telos of ethical criticism is to transvalue, to look at contemporary social values with detachment, as if one possessed 'the infinite vision of possibilities presented by culture' (348). Like Milton and John Stuart Mill, Frye argues that 'liberty can begin only with an immediate and present guarantee of the autonomy of culture' (348–9). This is the liberalism that Frye extends, to which he adds the humanist belief that human freedom is bound up with the acceptance of cultural heritage. The aesthetic and contemplative element of art is not the final resting place of art or criticism because as soon as we move from the single work to the total form of art, we move from aesthetic contemplation to the ethical, to participation in civilization. Frye realizes that he is in danger of moving from a poem to Poetry as an aesthetic object but says that he has balanced this tendency with rhetoric, the notion that all verbal structures are partly rhetorical and that our literary universe has expanded into a verbal universe in which no aesthetic principle of self-containment will obtain (348–9). The decades since *Anatomy* have borne out the expansion of criticism into cultural studies and the examination of the rhetorical and the 'literary' in other disciplines. Like mathematics, literature proceeds by postulates, breaks down the distinction between being and non-being and relates indirectly to common experience with a view to swallowing it. Metaphors are like equations (350–2). Perhaps myth and metaphor, in their original hypothetical form in literature, are the language of all verbal structures just as mathematics, with its equations, is the language of the sciences. Frye then gives a few suggestions on how to prove this claim, for instance, his observation that the myth of the sleeping beauty informs Rousseau's view of revolution, which, although distinctly Frygian and archetypal, prefigures de Man's rhetorical readings of philosophical texts, like those by Rousseau (353–4). With characteristic insight, Frye sees this relation of myth to argument as being proximate to Plato, 'for whom the ultimate acts of apprehension were either mathematical or mythical' (354). He also recognizes his and our blindnesses because as soon as we construct a system of thought to unite heaven and earth, we discover we can't; the story of the Tower of Babel recurs. He does, none the less, use a myth to identify this tantalizing reaching after the unattainable. Critics, in Frye's system, reforge 'the broken links between creation and knowledge, art and science, myth and concept' (354). This is a tall order that Frye didn't think was being met in the year of his death: even then, he thought that this work of unification without uniformity, of searching for identity in culture, was still as possible as it was desirable.

THE CRITICAL PATH

This book is subtitled *An Essay on the Social Context of Literary Criticism*, and is the shaping and expanding into an essay of revisions of lectures that examined the concern-and-freedom thesis and were given in 1968 and 1969 during the student unrest. Here, Frye recreates his central myth: 'One of my less perceptive reviewers remarked recently that I seemed to be rewriting my central myth in every book I produced. I certainly do, and would never read or trust any writer who did not also do so' (Frye 1971b: 9). He decides that the critical path between dogmatism and scepticism, as set out in the closing sentences of Kant's

Critique of Pure Reason, is the one to take, a decision made long ago when he chose to crack Blake's symbolic code through literature itself. In summing up his earlier efforts, Frye says that he wanted a theory of criticism that would account for the significant phenomena of literary experience and would describe the place of literature in civilization. He also rejected the view that criticism was part of literature, and a minor part at that (13–14).

Earlier, Frye had hoped that literary criticism, which was part of two undeveloped areas – mythology and a unified criticism of all the arts – would expand as it moved away from this parasitical view of itself. Frye attempted to concentrate on one of the two contexts of literature, the imaginative context of literature as opposed to that of ordinary intentional discourse, so that he could answer one of his main questions: 'How do we arrive at poetic meaning?' (1971b: 15). He reiterates a longstanding principle: 'As long as the meaning of a poem . . . is sought primarily within the context of intentional discourse, it becomes a document, to be related to some verbal area outside literature' (16). All documentary ideas of literature, Frye says, are allegorical conceptions of it, for instance, when poems are read as 'allegories of Freudian repressions, unresolved conflicts, or tensions between ego and id' (18). Three types of documentary criticism occur: the biographical, psychological and historical. Frye wants a historical criticism that sees literature as an important part of history. He calls 'the impulse to find the ultimate meaning of literature in something that is not literature' determinism (19). Marxism, for Frye, is perhaps the most serious historical perspective, but it focuses on one allegorical interpretation of the content of literature. He finds three limitations to documentary and external methods: they do not account for literary form, or for metaphorical and poetic language or for the negative relation the poet often has to his or her given context (19–20). New Criticism, according to Frye, was a form of rhetorical criticism that looked at the figuration of language rather than persuasion, but while it accepted poetic form and language as the foundation of meaning, it lacked the sense of context that documentary criticism had (20–1). In resisting determinism, including Marshall McLuhan's, 'in which communication media play the same role that instruments of production do in more orthodox Marxism', Frye says, 'It seemed to me obvious that, after accepting the poetic form of a poem as the basis of meaning, the next step was to look for its context within literature itself' (21). In giving the historical genesis of his own thought, Frye reiterates his central myth, calling poetry a technique of communication that engages the conscious and unconscious mind and observing that communicating is at least as important as the failure to resolve something for oneself. He recalls the structure of imagery that every poet, like Blake, possesses, and recollects how one structure was analogous but not similar to another, so that he discarded the idea of private symbolism. Here, he sets out his idea of identity, which allows for individuality while poets use the same images but not for the monotony and uniformity of similarity (22–3). Frye's historical criticism would be a genuine history of literature and not an assimilation of literature to another type of history. In his search for this historical method he saw the significance of archetypes, 'certain structural elements in the literary tradition, such as conventions, genres, and the recurring use of certain images or image-clusters' (23). For Frye, within literature, convention seemed to be more powerful than history because the poetic conventions change less than social conditions and the poet relates to earlier poets as the scholar relates to earlier scholars, adding something to an organic body of previous work (23–4). He argues for a sense of history as a balance between the history of literature's larger structural principles (conventions, genres and archetypes) and the history of literature in relation to its non-literary background (24–5). The critical path balances a study of the structure of literature and a turning outward to other cultural phenomena that compose the social environment. Criticism is not the narrative movement of reading but a subsequent examination of a text as a simultaneous structure. Frye wants to attach rhetorical readings to a deductive framework that derives from a study of the structure, so that its context will show what central images and ambiguities need analysis. He opposes the primary term of the New Critics, 'texture', to his own, 'structure', although it is not certain how one is necessarily any more of the premise of a hypothesis than the other (26). Can any primary term be the certain beginning or essence of literary study or any other discipline? In this recapitulation of *Anatomy*, Frye says that criticism is a structure of knowledge whereas the reading of a poem is unique and is unknowable (27). In other words, in one sense, criticism is 'a monument to a failure of experience' (27). Frye is not discounting reading, which is like Schiller's naive: instead, he says that the 'real reader' enters into a coherent structure of experience and can see that structure with the help of a criticism that studies literature in light of convention, genre and archetype – its organizing principles (29). In such a study the reader finds the objective 'identity' in literature, which is infinitely various and novel and does not stick to the 'greats' or the classics of the established canon, for his or her own identity (29). The 'sentimental' response is the beginning of criticism, which involves a reading of the unity of the text (30). With deconstruction, it is difference, and not unity, that becomes the work of criticism or theory. None the less, Frye realizes that the end of literature is less and less unity but more and more an intensity of experience, the conception of the ideal experience. He is basing this observation on modernist texts, for instance, the epiphanies in Joyce, and it may not apply to post-modernist texts that frustrate ideal experience. Has there been a radical break with tradition in the past few decades or is this a polemical stance to proclaim revolution and originality and to elide tradition and convention? This is a central question in assessing the relation of Frye's critical theory to the present context. He draws from the traditional Christian view in which 'literature, philosophy and religion at least are all articulate analogies of an experience that goes not only beyond articulateness, but beyond human capacity as well' (31). Through articulated analogies, of which literature is the central one, we identify ourselves or parts of ourselves with a world of ideal experience – the end of the critical path (32). Like Aristotle's middle way, Frye's critical path goes between extremes, in this case the centrifugal fallacy of determinism, or a movement to read the content of literature and to associate it with the non-literary, and the centripetal fallacy of direct experience, or the tendency towards evaluation and the critic's social anxieties (33).

Conventions, genres and archetypes develop historically from origins. Once again, Frye turns to Vico, who is rare in his understanding of 'the historical role of the poetic impulse in civilization as a whole' (Frye 1971b: 34). A society sets up a mythology from myths, which are stories that are of central importance for its religion, history and social structure and that have similar literary forms to legends and folk tales but stick together and have a different social function. When mythology crystallizes in the centre of a culture, a magic circle or *temenos* is drawn around it, and literature develops within certain limits, such as those of language, reference and belief (34–5). In *The Critical Path* Frye looks at the literary aspects of myth and, more specifically, at the way that as a culture expands it produces an encyclopedic mythology that elaborates the society's view of past, present and future, or the myth of concern (36). The myth of concern is there to hold a society together, and in it reality and truth are socially established, so that concern speaks the language of belief. European and American culture have inherited the Judaeo-Christian myth in the Bible and taught in the doctrine of the Christian church. The Bible has an encyclopedic form extending from creation to apocalypse. Concern also involves the anxiety of coherence and of continuity, so that dissent, especially in times of crisis, comes under a great deal of pressure (36–7). Frye observes that 'The influence of social concern on literature is to make it intensely traditional, repeating the legends and learning which have most to do with that concern, and which are as a rule well known to the poet's audience' (37). In a discussion of concern and its relation to oral and writing culture, Frye observes that 'A writing culture reverses the development of oral culture, as its tendency is toward continuous prose and discontinuous verse', which leads to a prose of logic and dialectic in philosophy and of a continuous narrative of events in history (42). A shift occurs from the language of commandment and myth to the language of belief (42–3). Frye admits that 'disinterested' is a relative term with no absolute, something to keep in mind when, in *Anatomy*, he claimed that literature was disinterested (44). This disinterest leads to his myth of freedom, which is the verbal expression of mental attitudes like tolerance, objectivity, suspension of judgement and respect for the individual when they become social attitudes. The beginnings of these attitudes are in a truth based on logic, evidence and verification. The myth of freedom, Frye says,

> is part of the myth of concern, but is a part that stresses the importance of the non-mythical elements in culture, of the truths and realities that are studied rather than created, provided by nature rather than by a social vision. It thus extends to the safeguarding of certain social values not directly connected with the myth of concern, such as the tolerance of opinion which dissents from it.
>
> (44)

The 'liberal' element in society, which is often a small educated or critical minority, is constituted in the myth of freedom, which counterbalances the conservative myth of concern (45). Frye reiterates the centrality of the Bible, that the Western myth of concern is originally a revolutionary myth (48–50). New supplementary and pluralistic myths, such as that of democracy and of the revolutionary working class, began to emerge from the eighteenth century (50). Marxism and Christianity share three aspects of a revolutionary movement: the belief in a unique historical revelation, a canon of approved or essential texts and the resistance to any kind of 'revisionism' (51). Liberals, from Origen through Erasmus to political liberals today, are taken, consciously or unconsciously, by radicals as being part of the establishment. But, in Frye's view, these very liberals are those who slowly expanded the myth of concern in Christianity to include a myth of freedom, which came to be reflected in literature and the visual arts, including the theatre (51–2). What we must do to be saved, although notions of salvation vary, is the central question of concern. There are two human worlds, the natural environment and civilization. Most myths of concern today leave for humans, and not for God, a creativity that involves a reality or truth connected with desire and practical skill, the relation between ought and is. When we hear that it is better to change the world than study it, we are hearing a myth of concern emerge that wants to subordinate all myths of freedom (53). Frye argues for a crucial tension between concern and freedom:

> When a myth of concern has everything its own way, it becomes the most squalid of tyrannies, with no moral principles except those of its own tactics, and a hatred of all human life that escapes from its particular obsessions. When a myth of freedom has everything its own way, it becomes a lazy and selfish parasite on a power-structure. Satire shows us in *1984* the society that has destroyed its freedom, and in *Brave New World* the society that has forgotten its concern. They must both be there, and the genuine individual and the free society can exist only when they are.
>
> (55)

Frye's work is liberal and conservative, revolutionary and traditional because these are the very tensions he sees within the literature he studies and the society in which he lives.

The humanist Frye describes shares much with him: both are encyclopedic and versatile, so that they can keep a social perspective and see the whole range of their society's culture, specialized to a degree as scholars but able to relate that 'specialization to a comprehensive social vision' (1971b: 62). Like the humanists and Milton, Frye has a deeply conservative devotion to order and discipline, but not an authoritarian view of society (64). This comparison is implicit and cannot be taken too far and should be balanced with the tension between Frye's myths of concern and freedom as they apply to his own ideas, but the humanists are background for him as they are for Sidney, whose defence of poetry he discusses at some length. In Sidney, 'The function of poetry . . . is to provide a *rhetorical analogue* to concerned truth' because the problem is that in writing culture non-literary writers set the norms of meaning, and poetry is thought to be oblique or ironic and must be justified as being useful and educational, especially in regard to morality (66). The poet, for Sidney, creates a distinctive use of language by combining the example of the historian with the precept of the moral philosopher in accordance with Aristotle's description of the two types of truthful statements (67). Frye returns us to Hopkins' overthought, or explicit meaning, and his underthought, or texture of metaphors and images, saying that the underthought is the poet's real thought (68). Thus, in Frye's view, there is no definitive rendering of poetic meaning, and a translation must give a literal rendering of the structure of this underthought (70). After Sidney, and particularly during and after the Restoration, humanists began to be preoccupied with classicism to the point that their successors, like Shelley, several of the German Romantics and Matthew Arnold, suggested that the real myth of concern was classical. With irony, Frye says that in 1969, a hundred years after Arnold's *Culture and Anarchy*, no one can write on this subject without recognizing that the confrontations of these two forces have taken a different turn from the one Arnold thought they would: humanist society has disappeared (72–5). With characteristic irony and satire, Frye observes of the post-humanist world: 'Today each intellectual is, socially speaking, in the position of Archimedes in Syracuse, who could perhaps move the world if he were standing in a different position, but, being where he is, is able to continue his work only so long as he is unnoticed by the murderous louts of Rome' (75). With the loss of the poet's authority to speak the myth of concern, which occurred in humanism, he or she turned to the imaginative and literary while other non-literary writers gave to the myth of concern a sense of reason, logic and historical evidence. Like Sidney, Marxists make poetry a rhetorical analogue to convince emotion and imagination of the truths of the reigning doctrine or ideology (75). The prophetic writer, such as Milton and Shelley, the one Christian and the other secular, proclaims liberty (77–8).

The more technologically advanced the society, the less primary and the more secondary a need poetry becomes. It is now an ornament or aesthetic object. With technological advancement, convention declines in art, a community of words in poetry. After Sidney, who thought of the poet as a potential religious teacher, the elements that make Homer the foundation of our poetic tradition, such as the formulaic, conventional and traditional, are those that become most abhorred and are swept aside for 'originality'. In the nineteenth and twentieth centuries, the poet no longer tells society what it needs to know and grows increasingly out of touch with ordinary social values. Instead, it is the 'man of action', like Jefferson, Lincoln, Lenin and Mao, who speaks and writes sententious prose and holds society together. The greater the sphere of writing and the disciplines it creates, the more isolated poetry becomes (79–82). In discussing the relation between poetry and science, Frye observes: 'Cosmological and speculative themes have been central to poetry throughout its history, but versified science and abstract conceptual language have always been eccentric to it' (82). In earlier periods, such as Dante's, what attracted poets to science was its mythical and schematic qualities, and the four elements still appear in the works of modern poets like T. S. Eliot and Dylan Thomas.

Poetry is founded on social concern (Frye 1971b: 83–4). It 'attempts to unite the physical environment to man through the most archaic categories of analogy and identity, simile and metaphor, which the poet shares with the lunatic and the lover, and which are essentially the categories of magic' (84). Poetry speaks the language of myth, and not the language of fact or reason. The literary critic assumes that people in the age of Lascaux and Altamira were as intelligent as we are and cannot accept evolution and its more sinister aspects after Darwin: 'Unhappily, evolution came to be regarded as the scientific proof of a myth of progress, and the combination became, as has often been shown, part of an imperialist ideology, designed to rationalize the aggressiveness with which the white man assumed his burden' (85). Throughout his career, Frye rarely misses an occasion to speak against imperialism, fascism and totalitarianism. The poet should not be the servant of the myth of imperial progress, although Virgil would occur to Frye as a problematic exception. Frye revisits and exposes a favourite book of his youth, H. G. Wells' *Outline of History*, as a misguided exemplar of the gradualist or progressive mythology in which the evidence, however flawed, creates a story in which inferior ancestors and races have given way to 'true men' who come later and survive the progress of history (86). This kind of snobbery, which Frye says is of humanist origin, is unworthy and can be found in its fossilized terms such as 'Dark Ages' and 'Enlightenment' (87). Frye can distance himself from the progressive myths associated with humanism and liberalism. Two teleological myths, the bourgeois myth of progress and the more plausible Marxist myth that the disasters that threaten the myth of progress are the 'death-agonies of bourgeois culture', dominate a good deal of our thinking, but, Frye says, more out of habit than conviction (87–8). Frye satirizes both views and thinks that the unhappiest people in our society are those who, in Charles Snow's words, 'have the future in their bones', who wait each night for Godot (88).

The poets' protest against technology, being like that of Snow's Luddites, 'is really a protest against the mechanical dehumanizing of life . . . and it only looks reactionary when its opposite is assumed to be beneficent' (Frye 1971b: 89). Poetry involves psychological primitivism and brings us back to the beginning of social attitudes, the speculations, hopes, despairs, emotions and desires that make us human. The primitive occurs existentially when a person admires a sunset, quarrels with a lover, demonstrates for peace or commits suicide. When technology and mechanics dominate society, the poet becomes socially alienated. The cases of Pound searching for a social role in his admiration for Mussolini and of D. H. Lawrence's lapsing into a regressive myth of historical primitivism demonstrate that the modern poet cannot be the focus of the myth of freedom. Poets are 'children of concern' who can be converted to dogmatism: their genius, in Frye's view, is of intensity as opposed to wisdom or serenity (89–91). Poets, who since Blake have inveighed against 'dark Satanic mills', have protested against mechanization. In one of Frye's favourite satires, Thomas Love Peacock's *The Four Ages of Poetry*, which is to be admired for being nearer to Vico than anything else in English literature, the poet is portrayed as a primitive, the kind of atavistic survival that Plato prophesied, in what is really, in Frye's reading of Peacock's ironic allegory, a satire on a society that could think such a thing (93–4). Shelley's defence places imagination above discursive writing, which posits theses that are half-truths implying their own opposites, because works of imagination cannot be refuted. Poetry includes; discursive writing attacks. Shelley's 'argument assumes, not only that the language of poetry is mythical, but that poetry, in its totality, is in fact society's real myth of concern, and that the poet is still the teacher of that myth' (95). For Shelley, the authority of the poet comes from the oracular power in his or her mind that was once ascribed to divine revelation. Adapting Snow, perhaps, Frye postulates two cultures that co-exist but are not connected: science and mythology. Frye says that poetry is primitive and therefore revolutionary, because, as Shelley says, it 'creates anew' and breaks down mental habits. With Shelley, Frye concludes that 'The imagination, which conceives the forms of human society, is the source of the power to change that society' and that we should read the underthought of a poem and not its surface anxiety, where the poet shares the prejudices of his or her society (97). Imagination is counter-historical and redeems time – here Frye calls on Shelley and the Bible in making this claim – 'and literature for it exists totally in the present tense as a total form of verbal imagination' (98). Frye finds his idea of total form in Shelley's insight that the total form of literature is a great poem that poets have built, like cooperating thoughts, since the beginning and calls this image a bridge to the other critical shore, where the reference and social context of criticism is located.

When humanism disappeared (Frye calls Arnold one of the last humanists), its elite society which functioned within an established framework of concern disappeared, so that, out of that context, its concept of the critic as judge made little sense any more. Frye differs from Erasmus and Arnold because his function as a critic differs. Literature is the language of concern, but not a myth of concern. Criticism is an expanding field, and literature displays the imaginative possibilities of concern, the total range of verbal fictions and models and images and metaphors out of which all myths of concern are constructed. The modern critic is therefore a student of mythology, and his total subject embraces not merely literature, but the areas of concern which the mythical language of construction and belief enters and informs. These areas constitute the mythological subjects, and they include large parts of religion, philosophy, political theory, and the social sciences.

(Frye 1971b: 98)

The criteria for the critic are those of the myth of freedom: he or she depends on evidence and verification. Freed from moral and evaluative criticism, the modern critic must be tolerant of all kinds of poets and poetic expression and not dislike any genre. Critics are subject to the anxieties of their age, and the poet's relation to his or her time is the 'liberal element' in their study (99). The critic links the present with its past and with its inheritors because 'a culture that is careless of its past has no defences against the future' (100). As a historical critic, he or she continues the humanist tradition, whose liberal quality derives much from its ability to study the past with detachment, but as a contemporary, he or she studies our own concern and looks at its relation to the past. In discussing William Morris' *News from Nowhere*, Frye says that freedom has two parts, contemplation and creative imagination (100–3). Literature as a whole and in individual texts says something, involving intuitions of human nature and destiny that are similar to, but more infinite and encyclopedic than, the formulation of concern in political or religious myths (103).

In moving from concern to imagination, Frye enters the fifth stage of his critical path. He provides tentative conclusions that arise out of his 'quasi-historical survey', for instance, that in this fragmented age 'the great dream of the deductive synthesis, in which faith and knowledge are indissoluably linked, seems to be fading' (Frye 1971b: 104). Thomism and Marxism have not provided adequate syntheses. Between ought and is, Frye says, there lies 'an existential gap, a revolutionary and transforming act of choice', so that it is 'an illusion of habit' to think that our choices are inevitably linked to things as they are, whether through God or nature, because we choose our beliefs and society from infinite possibilities (104–5). Mythical and logical languages are distinct. It also appears futile to think that one myth of concern will establish itself worldwide, because the more widespread it is, the more rifts appear within: it needs an enemy (105). There are closed and open mythologies. Democracy is open, although tolerance has its limits, because in practice it sets out the rules of the game in keeping the peace between a plurality of myths of concern. In theory tolerance is difficult to formulate (106–7). For Frye, the open mythology, as opposed to the closed one that demands adherence by all to a set of doctrines or beliefs, is the way to a world community because this openness 'establishes the relativity of each myth of concern within it, and so emphasizes the element of construct or imaginative vision in the myth' (107). The closed mythology insists on truth of correspondence, whereas the open mythology allows for truth of vision and renounces the finality of a person's comprehension of the truth (107–8). Perhaps the best myths of concern are those that answer to two standards: charity and intellectual honesty. Frye thinks that Nazism, a myth of concern, lacked charity and falsified history and science, so that these two vices may always go together. Only by recognizing the tension between concern and freedom can tolerance, or the plurality of concerns, exist in society (108). By example, educated people should show 'that beliefs may be held and examined at the same time' (109). Concern and belief occupy the entirety of the same universe. Knowledge by itself cannot give us the social vision to suggest what ought to be done with our knowledge (109–10). Ideology becomes one of Frye's central interests (see Chapter 7):

> What we really believe is not what we say or think we believe but what our actions show that we believe, and no belief which is not an axiom of behavior is a genuinely concerned belief. Marxism has a similar conception of unessential belief, the 'ideology' which is to be talked about but not acted upon, and which has the function of decorating the facade of a conservative attitude. Many of my readers would call what I am calling a myth of concern an ideology, and though, as I have indicated, I have specific reasons for using the term myth, those who prefer ideology may substitute it in most contexts.
>
> (112)

But, paradoxically, Frye believes in a myth of freedom that balances this will to demand a conformity of belief in the community.

Frye returns to the Bible and sees there a Jesus more mythical than historical. Myth is, Frye says, the language of the present tense. Although not an epic or a story-book, the Bible is closer to being a literary text than history or doctrine. In a culture with strict limits to experience and a developed sense of fact, concern passes through the language of imagination. Every myth of concern retreats from belief to imagination, and the standards of a myth of freedom – logic, evidence, a sense of objective reality – also represent approximations, are analogies of what Frye calls a model world or ideals of procedure (1971b: 113–19). Words cannot tell the truth of correspondence because a verbal structure *sui generis* involves fictional and mythical features and cannot be aligned to the phenomena it describes. Grammar is a fiction: words have a narrative shape (*mythos*) that the demands of narrative, a causality that does not correspond to any other sequence of events or kind of causality, partly shape (119). The mythical integrity of the Bible is closely related to its unreliability as history (119–20). In an open mythology Frye connects interpretation with 'the detached oracular structure of the prose of concern' and says that such commentary resembles criticism in literature, so that in the area of general concern, different forms of critical hermeneutics, whether of the Bible, Shakespeare, the American Constitution or oral traditions of an indigenous tribe, converge (123). He outlines four principles about the poet. Frye contrasts the teacher of a myth of concern, who is wise or inspired, to the poet, who can be a fool. The reader sets out to transfer the vision of the poet to himself or herself. There are no negative visions. Criticism is not evaluation or a critic creating a canon and thereby 'making literature a single gigantic allegory of his own anxieties' (127). When the myth of concern develops, its language becomes conceptual and poetry goes its own narrative, imaginal and metaphorical way. At this point, 'The critic begins to see literature as presenting the range of imaginative possibilities of belief, its stories the encyclopaedia of visions of human life and destiny which form the context of belief' (128). If, as Blake says, 'The Old and New Testaments are the Great Code of Art', literature, in Frye's view, is the great code of concern because through the universals of imagination, mythical stories that from the point of view of history and reason seem immature can become 'visionary sources of belief'(128). Literature has no connection with belief: therefore it has a great importance 'in indicating the horizons beyond all formulations of belief, in pointing to an infinite total concern that can never be expressed, but only indicated in the variety of the arts themselves' (128). Frye suggests the absent presence or telos of the ineffable vision, a suggestion he made to the end of his life (see Chapter 8).

Concern is part of the attempt to escape alienation: freedom is born of it and cannot exist without it, but, nevertheless, opposes it. Frye advocates a both/and world rather than one like Kierkegaard's either/or. He identifies the temptation to identify liberty with freedom of choice or free will with Kierkegaard and existentialists and with irony itself (Frye 1971b: 128–33; see also Hart 1992c: 229–31, 9–11). The return to vision recurs in Frye:

The only genuine freedom is a freedom of the will which is informed by a vision, and this vision can only come to us through the intellect and the imagination, and through the arts and sciences which embody them, the analogies of whatever truth and beauty we can reach. In this kind of freedom the opposition to necessity disappears: for scientists and artists and scholars, as such, what they want to do and what they have to do become the same thing. This is the core of the freedom that no concern can ever include or replace, and everything else that we associate with freedom proceeds from it.

(133)

In Frye's scheme freedom can be achieved only through vision and imagination that become translated through analogy to an existential process that imaginers, like scientists, artists and scholars can achieve. Although Frye doesn't say so, his views elsewhere would seem to indicate that he thinks that readers and anyone using imagination would have access to this core of freedom. Generally, he tends towards the democratic and away from the preserves of an elite or priesthood.

Two types of education occur in life, education in concern, a comprehension of assumptions and axioms on which people act or say they act, and education in schools and universities, which focuses on the truth of correspondence and the myth of freedom. Intolerance of the American way of life, as opposed to religious tolerance in the United States, shows that it is the central myth of concern in that country, although as a student moves higher in the educational system, he or she finds more means of criticizing this myth, of finding alternative social mythologies or of experiencing disillusionment or an 'identity crisis', which Frye empathizes with in those, especially those under thirty, who are opposing the Vietnam war (1971b: 134–5, 137–8). Once again, Frye brings up the importance of 'mythology' – Roland Barthes also concerns himself with this term – which many today call ideology: 'In a society that has what I have called an open mythology, there is a certain critical element in education, which consists in becoming increasingly aware of one's mythological conditioning' (135). In a closed mythology with its centralization of power, propaganda prevails; in an open mythology, the competitive market. Frye defends the university in the climate of student protests in the late 1960s not because he doesn't experience empathy for the alienated students but because, for him, the university is the place of the myth of freedom, which encourages criticism of the myth of concern or ideology and should not, no matter how dire the circumstances, be hijacked as a society of concern, an institution for coercion in the name of dogma.

Frye looks at the motivation of those who would like to cure the identity crisis of the late 1960s and early 1970s by returning to the radical strand in America, of Jefferson, Thoreau, Lincoln, Whitman and others, to recover that democratic and revolutionary myth of concern. Like all of us, Frye is better at prophesying the future in the past, of seeing prophecy as part of a mythical pattern, because much of the last two decades before he died was part of a revival of political conservativism: 'There is also of course a right wing that would like to make the American way of life a closed myth, but its prospects at the moment do not seem bright' (140; see also 138–9). The words 'at the moment' show Frye's propensity for the longer view or for the eternal now, for thinking of all time in the present moment, and his wiliness about thinking about prophecy as prediction, a saying before of what will happen after (see 151). The student protest and the hippie communes show affinities to nineteenth-century anarchism and utopian communities respectively. The existentialism of Kierkegaard and the French resistance also have their echoes in the movement. Frye seems to be more able to accommodate these influences than he is to accept the psychological, rather than political, basis of this middle-class disillusionment with its own affluence:

> This kind of disaffectation is not, like orthodox Marxism, directed at the centres of economic power: it is rather a psychologically based revolution, a movement of protest directed at the anxieties of privilege. It does not fight for workers against exploiters so much as attack and ridicule the work ethic itself. It does not see Negro segregation or the Vietnam war merely as by-products of a class struggle: it sees fears and prejudices involved in these issues as primary, and the insecurity that inspires them as the real enemy.
>
> (141)

Quite convincingly, Frye relates this radical mood to Bohemianism, which began in the nineteenth century and was revived in the twentieth century with Freud as its spokesman and drugs and sex as its symbols of social opposition. The myth here, as Freud is unmoored from his intention, is that bourgeois society represents a repressive anxiety-structure that the sexual instinct especially disturbs, so that to renew society is to emancipate that instinct and to associate it with creativity, as Blake and Shelley do (141–2). Taking off one's clothes is an attack on what is supposed to be ruling-class prudery because sex is available to all classes and so has to be devalued. Four-letter words are meant to disturb, but, in Frye's view, the really obscene and socially dangerous words are those that express religious, national and racial hatreds

(142–3). The arts can play a central and functional role in this kind of partially psychological revolution by helping to understand the poetic and mythical language of the emergent myth of concern. The growth of oral culture in this movement allows us to see that poetry is the centre of literature with literary prose in plays and novels on the periphery and with utilitarian prose outside that. This orality allows for a corrective in education, which has recently taught poetry as communication in unimaginative and paraphrasable ways and which has made the use of words for non-literary purposes the centre. Film and the popular contemporary poetry have helped to educate students, in spite of educators, about archetypes and symbols, the underthought of poetry. Frye is, of course, hopeful because these are at the centre of his critical theory (143–5). He is also encouraged by 'the tolerance for schematic thinking', in the I Ching, Tarot cards, astrology, Gurdjieff, Velikowski and so on, another centre of Frye's critical universe (145). The absorption of the poetic habit of mind into ordinary experience is a new situation, so that Frye can only speculate on its ramifications. He performs a reading of the 'people's park' crisis in the summer of 1969 at Berkeley, where he was a visiting professor, in which he does a mythological reading of it as a kind of 'archetype of the expulsion from Eden' (see Chapter 6) (146).

The revival of oral culture and the development of a radical sense of social concern appear to be part of the same process, and in a society where the distinction between art and social event often breaks down, literary critics cannot ignore the social context of their subject. We are, as Joyce realized, living in the age of the *perce-oreille*, a steady insinuation of implacable voices suggesting social attitudes and responses, selling and indoctrinating. It is not, Frye says, simply 'the voice we hear that haunts us, but the voice that goes on echoing in our minds, forming our social attitudes, our habits of speech, our processes of thought' (147). People resist the voice and its echoes with its erotic stimulations for us to be seduced into being consumers. The panic that we cannot escape, the voice leads to vicious and silly behaviour, like smashing and looting, that nevertheless represents 'acts of counter-communication, acts noisy enough or outrageous enough to shout down that voice and spit at that image, if only for a few moments' (148). The defiance has momentary success because 'hysterical violence is self-defeating' because, as counter-communication, it provokes worse words from that which it attacks, thereby creating a kind of circular verbal dance of lost direction. Releasing inhibitions can be as hysterical, compulsive and repetitive as repressing them. Advertising of luxury goods and privilege for a white elite can have explosive results for those who cannot participate in the gorging. When television is used as the advertisers use it, illegal narcotics, a wall of rock music and political separatism are all techniques used to wash out the voice of mythology or ideology. Marshall McLuhan, his colleague in the Department of English at the University of Toronto and an innovative observer of technology and the media, is never far from Frye's mind, sometimes in favourable terms, sometimes less so: 'If the world is becoming a global village, we should not forget that the primary characteristics of village life include cliques, feuds and impassable social barriers' (149). Technology has led to introversion without privacy and community, a prison, an image Frye might be using with Kierkegaard's view of hell as incommunication in mind. In this context Frye welcomes as an encouraging sign 'the growth of a sense of festivity connected with poetry and music, however noisy or strident' (150). Contra McLuhan, Frye says that the linear and simultaneous are mental operations, and the written document is what makes those responses and democracy itself possible by making the conditions of freedom possible. The electronic media intensify what Frye calls 'linear' panic and give us images, words and rhythms with the same message, and it is only a technical matter whether one is interested in resolution and tone. The message of painting may be paint, but in direct communication, as opposed to artistic, an awareness of form brings about a separation of content from it (151–2). Frye, who builds his theory on cycles, finds cycles in history outside literary history: 'In every generation the inexperience of youth revolts against the wasted experience of its elders, and repeats the cycle in its turn' (151). Nature with its seasons may have more to do with culture than we would like to admit.

The anxiety of continuity has as much to do with individual identity as with society. This identity can be surface habit and custom or a deeper sense of developing skills and ways to learn through habit and repetition, something that applies especially to the artist (Frye 1971b: 152–3). Repetition need not be rote and increases skill in education, a kind of insurance against the electronic media's intensification of the linear and the fragmented. The discontinuity of identity in the individual can manifest itself as a mechanical repetition of sexual experience with different female sexual objects. Frye implies a critique of pornography:

In the mechanical sexuality of so much of contemporary entertainment there comes back into our culture something of the fetishism that we have in that quaint little paleolithic object called the Venus of Willendorf, all belly and teats and gaping vulva, but no face. The confusion between the physically intimate and the genuinely personal is parallel to, and doubtless related to, the confusion between the introverted and the creative experience in the drug cults.

(154)

He says that the demand for 'relevance' in the universities has two principal sources, the threat to identity that the discontinuity in contemporary experience creates and a perceived lack of meaning when one feels that one's life is not connected to an adequately articulate myth of concern. Scholarship and sciences, which are specialized and pluralistic, appear to threaten identity and in isolation can lead to an indifference to human values, but in a society with an open mythology, scholarship must be autonomous and have a veto over any aspect of the myth of concern (155). The establishment or power-structure is a transient form of that society, so that social change is the release of the real form of society. Radical and conservative wings want a society with an open mythology to close its mythology. When identity is threatened, a myth of concern is more attractive with its 'convinced and final answers', but questions are our birthright. For the myth of freedom, the student must work on a subject and find its relevance. In Frye's allegory for the present – the time of student protests – to make a commitment to a subject is 'an act of historical significance' because to find a critical path between the 'dogmatism of unliberated concern' and 'the scepticism of unconcerned freedom' is to live in the history of one's time (156–7).

Two mythical conceptions polarize social mythology – social contract and utopia – which descend historically from the myth of the fall and the fulfilment myth of the city of God. Contract myth starts as a fiction about social authority and its transfer long ago but is an attempt to account for the structure of society in the present (Frye 1971b: 158). In discussing Edmund Burke and Tom Paine, Frye contrasts the conservative defence of the 'facade of society as though it were society', an uncritical rationalization of what exists in society, with the radical and utopian social view, which has gathered strength in the past century, that uncovers this lack of a critical attitude and suggests ways to be more aware of our social conditioning and to experience a loyalty we choose, often to a social ideal that does not exist yet as opposed to the established social order (159–61). In reading writers who explore ideal societies, like Plato, More, Locke and Rousseau, it soon becomes apparent that they are really writing about education (see Chapter 6). Through education, one learns the true authority of internal or inherent compulsion – of reason, accuracy, experiment and imagination. The educational contract, a legacy of nineteenth-century English liberalism and central to John Stuart Mill's view of liberty, Arnold's culture and Newman's idea of the university, is the source of spiritual authority in the present and projected into the future (162–4). It is the process by which the arts and sciences, with their methods of logic, experiment, amassing of evidence and imaginative presentation, actually operate as the source of spiritual authority in society. The university in society, which Frye so often defends, mainly stands for the educational contract because although the university is only the engine room of liberty, it sustains free authority in society as a whole. In the midst of the student protests Frye is trying to show that the university is easy to harass, but that to attack the place of freedom, where imagination, experiment, reason and evidence are fostered, is a mistake and that 'the tactics of trying to revolutionize society by harassing and bedevilling the university are not serious tactics' (164). This is the nub of Frye's disagreement with the student protesters and one that I later explore. Literature liberates the language of concern to express in society a wide imaginative range of concern, not a rhetorical analogue for the tactics of one social group (166). Arnold's classless society, rather than Marx's, serves as a model for Frye because it balances the fraternity, liberty and equality that the aristocracy, bourgeoisie and proletariat have each given us in history (166–8). Frye returns to the critical path between an existing world and the intelligible world of the thinker as well as the imaginative world of the artist. He resists 'the false form of imaginative pleasure, connected with what Kierkegaard calls the aesthetic attitude to experience, which is passive, a sense of a pleasantly stimulated subject contemplating an inscrutably beautiful object' (168–9). This 'idolatry of art' or aesthetic ideology will not do for Frye partly because art cannot be believed in. Whereas myths of concern are verbal constructions made for particular social purposes, myths in literature are disinterested, are forms of human creativity that 'communicate the joy . . . that belongs to pure creation' (169). Literature possesses an 'inner exuberance' that raises its myths clear of the horror and iniquity of the human life from which they form themselves. For Frye, 'Literature is unique among the arts in being able to reflect the world escaped from, in its conventions of tragedy and irony and satire, along with the world escaped to, in its conventions of pastoral and romance and comedy' (169). In threading his critical path between concern and freedom, Frye maintains the balance between them, not in Hegelian and Marxist dialectics but in an older philosophical tradition in which the ideal society or synthesis can only exist in a tension of opposites or antithesis (see 168):

But just as society is never free from hysteria, so individual freedom is never itself entirely free from a privilege that somebody else is partly paying for. It is out of the tension between concern and freedom that glimpses of a third order of experience emerge, of a world that may not exist but completes existence, the world of the definitive experience that poetry urges us to have but which we never quite get.

(170–1)

Frye ends *The Critical Path* with a sentence that embodies a conditional vision, the apocalyptic withering away of criticism in which the distinction between literature and life would disappear 'because life itself would then be the continuous incarnation of the creative word' (171). But the implication is that in life at least this withering away will not occur, so that the creative word frees us even if we cannot incarnate it. Poetry urges us to have a definitive experience we cannot have, but that informs our indefinite experience that life affords us. Criticism translates poetry into its society. Poetry and criticism are two parts of the worlds of consciousness, 'the intelligible and imaginative worlds, that are at once the reward of freedom and the guarantee of it' (170). Only individual, but not social, happiness is possible. This happiness involves 'unimpeded movement in society, a detachment that does not withdraw; and the basis of that sense of independence is consciousness' (170). An individual freedom and happiness that also involves the responsibility of concern is the middle way of the critical path. Life is not literature, but one informs the other, and literature is where ideology is, perhaps, only hypothetically evaded. Frye's third order or critical path is of concern and freedom but is neither.

4 *The Great Code*

Sciant autem litterati modis omnibus locutionis, quos grammatici graeco
nomine tropos vocant, auctores nostros usos fuisse.

Let all those conversant with letters know that our authors have used all
the figures of speech, which the grammarians have given the Greek name
tropes [*tropi*].

(Augustine, *De doctrina christiana* III.29)

In *The Great Code: The Bible and Literature* (1982) Frye begins to fulfil
his desire to write a book on the Bible which amplifies his comments on
the Bible and its centrality to English and Western literature and
mythology in many of his books, including *Fearful Symmetry*, *Anatomy
of Criticism* and *The Critical Path*. A prologue to *The Great Code*,
Creation and Recreation (1980), first delivered as the Larkin-Stuart
Lectures at the University of Toronto in 1980, looks at the ideas of
creation and recreation, the divine and the human, the religious and the
literary. His analysis of the Bible finds its completion in *Words with
Power* (1990) and *The Double Vision* (1991), which I discuss in
chapters 7 and 8. It suffices to say that Frye exercised a Miltonic
patience, and perhaps frustration, in completing his great task of
relating the Bible and literature together, something that probably
arose out of Frye's training in both theology and English literature at
university. This study of the Bible *and* (not as) literature was a personal
response as well as 'a study of the Bible from the point of view of a
literary critic' (Frye 1982b: xi). Frye explains the genesis of his book
from his undergraduate course on the Bible at Toronto.

He does not waver in his view of the critical operation, which he
thinks 'begins with reading a work straight through, as many times as
may be necessary to possess it in totality', the point at which the critic
is able to begin a formulation of 'a conceptual unity corresponding to
the imaginative unity of his text' (Frye 1982b: xii). Even though the

Bible is more like a library than a book and is an 'inconsistent jumble of badly established texts', it 'has traditionally been read as a unity, and has influenced Western imagination as a unity' (xii-xiii). Frye appeals to the external evidence of the reception of the Bible and the internal evidence of an 'Aristotelian' structure of beginning, middle and end as proof of the unity of the Bible. *The Great Code*, like Frye's course, looks at 'a unified structure of narrative and imagery in the Bible' (xiii). The unifying principle in the Bible is one of shape, not of meaning. Frye is still in search of a total structure and a body of archetypes or recurrent images. The Bible

> begins where time begins, with the creation of the world; it ends where time ends, with the Apocalypse, and it surveys human history in between, or the aspect of history it is interested in, under the symbolic names of Adam and Israel. There is also a body of concrete images: city, mountain, river, garden, tree, oil, fountain, bread, wine, bride, sheep, and many others, which recur so often that they clearly indicate some kind of unifying principle.
>
> (xiii)

Frye concentrates on the Christian Bible, and not on the Jewish or Islamic conceptions of the Bible, because that is the Bible which he knows and which is central to English literature and Western cultural tradition. More specifically, he uses the Authorized Version or King James Bible of 1611 because it is in the Vulgate tradition, and thus is near to the Bible known to European writers from the fifth century onwards (xiii). Frye is interested in concrete images, which translators are unlikely to get wrong and which make the differences between Protestant and Catholic Bibles unimportant (xiii–xiv).

The Great Code retains its original goal 'of introducing the general reader to a knowledge of the Bible and to some of the applications he can make of such knowledge in the rest of his reading' (1982b: xiv). As usual since *Anatomy* and perhaps in keeping with his work for the *Canadian Forum* in the 1930s and 1940s, Frye's desire here is for a democratic accessibility to, and application of, knowledge. He recognizes the strength and weakness of repeating himself in new contexts. Here is a critic whose work was probably more scrutinized by more contemporaries in more places than any critic before him in the twentieth century. Frye had heard many objections over the years. In addition to having to defend literature and criticism, he had to defend himself, his method of repeating his central myth in new contexts, like the reiterative imagery and generic structures he wrote about. Possibly, he sometimes slipped into a primary professional hazard for the literary critic and theorist, that is in imitating, consciously or unconsciously, the texts and field one studies. But Frye's *apologia* shows the vulnerability of the magisterial critic and his text, the power and the tentativeness that one can find even in his first two books, *Fearful Symmetry* and *Anatomy of Criticism*:

> In a sense all my critical work, beginning with a study of Blake published in 1947, and formulated ten years later in *Anatomy of Criticism*, has revolved around the Bible. Hence the total project is, among other things, a restatement of the critical outlook I have been expounding in various ways for years. I feel that it is now very far from being what I was afraid at first it would turn into, a rewritten version of the *Anatomy*, but I apologize in advance to readers who may often feel that they have been here before. All I can say is that I am aware of the dangers of restating what I have said elsewhere in a different context, and that the repetitions unavoidable here are not wholly that. In this volume such features as the categories of metaphor, the ladder of 'polysemous sense', the conception of literal meaning, and the identification of mythology and literature are presented in what I hope is a new framework.
>
> (xiv)

Is this repetition with a difference, which the anxiety to escape being stereotyped in the shadows of his most famous book reveals, or the fear that after such a long wait, his book will appear like old recycled stuff to his fellow scholars who hover in their unnamed absence behind the general reader, or both? One has the sense, as one did in Frye's classes in the mid and late 1970s, that this last great work on the Bible was his *summa*, a kind of retrospective culmination of, and sometimes brooding over, his career as a critic.

The teaching theme, for instance, serves such a purpose in one of its aspects. Frye taught up to his death at the age of 78: he needed to teach and apparently liked it. *The Great Code* grew out of his teaching and not his scholarship. His pronouncements are as true as they are modest: 'all my books have really been teachers' manuals, concerned more with establishing perspectives than with adding specifically to knowledge' (1982b: xiv). The figure of the teacher is something Frye takes seriously, so that his book addresses the position of the student and uses paradox and the pretence of naiveté, or Socratic irony, which are teaching tactics. He appeals to the teacher as portrayed in Plato's *Meno*, 'someone who attempts to re-create the subject in the student's mind ... to get the student to recognize what he already potentially knows, which includes breaking up the powers of repression in his mind that keep him from knowing what he knows' (xv). According to Frye, some have resented his use of teaching techniques, but, he says, that is because they are loyal to different teachers. He has also been criticized for being elusive as a result of his irony, but Frye appeals to the irony of Socrates, the parables of Jesus and the paradox of the teacher in Zen Buddhism as his defence. Great teachers are elusive. Jesus' parables are *ainoi* or fables with a riddling quality; the Zen Buddhist teacher answers with paradox: to answer a question, for Frye, 'is to consolidate the mental level on which the question is asked', so that 'Unless something is kept in reserve, suggesting the possibility of better and fuller questions, the student's mental advance is blocked' (xv). This explanation suggests why Frye does not like the word 'position' and seldom uses it in a positive way. He wanted to transcend or evade antitheses like scholarly/unscholarly and personal/impersonal. Like other people, academics begin with a personality 'afflicted by ignorance and prejudice' and attempt to escape from that personality, as Eliot said, by absorbing themselves in impersonal scholarship. Frye says that academics should then emerge on the other side and realize that all knowledge is personal but also having experienced some transformation as people (xv). The Bible attracted Frye not as a reinforcement for his 'position' but as a suggestive means 'of getting past some of the limitations inherent in all positions' (xvi). As a both/and critic who, like Frye, attempts to be open to possibility and to multiple points of view, I think that his resistance to setting out his position is not a political smokescreen but a conscious and admirable failure to conform to those editors of journals and presses as well as those students, teachers and critics who as theory police and ideology agents insist that one should at all times give one's position. If one performs this engraving of position, it must be done with some irony, for, as I have said elsewhere, unconscious motivations may be more interesting, indirect and complex than conscious ones. Professed belief or statement of position is not the lived ideology or being and action in the world. Not every critic has to declare, as in a show trial, where he or she stands. The elusiveness of irony, parable and paradox – the teacher as poetry – breaks down the rigid oppositions such as we/ they and the chosen/the banished. Frye is not advocating irresponsibility and apoliticism – there are too many atrocities to make a retreat into silence or selfishness a proper response – but he is opposing a kind of totalitarian desire to reduce things to either/or and people to sets of propositions, a domineering will that does not allow people to explore the ambivalences and complexities of their private–public lives. Frye, whenever he had the opportunity, slammed Nazism, and not after the fact. He did not, to use terminology from *The Critical Path*, want to let the myth of concern banish or dictate to the myth of freedom, to make him declare and harden into a position, like the student who gets the answer he or she is looking for. Education lives in the themes and the techniques of Frye's writing.

The Bible is more than literature and evades classification, but it has continually fertilized English literature, from its beginnings to the present, so that would it, Frye implies, share the formal principles of literature that are, like those of music, proper to literature? Value judgements are by-products of the critical process and not a major function of it. A study of a text leads the critic 'through literature into the broader question of the social function of words' (Frye 1982b: xvi). The Bible by-passes the barrier of evaluation and leads Frye 'outside literature into the larger verbal context of which literature forms a part' (xvii). He outlines two directions in biblical scholarship, the critical and the traditional. The former 'establishes the text and studies the historical and cultural background', while the latter 'interprets it in accordance with what a consensus of theological and ecclesiastical authorities have declared the meaning to be' (xvii). The critical biblical scholarship which has dominated biblical studies for over a century was not much help to Frye because it does not illuminate how a poet might read the Bible and because its textual scholarship has sunk into a state where the disintegration of the text has become an end in itself. For Frye, the only interesting question in textual scholarship is 'why the Bible as we know it emerged in that particular form', even if that form is the product of a long and intricate editorial process. Traditional biblical scholarship includes two approaches that interest Frye – medieval typology and Reformation commentary – because they assumed the unity of the Bible as a postulate and because they demonstrate how it can be comprehensible to poets (xvii). Frye also wants to provide a contemporary 'look' at the Bible as an aspect of present literary and critical concerns. For instance, he thinks that his assertion in *Anatomy* that literary criticism was approaching the social sciences has been borne out because language has been taken as the basis of investigation in many of the social sciences, so that the humanist concern with language can no longer be separated from other concerns. The genuine issues of contemporary criticism, Frye asserts, are closely related to a study of the Bible (xviii).

A major aspect of our imaginative tradition, the Bible tells us something about what Frye calls the mythological universe, a body of assumptions and beliefs arising out of the existential concerns of humans, who do not live directly in nature as animals do. Most of the mythological universe is held unconsciously, which means that our imaginations may recognize elements of it, when presented in art or literature, without consciously understanding what it is that we recognize. Practically all that we can see of this body of concern is socially conditioned and culturally inherited. Below the cultural inheritance there must be a common psychological inheritance, otherwise forms of culture and imagination outside our own traditions would not be intelligible to us. But I doubt if we can reach this common inheritance directly, bypassing the distinctive qualities in our specific culture. One of the practical functions of criticism, by which I mean the conscious organizing of a cultural tradition, is, I think, to make us more aware of our mythological conditioning.

(xviii)

Criticism becomes a mediation, a means of recognition through art and literature of our common psychology, a way of making us more conscious of our mythological or ideological conditioning. *Anagnorisis* reveals ideology, which in the guise of 'mythology' and the myths of concern and freedom preoccupy Northrop Frye from about 1968 to 1991. Recognition is an aspect of Frye's preoccupation with vision: not only does he speak explicitly about vision and the visionary throughout his œuvre, but he also uses metaphors and images of sight throughout.

If for prudential reasons Giambattista Vico had to avoid discussing the Bible in his theory of culture, Frye does not have to observe such taboos. Too many scholars today, Frye says, avoid the Bible even though so many cultural issues arose originally from it. For example,

Many issues in critical theory today had their origin in the hermeneutic study of the Bible; many contemporary approaches to criticism are obscurely motivated by a God-is-dead syndrome that also developed out of Biblical criticism; many formulations of critical theory seem to me more defensible when applied to the Bible than they are when applied elsewhere.

(xix)

Frye agrees with the Romantics – who realized that the traditional Protestant separation of the poetic element in the Bible from secular literature, as exemplified in Samuel Johnson, was irrational – and wishes that Coleridge and Ruskin had developed their views on typology more systematically. Critical theory, in Frye's view, is coming back into focus, especially in the work of Hans-Georg Gadamer, Paul Ricœur and Walter Ong, to whom, he says, he owes a debt (xix). Marxism is an 'heir of the revolutionary and socially organized forms of religion derived from the Bible', and if Hegel is Marx's spiritual father, Martin Luther is his spiritual grandfather (xx). The increased interest in Buddhist, Hindu and Taoist thought in the West would be even more illuminating if we understood better their counterparts in our tradition. Frye realizes how emotionally charged the subject of the Bible is and says that the academic goal is not to accept or reject it but to see what the subject means. He thinks that rejection of belief means little in terms of changing our mental processes, whereas the 'primitive' categories of metaphor, myth and typology involve much disturbance of ways of thinking. Insight is Frye's aim.

Irony is the teacher's strategy, so that the teaching of literature is like a game. Frye argues that 'Literature continues in society the tradition of myth-making, and myth-making has a quality that Lévi-Strauss calls *bricolage*, a putting together of bits and pieces out of whatever comes to hand' (1982b: xxi). Dante, Blake and Eliot made a system out of odds and ends of their reading. *The Great Code*, Frye says, is a *bricolage* about a work of *bricolage*, the Bible. By choosing this structure, he returns to the anatomy and to Burton's *Anatomy of Melancholy*, which has 'schematic arrangements that are hardly those of any systematic medical treatment of melancholy, and yet correspond to something in the mind that yields a perhaps even deeper kind of comprehension' (xxi). Burton's was the only book that could rouse Samuel Johnson from bed earlier than he wanted to be: Frye's *The Great Code* tries to follow in the anatomy tradition and also serves as its author's prefatory comments on the relation of the Bible to Western literature, especially the impact of the Bible on the creative imagination. The structure of the book is a double mirror like the Bible itself. The first part contains four chapters: Chapter 1 is concerned with the language people use to talk about the Bible and questions related to it and provides a context for examining the Bible as an imaginative influence; chapters 2 and 3 discuss myth and metaphor, especially how they relate to the literal meaning of the Bible; Chapter 4 deals with temporality and how it connects with the traditional way that Christians have read the Bible. The second part is a more direct application of critical principles to the structure of the Bible, only in reverse order, so that while the first part ends with a chapter on typology, the second part begins with one. In Chapter 5 Frye begins with the seven phases of revelation: creation, exodus, law, wisdom, prophecy, Gospel and apocalypse. He further breaks down apocalypse into two forms of vision (so that the seven phases are really eight), the last of which returns us to the role of the reader. Chapter 6 and Chapter 7 are inductive surveys of imagery and the narrative structures of the Bible respectively, where the book had its origin. The eighth and final chapter makes a second approach to what Kenneth Burke calls the 'rhetoric of religion' and looks briefly at polysemous meaning, which suggests a direction from literal meaning (xxi–xxii). By now it should be apparent that Frye has moved in his familiar circular, cyclical or comic structure, taking the reader through the still point of the turning wheel of typology at the centre of the book, perhaps like the famous moment in which Dante emerges at the centre of the *Divine Comedy* that Frye likes to refer to.

In the second study, which will turn out eight years later to be *Words with Power*, Frye hopes to look in more detail at Ruth, the Song of Songs and the folk-tale aspects of the Apocrypha, all of which have literary elements. He tries to conceive of his readers and assumes they are not that familiar with the Bible or at least the imaginative component. The readers he aims at are those in the middle way who do not have such an investment in religion that they will dismiss the book as 'sterile dilettantism' or those who think of the Bible as an establishment symbol connected with a primitive view of biology and with sexual inhibitions, a sign of infantile or authoritarian malaise. In the years that Frye has conceived of *The Great Code* he has felt like Milton's Satan who while journeying through chaos is surrounded by boundless vistas of an unknown territory, but in his moments of discouragement, he has used the haunting and moving phrase of Giordano Bruno, 'Est aliquid prodisse tenus', as a motto (xxiii, see xxii). Better to make a statement than not at all, if only to encourage the making of better books. This is the hope of scholarship, but few have produced better books than Frye in the domain of criticism, though some have produced different books that have contributed, along with Frye's, to what he considered to be the realm of genuine criticism.

In the rest of the chapter, I want to look briefly at some of the most significant aspects of *The Great Code* as it relates to literary criticism and theory. Frye divides the book into two parts, 'The Order of Words' and 'The Order of Types', which represents a double mirror or vision of language and typology or structure. In 'Language I' Frye says that a sacred book is usually composed with at least the concentration of poetry. Unlike the Koran and the Hebrew text of the Old Testament, which have been tied up with their respective languages, the Christian Bible relies on translation. St Jerome's Latin or Vulgate translation of the Bible was the Bible for a thousand years. Frye's interest is to discover what is the essential force or thing that a translation translates, the *langage*, or that which makes it possible to express similar things in different *langues*, such as German, French and English. He speculates whether there is enough of a positive linguistic force in *langage* to warrant a history of this 'sequence of modes of more or less translatable structures in words, cutting across the variety of *langues* employed, affected and conditioned but not wholly determined by them' and thereby provide a new historical context for the Bible (Frye 1982b: 5; see also 3–4). Frye returns to Vico, whom he had found helpful in *Anatomy of Criticism*, and translates, in terms of the Bible, Vico's three ages in a cycle of history, the age of the gods (mythical), the age of an aristocracy (heroic) and the age of the people, after which a return or *ricorso* occurs. Each age produces its own *langage*: the poetic, the heroic (noble) and the vulgar. The first involved hieroglyphs, the second allegory and the third description (5). Translating Vico, partly through Roman Jakobson, Frye calls his first three phases the metaphoric, the metonymical and the descriptive and adds a fourth, the *kerygmatic*. The metaphorical has a sense of identity of life, power or energy between humanity and nature (this is that) (7); the metonymic tends to become analogical, 'a verbal imitation of a reality beyond itself that can be conveyed most directly by words' (this is put for that) (8); the descriptive 'treats language as primarily descriptive of an objective natural order' (13); the kerygmatic, or proclamation, is the vehicle of revelation (29). The reason Frye comes up with the fourth phase of language, the *kerygma*, is that the other three phases, each of which supplements the other and shows the inadequacy of each phase by itself, are not adequate in considering the Bible (27). This chapter leads up to Frye's central conclusion 'that myth is the linguistic vehicle of *kerygma*, and that to "demythologize" any part of the Bible would be the same thing as to obliterate it' (30).

Frye makes many interesting points while building up this schema. Perhaps the most interesting is his discussion of the Bible in relation to the oral and the written. In the Introduction, Frye says, when setting out his general thesis, 'that the Bible comes to us as a written book, an absence invoking a historical presence "behind" it, as Derrida would say, and that the background presence gradually shifts to a foreground, the re-creation of that reality in the reader's mind' (1982b: xxii). Frye adjusts Eric Havelock's association, in *A Preface to Plato*, of the revolution in language with the development of writing to an association of 'the Platonic revolution with the development of continuous prose' (8). In the latter classical period, Frye says, Plato's superior order, in which only language can approach, combines with the *logos*, 'a conception of a unity of consciousness or reason' that in Stoicism and Christianity 'is seen as a possible means of uniting human society both spiritually and temporally' (9). In the metaphorical stage the god is a personal nature-spirit; in the metonymical God becomes the centre of the order of words; in the descriptive 'the word "God" becomes linguistically unfunctional' with a few exceptions (15). For Frye, 'mythological space', which is at the centre of his theory, 'became separated from scientific space with the new astronomy of the seventeenth century, and mythological time from scientific time with nineteenth-century geology and biology' (15). In the descriptive phase the answer to whether there is a God is no because such a question is ungodly. Nietzsche, who is important for Derrida and other deconstructionists, formulated the famous phrase 'God is dead', which, Frye says, in spite of the attention given to it, 'was incidental to his more important aim of de-deifying the natural environment, and in particular of removing the metaphor of "law" from ordinary consciousness to describe the operations of nature' (16). Other third-phase descriptive thinkers share with Nietzsche his attempt at 'demystification'. Machiavelli looked at the strategic use of illusion for rulers; Marx thought that metonymic language had become ideology; Freud considered consciousness to be a smoke-screen for other motives of speech (16). Frye is concerned not with the death or obsolescence of God but with 'what resources of language may be dead or obsolete', so that he looks for a fourth phase beyond the metaphorical and metonymical, which impose obvious limitations on the human mind, and the descriptive, whose distinction of subject and object does not often work (17).

The fourth phase is not meant to supplant but to supplement the other three. Although Frye does not like the term 'realism', he connects it to the descriptive phase, which he does not want to abandon but wishes to relate to 'a broader spectrum of verbal expression' (1982b: 17). Frye appeals to the growth of scientific knowledge, such as post-Einsteinian physics and its view of atoms and electrons as processes and traces, so that when he suggests that 'God' is 'a verb implying a process accomplishing itself', he may be expanding our sense of 'reality' (17–18, see also Levin 1963). The *logos*, which Derrida has made the decentre of his deconstruction of the logocentric, is a variable term, according to the phase of language in which it occurs. In the metaphorical phase the Gospel of John *logos* is metaphorical, an element of creative power, and in Genesis 1:4 and in Heraclitus it is metaphorical in a different sense, as an expression of the unity of consciousness and the physical world. Philo and the author of John combine the modes of the metaphorical phase. In Erasmus' translation, which is appended to his Greek New Testament, he uses a metonymic translation of *logos* (Word) as *sermo*. Goethe's Faust moves through the three phases from *das Wort* through *der Sinn* to *die That* (18). There is great difficulty in translating *logos*, and it is not certain what John meant by it, except that because it was made flesh, he thought it was an easily intelligible metaphor. None the less, Frye says, for descriptive writers, perhaps like Derrida, *logos* 'has no power to be anything but a word' (19). A further complication is that each of the three phases of language possesses 'a characteristic word for the human entity that uses the language' (19). In contemporary language, one would say that Frye is using a kind of Viconian history to differentiate and destabilize the notion of the human 'subject'. The metaphorical phase assumes a 'plurality of psychic forces' that correspond with the plurality of gods and that separate or disintegrate at death. In the metonymic phase a single 'body' and 'soul' correspond to one God. The descriptive phase involves a modulation from 'soul' to 'mind'. From Freud onwards, people have tended to revert to the pluralistic or metaphorical view of consciousness (19–20). To complicate matters more, a distinction occurs between soul and spirit, *nephesh* and *ruach* (Hebrew), *psyche* and *pneuma* (Greek) and *anima* and *spiritus* (Latin) as well as those in modern languages. These distinctions are not consistent in the Bible, although, Frye says, the important distinction that Paul makes between the spiritual body and the natural body had little effect on the traditional body–soul dichotomy. Paul also contrasts the spiritual with the soul–body, the *pneumatikos* with the *psychikos* in which the significant line occurs between spirit and soul and not soul and body (20; see also Frye 1990c, 1991b). The metaphorical gives immediacy and aliveness, whereas the metonymic offers a dialectic freed from nature. The greater the subjective order, the more restricted the subjective world seems. In English the 'subject' has two inseparable meanings: it means the observer of the objective and, in politics, an individual subordinate to the authority of a ruler or of the society. The observer, as in twentieth-century science, becomes a member of a community of observers, so that the only thing subjective that remains is a structure of language (including mathematics). Even here, the structure appears objective to each student of it (20–2). Humans become like subjects in the sense of the subject of a book: 'People are "subjects", then, not as people, but only to the extent that they form a community within a linguistic structure which records some observation of the objective' (22). But, from Frye's point of view:

> It is not a difficult step from here to the feeling, often expressed in contemporary criticism and philosophy, that it is really language that uses man, and not man that uses language. . . . It means . . . that man is a child of the word as well as a child of nature, and that, just as he is conditioned by nature and finds his conception of necessity in it, so

the first thing he finds in the community of the word is the charter of
his freedom.

(22)

While acknowledging Derrida here through allusion, Frye is also taking
up the 'liberal' and 'Romantic' call to freedom, the myth of freedom as
a means of supplementing the myth of concern, from which it is
inseparable. Culture is of nature but frees itself to some extent from its
necessity. Many contemporary literary theorists tend to come at it from
the opposite side to Frye, that all objectivity is subjectivity no matter
how apparently objective something like language appears.

Verse is more memorable and so is the vehicle for keeping tradition
alive in an oral culture. Frye also observes: 'As the critics of the god
Thoth, the inventor of writing, remark in Plato's *Phaedrus*, the ability to
record has a lot more to do with forgetting than with remembering: with
keeping the past in the past, instead of continuously recreating it in the
present' (1982b: 22). Like Shelley in *A Defence of Poetry*, Frye thinks
that it is the role of poetry to keep recreating the metaphorical phase of
language in an age that underestimates or loses sight of it (23).
Oratorical rhetoric, which comes through Cicero and relates closely to
the figuration in poetry, also changes with the 'ideology of humanism',
in which a cult of plain style occurs in the third and descriptive phase of
language. Frye also says that the Bible has an essential oratorical idiom
– whose two most important aspects are metaphor and concern – and
expresses *kerygma*, exhortation or oracle (27–9). Here the oral and the
written show their intricate inseparability.

In 'Myth I' Frye amplifies the notion 'that myth is the linguistic
vehicle of *kerygma*' and defines myth as '*mythos*, plot, narrative, or in
general the sequential ordering of words' (1982b: 30–1; see also my
chapters 7 and 8). He makes a point that Hayden White argues in
Metahistory (1973): up to a point in a history words appear to follow 'a
corresponding procession of antecedent events . . . but the selection and
arrangement of data involved in the verbal narrative is primary, and the
notion that the shape of the sequence comes from outside the words is
an illusion of projection' (32; see also my Chapter 5). For Frye, the
Bible is a story and therefore a myth. He sets out a secondary use of
'myth', stories that have a distinct significance, that tell the society what
is important to know. These are the sacred stories, or revelation, as
opposed to the profane stories, which are told for entertainment or other
more marginal purposes. This distinction may not hold in primitive
societies, but occurs later and can persist for centuries (contra: see
Bloom in Salusinszky 1987: 54–5). In this secondary sense, myth

'means being charged with a special seriousness' (Frye 1982b: 33). Whereas folk tales are nomadic and interchange their motifs and themes, myths occur in a canon or mythology. Mythical structures shape the rhetoric and metaphors of later structures. Myth, which has a haunting power, is a form of creative and imaginative thinking and is thus autonomous (33–6). Although in *Anatomy* Frye suggested that criticism was approaching the condition of social science, he complicates that position by saying with some irony: 'it apparently takes social scientists much longer than poets or critics to realize that every mind is a primitive mind, whatever the varieties of social conditioning' (1982b: 37). He also warns that one should not interpret the sequence of metaphorical-metonymic-descriptive language as a form of progress. As myth involves creative and imaginative thinking, it does not improve with an expanding technology or society, so that to infantalize mythology by identifying evolution with progress, as the Victorians did, leads to mistakes, like James Frazer's: 'This was obviously part of an ideology designed to rationalize the European treatment of "natives" on darker continents, and the less attention given it now the better' (38). Poets recreate the central line of mythology in every age. An identity, or perhaps a structural analogy, exists between sacred and profane stories. Frye examines the relation between history and fiction in the Bible. His view of the Bible as a mythology crystallizes in a central passage:

> Clearly, the Bible is a violently partisan book: as with any other form of propaganda, what is true is what the writer thinks ought to be true; and the sense of urgency in the writing comes out much more freely for not being hampered by the clutter of what may actually have occurred.
>
> The general principle involved here is that if anything historically true is in the Bible, it is there not because it is historically true but for different reasons. The reasons have presumably something to do with spiritual profundity or significance. And historical truth has no correlation with spiritual profundity, unless the relation is inverse.
>
> (40)

Myth is the motivating force in the Bible. The mythical structure of the Book of Judges, which is a synecdoche for that of the Bible, shows how the stories are shaped by editing into a myth of Israel (40–1). The Gospel writers/editors shape their stories through typology, the relation of their myths to those in the Old Testament. Biblical scholars have long known that 'the Bible will only confuse and exasperate a historian who tries to treat it as a history': the evidence for the historical Jesus is sealed in the New Testament (42). Similarly, Homer has a sense of history but is not writing history. Frye, who studied Blake's fearful symmetry so long in his youth, says that when one finds symmetry in any narrative, it means that mythical design and form have priority over historical content. Archaeology is the only hope for new historical evidence for the Viking voyages and for episodes in the Bible, but Frye recommends that we emphasize the mythical elements in these stories as a means of resisting the simplistic popular notion of a 'literal' meaning (43–5).

Once again, he anchors his distinction between history and poetry, as he applies them to the Bible, to Aristotle's distinction between them. In explaining why biblical myths are nearer to poetry than to history, Frye says: 'History makes particular statements, and is therefore subject to external criteria of truth and falsehood; poetry makes no particular statements and is not so subject' (46). The poetic expresses the universal in the event, the type of thing that always occurs. What is universal in history is its narrative shape or *mythos*. Although a myth can describe a given situation, it does not restrict its meaning to that particular situation. For Frye, the truth of a myth is in its structure. But he complicates his exploration further because he says that the Bible cannot be viewed as all poetry because while its mythic nature means that it has a story-structure, it also signifies that, as concerned knowledge, it has a social function. The Bible has a slippery relation to the historical because it presents simultaneously two conflicting views of history – *Weltgeschichte*, ordinary history, and *Heilsgeschichte*, the actions of God in the world and the relation of humanity to them: in the former nothing repeats exactly, but in the latter events are repeated and form a pattern (46–9). Myth is a story that is poetic and is recreated in literature, but it also has a social function that is a programme of action for a particular society. History shows what humans have done, literature, 'the dimension of the possible in the actual', which might explain the fertile field of fictional and possible world theory, as pioneered in Leibnitz and as recently exemplified in the work of Jerome Bruner and Thomas Pavel (49; see also Hart 1988).

Myth redeems history. Frye expands this controversial point, which might be a form of ideological delusion that oppressed peoples can find solace in myth and ignore historical change, by saying that we should learn to see illusion in the real and the real in illusion. From this point of view, the myth of deliverance is the central myth in the Bible, something that, by implication, brings together the real illusion and the illusory real. In distinguishing between nature and culture, what is and what is human-made, Frye also notes that 'There are no noble savages, in the sense of purely natural men for whom the integument of culture has disappeared' (1982b: 50). He also observes that myths become mythologies that explain an encyclopedic range of social concerns and can therefore become instruments of social coercion and authority, and he criticizes the unnamed Thomism and medieval revival for doing so about two generations ago and Marxism for its 'all-encompassing metaphysic' today (51). Instead, Frye thinks that 'cultural pluralism' cannot be stopped, and says that social concern can be right and wrong, depending on its circumstances. The myths of concern and freedom must balance 'inner integrity' and 'social relevance' (51–2). Frye's temperament or Christian training or both bring him back to hope, to the choosing of life over death, to an avoidance of a regression into the atavistic. He says that without integrity we would find that authority, with its superstitions and expediencies, would subordinate the creative and the scholarly, and without relevance, we would 'fly apart into a chaos of mutually unintelligible elites' where those closest to the centre of power would seize control (52).

Frye examines the imaginative and metahistorical aspects of what he calls the *Heilsgeschichte* vision, a godlike perspective that involves 'a concern for the continuation of human life in time that goes far beyond the purely imaginative, together with a view of the human situation that goes equally far beyond the purely historical' (1982b: 52). In 'Metaphor I' he argues that the Bible is not primarily literary but is contemporary with a metaphorical phase of language, which uses metaphors and poetic means and figures (such as puns) to convey many elements of verbal meaning (53). Explicit and implicit metaphors are plentiful in the Bible, and many of the central doctrines of traditional Christianity can be expressed only in metaphors (54–7). Frye concludes that 'Failure to grasp centrifugal meaning is incomplete reading; failure to grasp centripetal meaning is incompetent reading' (58). The centrifugal meaning is the dictionary or conventional meaning, whereas the centripetal is the contextual one. Implicit meaning that arises out of the juxtaposing of words is the general principle of *explication de texte*, a part of hermeneutics, which began in the exegesis of the Bible (57–9). The primary aspect of a verbal structure is its centripetal element 'because the only thing that words can do with any real precision or ✓ accuracy is hang together' (60). In the Bible the primary and literal meaning is the poetic or centripetal meaning, to which the secondary or centrifugal meanings (concepts, historical or biographical events) are subordinate. Literature involves the absence of 'a pattern of continuous descriptive reference', and the presence of the criterion of truth, if at all, 'emerges entirely from the inner verbal consistency' (61–2). The Bible, which is neither literary nor non-literary, 'is as literary as it can well be without actually being literature': its unity is that of narrative and imagery, of implicit metaphor, and not a unity of doctrine addressed to faith (62). As Frye states in *Anatomy*, reading involves two operations, the sequential and pre-critical and the spatial form or critical. One of the cruxes of Frye's argument is that while traditionally the narrative of the Bible has been considered to be literally historical and its meaning to be literally didactic or doctrinal, he regards myth and metaphor as the true literal bases (64).

Frye regrets that in the *Poetics* Aristotle had not spent more time in discussing myth, for which he shows some contempt in a brief reference to it in the *Metaphysics*, because without Aristotle's authority in the area, people have reversed the primary and secondary meanings by making myth secondary. He seems confident, for his argument at least, that had Aristotle spent more time thinking about the problem, he would have made myth primary, as Frye has. For Frye, who uses the myths in Plato's dialogues as an example, metaphorical meaning is to discursive meaning what myth is to history – primary. All verbal structures have a moving and static aspect. From praxis (where history is a primary verbal imitation of an action) we move through poetry as a secondary verbal imitation of an *action* and poetry as a secondary verbal imitation of *thought* to theoria (where philosophy is a primary verbal imitation of thought) (Frye 1982b: 64–5). Readings of myth in the metonymic phase tend to reduce them to an elite concealment of deeper meanings from the masses, a kind of allegorical rite.

But the Bible leaves history and knowledge of nature to humanity and involves itself with revelation in the realm of myth. The Bible condemns idolatry, the ascription of divine presence to nature, rather than the experience of it through and in nature (64–8). In discussing the metaphors of the earth goddess and sky god in the Bible, Frye doubts that we can assign a historical priority of one over the other and says that no god is ever new and that 'only a new emphasis may be given to a conception potentially present from the beginning' (70). By including an absolute beginning, the Bible does not make time an ultimate reality. In the New Testament 'resurrection' is an ascent from death to life. The kingdom of God is idealized in imagery of youth, spring, vigour and energy from the natural cycle and from creative and productive human work. Frye sees two great organizing patterns in literature, the natural cycle and the final separation of an idealized and happy world from a miserable and horrifying one. Comedy has the first kind of movement, tragedy the second. Greek literature sees misery as tragic: the Bible sees it as ironic (71–3). Frye thinks that the foregrounding of hell as an unending nightmare in Christian teaching is a foul doctrine: 'humanity owes infinitely more to the sinners who went on sinning in spite of it than it does to the preachers who tried to restrain sin by threatening it' (74). The central question of this chapter is 'What does the Bible look like when we try to see it statically, as a single and simultaneous metaphor cluster?' and the answer is 'a vision of upward metamorphosis, of the alienated relation of man to nature transformed into a spontaneous and effortless life ... in the sense of being energy without alienation' (76). It makes sense, in Frye's view, to identify the Bible and Christ as the Word of God from the point of view of history and even better sense from the vantage-point of metaphor. They are two aspects of the same thing (76–7). At the heart of Frye's view of the Bible is his notion of identity.

In 'Typology I' Frye shows the internal typological system of the Bible: it is circular and verifies itself without reference to external evidence. This double mirror is the Old and New Testaments reflecting each other but not the outside world: 'How do we know that the Gospel story is true? Because it confirms the prophecies of the Old Testament. But how do we know that the Old Testament prophecies are true? Because they are confirmed by the Gospel story' (Frye 1982b: 78). The writers of the New Testament regarded the Old Testament in terms of prefigurements of incidents in the life of Christ, so that everything that happens in the Old Testament is a type or adumbration of something in the New Testament and everything that happens in the New Testament is an antitype or realized form of something that the Old Testament foreshadows. The New Testament is presented as a key to, or an explanation of, the Old Testament. For Frye, typology is a figure of speech and a mode of thought (78–9). Here is Frye's central statement on the nature of typology:

> Typology is a figure of speech that moves in time: the type exists in the past and the antitype in the present, or the type exists in the present and the antitype in the future. What typology really is as a mode of thought, what it both assumes and leads to, is a theory of history, or more accurately of historical process: an assumption that there is some meaning and point to history, and that sooner or later some event or events will occur which will indicate what that meaning or point is, and so become an antitype of what has happened previously.

> (81)

When some call Frye anti-historical or unhistorical, what they are implying is that his concept of history is not theirs (see my Chapter 5). He thinks that the modern confidence in the historical process, that it has a telos, owes much to biblical typology. It seems that Frye also sees this tradition as being a precursor to Hegelian and Marxist dialectic.

Causality, which is at the core of historical writing, also interests Frye because it has played a large part in the metonymic and descriptive phases of language. He connects causality to continuous prose. In Frye's view, causality and typology are rhetorically alike in form: typology might be an analogy of causality, 'a development of Aristotle's formal and final causes' (1982b: 81). There are differences. Whereas causality is founded on reason, observation and knowledge, moves on the same temporal plane and relates to the past, typology is connected with faith, hope and vision, points to a transcendence of time and relates to the future. Kierkegaard's *Repetition* looks at these two terms as a psychological contrast. Typology is revolutionary thought and rhetoric because it makes us aware that life is a dream from which we should awaken (81–3).

History, then, is central to the Judaeo-Christian scriptures. According to Frye, the most significant 'historical fact about the Old Testament is that the people who produced it were never lucky at the game of empire' (1982b: 83). In Judaism, as well as in Christianity, the antitypes of prophecy in the Old Testament are the coming of the Messiah and the restoration of Israel. The Old Testament is, for Jews, typological without the New Testament. Frye observes that 'Judaism has also the great advantage, for a typological outlook, of keeping its crucial antitypes in the future', whereas the Resurrection's transcendence of ordinary experience in Christianity 'did not bring about an end of time in ordinary experience', and so a belief in the second coming was needed (83). The typological shape and structure of the Bible give it a diachronic mythology as opposed to the synchronic mythology found in most other religions, so that Judaism and Christianity have a distinctive sense of history. Frye sees the Torah, the first five books of the Old Testament, as presenting the types and the Talmud, commentary on the Torah, the antitypes, whereas, for Christians, the Old Testament is a book of prophecy (83–4). However oblique the approach of the Old and New Testaments to history, they treat real people and events, so that typology is not allegory, which 'is normally a story-myth that finds its "true" meaning in a conceptual or argumentative translation' (85). The typology of the New Testament proceeds in two directions into the future (apocalypse) and the eternal world (Last Judgement). The capitalist revolutions of the eighteenth century bring typological thinking into the secular sphere, so that democrats, Marxists, Christians and others have their own version of typology. In Nietzsche the ancient tension between the typological and the cyclical views of time occurs, and it is possible to observe this tension when comparing the cyclical aspects of the structure of *Anatomy of Criticism*, such as the seasonal cycles of the *mythoi*, and the typological double structure (in which the second half reflects in inverse order the first half) of *The Great Code*. When looking at Israel in the Old Testament and Jesus in the New Testament, the society is the type of which the individual is the antitype. Frye looks at what he calls the 'royal metaphor', an identification of individual with its class, especially as it relates to kingship (see Hart 1992d: esp. 3–87, 190–7, 241–6). A sovereign may be an icon or an idol. For the Jews, the Messiah is a legitimate ruler but also becomes the restorer of Israel and the end of history. Jesus as the Messiah is the point of difference between Christians and Jews. Jesus' claim that he is the real king is the symbolic end of history where master and servant represent the same thing, become the same person (85–9). Once again, Frye returns to Gibbon's *Decline and Fall*, which he considers as having the historical identity of being an eighteenth-century book, and applies the same principle to the Christian Bible as a text of the first century AD. More specifcally, in considering the history of this period of the New Testament, Frye says that the Bible does not think that the world ruler is necessarily evil but that he governs the kind of world that will make one of his successors into a tyrant (92–3). The cult of divine Caesar became obligatory and drove Christianity into revolutionary organization, what Marcus Aurelius called Christian *parataxis* or military discipline.

True to Frye's advocacy of textual or literary history as being a key and 'autonomous' part of history, he looks at the great consolidation of classical literature under Virgil and Ovid, especially Aeneas' crucial vision in the sixth book of the *Aeneid*, when he journeys to the lower world and 'sees the great wheel of history turning to bring Rome to world power' and Ovid's pagan counterpart to the Bible, in which the metamorphosis is an image of what is called the fall in the Bible (1982b: 96–7; see also 94–5). Frye concludes that Jesus came into the world at a historical time when history, in a dialectical confrontation, suddenly expands into myth and shows a dimension beyond history. The central royal metaphor – we are members of one body – was represented in the language of unity and integration, 'as the unity of a social body into which the individual is absorbed', so that the church said it was 'the continuing Body of Christ in history' (99). Only recently have people questioned the formulation of state and church authority as a body of which individuals are cells. Frye calls this subordination of the individual to the state or church 'the "Antichrist" complex', which we would now call totalitarianism, Frye's mortal enemy (99). Habit and tradition underpin totalitarian movements. He prefers democracy, in which a sense of individuality should grow out of society because 'the notion of a socially detached individual is an illusion' (100). Frye understands the totalitarian tendencies of organized religion and, following Paul at Galatians 2:20 and elsewhere, suggests that the royal metaphor be turned inside out, so that 'the total body is complete within each individual' (100). In other words, 'The individual acquires the internal authority of the unity of the Logos, and it is this unity that makes him an individual' (100).

Central to Frye's ideas is the 'metaphorical vision, or the application of metaphors to human experience' (1982b: 101). Frye is not advocating a selfish individualism but says that we are born into a social contract from which we develop our individuality, and the society's interests have priority over individual interests. Paul's concept of Jesus as the genuine individuality of the individual, which Frye thinks Simone Weil is following, reconstitutes 'the central Christian metaphor in a way that unites without subordinating, that achieves identity *with* and identity *as* on equal terms' (101). For instance, a moment of recognition occurs in which typology as revolutionary thought and rhetoric shows us that life is a dream from which we must awaken: 'When this individual awakens and we pass to resurrection and Easter, the community with which he is identical is no longer a whole of which he is a part, but another aspect of himself, or, in the traditional metonymic language, another person of his substance' (101). Frye wants to use the imagery and the narrative of the Bible to decentralize Christian metaphors, to achieve within Christianity a symbolic counterpart to 'the political ideal of democracy' (101). Having ideals is a necessary form of freedom for Frye, while for some, it is idealization.

Part Two of *The Great Code*, 'The Order of Types', is an expansion of Part One, 'The Order of Words'. In 'Typology II' Frye examines the phases of revelation. He says that the biblical religions, which are moral and voluntaristic, emphasize individual and social salvation (1982b: 105). His central question is 'What in the Bible particularly attracts poets and other creative artists of the Western world?' (106). Revelation is the content of the Bible, which involves a sequence or dialectical progression in seven phases: 'creation, revolution or exodus (Israel in Egypt), law, wisdom, prophecy, gospel, and apocalypse' (106). Each phase – offering a wider perspective, but not an improvement, on its predecessor – is an antitype of the type that immediately precedes it. Frye says that three questions arise in studying the creation myth in the Bible: Why is the deity so patriarchal? Why does creation occur in the image of a week? What does it mean to say that with the fall death came into the world? He wants to move beyond the most obvious answers: a patriarchal society rationalizes its ethos with a patriarchal God; the week rationalizes the sabbath; natural death is rationalized as unnatural. Supplementary answers are that the maleness of God appears to be related to the Bible's resistance to the natural cycle as our highest mental category; the beginning is a wakening from sleep and not a birth, which affects notions of death (107–8). Frye also says that human creative power is 're-creation, a transforming of the chaos within our ordinary experience of nature' (112). Christianity steered a middle course between the pagan adoration of nature and the Gnostic contempt for it (112–13). Human creativity no longer means to us an imitation or restoration of an original divine creation of nature, but the creation myth is, rather, a type whose antitype is the new heaven and earth that Revelation 21:1 promises (113–14).

The second phase is revolution. God's sixth testament or contract is with Moses. If the biblical story had begun with a colloquy between Moses and God in the burning bush, then, Frye notes, the dreary problem of theodicy, how a good God could remain good after allowing evil in the world, could be dispensed with (1982b: 114). The burning-bush contract introduces a revolutionary element into the Bible that persists through Christianity, Islam and Marxism. This element relies on a belief in a particular historical revelation as a beginning, the adoption of a specific canon of texts and a dialectical mind-set that divides the world for and against us. The contribution of the Israelites to history was their belief that all other gods were false (114). The principal historical preoccupation of Judaism and Christianity was 'the expectation of a *culbute générale* in the future, a kind of recognition scene when those with the right beliefs or attitudes would emerge on top with their now powerful enemies rendered impotent' (115). In Christianity, Islam and Marxism there is a general feeling that only when the world is united in the correct beliefs will it be a good place (115). Metaphors of the ear in the Bible, and not those of the eye, express this revolutionary aspect (116). Frye observes that 'The revolutionary tradition in Judaism, Christianity, and Islam has tended to a good deal of prudery about the naked body, to iconoclasm, and to a rejection of spectacular art, especially when representational' (117). He is glad for the Greek tradition that has counteracted the neuroses of the Western revolutionary religious tradition, although he notes the genuine revolutionary impatience with idolatry, with a passive attitude towards nature, with 'any lotus-eating surrender to fate and the cycles of nature' (117–18).

The third phase is the law, which is given after the revolution and which gives a sense of the people (Frye 1982b: 118). Two aspects of the law exist: 'our obligations to society and the human observation of the repeating processes in nature' (119). Natural law was an attempt to connect these two separate levels and was an extension of divine creation. It causes difficulties today because, as Sartre observed, we cannot work out the problem of human freedom within the categories of humanity as we know it and nature as we see it (119–21).

The fourth phase is wisdom, which 'begins in interpreting and commenting on law, and applying it to specific and variable situations' (121). In such wisdom two wider principles exist: the wise person follows the accepted way, whereas the fool has a new idea that turns out to be an old fallacy; wisdom faces the past, while prudence is wisdom facing the future (121). The Book of Ecclesiastes, which is said to be written by Koheleth, is the centre of the idea of wisdom in the Bible. Koheleth translates conservative popular wisdom into continuous mental energy and expresses his central intuition in a paradox: 'all things are full of emptiness': in Frye's view, the secret of Koheleth's wisdom is 'detachment without withdrawal' (123). Frye interprets 'There is nothing new under the sun' paradoxically: 'Only when we realize that nothing is new can we live with an intensity in which everything becomes new' (124). The old world becomes new, but not entirely in the way the brave new world is new to Miranda but not to Prospero. Wisdom is the way out or through the fog of vanity. All this leads to vision, which lies at the heart of Frye's work (see my Chapter 8). In Proverbs 8:31, we find 'Ludens in orbe terrarum', which, Frye reminds us, means playing all over the earth, which the Authorized Version renders into the anaemic 'rejoicing in the habitable part of the earth'. In verse 30 the Authorized Version also translates the Vulgate's 'Ludens' as 'rejoicing'. In Frye's interpretation of verse 31 we can find the key to his own visionary wisdom:

> Here we finally see the real form of wisdom in human life as the *philosophia* or *love* of wisdom that is creative and not simply erudite. We see too how the primitive form of wisdom, using past experience as a balancing pole for walking the tightrope of life, finally grows, through incessant discipline and practice, into the final freedom of movement where, in Yeats's phrase, we can no longer tell the dancer from the dance.
>
> (125)

Wisdom is the highest form of ordinary society, but prophecy distinguishes Old Testament culture.

The fifth phase of revelation is prophecy, which 'is the individualizing of the revolutionary impulse, as wisdom is the individualizing of the law, and is geared to the future as wisdom is to the past' (Frye

1982b: 125). Like the oracle priestesses in Greece, the prophets 'arose out of a primitive reverence for people with ecstatic powers' (126). In the Old and the New Testaments a sharp distinction occurs between accredited prophets and ecstatics (127). In the Bible, prophecy is a comprehensive view of the human situation. It surveys from creation to deliverance, is the extent of creative imagination, and enlarges, while it incorporates, the perspective of wisdom. In the contemporary world, cultural pluralism corresponds to the authority of the prophet because scientists, historians and artists find the inner authority of their subjects and make discoveries to which they owe loyalty even when they conflict with social concern and meet with opposition from society (128).

The sixth phase, the Gospel, further intensifies the prophetic vision, which has two levels, the present moment and a level above it that represents the original and ultimate identities of humanity with God (Frye 1982b: 129). The return to a spiritual world is the Resurrection, which involves a distinction 'between those who think of achieving the spiritual kingdom as a way of life and those who understand it merely as a doctrine' (129). This way of life begins in *metanoia*, or a 'spiritual metamorphosis, an enlarged vision of the dimensions of human life', a vision that means detachment from a primary community and an attachment to another (130). Sin is an attempt to block the activity of God, which results in a curtailment of human freedom, of the sinner or his or her neighbour. The Gospel of *metanoia* makes humans new creatures (II Corinthians 5:17), where nature, original and fallen, becomes a mother giving birth to a recreation that the union of God and humanity makes (Romans 8:21). Frye uses Plato and the Bible to illustrate his argument. The *Republic* is a powerful vision, an allegory of the wise person's mind, but as an ideal social order, Frye says, it would represent 'a fantastic tyranny' (131). Frye sees a prophetic rather than a legal basis for the Sermon on the Mount, which is, in part, a commentary on the Ten Commandments, where 'the negative commands not to kill or commit adultery or steal are positively stated as an enthusiasm for human life, a habitual respect for the dignity of a woman, a delight in sharing goods with those who need them' (131–2). But society, past and present, cannot put up with Socrates and Jesus (132–3). The prophet confronts society in Judaism and Christianity but not in most Oriental religions (133). Jesus attacks Pharisaism, a kind of elitism, in his society, but this elitism exists in all societies, including Christian ones, and is therefore no pretext for anti-Semitism, which is a corruption (133). The Gospel also brings a new conception of 'Israel' as citizens of the kingdom of God, a notion that will not abide any view that there are second-class citizens, such as women or slaves (134–5).

The seventh phase is apocalypse, which derives from the Greek word for revelation, *apocalypsis*, a kind of uncovering. Repression is the block to truth and an emerging revelation. Frye says that Revelation or Apocalypse, the last book of the Bible, 'is a mosaic of allusions to the Old Testament . . . a progression of antitypes' (135). The author, the seer in Patmos, has a vision of 'the true meaning of the Scriptures', the general material of which 'is the familiar material of prophecy: there is again a *culbute général* in which the people of God are raised into recognition and the heathen kingdoms are cast into darkness' (135). This true vision can occur at any time (136). The incredible wonders in Revelation are, for the author, their inner meaning, the inner form of present events. Frye concludes that humanity creates 'history as a screen to conceal the workings of the apocalypse' from itself (136). Mystery turns into a revelation of how things really are, while the power of Nero turns back into the mystery of the corruption of the human will out of which it came. The Scriptures symbolically destroy nature as a means of destroying the way people see nature, a view that keeps people confined to the world of time and history (136). There are two aspects of apocalyptic vision: the panoramic apocalypse (Frye's term) and the reader's apocalypse (my term derived from Frye). The first is 'the vision of staggering marvels placed in a near future and just before the end of time' and 'ends with the restoration of the tree and water of life, the two elements of the original creation' (136–7). But, Frye suggests, this restoration, like other ones, is the type of an antitype that represents 'a resurrection or upward metamorphosis to a new beginning that is now present' (137). This second apocalypse begins in the mind of the reader after reading, in a vision that passes through legalized vision (ordeals, trials, judgements) into a second life, where the antithetical tension between creator and creature, divine and human no longer exists and the sense of an object-subject split and of a transcendent person ceases to limit our vision. The Bible invites the reader to identify himself or herself with the book, so that 'the reader completes the visionary operation of the Bible by throwing out the subjective fallacy with the objective one' in experiencing the apocalypse as 'the way the world looks after the ego has disappeared' (138). At the end of the Book of Revelation, Frye asserts, 'we reach the antitype of all antitypes, the real beginning of light and sound of which the first word of the Bible is the type' (138). Re-creation in the reader is a central conception in most of Frye's work, a kind of selfless self-recognition.

In 'Myth II', which discusses imagery, he begins a summary of the Bible in terms of practical criticism, and in subsequent chapters proceeds to an examination of narrative and rhetoric. This practical criticism is dense with detail, so I shall touch upon only a few points that are particularly relevant to his theoretical framework. Natural images are a primary feature of the Bible. There are two levels of nature, lower and higher, the one to be dominated and exploited by humans and the other to which humans can belong with redemption. Between lower and higher nature there are images of work, pastoral, agricultural and urban imagery that evoke a nature that humans have transformed and made intelligible. The structure of imagery in the Bible involves 'the imagery of sheep and pasture, the imagery of harvest and vintage, the imagery of cities and temples, all contained in and infused by the oasis imagery of trees and water that suggests a higher mode of life altogether' (139). All these images constitute part of what Frye calls the 'apocalyptic world', the vision that the human creative imagination sees, the model that human energy attempts to bring into being, and the blueprint that the Bible presents as a structure of revelation (139–40). As the nations outside Israel, such as Egypt, Assyria, Babylon and Phoenicia, were generally more prosperous and successful than Israel, their success is shown in a context of demonic parody, a temporary success or an imminent waste. Frye notes that 'In between the demonic and the apocalyptic come the Old Testament types, which the Christian Bible regards as symbols or parables of the existential form of salvation presented in the New' (140). As an illustration of this structure, Frye examines the female figures in the Bible, mothers and brides (140–2). He also performs a useful reading of the sequence of pastoral, agricultural and urban images in the history of Israel, for instance, those in the story of Cain the farmer and Abel the shepherd, and gives a suggestive interpretation of water and tree imagery in the Bible, for example, the tree of life, the tree of the knowledge of good and evil and the body of Christ (for instance, on the crucifix) all being identified (142–58, 162). As usual, Frye makes some interesting observations, such as the shrinking of sacred space as the Bible proceeds (158–60). He observes the vicissitudes of the royal metaphor as it occurs in the Trinity, which appears only at I John 5:7, a verse not in the Greek manuscripts, added to the Latin Vulgate, translated into Greek, included in Erasmus' Greek New Testament and then in the Authorized Version, but left out in modern translations without even a note about the ideological and historical significance of this interpolation (163). Frye illustrates the structure of the imagery in the Bible with a double table of the apocalyptic and demonic imagery. The table of apocalyptic imagery was frozen as a hierarchy of being from early Greek times to the eighteenth century, but in its apocalyptic context it is a vision of plenitude in which everything is identical with everything else the way it would be in a reality after the ego had disappeared (165).

In the apocalyptic vision the body of Christ is the metaphor that holds together in an identity all categories of being and gives us a world where there is only one knower for whom nothing is dead or insensible because there is nothing outside the knower, the real consciousness in everyone (Frye 1982b: 166). Rather than be interested in faith, Frye is concerned with 'the expanding of vision through language', especially when metaphorical structure is turned inside out from that of unity and integration to that of particularity, 'the kind of vision Blake expressed in the phrase "minute particulars"' and the Buddhist notion of interpenetration when each has individuality but also something universal, a vision that reminds Frye increasingly of the Book of Revelation and like forms of vision in the Prophets and the Gospels (167–8). As Frye has noted before in *The Great Code*, because metaphors of unity and integration come from the finiteness of the human mind, they can take us only so far, so that in order 'to expand our vision into the genuinely infinite, that vision becomes decentralized' (168). Then we reach the state of innocence of the sheep in the twenty-third psalm, where we wander without being lost to Wallace Stevens' imperfect paradise, 'a world that may change as much as our own, but where change is no longer dominated by the single direction toward nothingness and death' (168).

'Myth II' discusses narrative in the Bible, which is a divine comedy and has a U-shaped structure, a story in which humanity 'loses the tree and water of life at the beginning of Genesis and gets them back at the end of Revelation' (Frye 1982b: 169). The middle of the story involves the narrative of Israel, which is 'a series of declines into the power of heathen kingdoms, Egypt, Philistia, Babylon, Syria, Rome, each followed by a rise into a brief moment of relative independence' (169). The account of the disasters and restoration of Job and the parable Jesus tells of the prodigal son also use the U-shaped story. Frye isolates seven falls and rises from the many. All the high and low points relate metaphorically with one another:

That is, the garden of Eden, the Promised Land, Jerusalem, and Mount Zion are interchangeable synonyms for the home of the soul, and in Christian imagery they are all identical, in their 'spiritual' form (which we remember means metaphorically, whatever else it may also mean), with the kingdom of God spoken of by Jesus. Similarly, Egypt, Babylon, and Rome are all spiritually the same place, and the Pharaoh of the Exodus, Nebuchadnezzar, Antiochus

Epiphanes, and Nero are spiritually the same person. And the deliverers of Israel – Abraham, Moses and Joshua, the judges, David, and Solomon – are all prototypes of the Messiah or final deliverer.

(171)

Israel is the type, Jesus the antitype. Just as Moses organizes the twelve tribes of Israel, so too does Jesus bring together twelve disciples. By crossing the Red Sea, Israel achieves its identity as a nation; when Jesus is baptized in the Jordan, he is recognized as the Son of God. The crossing is also a type of the Resurrection (172–3). As a narrative, the Christian Bible is like a romance because it has as its hero the Messiah, who emerges 'with his own name and identity only near the end' (174). Although Frye has shown the anti-cyclical bias of the Bible, he says that the messianic quest can be read as a cycle because every apocalyptic image has a demonic parody and because there is no change for the divine nature, so that its quest is cyclical for it (175–6). As the hero of the Christian Bible, Christ is an authority: prophet, priest and king (178). Frye also observes that 'The writers of the Gospels found that in telling the story of Jesus they needed the imagery of the executed kings and Absalom quite as much as that of the figures of glory and triumph' (180). The Bible, Frye notes, is not given to tragic themes, so that except for the Passion, it has an ironic approach to victims. He suggests that Job is a special case and finds the story of Saul tragic (181–2). All human societies express anxiety over a clear and settled succession, the England of Shakespeare's history plays as much as the Israel of the Bible (182). The Bible is concerned with human sacrifice: many types lead up to the antitype of the crucified Christ (183–6). In a myth older than the Old Testament, an old and impotent king rules over a wasteland that is threatened by a monster from the sea until a hero arrives who saves the king's daughter, who is to be sacrificed to the monster, and becomes the new king. This myth underpins the creation of the firmament in Genesis, and the dragon in the Old Testament is called Rahab or Leviathan (188–92).

Frye's summary of the narrative of the Bible, which he describes as 'a sequence of events in human life', is very helpful in focusing his interest in typology and his penchant for perspective. The narrative

becomes a series of ups and downs in which God's people periodically fall into bondage and are then rescued by a leader, while the great heathen empires rise and fall in the opposite rhythm. At a certain point this perspective goes into reverse, and what we see is something more like an epic or romantic hero descending to a lower world to rescue what is at the same time a single bride and a large host of men and women. In this perspective the *sequence* of captivities and redemptions disappears and is replaced by a unique act of descent and return. But the act, if in itself unique, has many symbolic settings.

(Frye 1982b: 192–3)

In a further observation about the structure of the Bible, Frye says that the Book of Job is an epitome of the narrative of the Bible just as the Book of Revelation is the epitome of its imagery (193). Frye gives a detailed reading of Job and thinks that the climax of the poem, the conclusion of Job's summarizing speech (Job 29–31), is without parallel in literature for its powerful statement on human dignity in an alien world. Although technically a comedy because it has a happy ending, the Book of Job is also tragic (193–8). Job, Frye says, has gone the whole way of the Bible's narrative, from creation and fall through the plagues of Egypt, the law and wisdom of the fathers, the prophetic insight that breaks the chain of wisdom to 'the final vision of presence and the knowledge that in the midst of death we are in life' (197). The prophetic aspect of the Book of Job is linked to its U-shaped narrative just as Job is delivered from his story when there is no further need of time; so too Jesus is delivered in the Passion narrative because time helps and hinders narrative and 'disappears only when all that can be experienced has been experienced' (198). The Bible is more narrative than the Buddhist sutras or the Koran. Its narrative framework 'is a part of its emphasis on the shape of history and the specific collision with temporal movement that its revelation is assumed to make' (198). Only through time is time conquered.

In 'Language II', which serves as an end but not a conclusion to *The Great Code*, Frye returns to rhetoric in the Bible. He sets out the achievement of the Israelites in the realm of language as opposed to architecture or any other visual art and suggests that the verbal endures more than the monumental, citing the commitment of Josiah, one of the last kings of Judah, to the availability of written documents to his people as a turning point in history, as a step towards democracy (Frye 1982b: 199–202). Returning once more to the question of historical and textual scholarship of the Bible, Frye says that the anxieties in such nineteenth-century arguments and their successors 'are based on modern assumptions about bookmaking and writing which are irrelevant to the Bible' (202). Authorship is of too little importance in the Bible for inspiration to have a function: most of the biblical books are edited compilations of various documents. In speaking of the Pentateuch, Frye says: 'There is no way of distinguishing the voice of God from the voice of the Deuteronomic redactor' (203). The relation between the author and the reader, like that between the orator and the listener, is a central rhetorical relation, and that is why Frye needs to view its complexity in examining the rhetoric of the Bible. Between the anonymity of oral tradition and the identified authorship of writing tradition lies pseudonymous authorship, which occurs inside and outside the Bible and which regards all that is sacred as secret, left to oral communication only (204). If we were to leave out parts of the Bible that were pseudonymous, most of the Bible would be thrown out (206). Here again, Frye is countering what he considers to be an undeveloped historical imagination. The Bible is a mosaic of genres, from pericopes through marginal glosses to ecstatic visions, of which Frye lists twenty-six kinds but which are, he says, indefinite in number (206). Like Homeric scholarship, biblical scholarship, or at least Frye's readers, should be 'rid of the fetish of individual authorship' (206). One of the central themes of *The Great Code* is a kind of Blakean movement from innocence through experience to a higher innocence, a perspective that takes us through to the other side: 'The Bible, however unified, also displays a carelessness about unity, not because it fails to achieve it, but because it has passed through it to another perspective on the other side of it' (207). The question of authorship relates to translation as much as to editing. The Authorized Version does not distinguish verse from prose and prints each verse as a paragraph, so that it produces a rhythm that is between prose and verse and that captures the paratactical structure of biblical Hebrew, in other words its constant use of 'and' (*wa*) that seems neither to coordinate nor to subordinate (207–8). The Authorized Version is also designed to appeal to the ear of congregations in the churches, as its title page says.

From this discussion of the Authorized Version or King James Bible, Frye derives two critical principles. First, the linguistic conventions of the Bible are close to the conventions of the oral tradition and of the spoken world. Second, each sentence is ideally the key to the Bible, a king of linguistic monad. Frye is interested in shifting from Dante's view of the Bible as unified and continuous to a decentralized perspective in which it is epiphanic and discontinuous (209). That the Old Testament is in prose shows that its present form is from a relatively late cultural stage, although traces of poetry occur in it no matter how much the editorial process has tried to wipe them out (210–11). The simplicity of the Bible is that of majesty and of the voice of authority or impersonality and not, as in our descriptive prose, of democratic authority (211–12). In the discontinuous prose of oracles or aphorisms, silence surrounds each sentence: the Bible's prose uses a similar style to move towards ethical action, to do battle rather than to remove to the cloister. The metaphysic of presence predominates in the Bible, the spoken word having precedence over the written word, or at least lying behind it, and writing being transient (213). Here is the tradition, like Plato's, that Derrida calls into question in his discussions of logocentrism. Frye extracts a general principle from a study of the rhetoric of the Bible: 'The more poetic, repetitive, and metaphorical the texture, the more the sense of external authority surrounds it; the closer the texture comes to continuous prose, the greater the sense of the human and familiar' (214). The Authorized Version emphasizes the oracular and discontinuous rhythms of the Bible. Vast rhetorical difficulties occur: 'The rhetorical problem posed by the Bible is insoluble for the translator, who can only do his best and cut his losses; perhaps some aspects of it were insoluble for the original writers and editors as well' (215). In discussing the degrees of authority and persuasive power, Frye wants to explore the point at which sacred and literary texts meet (216). He speaks of the paradox of the uniqueness and impersonality of great art, of Bach and Mozart creating distinctive music that expresses the impersonal voice of music just as Sophocles and Shakespeare are distinctive as they express the voice of drama. We experience the individual compositions of Bach and Mozart in the total context of music, and Sophocles and Shakespeare in the total context of drama. Characters from Shakespeare and Dickens take on a function beyond their plays and novels respectively, and Shakespeare's *sententiae* have a similar supplementary and existential role as they become guides to living and means of education. This is the decentralizing role that Frye says connects literature and the Bible (216–17).

In the Bible a specific statement in a specific context takes on a universal meaning: Frye calls this 'resonance'. Resonance depends on an original context and a power to expand away from that context. The unity of context, the real structure of the Bible, is not doctrinal but imaginative and is therefore founded on metaphor, 'an identity of various things, not the sham unity of uniformity in which all details are alike' (Frye 1982b: 217–18). In William Blake's 'Auguries of Innocence', the commandment 'Thou shalt not kill' in the Old Testament and Jesus' exhortation are 'parts of a vision of an "innocent" world, and it is that vision which is the guide to practice' (219–20). In Shakespeare and in the Bible we find a precision that conveys and that is an aspect of the decentralizing element (220). Frye returns to something dear to his heart, the core of *Anatomy of Criticism*, 'the traditional but still neglected theory of "polysemous" meaning' (220). He considers this kind of signification to be a feature of all deeply serious meaning, of which the Bible is a model. For Dante, 'polysemous' implies 'a single process growing in subtlety and comprehensiveness, not different senses, but different intensities or wider contexts of a continuous sense, unfolding like a plant out of a seed' (221). Although Frye says that some texts invite more and more interpretations, he still wants to avoid the illusory upward path of discovery or the witch's house of value judgements (221–2). He thinks that polysemous meaning is a single dialectical process like the one Hegel describes in the *Phenomenology* which turns out to be a theory of how verbal signification takes shape. He wishes to redeem and reveal the complexity of Hegel's dialectic and to keep it from parodic reduction. This dialectic combines with its own opposite or otherness, and in so doing negates itself but passes through that negation into another stage, 'preserving its essence in a broader context, and abandoning the one just completed like the chrysalis of a butterfly or a crustacean's outgrown shell' (222). Dante's understanding of the Bible moves from the literal level (the centre of sense experience) to the allegorical level (the centre of contemplative reason) to the moral level (faith that transcends and fulfils reason) and to the anagogic level (the centre of beatific vision that fulfils faith) (see Jameson's discussion of Frye's alterations of Dante's four levels in my Chapter 7). The reason Dante will not do for contemporary criticism is that he assumes an exclusive truth in one interpretation of the Bible and subordinates the Bible to something else that he assumes is more real (223). In *Anatomy*, Frye says, he attempted this polysemous expansion by beginning with a symbol and not, like Hegel, with a concept, so that his unit of poetic expression would lead to 'a verbal universe in which the symbol has become a monad, though one that interpenetrates with all the other monads' (224). Frye admits that his procedure is closer to Dante's, but would begin with a different idea of literal meaning and would not follow his subordination of words to non-verbal 'realities' (224).

Here begins Frye's coda on his great code. He presents an admirable summary of the movement of his book:

Literally, the Bible is a gigantic myth, a narrative extending over the whole of time from creation to apocalypse, unified by a body of recurring imagery that 'freezes' into a single metaphor cluster, the metaphors all being identified with the body of the Messiah, the man who is all men, the totality of *logoi* who is one Logos, the grain of sand that is the world. We also traced a sequence of manifestations of this reality, each one a stage more explicit than its predecessor. First is the creation, not the natural environment with its alienating chaos but the ordered structure that the mind perceives in it. Next comes the revolutionary vision of human life as a casting off of tyranny and exploitation. Next is the ceremonial, moral, judicial code that keeps a society together. Next is the wisdom or sense of integrated continuous life which grows out of this, and next the prophecy or imaginative vision of man as somewhere between his original and his ultimate identity. Gospel and apocalypse speak of a present that no longer finds its meaning in the future, as in the New Testament's view of the Old Testament, but is a present moment around which past and future revolve.

(Frye 1982b: 224–5)

Frye is interested in the way that the Bible has a capacity for 'self-re-creation'. In building up his four-level theory he takes one aspect of the literal Bible of myth and metaphor and derives two principles from the fact that it is a written book. First, each text is a type of its reading and the antitype begins in the reader's mind (226). To reconsider the Bible, one should reconsider language, including the structures, like the literary ones, it produces. The aim of the reconsideration would be directed to 'the open community of vision' rather than 'a terminus of belief', to a charity that takes us beyond faith (227). Frye interprets the image of the prison-house of language, which Fredric Jameson borrowed from Nietzsche for the title of a book (1972), to mean the creative doubt of limits that would carry us 'beyond the limits of dialectic itself, into an infinite identity of word and spirit that, we are told, rises from the body of death' (227). Second, the written book is connected with the arts of magic, and the poetic impulse arises through a renunciation of magic or its practical goals. The written word has the power to mesmerize, not simply to weaken the role of memory in society as the critics of the god Thoth feared (227). The Bible grows out of the world of history and concept and points to it, but not as a criterion for its worth or truth (228). Humans create their gods in their own image, what Frye calls the Feuerbach principle. Frye returns to the royal metaphor in which individuals of every class form one body, a kind of 'real universal': 'Whether we think it *is* true or not matters little, in actual life: there, it is the determination to make it true, to live *as though* individual and class were an identity, that is important' (228). By relating one's literal understanding of the Bible to our knowledge, especially of the Bible in history and culture, we soon move to an existential level, from Dante's allegorical to his tropological, from aesthetic pleasure to ethical freedom – to faith (228–9).

Faith can be professed or actions that show what we believe. Professed faith is 'instinctively aggressive', bearing out Swift's remark that people have enough religion to hate each other but not enough to love (229). Faith is militant and its structures are those of unity and integration, a reflection of the human mind's finitude. A sentence that might describe the middle way of Frye's career and œuvre is 'The mind seems to want to expand, to move from the closed fortresses of believer and sceptic to the community of vision' (230). Faith and doubt complement each other. The nothingness of death is a leveller because no one understands the meaning of death. In the final anagogic level we ask what speaks to us across (our own) death. Paul's moment of enlightenment (II Corinthians 12) involves a dissolving of the ego until it is difficult to say to whom the experience happened and an uncertainty whether the experience was in or out of body or whether that distinction matters. The new language that Paul describes is one that escapes from argument and refutation and divides life from death. The language of the Bible is the language of love. A symbolically male God addresses a symbolically female body of readers in the biblical *kerygma*, or rhetoric of proclamation. In literature and the arts, where a human imaginative response occurs, language is imaginative and hypothetical, and the text is the daughter of a Muse, a female symbol.

Only through a study of imaginative works, Frye suggests, can we make contact with vision beyond faith. Here Frye answers his own question that is central to his entire book, if not career, that such vision is the quality that enables religions to be associated with products of human imagination and culture that have for their limit the conceivable and not the actual. Frye implies that Nietzsche's creative doubt about whether a limit is really a limit comes into play (1982b: 230–2). One must get beyond the limits of the legal perspective, beyond the doctrine of original sin, which Frye defines 'as man's fear of freedom and his resentment of the discipline and responsibility that freedom brings' (232). He cites Milton as someone who exemplifies the combination of biblical and secular societies and addresses the problem of freedom, which humanity achieves only because God wants it to; but it prefers to collapse back into the master-slave duality in 'nature'. For Frye, the history of the Bible's influence in Western culture may show us where the failure of nerve comes in this quest for freedom. If Milton's view of the Bible as a manifesto of liberty is helpful, then the Bible should be written in a revolutionary language that would smash the anxiety-structures that surround human social and religious institutions. But anxiety distorts language.

Frye tells a parable of the Bible as Samson based on an Old English riddle: however much humans want to act on their anxieties and reduce a great cultural achievement like the Bible to aggression and prejudice, it is possible that the Bible in its analogical blindness will find strength, perhaps, I might add, like the antitype Christ in Revelation. Then the cultural work of the Bible would redouble its theme or structural movement to resurrection as an ideal in the human mind. This is the kind of vision beyond the limits of faith and doubt that Frye reaches for from his early study of Blake to his last books, which express words with power and a double vision. It is for the vision to transform the society that always falls short of it, to let freedom lead the concern out of which it grows without becoming its slave in the ideological idolatry of the natural.

5 History

The greatness of Frye, and the radical difference between his work and that of the great bulk of garden-variety myth criticism, lies in his willingness to raise the issue of community and to draw basic, essentially social, consequences from the nature of religion as collective representation.

(Jameson 1981: 69)

I wanted a historical approach to literature, but an approach that would be or include a genuine history of literature, and not simply the assimilating of literature to some other kind of history. It was at this point that the immense importance of certain structural elements in the literary tradition, such as conventions, genres, and the recurring use of certain images or image-clusters, which I came to call archetypes, forced itself on me.

(Frye 1971b: 23)

Northrop Frye has a history and is, on his own terms, a critic in tune with literary history. While rumours swirled around Frye – he was a formalist without regard for history – few of his fellow critics noticed Frye's practice of literary history, as a record of conventions and genres in Western literature from Homer onwards. Some critics, of course, were genuinely concerned with what they perceived to be Frye's penchant for the synchronic even when he was discussing history and literary history. In the 1940s and 1950s he was reacting to the positivist approach to history or historicism that was pursued, along with New Criticism, in departments of literature. He seems to have thought that intellectual history, as practised by Arthur Lovejoy and E. M. W. Tillyard, was less subject to correction or reorientation. Frye's sense of irony and satire made him aware of the capricious and labyrinthine nature of the House of Fame. He probably understood that he was, in part, attacked and praised in proportion to his success. A leading critic at a given time fulfils the needs of a historical period and expresses its

anxieties and desires, so that the very systematic overview that
Anatomy enabled soon became subject to critique. What gave Frye his
strength soon provided his weakness. Reputation can pare away the
complexities of the work of a writer or critic. I am trying to recollect
Frye's complexity by reintroducing his intricate view of history. In this
chapter I want to go to the work that sets out Frye's theory of literature,
his system, *Anatomy of Criticism*. Here, I shall concentrate on the
'Tentative Conclusion' of *Anatomy* because it is a leaving off and a
point of departure since it ends a study of literary form and convention and begins a phase in Frye's career which is a transition to a
consideration of history, society and ideology.

Anatomy of Criticism can keep company with Aristotle's *Poetics* and
Samuel Johnson's criticism, so that it has become a target as much as a
relic. But I am not interested in presuming to dissect Frye's great
Burtonesque critical body again, impugning him for a fading formalism
or a theory of archetypes and myths at rest with Cornford, Campbell and
Jung. The penchant that the present has for celebrating its moment as the
moment, as if the past were made for drudges, sometimes heroic
drudges, represents a form of ironic blindness. In such a scheme the very
distance the present has from the past enables it to see the shortcomings
of the past, but by a similar logic, the future will preside over the past we
now call the present. Frye himself was fond in his lectures of reminding
students that the present was already always past. I want to find what
still lives in his work. Frye has passed into literature, and to deny the
elegance and importance of his thought is to be professionally irritable
in a blindness that amounts to neglect or malpractice. We who live in an
age of historical criticism should not turn away from formal criticism.
History too has a shape. Herodotus knew this, and, in the past twenty-
five years, Roland Barthes, Hayden White and others have questioned
the difference between fictional and historical narratives (Barthes 1967:
27, White 1973: 1–57; see also Frye 1947b).

Frye is more than a formal critic. Even if for polemical reasons Terry
Eagleton has tried to reduce him to an American New Critic, Frye
remains stubbornly Canadian and is neither a New Critic nor a proto-
structuralist (Eagleton 1983b: 91–4, 199, 204, 224–5; see also Wimsatt's
critique of Frye, Wimsatt 1966: esp. 79–82). Historical critics need not
formalize Frye – to classify the critic they consider to be the great
classifier represents the very formalism they criticize. When criticizing
formalism, historicists need to recognize the formal properties of
history. Philosophy, poetry and history cannot escape one another, but
each will always seek priority over the other. One myth in literary
history might go as follows: historical critics have languished for

decades in the wilderness as old historicism and Marxism faded while New Criticism and 'formalism' generally flourished in the English-speaking world. As my introductory epigraphs show, at least two critics, Fredric Jameson and Frye himself, consider Frye a historical critic (Krieger 1966a:11, 14 assumes Frye's regard for history, whereas Wimsatt 1966: 97–9, 107 does not). Frye wanted his historical criticism to be a history of and from literature and not a history of which it was an incidental or minor part. Literature and criticism, which was a theory of literature, was not to be secondary to the other great subjects. Frye's history is inductive and not an importation of the historian's craft. This is one of the major ways in which Frye differs from many of his historicist successors, for while they often hide their formalist interest and styles, they appeal to history as some fundamental and unassailable discipline.

Actually, philosophical, historical and poetic criticism coincide, but one model tends to gain prominence for a while. Individual critics, at least those worth reading, often emphasize different models or methods in different works. History, or at any rate the literary and rhetorical kind of history, is prominent once again. It is, however, a mistake to say that anything that is not primarily historical criticism is formalism. Writing is by its nature selective and symbolic, so that all writing, historical and otherwise, can be dismissed as idealist and abstract. Writing is more and less than the complex human and natural worlds it represents. As part of a collective archive, it outlasts our individual lives, but it cannot encompass the vast and profound world in which we live. Jameson's reading of Frye is exemplary because he takes seriously Frye's ideas, including those about symbolism, even though the two theorists do not share Marxist ideology (1981: 69–75; see also Salusinszky 1987: 38–9). Where we diverge most from the text we are interpreting, there should we try hardest to understand it. Perhaps the most neglected aspect of Frye's theory among his critics is his social and historical thought. My interest here is in Frye the historicist, the Frye we find most in the 'Tentative Conclusion' to *Anatomy* rather than the synoptic Frye in the 'Polemical Introduction'.

Before I interpret the ending of *Anatomy* in the light of its view of history, I wish to examine briefly its historical context, particularly the writings for which it was a prolegomena rather than the earlier writings, like *Fearful Symmetry*, of which it was an epilogue, or at least a later movement in the music of Frye's ideas (see my Chapter 2). I do not want to play down Frye's view that literature is autonomous. Rather, I wish to stress that Frye argues that literature is autonomous and has its own kind of history in relation to other histories. For Frye, his 'formalism' is only apparent because each work is read in the context of the other works in that genre, or using that convention, or representing the same imagery. All literature becomes the historical context for a single literary work. This is the major way in which Frye differs from the New Critics, although he shares with them the idea that the basis of poetic meaning is poetic language and form. In *The Critical Path* Frye says that the New Critics soon realized that their criticism lacked context, so that many fell back on history (Frye 1971d: 20–1). When he had the opportunity of addressing a large popular audience on CBC late in 1962, he stated his position clearly: 'Our principle is, then, that literature can only derive its forms from itself: they can't exist outside literature, any more than musical forms like the sonata and the fugue can exist outside music' (Frye 1963b: 15). But paradoxically Frye admits that the motive for metaphor, the very use of literary language, is to associate the mind with the world, whereas the motive for writing outside literature is to describe the world (1963b: 10). He sees identity, rather than separation, as the aim of writing literature. Even if literature has a refractory relation to the world by attempting to erase the difference between word and world, it stems from moments of identity in experience (1963b: 4). These fables of identity, which Frye elaborates in *Anatomy* and a collection of essays on poetic mythology, rely on the unifying structure of imagery that is larger than a verbal structure. Literary forms and conventions, Frye argues, are received and enable imaginative expression of human experience (1963c). In *The Well-Tempered Critic* he places style more in a literary than a social context (1963e).

But, like all great critics, Frye is hard to pin down. His protean nature is apparent in his interest in Canadian literature and culture. Like the annual reviews of Canadian literature in the *University of Toronto Quarterly*, which were collected as part of *The Bush Garden*, and the later collection of essays on Canadian culture, *Divisions on a Ground*, *The Modern Century* is unabashedly Canadian in its terms of reference, including the titles of the three chapters (and the original three talks that comprised the Whidden Lectures at McMaster University in 1967) that are taken from the Canadian poets Archibald Lampman, Irving Layton and Emile Nelligan. Frye actually puts into context the relative obscurity of Canadian Confederation in 1867, whose Centennial was being celebrated during the year in which he was delivering the lectures. The purchase of Alaska, the passing of the Second Reform Bill and, above all, the publication of the first volume of *Das Kapital* over-shadowed the independence of Canada over its domestic affairs (1967b: 14). Frye argues that Canada has in its first hundred years as a nation moved from pre-national to the post-national consciousness. He sets out 'to consider what kinds of social context are appropriate for a world in which the nation is rapidly ceasing to be the real defining unit of society' (1967b: 17–18). For those who would blindly take Frye's usual emphasis on the forms and autonomy of literature to be his only interest, his social criticism and prophetic musings seem forgotten.

The clash between Frye and some political critics, such as some Marxists and cultural materialists, is that while he considers mythology to be prior to ideology, they see mythology (and Frye's view of it) as a form of ideology (see, for instance, Eagleton 1983b: 204, Frye 1971b: 49–51). This disagreement between Frye and some of his political successors does not follow necessarily. Frye himself later admits that his use of 'mythology' can often be equated to 'ideology' (see my Chapters 3 and 4). Jameson, a Marxist, sees the importance of Frye's work just as Frye understands the significance of the Marxist project. When Jameson recognizes that the need to 'transcend individualistic categories and modes of interpretation' is basic for a doctrine of the political unconscious – interpretation in the light of the associative or collective – he shifts from the Freudian hermeneutic to Frye's archetypal system. Like Freudianism, this system valorizes desire but also explicitly conceives of the function of culture in social terms. Jameson asserts that for any contemporary re-evaluation of inter-pretation, the 'most vital exchange of energies' occurs between psycho-analysis and theology. Although Jameson wants to move beyond Frye's theological grounding, he admits its importance (Jameson 1981: 68–9). Frye values Marxism as a necessary critique of bourgeois society and an integral part of the Western imagination, but he is sceptical about it as a practical political system that enhances human freedom (Salusinszky 1987: 38–9). He thinks that the social democracies of the West were the first to develop a cultural dialectic in society between two mental attitudes, the active and the passive, characterized by the creative and the communicating arts respectively. The active response to con-temporary society is an important function of the arts. Frye describes the activists:

> On one side are those who struggle for an active and conscious relation to their time, who study what is happening in the world, survey the conditions of life that seem most likely to occur, and try to acquire some sense of what can be done to build up from those conditions a way of life that is at least self-respecting. ... The subject matter of contemporary literature being its own time, the passive and uncritical attitude is seen as its most dangerous enemy.

Many aspects of contemporary literature – its ironic tone, its emphasis on anxiety and absurdity, its queasy apocalyptic forebodings – derive from this situation.

(1967b: 18–19)

These are not the words of a critic who thinks that literature is not produced in social, political and historical conditions, someone who would seal the writers or readers of literature from society. Later, in the second and third chapters (lectures) of *The Modern Century*, Frye defines a social role for art and education, an issue that recurs in the body of his criticism and theory throughout his career. In his scheme the artist is a liberator who opposes political repression and illusions of universal progress, and education assimilates the arts into society. Frye proposes that humans create open myths for democracy as opposed to the closed myths based on a religious past. Religion and poetry are, for Frye, open mythologies, although in the past many have considered religion in a closed and doctrinal way, so that these two subjects suggest that there are no limits to the human imagination. This discussion of the shift from divine to human myths also occurs later in *Creation and Recreation*. With a prophetic hope, which has much to do with the Canada of the 1990s, Frye suggests that we imagine a better or ideal society that casts across the blaze of lies, power and alienation that comprise our world, to dream 'the uncreated identity of Canada' (1967b: 116–23). Here is the Blakean Frye trying to build a New Jerusalem amid sectarian strife, sceptical about his chances but dreaming, none the less.

Once started on Frye's social criticism it is difficult to stop. It is a major part of his corpus. The Conclusion to the *Literary History of Canada* – which is reprinted as part of *The Bush Garden – The Critical Path* and *Spiritus Mundi* also examine the contexts, and especially the social conditions, of literary criticism (Frye 1965, rpt. 1971a; 1971b, 1976c). In *The Critical Path* Frye discusses disparate topics, such as Renaissance humanism, Marxism, the youth culture of the 1960s and McLuhanism. Frye's central ideas in this study are two opposing social myths – the myth of concern and the myth of freedom. The first myth emphasizes the conservative and communal, authority, belief and coherence. The second stresses the liberal and individual, tolerance, objectivity and correspondence. Frye says that the two myths combine to produce the social context of literature (1971b). Eagleton, in a moment of inattention or with a strange trace of imperial indifference, dismisses Frye's two myths, which begin with Homer and end with the kingdom of God, as a position between a conservative Democrat and a liberal Republican (1983b: 94; see also Wimsatt's implied elision of Frye into 'American criticism', 1966: 85; Frye, Wimsatt and Eagleton are all gifted polemicists). Although Eagleton is always challenging because of his satirical élan, he translates these American parties north and neglects Frye's suspicion of party politics and his preference, if any, for Canada's socialist party, the New Democrats, which would not be tolerated, let alone popular, in the United States. One of Frye's related concerns, which he discusses in *The Critical Path* and *Spiritus Mundi*, is social contract theory.

What is Frye's place in our contemporary social, intellectual and historical context? This is too big a question to raise here, except that suggestively Frye has made his views known about the nature of his theory and its context, discussing, for instance, his relation to other theorists like Bloom and Derrida, the difference between his myth of concern and ideology and his relation to Marxism (Salusinszky 1987: 30–42; see also Hart 1990, Krieger 1966a: esp. 14–24, Dolzani 1983: esp. 65–6). Geoffrey Hartman may be considered as someone whose theoretical work demonstrates a movement towards deconstruction and away from Frye's position. For instance, in 1966 Hartman could praise Frye's universalism, democratization of criticism and recovery of romance for the imagination, whereas in the 1980s Hartman is more ambivalent towards Frye but less so than those who chart the rise and fall of critical schools might imagine. Unlike W. K. Wimsatt, whose New Criticism Frye's *Anatomy* was displacing and who is said to have stormed out of the English Institute meeting in 1966 that was dedicated to a discussion of Frye's work, Hartman, whose deconstructive 'school' was displacing *Anatomy*, shows sympathy for Frye's position and admiration for the brilliance of its expression (Ayre 1989: 306). Hartman opposes Frye where Frye resists absorption to deconstruction: encyclopedic systemization, devaluation of language and close reading that resists systems, and anti-relativism in method (Hartman 1966, 1970, 1980, 1984, Salusinszky 1987: 74–96). If in 1957 Frye was walking the middle way between the historical critics – the philologists and so-called old historicists – and the textual interpreters, the New Critics, from the late 1960s to the early 1980s deconstructionists and post-structuralists became the most influential theorists, and from about 1980 onwards the new historicists and cultural materialists began to displace the deconstructionists (see Alteri 1972, Felperin 1985). In reviewing *The Stubborn Structure* Raymond Williams, who influenced a generation of cultural critics, most notably Terry Eagleton and Jonathan Dollimore (who called Williams the inspiration for cultural materialism), admires Frye's work but faults it for neglecting contemporary experience and fostering abstraction, for succumbing to Matthew Arnold's belief in salvation through poetry (Williams 1970; Dollimore 1985: 2–3). When Stephen Greenblatt, the leading new historicist, reviewed *Northrop Frye on Shakespeare*, he contrasted unfavourably this transcendental and prophetic work with the 'startling architectonic power' of Frye's *Anatomy* and of two earlier works of Shakespearian criticism, *The Fools of Time* and *A Natural Perspective* (1986: 44). For Greenblatt, in *Northrop Frye on Shakespeare*, a collection of undergraduate lectures, Frye places history below poetics, neglects the critique of the binary opposition of history and poetry, and is thereby indifferent to new historicism, which has 'called attention to the ways in which specific cultures produce systems of meaning and hence to shifting interests encoded in any given conception of the past', and, more generally, to 'the theoretical turmoil of the past few years' (Greenblatt 1986: 45; for more on new historicism and Greenblatt, see Hart 1991a, 1991b). Other methods or positions, some textual and some contextual, have exhibited great strength since the 1960s. Hayden White's metahistorical methodology, which flourished especially from the mid-1970s to mid-1980s, is indebted in part to Frye's theory, particularly in the use of *mythos* or the emplotment of narratives (see White 1973; and 1989 for his critique of new historicism). Feminism, post-colonial discourse theory, cultural studies and other contextual positions have been influential and have moved away from some of Frye's concerns. Post-colonialism and feminism are rapidly becoming the most active areas of literary studies (see, for instance, 'Post-Colonialism and Post-Modernism' 1989; Belsey and Moore 1989; Newton 1989). Post-colonialism has been gathering increasing notice since the mid-1980s, and feminism has never lost its momentum but has become increasingly multifold, dynamic and suggestive for many areas of literary theory. Post-colonial writers and critics often focus on Shakespeare's *The Tempest*, one of Frye's favourite texts, and emphasize the political problematics rather than the redemptive mythic patterns (Nixon 1987). These two positions are suspicious of the master narratives Frye examines and might resist the grand argument he produces (Lyotard addresses grand narratives; see Chambers 1991 (esp. xi-xx) for a fine discussion of oppositionality, which includes a consideration of Lyotard). With Greenblatt and the new historicists, whose debt to Foucault produces a similar hermeneutics of suspicion, these feminist and post-colonial oppositional critics resist logocentrism. Without parodying these complex and variegated movements (feminisms is an understatement), some of these critics have not found Frye to be their kind of revolutionary. For them, Frye's words with power appear to represent a phallocentric and logocentric power, stemming from the Bible. Frye's revolution is not theirs.

In some ways new historicism, which uses techniques from New Criticism, structuralism, post-structuralism and feminism, is aligning itself with post-colonialism (see Hart 1991a and b). The object of study is the new world narratives, particularly Columbus' diaries and the writings of early English settlers in North America (see Greenblatt 1976 and Nixon 1987). These 'non-literary' texts were not Frye's focus. By moving the Renaissance to the Americas, these oppositional or cultural critics (and I include some of my work, especially on new world narratives, in this 'position') are trying to de-centre the European Renaissance. One of the dangers is that the Columbus whom the American academy subverts and problematizes may serve in its sub-version to reinforce the power of an imperial state as opposed to the ongoing critique (not merely for 1992) that post-colonial writers, say, in the Caribbean, have been representing in their songs, poems, novels and other works. This coalition may also contain a world of difference. How does one reconcile the traces of the European past, even in their translation to the Americas, that are found and that founded universities in this hemisphere with the oppositionality to the institution by those who have benefited from that institution? Our very positions exist because of that European past. How am I not implicated in the very systems I seek to criticize? The same problems do not occur for dispossessed aboriginal peoples so often outside the universities, although other problematics – more urgent and pressing, like survival, alienation and taking destiny into their own hands – preoccupy them. Possibly, critics like Frye did not think it wise to speak for others outside their tradition: perhaps these critics considered such a repre-sentation for others presumptuous.

Whereas oppositional critics are discussing counter-narratives of the dominant gender, ideologies, and empires, Frye considered literature a counter-narrative of identity against the everyday world of alienation. I am not interested in being for or against Frye but only in complicating our notions of his work. In the polemical and dialectic world of criticism and theory it is easy to parody those who do not share our positions. The trouble with and beauty of grammar and style are that they close down at least as many semantic options as they open up. Frye wrote enough on Canada to understand this project. He discussed his fairly obscure home in the Americas long before many others talked about less obscure places in the hemisphere. He understood the movement to the post-national. He said that all European settlers could do was to bring their sensibility to the new land. But the generation of

1968, many of whom are leaders among the oppositional critics, was one that Frye could not always fathom (see Chapter 6). The post-structuralist and post-modernist view that history makes no sense except what we make of it is only one option. As opposed to the 'deconstruction' of narrativity that the post-structuralists bring about, Frye wants to argue for sense recreated in the imagination through the places literary texts give the reader. Frye understands the problems of communication but believes in communication (1971d: 22). Construction and recreation of meaning, rather than deconstruction, provide his focus. New historicist, feminist and post-colonial criticism is making use of more fragmentary counter-narratives, so that narrative remains important to literary studies. Each of these 'schools' may have its own implicit grand design or narrative, but each contains within it conflicting positions. As Hayden White says, and I have long maintained, 'the conviction that one can make sense of history stands on the same level of epistemic plausibility as the conviction that it makes no sense whatsoever' (1987: 73; see also 37–8). But I also agree with White that the choice of either option has implications for politics. Some writers do not want to conflate history and literature. For Frye, like Stephen Dedalus, the myth-building of literature may make sense of the nightmare of history (experience). Some of the teachers and students (now teachers) of the generation of 1968 also still resist the idea of the university that Frye so often defended (Salusinszky 1987: 37–8, Frye 1972a, 1988, Greenblatt 1986: 44). 1967 is the year after Derrida 'arrived' in America and the year that Frye gave *The Modern Century* as lectures. The post-modern world was being born while the modern world was being proclaimed (see Lyotard 1984, Jameson 1984, Hutcheon 1988, Belsey 1990). But history is not necessarily about progress. Frye thought that literature was an active force in negotiating the world. I think that he might admire this imagining and creation of a new world, a liberation for those enslaved by indifference and tyranny, even if he might not agree with the means of the revolution. This was one of the questions I wanted to ask him in an interview.

I leave it to Frye himself to chart his way back to *Anatomy* from his two volumes on the Bible. In *The Great Code* Frye defends a specific prophetic pronouncement in his great work from the 1950s:

In my *Anatomy of Criticism* I remarked that literary criticism was approaching the area of the social sciences. The statement was strongly resisted, as it cut across the conditioned reflexes of most humanists at the time, but language since then has been taken to be a model of investigation in so many fields, and the theory of language has revolutionized so many approaches in psychology, anthropology, and political theory, to say nothing of literary criticism itself, that no one can any longer regard the humanistic concern with language as separable or even distinguishable from other concerns.

(Frye 1982b: xviii)

Frye's interest in language is more akin to the structuralist (and even post-structuralist) view that language is a concern in all writing. The New Critics wanted a heightened and distinctive literary language that one could find most readily by a close reading of a lyric. But Frye is ambivalent about contemporary theory, avoiding specific discussions of it in *The Great Code*, except to say that some of the developments in that theory are temporary because they are irrational or paradoxical dead-ends (xviii; see also my Chapter 4). He tempers this kind of dismissal with an acknowledgement of Derrida. Soon after using the topos of inexpressibility (in this case a great theorist being a teacher who does not want to overcomplicate his argument and so leaves off the discussion for a vague future time and place), Frye includes Derrida in a statement of the book's general argument: the Bible is a written text, 'an absence invoking a historical presence "behind" it, as Derrida would say', the recreation of such an actuality in the mind of the reader (xxii). As usual, Frye is perceptive because he recognizes that history lies behind the textuality of deconstruction. In a move akin to reader response theory he sees the central importance of the reader. The recreation of reality in the reader's mind is less problematic for Frye than it is for Stanley Fish, although reception theory and reader response theory exhibit many positions (Fish 1980; see also Iser 1990). Frye echoes Derrida as a means of asserting the context behind text, the absence made present in the reader's mind, but he may differ from Derrida over the stability or even possibility of meaning. Is history just another text?

In *Words with Power*, Frye does discuss critical theory and history at greater length. He characterizes this, his last long book, as a successor to *Anatomy* and *The Great Code*, as a summing up (Frye 1990e: xii; see also my Chapter 7). The basic position of *Anatomy*, Frye says, is based on the identity of mythology and literature and on how the structure of myth, as well as legend, folk tale and related genres, informs the structures of literature (xii). He says that one of the misunderstandings about comparative mythology is its most important extension into 'literature (along with criticism of literature) which incarnates a mythology in a historical context' (xiii). Conversely, Frye argues, a literary criticism that cuts off, in mythology, its own historical and cultural roots becomes sterile. In a significant but oblique critique of some contemporary theoretical positions, he asserts that some forms of literary criticism 'stop with an analytic disintegrating of texts as an end in itself; others study literature as a historical or ideological phenomenon, and its works as documents illustrating something outside literature' (xiii). This position is like that of the 'Polemical Introduction' to *Anatomy*, but the textual 'disintegration' of the deconstructionists echoes that of textual editors and has replaced the textual integration of the New Critics, and, perhaps, the new historicists and cultural materialists have joined the Marxists in primarily ideological and historical criticism. As Frye himself acknowledges, his position has not substantially changed since *Fearful Symmetry* but has been an extension and refinement of his theory (xi; see also 1971d: 9). The structural principles of literature – the derivation of literature from myth – are 'conditioned by social and historical factors and do not transcend them, but they retain a continuity of form that points to an identity of the literary organism distinct from all its adaptations to its social environment' (xiii). These principles allow literature to communicate through ideological changes throughout the centuries. Here, Frye opposes the challenge to structure and meaning that the deconstructionists and many post-modern theorists and critics have taken up. From *Anatomy* to the two volumes on the Bible and Western literature, Frye is led to the oppositions between, and shared ground of, religion and literature (xiv). True to his theory, Frye is interested in similarities rather than in differences. He says that the best critics from various 'schools' differ on the surface about the nature of literature but share 'an underlying consensus of attitude' that should lead to 'some unified comprehension of the subject', a construction as opposed to a deconstruction (xviii). He argues for a coherent criticism, not a wandering between 'aimless paradoxes' that make texts all or nothing. For Frye, an address to students and a general public is the only way to break the bickering between theoretical schools (xix). He wants the humanities to educate a public that needs education and not be an exercise for a coterie. He explains the arc of his career that begins in earnest with *Fearful Symmetry*, takes off with *Anatomy* and culminates with *The Great Code* and *Words with Power*:

> The view of critical theory as a comprehensive *theoria* may help to explain the role of the Bible in my criticism. The theory of genres in *Anatomy of Criticism* led me up to the sacred book, along with secular analogies or parodies of it, as the most comprehensive form that could reasonably be examined within a literary orbit. It then occurred

to me that the perspective might be reversed, starting with the sacred book and working outwards to secular literature.

(xx)

Frye gives the double perspective of the main part of his career. In *The Great Code* he implies that he has been rewriting the same book throughout his career when he says that all his critical work revolves around the Bible (Frye 1982b: xi, xiv). The task he set for himself is such an immense labour that it might take for its title *The Bottomless Dream*, his personal choice of title for *A Natural Perspective*. Perhaps this double perspective comes clear in an *anagnorisis* just as in *Twelfth Night* Orsino, the Duke of Illyria, recognizes that the male twin and female twin (disguised as a male) are two different people – 'A natural perspective, that is and is not!' (5.1.217; see Frye 1965b: ix). To begin with the Bible is to be historical. Frye implies that literary critics usually exclude the Bible from discussions of literature. He sees the connection between the scriptures and the secular scriptures as poetic language and the principle of the 'great code' that the structures of these two 'scriptures' reflect each other (1990c: xxii). Metaphor is the ground for social and individual experience (xxiii). Paradoxically, an important function of Frye's great schemata is to serve as a formalized historical context for close readings (xxii). It may be helpful to take up his challenge and try to explore the underlying connections between his work and those works of other theorists. To do so, I want to concentrate on the final movement of his central composition, *Anatomy of Criticism*.

To return to Frye's 'Tentative Conclusion' to *Anatomy* is to reiterate the central role of history in it. Frye is more suggestive, tentative and historical than many other critics consider him. The very power of his suggestions became systematized in the minds of many of his readers in essays like the 'Polemical Introduction'. Although in 1966 Angus Fletcher argued that there need not be a conflict between Frye's textual archetypes and the texture of history, that Frye uses a utopian historiography to make his view of temporality coherent and that *Anatomy* does not slight history, and although in 1978 Frank Lentricchia discussed historicity in *Anatomy* and the ways it goes beyond New Criticism, a similar argument needs to be made today because these voices have not been properly heeded (Fletcher 1966: esp. 34–5; for an expansion of his earlier position, see Lentricchia 1980: 3–26). My argument concentrates on the sense of *Anatomy*'s ending and why it is not the hermetic seal to an airtight formalist schema. While Frye's emphasis is not primarily historical, what he says about the relation between history and literature is apt and not too far from his more historical successors among literary critics and theorists.

Frye cannot be reconstructed as a new historicist or cultural materialist – he was in his last decade when the last two kinds of critics began to gather institutional strength – but some of his views are surprisingly like the ones these critics hold. As a polemicist, he probably understood their use of polemics. He would recognize their appeal to history, for he himself had appealed to it, but he might wonder at their return to literature despite their insistence on contextualizing it with 'non-literary' texts. In 1971 Frye could impugn political and personal criticism as pre-critical anxiety and not genuine criticism (1971d: 32–3). It is here that he parts company with the personal experience of seriatim explication and the political determinism of thematizing one social aspect of the content as if it were the work itself. Frye thereby differentiates himself from many of his predecessors (Marxists, critics of taste, some New Critics) and many of his successors (new historicists, ficto-theorists). In a world that has always been short of time it is easy to stereotype rather than to understand. Readers of Frye can now read him polemically without reprisal. The dead only talk back through text and memory. Although Frye himself was a polemicist, he thought that we could imagine a free space of understanding even if it would never exist in the world. In the 'Tentative Conclusion' he states that it would be folly to exclude the different kinds of critics that he has discussed in *Anatomy*, including historical critics (1957: 341). He says that he attacks only the barriers between the various methods of archetypal or mythical criticism, aesthetic form criticism, historical criticism, medieval four-level criticism and text-and-texture criticism (341). For Frye, historical criticism is one of the options, but a critic must have more than any one method in order to achieve a wide understanding of the complexity of literature.

Although Frye sometimes sounds like our contemporary by way of a Marxist turn of phrase or an observation that perceives the material nature of culture, he also questions the critical practice of making contacts with other disciplines rather than with other literary critics. This practice, he suggests, can lead to literary essays that sound like bad comparative religion, bad semantics, bad metaphysics and so on. Instead, Frye suggests a central role for archetypal criticism, which is to be expected. How central that role is today is debatable. Frye uses archetypal criticism as that which illuminates the shape of literature as a whole, as a complementary supplement to allegorical criticism or what is more commonly known as textual commentary. There is, then, in Frye's criticism a movement between the whole and the part. He wants a breaking down of the boundaries within criticism, whereas many critics and theorists today want to break down the boundaries between disciplines and to intensify contacts with other disciplines. The difference between Frye and his successors is not as great as it appears. Critics often mediate the contact with other disciplines for other critics. Another way of stating it is that critics translate the work of theorists outside literary theory in terms of literary theory. Many critics in North America heard about Clifford Geertz and Foucault through Edward Said, Stephen Greenblatt or some other prominent literary critic and then went to Geertz and Foucault. The conference at Johns Hopkins, the Yale literary theorists, Gayatri Spivak and others helped translate Derrida's philosophy for North American literary critics and theorists. Julia Kristeva came to be known on this continent partly through the efforts of, and disagreements with, American feminists. Anthropology, history, Marxism, philosophy and psychoanalysis are all mediated through the avant garde of literary criticism and theory before being absorbed into the critical and theoretical mainstream. Whether this process, to use Frye's value judgement, is bad or invigorating, or whether Frye would consider this critical and theoretical mediation a dialogue between critics is itself a judgement call. Quite possibly, Greenblatt's history is more literary than his literary criticism is historical.

Before Derrida and Hayden White, though not with the same emphasis, Frye suggests that the language of all disciplines, including literary criticism and history, is rhetorical, and more specifically, metaphorical. Frye partakes in, but recognizes the ironic limits of, organic metaphors to describe history, such as the 'quasi-organic rhythm of cultural aging' as postulated by modern philosophical historians or the decadence of capitalism as described by Marxists (1957: 343). He takes as a commonplace of criticism that art does not evolve or decay (344). What Frye does share with Christianity, Marxism, and nineteenth-century economic theory is a myth of progress, a telos. He suggests: 'What does improve in the arts is the comprehension of them, and the refining of society which results from it' (344). But, unlike Marxists, Frye concentrates on the educated imaginations of individuals, who, as a body, then improve the society. The consumer, and not the producer, finds improvement through literature. Frye's 'humanism' is not an arid formalism. Cultural production may be quasi-organic and half-involuntary, but cultural consumption is 'a revolutionary act of consciousness' (344). This act is spiritually productive and not politically productive in a Marxian sense. The humanistic tradition, Frye says, arose from the printing press, a view not too different from McLuhan's and Ong's (McLuhan 1962, Ong 1989, but see also Frye 1971b: 8, 26). Frye says that this invention codified past art more than it stimulated new culture.

Nor is Frye a dreaded essentialist dredging up inner essences to be fixed in marmorial certainty and eternity. The terrible bugbear – aesthetics – is to be understood historically in the schemes of Raymond Williams and Northrop Frye. Williams says, quite sensibly, that to enter into the history of aesthetics actively means that 'we have to learn to understand the specific elements – conventions and notations – which are the material keys to intention and response, and, more generally, the specific elements which socially and historically determine and signify aesthetic and other situations' (1977: 157; see also my Chapter 7). Although Frye does not pursue this historical perspective, he recognizes it. He understands a kind of Brechtian alienation effect in history as well as the Aristotelian conception of art:

> Nearly every work of art in the past had a social function in its own time, a function which was often not primarily an aesthetic function at all. The whole conception of 'works of art' as a classification for all pictures, statues, poems, and musical compositions is a relatively modern one. . . . Thus the question of whether a thing 'is' a work of art or not is one which cannot be settled by appealing to something in the nature of the thing itself. It is convention, social acceptance, and the work of criticism in the broadest sense that determines where it belongs. It may have been originally made for use rather than pleasure, and so fall outside the general Aristotelian conception of art, but if it now exists for our pleasure it is what *we* call art.
>
> (Frye 1957: 344–5)

Intention and reception concern both Williams and Frye. Even though Frye might not view the aesthetic object with the same hermeneutic suspicion as Williams does, they both understand that the constitution of literature changes for historical reasons. Frye's critical schema is rhetorical because it makes room for the writer and reader. If anything, Frye shares with reception theory the liberation of the reader. In the reader's imagination we find the revolution of our times.

For Frye, we are alienated from the original intentions of the author, as well as from his or her society. Historical criticism involves alienation because, he implies, history involves difference between one time and another. Frye declares: 'Even the most fantastical historical critic is bound to see Shakespeare and Homer as writers whom we admire for reasons that would have been largely unintelligible to them, to say nothing of their societies' (1957: 345). As much as Derrida, and even the New Critics who proclaimed the intentional fallacy, Frye understands the difficulty, if not impossibility, of discovering original intentions. 'One of the tasks of criticism', Frye says, 'is that of the recovery of function, not of course the restoration of an original function, which is out of the question, but the recreation of function in a new context' (345). Intentions and functions are recreated in the mind of the critic, whose different social context makes it impossible to secure the original. With our Promethean fire, with its allusions to classical myth, of the inner light of the non-conformists and the Romantic revolution of the imagination, the critic must recreate the past, which 'is all that is there' (345). Plato's allegory of the cave is too gloomy a metaphor: Frye suggests that, rather than shadows flickering on an objective world, the shadows are within us, 'and the goal of historical criticism, as our metaphors about it often indicate, is a kind of self-resurrection, the vision of a valley of dry bones that takes on the flesh and blood of our own vision' (345). Frye celebrates the subjective, while Plato holds up the objective. The culture of the past is our buried life that we must make new (346). Frye's Romanticism supplements Plato's classicism. All genuine historical critics must show 'the contemporary relevance of past art', by 'supporting a cause or a thesis in the present', so that Frye might consider Greenblatt as an able historical critic (346).

Frye is not the pillar of the establishment that some critics have made him, though it is possible for all of us to be contained, or at least diffused, by the forces of establishment (for an extreme polemic, see Kogan 1969). Although Frye recognizes class conflict, he thinks that Matthew Arnold's view that culture attempts to do away with class conflict is a more productive position than dwelling on that friction (1957: 346–7). Cutting through history, Frye asserts, we find a cross-section that we may call a class structure. Culture is not a series of isolated texts but 'may be employed by a social or intellectual class to increase its prestige; and in general, moral censors, selectors of great traditions, apologists of religious or political causes, aesthetes, radicals, codifiers of great books, and the like, are expressions of such class tensions' (346). In studying the pronouncements of these groups, Frye says, we soon realize that the only consistent moral criticism of this kind is that which is 'harnessed to an all-round revolutionary philosophy of society', like Marx's and Nietzsche's, in which 'culture is treated as a human productive power which in the past has been, like other productive powers, exploited by other ruling classes and is now to be revalued in terms of a better society' (346). This ideal society, Frye argues, can only exist in the future and is only valued in regard to 'its interim revolutionary effectiveness' (346). Like Plato, whose *Republic* is an early example of looking at culture in a revolutionary way, ethical critics can make culture in a definite future image and purge from the tradition any writers who do not fit. If historical criticism goes uncorrected, it relates culture only to the past, and if ethical criticism goes uncorrected, it relates culture only to an ideal future society that might be brought about through the proper education of our youth (346). Frye also observes what has become an unlying commonplace in Foucault, Greenblatt and Dollimore: 'The body of work done in society, or civilization, both maintains and undermines the class structure of that society' (347). Rather than approve of revolutionary action, in which one class has a dictatorship over the other classes, or celebrate dialectical materialism – even though Frye thinks that when people behave as if they are material bodies this philosophy seems true – Frye wants to avoid the extreme dialectic that operates in actual wars and in verbal or mimic wars, where the ghosts of social conflict dwell (347). Even if no society can be free, classless and urbane, we must, in Frye's view, exercise our utopian imaginations as a form of spiritual liberation (347). In a statement that would provoke the opposition of many of our contemporaries, Frye declares: 'The imaginative element in works of art, again, lifts them clear of the bondage of history' (347). The works of art that form part of liberal education, no matter their original intention, and the readers become liberated through the experience of criticism. If there is no free space in society, there is in the imagination.

Northrop Frye seems to partake in a secular apocalyptic and messianic vision that is akin to the utopian aspect of Marxism. He does not think that beauty can be studied as formal relations in an isolated work of art, but asserts that the work must be viewed socially and against the ideal of a complete and classless civilization, which is also the standard for ethical criticism (Frye 1957: 348). This social ideal is the culture in which we try to educate and free ourselves. For Frye, ethical criticism involves a transvaluation, 'the ability to look at contemporary social values with the detachment of one who is able to compare them in some degree with the infinite vision of possibilities presented by culture', a state of intellectual freedom (348). Frye disdains as a kind of defeatism that arises from a social malaise the notion that we cannot be detached from our own lives. Rather, in Frye's view, *theoria*, or withdrawn vision, enables the means and end of action and makes it purposeful by enlightening its goals (348). Perspective makes social action possible rather than represents a turning away from social responsibility. If there is no theory, the action becomes paralysed. Milton's *Areopagitica* and Mill's *On Liberty* are great examples of this kind of theory (348–9).

Although Derrida and the deconstructionists, and some feminists and ficto-theorists, have contributed a great deal to the breaking down of the binary opposition between creative and critical writing, the cultural tradition of giving precedence to the writer over the critic, Frye before them attempted to dignify criticism by making it different from, but equal to, creative writing. Frye tries to dispel the parasite fallacy of criticism in which the critic is a leech who feeds off literature and ruins it in his or her very analysis (349). He claims that his archetypal criticism does not argue for the aesthetic or contemplative aspect of art as the final resting place but, instead, facilitates, through a movement from a consideration of the individual work to the 'total form of the art', an ethical criticism that participates in the work of civilization (349). He says that the patterns of words – like scripture, liturgy, a written constitution and a set of ideological directives – can remain fixed for centuries but that the interpretation of them will change historically, so that criticism occupies a central role in society (349).

The danger in Frye's method, as he recognizes, is 'substituting Poetry for a mass of poems', but he attempts to avoid an 'aesthetic view on a gigantic scale' by assuming 'that all structures in words are partly rhetorical, and hence literary, and that the notion of a scientific or philosophical verbal structure free of rhetorical elements is an illusion' (Frye 1957: 350). He recognizes, as Derrida and others later do, that if all structures of words are, to some extent, rhetorical, the literary universe has become a verbal universe, and no aesthetic principle will contain the literary (350). In 1957 Frye was suggesting the relation of literature to old and new disciplines, from mathematics to cybernetics. Frye compares in some detail literature and mathematics: 'Both literature and mathematics proceed from postulates, not facts; both can be applied to external reality and yet exist also in a "pure" or self-contained form' (351). By using an analogy to another discipline, Frye attempts to find a principle that is not strictly aesthetic to define literature as being and not being self-contained. Equations and metaphors are tautologies that postulate being and non-being simultaneously (352). Verbal structures are, according to Frye, representative and constructive, which are the two main views of language since Plato (352–3; see also Waswo 1987: 1–47, 284–305). From descriptive representational language we construct metaphors that become 'units of the myth or the constructive principle of the argument' (353). None the less, Frye differs from some of his more rhetorically committed successors because he warns that it would be silly to reduce rhetorically other disciplines to myths and metaphors for polemical reasons because our proofs would be just as mythic and metaphorical. Criticism of truth, for Frye, has to do with content, but myth has to do with form, which is the kind of assertion that makes some critics think of Frye as a proto-structuralist (353). But in Frye's schema the myth is the source of coherence for an argument and so cannot be separated from content. Here, Frye admits to a Platonic affinity because Plato thought that the ultimate apprehension was either mathematical or mythical. Language – mathematics and literature – represents no truth but provides the means of expressing many truths (354). Frye closes his 'Tentative Conclusion' to his *magnum opus* with two myths – the Tower of Babel and the last chapter of *Finnegans Wake*. We cannot unite heaven and earth, Frye says, because when we try to think such thoughts, we discover their inadequacy and the plurality of languages. If Joyce's dreamer cannot remember his communion with a vast body of meta-phorical identifications, the ideal reader, or critic, can. Frye envisages the work of the critic as repairing the ruins of a fallen nature until we are happier far. Critics will use imagination to reforge 'the broken links between creation and knowledge, art and science, myth and concept', so that if critics continue their criticism this reforging will be 'the social and practical result of their labors' (354). Here we witness Frye's emphasis on society, practice and work, hardly the terms that make up typical contemporary characterizations of him. These last words of the body of *Anatomy* are not those of a Wildean aesthete but echo Milton and Blake to break the mind-forged manacles and build with myths a prophecy that is and is not historical.

Part of the historical as well as literary endeavour involves visions of utopia (see Fletcher 1966; see also my Chapter 8). The utopian impulse in literature and literary criticism has persisted and will persist. Writers in each historical moment, even if its texts speak to people through the translation of time but speak none the less, prophesy by trying to perform the improbable but important task of projecting the present beyond the present in the present. Frye's utopian or positive hermeneutic is obviously not Jameson's, which appeals to the material over the ideal, but both dream a systematic dream of a better future by interpreting the dream of literature, both with a firm idea of the imperfect, and sometimes barbarous and dystopic, form of their societies. Both Frye and Jameson contemplate the collective nature of art (Jameson 1981: 291–2). Frye's view of history and society as they were, are and will be provides us with a great reading of culture whether we agree with all of it or not. Contemporary critical theory and literature cannot afford to give the difficult dream of something better. It is no wonder that Frye's favourite Shakespearean play was *The Tempest*, where dystopic and utopian elements contend and interpenetrate, and that Jameson and others have found so much that is positive in Frye (Felperin 1992). Frye will be translated over time: his great work never was designed to escape the political and social only to translate them through literature. In literature Northrop Frye found something positive between the nightmare of history and the no place of the future: one possible positive mediation was the dreaming body of the literary critic.

6   On education

I saw the best minds of my generation destroyed by madness, starving
   hysterical naked . . .

angelheaded hipsters burning for the ancient heavenly connection to
   the starry dynamo in the machinery of night . . .

who passed through universities with radiant cool eyes hallucinating
   Arkansas and Blake-light tragedy among the scholars of war,
who were expelled from the academies for crazy & publishing obscene
   odes on the windows of the skull . . .

                              (Allen Ginsberg, *Howl*, 1956)

During the late 1950s and the 1960s, Frye was asked to lecture on
historical events he was living through. These events culminated in the
student protests at North American universities. In the 1950s the cries
of 'Blake-light tragedies' belonged mainly to the beat generation, but
by the 1960s the revolution had spread to the campuses and drew to its
cause a body of students. Ginsberg's *Howl* was published a year before
Frye's *Anatomy of Criticism*, and both men had their own ideas of
Blakean apocalypse, from translations of Moloch to those of eternity in
time. Frye's idea of a regained paradise differed from the prophets of
alternative ways of life and counterculture. What became the generation
of 1968 are the heirs to the beat generation and became important
proponents of the counterculture as it was translated into the academy in
the forms of cultural critique or post-structuralism. This is the generation
that, increasingly, turned away from 'humanism' and the values that
Frye expounded, from modernism to post-modernism. It was a generation that included many who admired Frye's brilliance but who could
not follow him down the critical path that he illuminated with his wit
and learning. Where he sought unity and meaning, they sought disintegration and indeterminacy; where he created a system and a grand
narrative, they opted for *petits récits*. The professorial heroes of 1968,

if that is not too much of an oxymoron, were not always too different in age from Frye (born 1912). Jacques Lacan was born in 1901, Claude Lévi-Strauss in 1908, Roland Barthes in 1915, Louis Althusser in 1918 and Paul de Man in 1919. Even Michel Foucault (1926) and Jacques Derrida (1930) were well advanced in their careers in 1968. The late structuralist and post-structuralist revolution in literary studies, which has challenged Frye's poetics since the late 1960s, has led to a new generation of political or oppositional critics, many of whom were born during the 1940s and who advanced the causes of feminism, subaltern studies, post-colonialism, new historicism and cultural materialism, Julia Kristeva, Gayatri Spivak, Stephen Greenblatt and Jonathan Dollimore among them. For most of the theorists and critics working in these new 'schools', politics, ideology and literature are inseparable. This is the generation who studied in the universities during the 1960s. Frye placed myth as something enduring behind transitory ideology, but many in the 1960s and after have a hard time believing in the transcendental and transhistorical. Here is one of the major differences between Frye and the post-structuralist/post-modernist movement that I have been characterizing.

I am younger than Frye and the university students of the 1960s. In 'Do It' Jerry Rubin describes my age-group (the younger brothers and sisters) under the satiric, prophetic and McLuhanesque rubric – 'Every Revolutionary Needs a Color TV':

> The first student demonstration flashed across the TV tubes of the nation [the US] as a myth in 1964. That year the first generation being raised from birth on TV was 9, 10, and 11 years old. 'First chance I get', they thought, 'I wanna do that too.'
>
> The first chance they got was when they got to junior high and high school five years later – 1969! And that was the year America's junior high and high schools exploded! A government survey shows that three out of every five high schools in the country had 'some form of active protest' in 1969.
>
> (Rubin 1984: 442)

But the demonstrations in France were not always the same as those in the United States. And it is a good antidote to that generation born in the 1940s, and those of us who came after, to avoid slipping into confession or self-indulgent autobiography. Gayatri Spivak makes this point clearly and bluntly:

> We live in a post-colonial neo-colonialized world. And we should teach students to find a toe-hold out of which they can become critical

so that so-called cultural production – confessions to being a baby-boomer and therefore I'm a new historicist – that stuff is seen as simply a desire to do bio-graphy where actually the historical narrative is catachretical. If you think of the '60s, think of Czechoslovakia, not only Berkeley and France, or that the promises of devaluation didn't come true in some countries in Asia in '67. So one must not think of one's cultural production as some kind of literal determinant of what one can or cannot do.

(Spivak 1989: 290–1)

Criticism in any generation is not monolithic, so it is no surprise that political critique during the 1960s and since has been diverse and contentious. Those who oppose Frye's vision sometimes oppose each other. This dialectic, this reading against the grain, is vital to the health of literary and cultural studies.

In this chapter I want to concentrate on the 1960s in Canada and North America, particularly on the universities, and then to examine Frye's ideas, especially in regard to education. In this idea of what education and the university are resides the difference between Frye and what I have called the 'generation of 1968' (realizing the differences within that generation here and elsewhere).

I

Because Northrop Frye's fame was probably at its peak during the 1960s and early 1970s and made its greatest impact in American universities, I would like to give a brief background to the movements of the 1950s and 1960s that may have influenced the reception of his works in universities in the United States and Canada. As has almost always been the case in the history of Canada, events in the United States could not help but influence those in this country. In 1951 a federal judge sentenced Julius and Ethel Rosenberg, two alleged Communists, to death for conspiring to spy against the United States. In 1954 the American Supreme Court declared that segregation in public education was illegal. In 1955 Rosa Parks was jailed in Alabama for not giving up her seat on a bus to a white person, and this protest led to a successful boycott of the city's bus system. In February 1960 black students staged a sit-in at a lunch counter in Greensboro, North Carolina to protest against segregation, and in the next two months about 50,000 people had participated in similar demonstrations at lunch counters throughout Southern cities (Albert and Albert 1984: 2–6). The history of the Civil Rights Movement after 1960 is better known.

There are parallel movements. The rise of the New Left is particularly important on university campuses across North America, and it was a group with which Northrop Frye often disagreed. In 1962 an organization of college students, Students for a Democratic Society (SDS), wrote and published *The Port Huron Statement*, a collective statement that described American society as militaristic and undemocratic (Albert and Albert 1984: 10). This statement identifies the degradation of blacks in the South and the Cold War, fought in the shadow of the Bomb, as the cause of their move from quietism to activism (176–7). The universities, which are never far from the minds of the New Left, are part of the state's ideological apparatus. The authors of *The Port Huron Statement* lament:

> But neither has our experience in the universities brought us moral enlightenment. Our professors and administrators sacrifice controversy to public relations; their curriculums change more slowly than the living events of the world; their skills and silence are purchased by investors in the arms race; passion is called unscholastic. The questions we might want raised – what is really important? can we live in a different and better way? if we wanted to change society, how would we do it? – are not thought to be questions of a 'fruitful, empirical nature', and thus are brushed aside.
>
> (Albert and Albert 1984: 179)

The collaborators on *The Port Huron Statement* also observe the potential of the university while outlining its ills. They assert that university students are separated from the social reality they study and that a similar alienation of faculty occurs as a result of over-specialized research. According to the collaborators, academic bureaucracy, which is generated through the massive size of universities, transforms the searching of many students into a ratification of convention, creating a numbness that will lead to imminent catastrophes, and moves the university towards the mentality of business and administration. Foundations and private-interest groups, they say, help finance the university and make it more commercial and less critical of society. Moreover, the collaborators argue that scientists and social scientists serve corporations and the arms race, that, like television, the university passes on stock truths, and that the university is a socialization to accept minority elite rule and comfort. By contrast, the potential good of the colleges and universities is that they could serve as a 'source of social criticism and an initiator of new modes and moulders of attitudes' (Albert and Albert 1984: 184–5). *The Port Huron Statement* is a self-conscious manifesto of the New Left that attempts to be measured and positive, to suggest a new way as well as criticizing the old way. This manifesto demonstrates an understanding of the strategic nature of the university in a movement for social change: 'Social relevance, the accessibility of knowledge, and internal openness – these together make the university a potential base and agency in a movement of social change' (195; see also 194). The students and faculty have united and should continue to unite in the democratic struggle for peace, civil rights and fair labour practices, and fight to remove academic cant with debate and controversy to assault the powers that be (196).

Polemics crossed the lines between professors and students. A Yippie like Abbie Hoffman quoted Marshall McLuhan as an authority on the relation between media and myth (1984: 422; contra, see Frye 1968a, 1971d: 8, 149–52, 1986: 106). Jerry Rubin could also adapt McLuhan, a professor at the University of Toronto, for his purposes, but, in advocating live political theatre, off-beat happenings to put the established powers off-guard and off-balance, Rubin incited students to drop out. By offending his enemy through the use of obscene language and aphoristic slogans, Rubin calls schools and colleges the biggest obstacles in 'Amerika' and prefers social action to abstract thinking: 'Abstract thinking is the way professors avoid facing their own social impotence' (1984: 446). Rubin calls professors put-ons, school an addiction (447). His technique, which is characteristic of polemics and often occurred in the 1960s, is the overstatement, distortion, fragmentary assertion and moral indignation of satire:

> Why stay in school? To get a degree? *Print your own!* Can you smoke a diploma?

> We are going to invade the schools and free our brothers who are prisoners. We will burn the buildings and the books. We will throw pies in the faces of our professors. . . .

> The same people who control the universities own the major capitalist corporations, carry out the wars, fuck over black people, run the police forces and eat money and flesh for breakfast. They are the absentee dictators who make rules but don't live under them.
>
> (448)

It was difficult for members of the counterculture to forget the demonstrations at the Democratic National Convention of August 1968 in Chicago. As the demonstrators chanted before the cameras, 'The whole world is watching' (35). And much of it did. Well known but less 'spectacular' events occurred at Columbia University in 1968, where a long strike paralysed the institution and, in 1969, at Berkeley, where violent clashes between police and demonstrators also took place at the 'People's Park' (Albert and Albert 1984: 30–1, 39–40; for a diary of these times, see Colebrook 1979: 231–334). Northrop Frye was at Berkeley during the time of the People's Park (Ayre 1989: 322–3; for the Canadian context, see Hart 1993b; see also *The University Game* 1968).

II

Many of Frye's ideas on education in the 1960s, whether they occur in oral addresses or essays on education or as part of a discussion on the nature of literature and criticism, are later versions of those expressed in the 1940s and 1950s, when Frye wrote a series of articles on education and culture for *Canadian Forum* and other journals. In 1940 he writes that democracy is *laissez-faire* in art, science and scholarship and predicts a decentralization of culture after the war (1940c). In an article in 1945 addressing views that prefigure the debate on technical education for global competition in the 1980s and 1990s, Frye defends liberal education against Conservative politicians and capitalists who want vocational training and says liberal education emphasizes that the great works of culture represent a vision of reality that is human and understandable but a little better than we can have in life. Frye asserts that *laissez-faire* philosophy was once liberating but is now reactionary and that the only coherent form of socialism is one based on the liberal theory of education – which is the tradition in which Frye's theory falls (1945a). But Part Two of this article tries to go both beyond the vocational view, that students should be prepared for the actual social surroundings, and the liberal view, that they should be trained for the ideal environment. Frye says that the proper purpose of liberal education is to effect 'neurotic maladjustment' in students in order to help develop critical thought (1945b). He finds spiritual freedom in Christianity and in the humanities through the form of a book and says that in times of crisis people return to the humanities because they lead us away from ordinary life and towards that freedom (Frye 1947b). In 1950 he outlines the ideological causes that seem to make apocalypse imminent in modern life: fascism, communism, *laissez-faire* utopianism, technology, and atheistic parodies of religion (1950c). Frye relates the church to various secular institutions like the university (1952a).

Frye's idea of education finds earlier affinities in Newman's idea of the university as a social place, Arnold's conception of culture and Mill's concept of an area of free discussion (Frye 1988c: 24–5). A university, Frye says in 1957, trains its students 'to think freely' or, in other words, to reason, to decide based on habit. His own use of amplification is related to the learning and teaching technique of habit and practice memory. For Frye, 'The process of education is a patient cultivating of habit: its principle is continuity and its agent memory, not rote memory but practice memory' (1988c: 26). At the basis of Frye's idea of education is the book, which he thinks is an admirable and durable piece of technology. The book, 'a model of patience', 'always presents the same words no matter how often one opens it; it is continuous and progressive, for one book leads to another, and it demands the physical habits of concentration' (27). The mass and popular media are, according to Frye, discontinuous, news-bearing and reflective of the change and dissolution of the present. In a statement that might glance at McLuhan, Frye says: 'It is often urged that these media have a revolutionary role to play in education, but I have never seen any evidence for this that I felt was worth a second glance' (27). Frye's view of the university is that it informs the world and not the converse. The function of the critic and teacher may, like that of the writer, not always be approved of by society, and so professors may have to demonstrate courage and integrity in the face of hysteria and support each other in a community with a common cause (28).

The Frygian revolution in education has some differences from what the student activists of the late 1960s proposed. With Milton, he would view their idea of liberty as an expression of licence. The centre of the university resides, for Frye, as he expressed it in an address to the Royal Society of Canada in 1960, in the critical discipline, by which he means 'criticism' in Matthew Arnold's sense (1988c: 30; see also 1961b). Frye's university demands that the student recognize a cultural environment that is at right angles to the social environment and that provides, through human imagination and thought, the criteria for judging society and one's actions (32). The student in Frye's scheme voluntarily removes himself or herself physically and mentally from society and discovers in the university academic freedom, which involves intensive study of ideas and works of imagination 'without reference to ordinary society's notions of their moral or political dangers' (32). Another unpopular but, I think, apt observation Frye makes is that scholarship in a subject should teach itself and 'that the university's practice of regarding teaching as a by-product of scholarship is apparently a sound one' (33). In the university, education yields to subjects, to organized bodies of knowledge, like literature, and the teacher is judged by how well he or she knows the subject. The university does not teach but calls forth a subject. For teachers to remain independent they must align themselves to their cultural, as opposed to their social, environment (33–4). Frye's ideas fly in the face of students, like those at Port Huron, who want universities to be more socially relevant or a tool for social change by being more of society, or of Althusser's view of the schools (and presumably the university) as the educational ISA or Ideological State Apparatus and literature as part of the cultural ISA, which are not RSAs or Repressive State Apparatuses, like the army, but which are on the side of the state (see Hayim 1982: 101 on the dangers of generalizing about the loose array that came to be called the New Left). Frye shares neither the utopian beliefs in society of the writers of the *Port Huron Statement* nor the view that all institutions are of an often unseen and unconscious ideological ether in Althusser's revisionary Marxist schema. In fact, Frye would probably find more affinity with Marx's view of ideology, that of false consciousness or inversions of the real in the world, as expressed in *The German Ideology*, than with Althusser's revision (Marx 1977: 164). Frye values the revolutionary impulse:

> Whatever one studies at a university, whether humanities or science, one is studying a subject in a state of continual intellectual ferment, which has gone through many revolutions of perspective in the last century and is certain to go through many more in the next one. Such a mental training is becoming almost indispensable for living in a society of which great revolutions in perspective will also be demanded.
>
> (36)

The advantage Communism has over democracy is that, being closer to its beginnings, it has not forgotten its roots, as democracy has. So Frye contends and adds that original sin is an idea that needs to be regained – even though students do not like the idea – because it is at the foundation of democracy and will allow the citizens of democracy to exercise their cultural memories and meet the social changes that are occurring. Frye's rhetoric is deliberately polemical, ironical and paradoxical:

> The university can best fulfil its revolutionary function by digging in its heels and doing its traditional job in its traditional retrograde, obscurantist, and reactionary way. It must continue to confront society with the imaginations of great poets, the visions of great thinkers, the discipline of scientific method, and the wisdom of the ages, until enough people in the democracies realize that a way of life, like life itself, must be lost before it can be gained.
>
> (37)

In 1960 Frye was sounding Miltonic in his educational typology. His notion of discipline for freedom, as well as his actual experience as an undergraduate at Victoria College, was what made the strict Honours Course at the University of Toronto so important to him. To be radical was not to be lax but to be rooted and ready for change. It was hard work to regain the paradise lost without and within us. The fascination with what's difficult is a rare thing in the details of labour, and sometimes when people seek paradise through religion, drugs or politics, the quick fix is more popular than sweat and patience.

III

Although Frye inveighs against the trash of the mass media, he seems to exempt programmes on CBC radio and television in which he participated. These media could, if used properly, be aids to education or to dissemination of knowledge. Public broadcasting appears in practice to escape Frye's general criticism. He opposes the limits and the vapidness of the mass media to the knowledge imparted in books, but combines the two forms. A famous example of Frye's media script becoming a book, or his book being used as a media script, is *The Educated Imagination* (1963), broadcast as the Massey Lectures on CBC radio in November and December 1962. The public lecture turned book, or its opposite, represents his favourite genre. He probably thought in books but also wrote with oral delivery and the silent speaking voice in mind. Public education taken beyond the classroom became Frye's mission in the last three decades of his life. Public lectures and lecture series at universities throughout the world spurred him into critical production. Frye used to say in class that all his books were teaching books, an endearing boast in the age of research universities devoted increasingly to scholarly production, and he silently assumed this movement from the classrooms of the 1940s and 1950s to the lecture circuit of the 1960s and beyond. This is hardly a man who wanted an elitist cabal to enjoy education. The academy without walls became Frye's model: he wanted an open university.

Frye's basic question in *The Educated Imagination* – 'What good is the study of literature?' – has no solution but only answers in the present (Frye 1963b: 1). He also outlines corollaries of this question: does literature improve our ability to think, feel or live? What is the function of the teacher, scholar and critic? What difference does the study of literature make to social, political or religious attitudes? These are the big questions Frye says he thought naive when he was young. The fundamental question that he asks is a variation on the most basic critical and theoretical question – What is literature? – that may have

been framed well before Plato and Aristotle asked it in its earlier form
– What is poetry? But Frye inserts the words 'good' and 'the study of' in
his basic question. There seem to be two emphases in the foundational
question: the moral and the aesthetic. Plato wants to know what good
poetry is and thereby asks a moral question. Aristotle describes what
poetry is and in doing so attempts to give aesthetic answers. But Frye's
'good' may also have to do with utility – as in what kind of work does
it do? Is it any good? This utilitarian echo would be familiar to Frye's
radio audience in late 1962 because even if many of its members were
sympathetic to poetry and literature, many English Canadians would be
familiar with the pioneer, commercial, practical and parish view that
poetry wasn't honest work and that a 'man' couldn't make a living at it.
Frye's 'good' might share something with John Stuart Mill's and
Plato's concepts of the good. All three were enchanted with poetry,
although Plato seems to have resisted its charms as he created it. Frye's
question about the function of the critic in 1962 echoes Matthew
Arnold's 1864 essay, 'The Function of Criticism at the Present Time'.
Poetry had to have a use. The apologetics for poetry, as for theatre,
probably begins in earnest with the reaction to Plato. In Western
European languages, defences of poetry and theatre abound. In English
the defences by Sidney and Shelley are the best known. But Frye's book
is more in the tradition of Pope's *An Essay on Criticism* and Coleridge's
On the Principles of Genial Criticism concerning the Fine Arts, in which
the subject shifts in part from literature to criticism. *The Educated
Imagination* is one work in an important line that examines the
imagination: Locke's *Essay concerning Human Understanding*, Addison's 'The Pleasures of the Imagination', and Coleridge's fragmentary
comments on imagination in *The Statesman* and the *Biographia
Literaria*. Frye's study of Blake, who champions imagination, is more
central to his thought than Locke (a primary target of Blake's) or
Addison, but it is in the tradition of discussing imagination that I am
interested. Another tradition that Frye is working in here is the defence
or reconstitution of education in works like Locke's *Thoughts concerning Education*, Rousseau's *Emile* and Newman's *The Idea of a
University Defined and Illustrated*. Returning to Arnold's essay on the
nature of criticism and imagination, we can observe that whereas he
rates criticism highly, Frye gives it an even higher place, because
Arnold explicitly ranks criticism below creative writing. For Arnold,
creative power is the highest human function through which 'men' may
achieve true happiness. They may also obtain this happy state in 'well-
doing', learning and 'even in criticising' (Arnold 1970: 453). Frye also
thinks of making literature and poetry as creative acts. He is an

intermediate step on the way from Arnold to deconstructionists, who collapse the difference between creative and critical writing.

The Educated Imagination also consolidates Frye's ideas on education that he discusses elsewhere in many short and long essays. The motive for metaphor, Frye says as he echoes Stevens, is the association of our minds with the world through the primitive forms of metaphor, which relies on identity, and simile, which depends on analogy (likeness) (1963b: 10–11). This is the archetypal critic, Frye, who shares a desire for the occasional moment of unity with the New Critics and structuralists, for an imaginative atonement or epiphany, as opposed to the desire of deconstructionists to be suspended between the construction and dismantling of the identity of poetic or imaginative meaning. Frye cannot avoid discussing literature when exploring the human imagination. In primitive societies, he says, literature is embedded in other aspects of life like religion, magic and social ceremonies. In time forms of literary expression that are social practices, like funeral laments and lullabies, become traditional literary forms (13–14). Literature then derives its forms from itself as music does (15). This last principle combines with Frye's concern for Canadian literature and culture. Many of Frye's talks and essays on education are addressed to Canadian audiences. In speaking about literature making its generic forms from itself, Frye declares:

> This principle is important for understanding what's happened in Canadian literature. When Canada was still a country for pioneers, it was assumed that a new country, a new society, new things to look at and new experiences would produce a new literature. So Canadian writers ever since, including me, have been saying that Canada was just about to get itself a brand new literature. But these new things provide only content; they don't provide new literary forms. Those can come only from the literature Canadians already know. People coming to Canada from, say, England in 1830 started writing in the conventions of English literature in 1830. They couldn't possibly have done anything else.

> (15–16)

Frye always insists on the conventionality of writing, which means that works of literature are individual but of a kind (16–18). The heart of this conventionality, from which we cannot escape, is the archetypal myth or story. In popularizing the central theses of *Anatomy* Frye sets out this central myth by citing a string of Romantic poets and their quests: Blake's desire to restore the golden age; Wordsworth's for paradise, the Elysian fields and Atlantis; D. H. Lawrence's for the Hesperides, and

Yeats' for Byzantium. The singing school of literature has one central tale to tell: 'This story of the loss and regaining of identity is, I think, the framework of all literature' (21). For Frye, literature uses irony to separate a vision of identity from the wretched world itself (21–2).

To close off his second 'lecture' in *The Educated Imagination*, Frye sums up clearly the basic attributes of his theoretical and critical writing:

> We have to look at the figures of speech a writer uses, his images and symbols, to realize that underneath all the complexity of human life that uneasy stare at an alien nature is still haunting us, and the problem of surmounting it is still with us. Above all, we have to look at the total design of a writer's work, the title he gives to it, and his main theme, which means his point in writing it, to understand that literature is still doing the same job that mythology did earlier, but filling in its huge cloudy shapes with sharper lights and deeper shadows.
>
> (Frye 1963b: 22)

This precedence of mythology has become, since the re-emergence of political criticism as a strong force in literary studies, a point of question (see Chapter 8).

In the third lecture, 'Giants in Time', Frye asks what kind of reality literature has and explores its imaginative power (1963b: 23). Literature expresses universals and is a complete world made up of individual literary works; it takes over the historical figure and the poet, so that there is no such thing as self-expression in literature (24–9). Frye's poet, like the magician, is an identifier: 'everything he sees in nature he identifies with human life' (31). But literature is not a world of belief. Instead, it opens up possibilities, so that our beliefs become some among many possible assumptions and we can see the power of other people's beliefs. This imaginative possibility, or detachment that arises from the imagination, allows for tolerance. The writer is not, for Frye, a dreamer or a watcher but participates in literature that swallows life through imagination. The imagination defeats time through literature by creating a universe possessed by humans. We cannot believe in this world, but the vision of such an imaginative place keeps alive what may be most important to us (31–3).

Frye's fourth lecture, 'Keys to Dreamland', asserts the conventional nature of society and literature. Whereas social conventions seem natural to us because we are immersed in them, literary conventions do not, because few of us are deeply familiar with them. In fact, Frye says, literary convention is as far from that of society as possible (1963b: 34–5). In ordinary life, goodness and beauty are conventions or what we are accustomed to, 'and even truth has been defined as whatever doesn't disturb the pattern of what we already know' (35). Frye also makes a wry suggestion: 'So however useful literature may be in improving one's imagination or vocabulary, it would be the wildest kind of pedantry to use it directly as a guide to life' (36). The more lifelike literature is, the more its imaginative effect diminishes (36–7). One of the recurring central principles in Frye's career is that literature imitates literature, not life. Prose is not the natural language of literature but a convention of literature. Other kinds of writing are for conveying information and are acts of will and intention, whereas literary writing means what the words on the page say and not the intended meaning of the author (37–8). One of the problems of Frye's division is that although history refers to actual events in the world, it uses figurative language: the intention of the historian is, therefore, mediated through 'literary' or rhetorical language, which complicates the issue. Frye illustrates his axiom that literature and life are not connected with the example of censorship: literature is not moral or immoral because moral effect relies on the reader (38–9). The human imagination is the reality of literature. In Frye's view literature represents a world that is better and worse than our own. The absorbing world of the sublime is the better habitation. Frye's notion of literature as a world that refines our sensibilities owes as much to Aristotle's notion of catharsis as to the eighteenth-century refinement of sensibility to which he refers (40–2). Value judgements disappear with our separate identities in the experience of literature: 'as a reader of literature I exist only as a representative of humanity as a whole' (42). This view of identity may be Frye's more optimistic equivalent of the subject position in ideology that Althusser and those influenced by him assert. We are constructed and made by the structures of something greater than us, in Frye's case, by literature, but in Althusser's by social structures based on the material conditions of economics. Frye alludes to Aristotelian universals, political critics of the 1980s and 1990s to contextual particulars. For the two sides, Blake's minute particulars or seeing the world in a grain of sand means something quite different. Frye's universal reader would be, for some, a gesture of the hegemony of European males. For Frye, I imagine, that response would be reading literature by the conventions of the world. Literature is oppositional to life in Frye's theory.

Literature gives us the imagination that life experience cannot (Frye 1963b: 42). Rather than be a dream world, literature, according to Frye, is two dreams, one of wish-fulfilment, the other of anxiety, focused together in a fully conscious vision. Here, Frye cites Plato, Keats and

Joyce to make his point. Life makes community, literature communication; life a private subconscious, literature a public one. Literature is
myth-making. In this century the greatest example of this point is
Finnegans Wake (43). Poets and critics, creation and understanding, are
necessary to literature. The critical response helps to make the pre-
critical response of first reading or viewing more accurate and sensitive.
Like Matthew Arnold, Frye is concerned with the critic's role and with
literature as a new kind of religious experience:

> The critic's function is to interpret every work of literature in the
> light of all the literature he knows, to keep constantly struggling to
> understand what literature as a whole is about. . . . Literature is a
> human apocalypse, man's revelation to man, and criticism is not a
> body of adjudications, but the awareness of that revelation, the last
> judgement of mankind.
>
> (44)

Frye's Romantic ideas of the imagination, what one might call the
emanation of Blake, is never far from his vision of literature and
criticism. This is a religious experience of literature and perhaps a
literary experience of religion. Frye is a critic of unity and of making the
unconscious or experiential seriatim into a coherent view, so that
although he can see the important function of deconstructive techniques, pulling the thread for Theseus to escape the maze is done in
order that he can see its architecture better. Literature is not to be
abandoned like Ariadne for other discourses that society has deemed
more powerful and relevant because they are closer to social conventions and the 'nature' in which society finds itself.

Literature is at the centre of Frye's theory of education. In 'Verticals
of Adam', the fifth lecture, Frye wants to test his theory of literature by
seeing if it can help in the question of teaching literature, particularly to
children (1963b: 45). The wonderful power of *The Educated Imagination* is that it illustrates its complex argument with such simple and
elegant clarity that it cannot help but be a teaching book, to be the very
test of coherence and pedagogy that Frye demands of his literary theory.
Here, for instance, is one of the clearest skeletal statements of the
historical and conceptual underpinnings of his theory of literature:

> My general principle . . . is that in the history of civilization literature
> follows after a mythology. A myth is a simple and primitive effort of
> the imagination to identify the human with the non-human world, and
> its most typical result is a story about a god. Later on, mythology
> begins to merge into literature, and myth then becomes a structural

principle of story-telling. I've tried to explain how myths stick together to form a mythology, and how the containing framework of the mythology takes the shape of a feeling of lost identity which we had once and may have again.

(45)

Frye's interest in identity, both of the individual and the society, is still very much with us, but in translated forms. These translations and revisions occur in the post-structuralist or post-modern age, from Barthes and Foucault on the death of the author or author function to Lyotard's *petits récits*, those small narratives that disrupt the grand narratives, or *grands récits* that have dominated European history to the debate over the possibility of experience, essence and identity between French feminists like Cixous and Kristeva on the one hand and American feminists like Showalter on the other (see *For Alma Mater* 1985 and *The Feminist Reader* 1989).

But the mythology Frye sets out is best observed in the Bible, so that Frye recommends introducing the Bible to children at the earliest age, in order that they can immerse themselves in mythology as a basis for their understanding of literature (1963b: 45–6; see also 1966: 142). Frye realizes that this is the most contentious of his proposals for education and literary theory because of the secular nature of those fields and, more implicitly, that those who are more inclined to the classics or to the assumption that literature is of society and not opposed to it would not want to make the Bible the basis for literary education or education with literature at its core. It is the literary structure or shape – the myth – of the Bible that should be taught in literature and not its religious dimension (46; see also my Chapter 4). The next element Frye would add to this early education is classical mythology, without which it is difficult to understand the Western literatures (46–7). The Bible and classical myths are sometimes similar – they move from stories of creation, fall and flood to actual history – because 'the same literary patterns turn up within different cultures and religions' (47).

For Frye, the next stage in literary education is to learn the structure of genres or literary forms, which derive from myth, beginning with the simpler and primary genres like comedy and romance and proceeding to tragedy and irony in secondary school. To detach oneself and grasp the total structure of a literary work is the student's goal (1963b: 48). Frye laments that too many people do not learn to distinguish between imaginative and discursive writing and so expect the former to convey information. Indeed, many of Frye's successors in the post-modern and post-structuralist schools insist on breaking down such a distinction,

which, for him, must have seemed misguided. Children should learn to
listen to stories as stories as early as possible. Later, in Frye's scheme,
a student should try to write as a way of understanding in his or her
reading the difficulties that the writer faces (49). Frye says there are two
contexts for the study of English: first, languages other than English,
and second, arts other than literature. The humanists have always
studied other languages, especially those that form the heritage of
English – Latin, Greek and Hebrew – and learnt to think in linguistic
conflict because it questions the 'natural' assumptions of one's native
tongue. The other arts help to show that 'the imagination is the
constructive power of the mind set free to work on pure construction,
construction for its own sake' because the constructive units can be
tones, colours, bricks or marble and not just words (50). This statement
may sound too much like Pater or Wilde for some today, especially
those who read, even unconsciously as a subtext or hidden ground,
cultural semiotics and cultural poetics as if culture were a verbal text
writ large rather than a construction of signs that can be linguistic,
visual, aural and tactile. The third context for literature is other
subjects, like philosophy and social sciences, built out of words. In the
teaching of literature we should begin at the centre – poetry – and work
outwards. Poetry is central because it is more primitive than prose and
is more like the speech of children with all its rhythm (51–2). Although
literature should be studied first as literature, 'a great work of literature
is also a place in which the whole cultural history of a nation that
produced it comes into focus' (52; see also 53). That is why it is
important, according to Frye, for Canadians to pay attention to Canadian
literature. All things vanish in time: only the imagination makes people
Proust's 'giants in time'. This is Frye's metaphor of the relation
between literature and history (53). The place of literature in education
is its relation, as a procedure that makes assumptions and postulates, to
other studies built out of words, such as history, philosophy, the social
sciences, law and theology, just as pure mathematics proceeds by
similar methods in relation to the physical sciences. In Frye's view the
lyric is the poetic equivalent to pure mathematics (54). The practice or
production of literature and the theory of literature or criticism are both
important aspects of literary study. By criticism, Frye means 'the
activity of uniting literature with society, and with the different
contexts that literature itself has' (55). All critics are contextual critics,
and Frye is a different kind from the contextual critics of the 1980s and
1990s. Most criticism occurs in the classroom at all levels of education,
less in reviewing and still less in the central activities of research and
scholarship. Literary teaching should transfer 'imaginative energy from

literature to the student' – this is the educated imagination that does work in society (55).

In the sixth and last lecture, Frye discusses the vocation of eloquence, to borrow a phrase from St John Perse. Of course, Frye knows that imagination is used during our waking and sleeping lives and that literary language, ordinary speech and the discourse of conveying information overlap (1963b: 56–7). He is not sealing literature off from society. Instead, Frye argues that our whole social life is based on imagination and that we live rhetorically in our public lives. In other words, we cannot express our intellect or emotions directly but speak through our bodies, clothes and social sense. In the social or public use of words, as Frye defines rhetoric, 'we realize that even in the truth there are certain things we can say and certain things we can't say' (57). In the eyes of society saying the right thing at the right time is more important than telling the whole truth or even the truth (57–8). The rhetorical situation or the social vision of rhetoric is like people dressed up in Sunday clothes and maintaining the polite, necessary but not necessarily true assumption that they are what they seem (58). With imagination each individual develops a vision of society, so that he or she can select from what it offers and cut through the illusions, those in advertising or politics, for instance, that do not appeal to that vision (58–60; see also Frye 1967b: 28).

Every society has a social mythology with its own folklore and conventions. Its purpose is to have us accept it and adjust to society. The main elements of social mythology, as Frye sees it, are appeals to status symbols, like those in advertising; clichés, especially in politics; jargon, which can disguise reality, like bureaucratic language that covers up the terrible wreckage of war; and nostalgia, like the pastoral longings for some imaginary good old days (60–2; see also 1966: 143, 1967b: 29–30). The educated imagination works against these illusions: it opposes archetypes to stereotypes. Frye makes a passionate liberal plea for free speech, which is quite different from licence or ready opinion, but comes from the imaginative power of the discourse itself:

I don't see how the study of language and literature can be separated from the question of free speech, which we all know is fundamental to our society. The area of ordinary speech, as I see it, is a battleground between two forms of social speech, the speech of the mob and the speech of a free society. One stands for cliché, ready-made idea and automatic babble, and it leads us inevitably from illusion to hysteria. There can be no free speech in a mob: free speech is one thing a mob can't stand. You notice that the people who allow

their fear of Communism to become hysterical eventually get to
screaming that every sane man they see is a Communist.

(64)

Frye is writing with McCarthyism at his back and in the shadow of the
Cuban missile crisis of October 1962. His free speech is highly trained
speech fostered through imagination. One is free to speak freely just as
one is free to play Bach, after much training. Free speech is cultivated
speech plus a social vision. However, there are exceptions, Frye
concedes, in times of crisis: for example, when, in a critical fight over
desegregation in New Orleans, a woman with little formal education
spoke with an eloquence equal to that of the Declaration of Independence
(1962b). A minority learns free speech, but it is that minority that makes
Canada a better place to live than East Berlin or South Africa (64).

To feed our imaginations, that is our task. If we have two worlds, that
of our society and that of our ideal society in an impersonal sense, we
can use the ideal vision to criticize and work on our practical social
environment, a kind of social function for the utopian imagination as
Frye suggests in another work (1963a, or 1988c: 70). The educated
imagination trains the mind and provides for social and moral development (1963b: 65–6). In the tradition of Plato, Blake and Arnold
the ideal world of our imaginations is 'the real world, the real form of
human society hidden behind the one we see' (1963a: 66 or 1988c:
70–2). The crux of Frye's argument, to which he alludes directly, is
Arnold's idea of the actual environment and the ideal environment. The
latter, which Arnold called culture, was suggested in our education, and
he deigned it the best that has been thought and said (Frye 1963b: 66; see
also 1971b: 166–8). The cultural environment provides the standards
and values we need to do more than adjust to society (1963b: 66; see
also 1963a or 1988c: 73). In an apt warning that displays an understanding of satire – because in my view a satire has to be a satire on satire
(and the satirist) as well as of individuals and society – and the self-
reflexive nature of imaginative social criticism, Frye says: 'There's
something in all of us that wants to drift toward a mob, where we can all
say the same thing without having to think about it, because everybody
is all alike except people that we can hate or persecute' (1963b: 67). The
power of imagination makes from words philosophy, history, science,
religion and law. Their contents are bodies of knowledge, but their
structures are myths, or imaginative verbal structures, which connect
them with literature.

Frye brings *The Educated Imagination* to a conclusion by two means,
a coda and an image of the organizing myth for the book, the Tower of

Babel. Frye concludes: 'So the whole subject of the use of words revolves around this constructive power itself, as it operates in the art of words, which is literature, the laboratory where myths themselves are studied and experimented with' (1963b: 67). The Tower of Babel, a work of imagination whose main elements are words, is our giant technological structure that is precarious and may collapse with the confusion of tongues. The real language of the imagination is the language of human nature: the language of poetry, that of Shakespeare and Pushkin, allows for the social vision of Lincoln and Gandhi. We need to listen to that language in leisure, words that tell us on the Tower that we are no closer to heaven and that it is time to get back to earth (67–8). Human nature is a highly contested construct today, especially for those who see it as transcending history, but Frye suggests that we imagine ourselves through a language given to us and, through the arts of language he calls literature, we fashion a social vision that allows us to oppose and change our society through free speech. This freedom is not the same as everyone of us speaking our prejudices like a reflex: this popular version of freedom of speech is wilful licence. Frye is of the liberal tradition of Locke and Mill, speaking of tolerance, as Lincoln and Gandhi did (see 1967b: 115–16). Frye's liberal imagination, as Lionel Trilling would understand, seeks justice and tolerance through heuristic possibility and the liberation of discipline (see Trilling 1972: 171–2). This liberating discipline may be an oxymoron to some, especially when liberalism is not held in as high regard as it once was, but it was anything but that for Frye. It was, and is as we read Frye, the centre of his idea of education.

IV

From the fullest and most coherent of Frye's accounts of education, it is possible, briefly, to discuss some of his other writings on education that speak in and to the turbulent 1960s. In *The Modern Century* Frye argues that educators and advertisers represent in democracies the equivalent to party workers in Marxist regimes (1967b: 88). In 1967 Frye can argue, although in the 1990s we may not be able to be so optimistic about our economy's ability to generate productive leisure for more people, that the technological revolution has brought leisure and that education is a positive element of leisure (89). Education involves institutions like schools, universities, churches, museums, art galleries, theatres and so on, but also includes leisure activities or the leisure structure. For Frye, what government does in regard to the leisure structure is of revolutionary importance to social development (89–92).

In the future, Frye says, adult education will become more important and we shall have to come to terms with the university as a place of education and not of training (92–3). He reiterates the importance of the close relation between artists and scholars and the appearance of artist-scholars (97–9; see also 1961a). He wishes that the North American university would concentrate on the historical dimension because it has become obsessed with the contemporary (103–4). Teaching literature in a social context, the contemporary in relation to the past, is at the centre of Frye's notion of the emancipatory, tolerant and social nature of liberal education, partly because detachment and perspective are necessary to show what is silly and reactionary in contemporary culture (104–5). Frye's university students would study the disciplines and find in their liberal education a vision of society or mythology. This mythology is about a human's concern with himself or herself, his or her relation to God and society, about the origin and fate of humanity or himself or herself and is, therefore, a human-centred view of the world (105). The old myth, a synthesis of biblical and Aristotelian sources in the Christian church, is based on the subject-object relation and the use of reason (106–7). The new myth is that humans are responsible for their own civilization, asserting, for instance, that liberty is not what God gave and humans resisted but what most people want in opposition to those who, appealing to their own gods, would try to keep them from getting (109). Modern mythology reaches us on two levels, social mythology and the myth of concern, the cliché and stock responses of family, teachers, neighbours and media on the one hand and a sense of human hopes and fears and something which scholarship modifies on the other. Frye advocates a democratic open mythology, not a closed mythology of belief, and prefers Mill's free discussion and Arnold's culture to the anarchy of doing as one likes and the stock response of social and political activism (110–18). Innocence and experience interpenetrate, as Blake sees and as Frye asserts with a backward glance to the poet and a prophecy, perhaps, for a dialectical and deconstructive age: 'No idea is anything more than a half-truth unless it contains its own opposite, and is expanded by its own denial or qualification' (116). The arts are not substitutes for religion because they are not structures of belief, although poetry and religion share mythical language. Appealing to Blake's 'The Lamb' and 'The Tyger', Frye asserts that we exist more in a world of experience, the subhuman world of nature, without design, the world of the tiger, where humans are the only creative force and they are mostly destructive. It is to the creativity of the imagination, to our education in social vision, that Frye appeals. His final question in *The Modern Century* is to what do Canadians owe loyalty in their

Centennial year when they are alienated from their economy (in Marx's sense), live in an all-too-human democracy (in Nietzsche's terms) and have only perfunctory symbols to hold them together (119–21). Frye reaches again for the idea of the real behind the illusory society that he discusses in *The Educated Imagination* when he concludes, 'The Canada to which we really do owe loyalty is the Canada we have failed to create', and suggests that this absence is our identity, to the ideal culture for which we strive and can never attain amid the lies, political hypnosis and suppression of freedom and criticism (122–3; see also p. 257 below).

In 1968 and 1969, Frye finds himself speaking on education in the midst of student protests. Speaking to the Canadian Association of School Superintendents and Inspectors on the social importance of literature, he says that the student protest has shallow roots (1968b). At the University of Saskatchewan convocation, he says that the student movement is more psychological than political and that it lacks the heroic vision of the educated imagination based on science, the humanities, religion and the arts (1968d). At Queen's University, Frye compares the student radical movement of the 1960s with that of the 1930s. He argues that permanent revolution occurs in the society's critical dialogue with itself. Frye thinks that the university is the best institution for enabling that critique, whereas the students of the 1960s seem to want a religious experience (1969a; see also 1971c). At Duke University, Frye contextualizes the New Left by comparing it to Communist, religious and American populist and revolutionary movements. In the New Left, Frye observes the discontinuity and hysteria of modern life and the movement's religious anxieties. Whereas he stresses that knowledge is continuous and structured, radicals prefer commitment and engagement. For Frye, education gives us such knowledge, but, for the New Left, education is irrelevant (1969b). In 1969, at York University, Ontario, Frye asserts that the student protests, like the one at Berkeley, arise from a lessening of social coherence, and that the university alone can provide us with the revolutionary and democratic social vision necessary to pull out of the crisis (1969c; for similar views, see 1970a, 1971d, 1971e, 1976a). For Frye, the student radicals want answers to existential problems, whereas the university offers them critical detachment from the society in order that they may develop a social vision as a utopian ideal with which to transform the society. None of Frye's response comes as a surprise to someone who had heard or read *The Educated Imagination* in 1962–3, which in turn brought together and developed Frye's earlier musings on education.

But Frye is much more sympathetic to the student protestors than these brief comments can convey. To redress the balance, I want to concentrate on some of Frye's more readily available writings on education in this period. In 'The Social Importance of Literature' (1968b) Frye concentrates once more on the university and addresses the student unrest. Frye contrasts the New Left with the old Marxist left. Whereas the old Marxist left accepted the work ethic, the New Left attacks it. And the modern leftist student in North America, if he or she is protesting against Negro segregation or the Vietnam war, does not think of those things as a Marxist would do, as mere by-products of a class struggle. He or she sees rather the emotions and prejudices involved in these issues as primary and as the real target to be attacked. Consequently, the new protest movement is anarchist, rather than Communist; it is much more deeply concerned with the imaginative and the emotional and it raises even more directly the question of the vision of society which one should have here and now (1988c: 76; see also 1968b). There is still a debate between Marxist and new historicist critics that, at least in its polemical manifestations, manifests some of the distinctions that Frye is making (see Gallagher 1989: 37–48, Franco 1989: 204–12, Fox-Genovese 1989: 213–24, Spivak 1989: 277–92). Frye understands that historical conditions, including the Sputnik crisis, have created a university in process where students participate in education as an end and not a means, as adults and not as those who are waiting to become adults (1988c: 76–7). Although Frye thinks that the student movement, unlike the black movement, has shallow social roots because it does not arise from longstanding social injustices, he says that he should support the students on the grounds of general fairness (77–8). He supports authority that is in the subject studied at university, the completion of freedom, not its limitation. His freedom is impersonal, whereas the freedom of the student protester is personal (79–80). Frye never tires of putting literature at the centre of the curriculum: 'The study of literature is a training in a constructive and imaginative vision of man's own sense of his social goal.' It does not solve social problems but bases 'education on the sense of a participating community which is constantly in process and constantly engaged in criticizing its own assumptions and clarifying the vision of what it might and could be'. It helps in the fight for human sanity (82).

In the Convocation address at the University of Western Ontario on 27 May 1969 (the talk was later called 'The Day of Intellectual Battle'), Frye reiterates his distinction between the myth of concern and of education, but he also opposes student radicals who attack the university, an institution that he so loves:

It is students, today, who repeat the formulas of the ignorant and stupid of a generation ago, that the university is a parasitic growth on society, that academic freedom is old-hat liberal rhetoric, that because complete objectivity is impossible degrees of objectivity do not matter, that the university seeks for a detachment that ducks out of social issues, that scholarship and research are all very well but of course aren't real life.

(1988b: 84)

Frye is ambivalent towards the students of the late 1960s: some are genuinely interested in social change, but others are interested in barbarism and totalitarian measures. Frye left Berkeley to visit Western, and recounts his experience in California, in particular with the 'People's Park' (1988b: 84–5). Frye feels for the students, his students, ordinary students, 'who were clubbed and beaten and gassed and prodded with bayonets while trying to get to lectures or enter their own residences' (85; see also 1971b: 146). As a liberal, Frye likens the SDS to Ronald Reagan, governor of California, the militant left to the militant right, because they would both like to destroy or transform the university (1988b: 85–6). And Frye is not afraid of change, but is glad the university is resisting left and right anti-intellectualism: 'The university is changing and will change more, but change is simply adaptation to new social conditions: it is not itself a good thing or a bad thing' (87).

V

A couple of works from the early 1970s, with reference to the 1960s, round out Frye's intense thinking on education during the crisis of the 1960s. In the Convocation Address at the University of Windsor on 17 October 1970 (the talk was later called 'A Revolution Betrayed: Freedom and Necessity in Education' and delivered at the time of the FLQ or October Crisis), Frye returns to the subjects of concern and convention. The university is not about Olympian detachment but 'the challenge of full consciousness' (1988c: 89). The university offers a world of intellect and imagination. Freedom is defined only in the university: 'The authority of the logical argument, the repeatable experiment, the compelling imagination, is the final authority in society, and it is an authority that demands no submission, no subordinating, no lessening of dignity' (90). Frye calls this a neofascist age when people hate the idea of freedom and attack academic freedom (90–1). He praises the convocating students for having the courage to educate themselves rather than to listen to all the distractions and detractions that might have deflected them from their purpose (91). As at Western, Frye addresses the students as becoming the embodiments of an academy without walls, taking with them the vision of the university into the rest of their lives wherever they may be (91–2).

The Critical Path (1971) revises lectures given at Cornell, Queen's and Duke in 1968 and two lectures at Berkeley on 'the concern-freedom thesis' and another at Bellagio, Italy in 1969 (Frye 1971b: 7). The myth of concern uses words and, as much as they are able, holds society together (36). For traditional Christianity, God designed the world in which one tried to move from anxiety to salvation, but today our myths of concern centre on a human-made world whose truth or reality is based on human desire (53). We need both concern and freedom, which operate in a dialectic in which they interpenetrate (55–6, 109–10, 134). Frye restates the problem facing the university, which is the social centre of the myth of freedom: there is a strong desire in society to change that institution into a place of the myth of concern, like a political party or church. Frye does admit a genuine radical tradition in the United States, of Jefferson, Whitman, Thoreau and Lincoln, which shows some affinity, in Jefferson and Thoreau, to the anarchism of the student radicals. The emphasis on individuality and psychology distinguishes this movement from Marxism (138–57; see also 79). Speaking of the 'People's Park' crisis at Berkeley in the summer of 1969, Frye says: 'Here a vacant lot with a fence around it became assimilated to the archetype of the expulsion from Eden, dramatizing the conflict of the democratic community and the oligarchical conspiracy in a pastoral mode related to some common conventions of the Western story' and notes that the police obliged as the demonic expelling angels (146). Frye also argues that the open mythology of democracy should allow the society to recognize the pluralism, specialization and autonomy of scholarship and its power of veto over any concerned mythology as it may produce evidence that contradicts this latter myth (155). At the heart of education is the right to ask questions, and it is the student's role to find relevance in study (156). Frye encourages the responsible student for following the critical path between unliberated concern and unconcerned freedom: he praises him or her for making a commitment amidst confusion, for an 'act of historical significance', and for realizing that civilization is the burden of the sane person (157).

Social mythology, Frye says, is divided into two mythical ideas: social contract and utopia (158). Behind the great writers of and on utopias, like Plato, More, Locke and Rousseau, Frye sees theorists of education (162). Frye focuses on the educational contract, the process by which sciences and arts, through logic, experiment, evidence and imagination, operate as a source of spiritual authority in society, a coherent community free of external compulsion. The centre of this contract is the university (163–4). The social vision of the wise person's mind in Frye's utopia is, in Freudian terms, the mind in which the principle of sanity is battling for its life against chaotic impulses, which must be indulged and humoured and not simply repressed (165). For Frye, the idea of equality provides the core of most modern myths of concern (167). The critical path uses an ideal world to contrast with the actual one. Frye says that the pleasure of the arts arises from the lively feeling of the world's absence (168). Through barriers of belief and cultural difference, literature haunts the imagination and grows in the form of criticism (170). Concern, on the other hand, cannot tell a community from a mob. We live between the freedom literature offers us and concern in society, so that criticism mediates between the society of which we are a part and the literature that society gives us the privilege of studying. If we could live naked in the utopian world that poetry invites us to, then the distinction between life and literature would dissolve 'because life itself would then be the continuous incarnation of the creative world' (171). This is Frye, the visionary, seeing the union of the individual and social body, the human body divine, with Blake one on side, but feeling his feet on the ground, and with Aristotle on the other.

VI

Today Frye is refuted but still stands, like the philosopher he describes.

In 1988, in the Preface to a collection of his essays from 1957 to 1985, *On Education*, Frye looks back on the student unrest of the late 1960s and says that although the reader might think that all the references to these events showed that this subject was a personal obsession, actually he was asked to talk about it because it was an obsession of the society of the time. The reader will still be the judge. Frye summarizes his position from hindsight but maintains the same stance he held then:

> I had little sympathy for the unrest: it seemed to me to have, like feminism or the black movement, no genuine social roots. Those who sympathized with it because they were remembering their own left-wing enthusiasms in the thirties were prisoners of their own metaphors: this movement was anarchist and neo-fascist in its tactics. It enlisted a very small minority of students, most even of them, I suspect, egged on by television cameras, who created 'mass demonstrations' with a totalitarian skill. But if I had no use for the

protest, I had if possible even less for the kind of opposition organized against it.

(1988c: 6)

Frye seems to have decided that the women's movement acquired deeper social roots from 1968 to 1986, because in a speech in 1968, he suggests shallow roots for that movement fifty years before. None the less, he says he would have supported the women's movement then out of fairness and a conviction that it is never good to create proletariats in society (1988c: 78). It remains to be seen whether the student unrest may also have been a flash point in a social change based on legitimate social grievances. The recent debate on political correctness may be a media event that *Newsweek* and George Bush got going in the United States and then Canada (the *Toronto Star* and other media organs rushing in where others feared to tread) or a renewal of the debate, which has never died, from the late 1960s about the nature of the universities and other social institutions on this continent.

Frye also had a great and positive effect on his students. Some of his students, particularly Margaret Atwood, have helped to shape a vital Canadian literature from 1960 onwards. In that same Preface in which he discusses the student unrest of the late 1960s, he claims: 'This maturing of Canadian literature (mainly English Canadian, despite so many wonderfully impressive French figures) is the greatest event of my life, so far as my own direct experience is concerned' (1988c: 7). This is Frye the teacher speaking, the internationalist who crusaded for Canadian art and literature.

To return to the Blake of Frye and of the radical movement of the late 1960s: Milton Klonsky is a representative of the latter position. He says that Blake insisted that rather than metaphysics and abstractions, minute particulars are the place where we can perceive, in our personal ways, the infinite. The seer must see by himself, alone. And Klonsky proceeds with a personal reminiscence, which begins: 'For better or for worse, Blake's words from *The Marriage of Heaven and Hell* were deeply etched upon my mind one day about ten years ago, at a beach on Fire Island, New York, when for the first (and also the last) time I "tripped" on LSD' (1977: 7; for a relation of Blake and counterculture, see Roszak 1969: epigraph and xiii–xiv, Nuttall 1968: 72–3, Trilling 1972: 171–2). A similar personal approach to Blake, a poet who was supposed to have an inscrutable private mythology, Frye discovered in the 1930s as a student. In the Preface to the 1969 edition of *Fearful Symmetry*, Frye's confession is personal but witnesses the poetic revolution of Blake as a social and not as an isolated event. Blake's cosmology is a revolutionary vision of the world as humanized through the imagination, a vision of possibilities for the world and not its actualities. Blake preferred reason to rationalization and saw human life as a revolt against the repression of desire and energy. In Chapter 1 I quoted a similar passage to the one I am about to quote, and do so because it is a point to which Frye returns throughout his career and because it demonstrates in ever-changing contexts Frye's hope in the chaos of history. He typifies Blake's time, the time Frye was writing his book on Blake and the time of the Preface for the revision:

> I wrote *Fearful Symmetry* during the Second World War, and hideous as that time was, it provided some parallels with Blake's time which were useful for understanding Blake's attitude to the world. Today, now that reactionary and radical forces alike are once more in the grip of the nihilistic psychosis that Blake described so powerfully in *Jerusalem*, one of the most hopeful signs is the immensely increased sense of the urgency and immediacy of what Blake had to say.
>
> (Frye: 1947a: Preface 1969 edn)

Frye's thoughts on Blake led to *Anatomy*, which iterates what later books, like *The Educated Imagination*, *The Critical Path* and *Words with Power*, reiterate, amplify and refocus. Blake was at the centre of Frye's education and Frye's theory of literature, and because literature was at the centre of Frye's theory of education, so too was Blake.

In the 1960s, when education and the university were experiencing crisis, Northrop Frye looks backwards and forwards. His ideas of education began early and stayed with him all the days of his life. Whether his quarrel with the generation of 1968, ambivalent as it was, was a conflict of generations is something I leave to a growing detachment we may have in the 1990s about a decade that is still with us. But only in the wide gap of time will the interest in the debate be less immediate, and, perhaps, a natural perspective on Frye and the student unrest will arise there. Perhaps then, like Blake's, Frye's evangelical and radical sympathies and his importance to the university and in the decade, well beyond the boundaries of Canada, will come into an even sharper focus.

7   Mythology and ideology

Did I fear a great multitude, or did the contempt of families terrify me,
that I kept silence, *and* went not out of the door?
                                    (Job 31: 34, Authorized or King James Version)

Si expavi ad multitudinem nimiam,
Et despectio propinquorum terruit me;
Et non magis tacui, nec egressus sum ostium.
                                    (Job 31: 34, Biblia Vulgata)

Consciousness can never be anything else than conscious existence, and
the existence of men is their actual life-process. If in all ideology men and
their circumstances appear upside-down as in a *camera obscura*, this
phenomenon arises just as much from their historical life-process as the
inversion of objects on the retina does from their physical life-process.
                        (Karl Marx, *The German Ideology*, 1932), in Marx 1977: 164)

There are a great number of 'myths' about Northrop Frye. Two such
myths persist – that he sought to seal literature off from the world and
that he denied ideology. 'Ideology' may be the key term in literary
criticism and theory over the past decade. My discussion of Frye and
ideology is twofold. After discussing briefly critical responses to Frye's
'ideology', I shall concentrate on his understanding of ideology. This
chapter should contribute to a better knowledge of some of the myths
about Frye, in the popular sense of misconceptions. My comments will
concentrate on the last book in a two-volume study of the Bible and
literature that Frye considered to be the culmination of his career,
Words with Power, and relate this book to *The Double Vision*, the brief
posthumous volume that bears a relation to *Words with Power* similar to
the relation that *The Educated Imagination* bears to *Anatomy of
Criticism* – it is a shorter and more popular version primarily meant for
oral delivery.

In the light of Frye's death in January 1991, it is an appropriate time to assess the misconceptions. By reducing Frye to a systematizer and a myth critic, we are more prone to blindness than to insight. Frye's schema is only part of his œuvre, and the schema is fluid, open and accommodating. He recognizes the debased form of myth as misconception and delusion, but he also realizes its structural, narrative, cognifive, existential and social dimensions. In Frye's critical theory language is of primary importance, so that myth and metaphor are interpenetrable aspects of literature, criticism and human culture. Increasingly, since the late 1960s, but especially in the last decade of his life, Frye often discussed mythology in relation to ideology. He took ideology seriously and thought of mythology as expressed through the imaginative and hypothetical nature of literature as something more fundamental than ideology but more marginalized and vulnerable. Paradoxically, mythology as translated in literature and as explained in criticism might resist the power of dominant ideologies and the political pressures brought to bear on writers, scholars and critics. Myth was Frye's hope against the desolate record of human history, the tyrannies that have oppressed so many in this century. For him, myth in literature was the rising up of the proletariat into a classless society and the return of the repressed. He returns to Marx and Freud, as well as to Blake and others, to help create his vision of hope and regeneration. The social function of literature, in Frye's view, is to create a human community that cares for the basic needs of its members – the desire to live, eat, love, create, and move about freely. Frye's theory is a later and important contribution in the tradition of defences of poetry that Sidney and Shelley helped to build in English. Frye is part of a European tradition that defends against the attacks on fiction – especially in poetry and in the theatre – that begins with Plato and Aristotle, gathers momentum with the church fathers, and continues through the closing of the theatres in England in 1642 (see Barish 1981). In this attack on the making or representation of fictions, poetry, theatre or novels are not considered morally, theologically, or philosophically serious enough. Literature and drama were demonic and parodic – the work of the devil, or at least a class of lying poets. Frye defends the dignity, autonomy and significance of literature in the political, social, ethical and semantic systems that he considers to be human constructions. Literature is a human construction that, for him, only needs defending because of human ignorance and ideology, because it offers us means to regenerate ourselves and our society. Although Frye may sound as if he is emulating Matthew Arnold in making faith in literature a substitute for the loss of faith in religion, and to some degree he is, he does not follow Arnold in this metonymy or displacement, because he relates the Bible and literature but also distinguishes them.

In the last book published in his lifetime, *Words with Power*, Frye presents a view of the ideological, including literature as a critique of ideology, that needs to be set in the context of contemporary views on the topic. The debates on ideology are too vast to discuss as a whole, so I hope to address only a few main points on ideology by a few important theorists. For the most part, because the debate on ideology is most active among post-modernists of the left and new Marxists, almost all of my contextual discussion will concern itself with important critics in these groups. In the last decade of his life, Frye himself often had those in mind, Marxists and deconstructionists, who had performed a critique of the aesthetic ideology. In discussing ideology, one of my main points is that 'ideology' is a term that represents a necessary debate on the relation of writers and critics, literature and criticism, to society, but that it is a fractured term that can range from meaning false consciousness to an all-pervasive condition of human existence (for definitions, see Plamenatz 1985: 15–31, Kavanagh 1991). Frye's contribution to the discussion of ideology will neither suit nor please everyone, but it helps, as do the positions of Althusser, de Man, Eagleton, Belsey, and others, to clarify and further the debate. It is also important that no matter how important Marxism is to the debate on ideology, other positions are considered. Frye's 'liberal humanist' stance may seem eccentric to this generation of theorists, but it is this 'eccentricity' that may prove informative. Perhaps the liberal humanist position is no longer dominant in the universities and needs to be heard from another historical context. But these classifications are not always helpful, because Frye is much more than a straw version of the 'humanist', a term that has changed so much in the past five centuries or more. I am not interested in classifying the schools of ideology but in the debate itself. Assumptions are beginnings that can begin anywhere.

I

Frye discusses mythology and ideology. The use of the term 'mythology' is, as Frye acknowledges, sometimes equated with illusion or lies. In *Mythologies* (1957, trans. 1972) Roland Barthes attempts to find ideology behind mythology, to demystify the uses of myth in European culture. Barthes is attacking mythology in the same year that Frye is making it his foundational notion. This is the primary reason for my prefacing this section on myth and metaphor with Barthes' view. The conceptions of Frye and Barthes on myth balance each other, or at least

effect a mutually creative tension. In a book on Frye I must concentrate on his view, but it seems partially-sighted to leave out
Barthes' powerful analysis. Like McLuhan, Barthes turns his sight on
signs in our society in a kind of semiotics of popular culture. He
attempts to demystify wrestling, guidebooks, the Tour de France and
other popular items or pursuits and their relation to the ambiguous and
mystified meanings that society produces. Barthes equates 'myth' with
doxa. By *doxa* he means a widespread, unexamined premise or
assumption rooted in the dominant ideology or political order, in this
case the bourgeoisie. The problem with the bourgeoisie, in Barthes'
view, is that it is incapable of imagining the other. In discussing
mythology today in the last essay in *Mythologies*, Barthes proposes a
method for reading or interpreting myths which derives from semiotics, the study of sign systems and of signification. Barthes is interested
in the gap between the literal and the symbolic or mythical meanings
of signs. For instance, Barthes, as a 'mythologue', teaches us how to
read the repressed or unstated mythological meanings in images and
signs, like those of French imperialism in 1957, to be more sceptical of
the way we are being manipulated (Bathes 1957: 109–59, Sturrock
1979: 61–4). Like Brecht, Barthes is suspicious of the 'natural' or
'realistic' that hides its history and its construction. Literature is
produced – like other products – in different historical periods and not
something magical or inspired (Hart 1989a: 61–5). Barthes is suspicious of the Romantic myth of genius, which Frye is ambivalent
about but does not entirely deny. Like Frye, Barthes thinks that realism
can be an anti-art, a kind of instrumental and mimetic work, and that
literary language is purposeless and does not do anything (see Sturrock
1979: 64–5). Barthes' notion of the term 'mythology' extends what
Frye calls bad mythology to all of mythology, whereas Frye argues
that myth in literature is related to literary language, to metaphor, and
is purposeless. It asserts or affirms nothing. For the most part, Barthes
and Frye agree on these matters, but whereas the one equates
mythology and ideology, the other will not.

Frye discusses myth in the context of literary criticism, so that myth
means '*mythos*, story, plot, narrative' (1990b: 3). His view of possessing
the total structure of a story is open-ended because in a Shakespearian
play or any 'classic' there is an indefinite series of these final
apprehensions. As soon as we reach an understanding, we become
dissatisfied and try to come to a better understanding, in a process that
can last a lifetime (6). (Frye says that myth and metaphor are
inseparable because myth annihilates the space between A and B in time
and metaphor does the same in space: we are here and now even as we

speak about the past or the future.) Both myth and metaphor are counterlogical (7–8).

Raymond Williams (1921–88) helps to clarify the debate on ideology. Ideology, as Williams says, did not begin with Marx, but it is an important idea in Marxist formulations about culture, especially about ideas and literature. Williams calls attention to the three main meanings of 'ideology' that may also be found in Marxism: a system of beliefs of a class or group; a system of false ideas or consciousness in contrast with true or scientific knowledge; the process of producing ideas and meanings (1977: 55). Except in polemics, he says, a correct definition of ideology is not possible. Instead, he finds the origin of the term in the work of Destutt de Tracy, a French philosopher of the late eighteenth century whose science of ideas is part of the empiricist tradition and is a part of zoology, and Williams proceeds to give a history of ideology (56; see also Plamenatz 1985: 15). Williams observes the central element of Marx's argument: 'Consciousness is seen from the beginning as part of the human material social process, and its products in "ideas" are then as much part of this process as material products themselves' (59–60). In 'ideology', Williams implies, there is an ambivalence or even multivalence that can lead to contradiction. He thinks that the limiting condition in 'ideology' as an idea, since Destutt, has been to limit processes of meaning and value to formed and separable theories or ideas. He also criticizes as a persistent error the attempt to take these processes back to sensations or practical consciousness, a 'material social process' that excludes these basic processes of signification. The practical connections, Williams argues, between ideas and theories on the one hand and the 'production of real life' on the other are in this material and social signifying process. If this realization occurs, then, in Williams' view, art and literature, which are products of the processes of culture and language and are not theories or ideas, may be approached in new ways. The old ways that Williams wants to avoid are abstraction, reduction and assimilation. This is the contribution that Williams sees Marxists making to literary and cultural studies in the 1970s (70–1). In 1977, Williams is asking what Frye and others have also asked for some time: will the terms 'ideology' and 'ideological' do?

Although I would like to discuss Louis Althusser and other theorists of ideology, I shall limit my discussion to those who respond directly to Frye (see Hart 1994 for a fuller discussion). Paul de Man criticizes Romantic aesthetic ideology, which sometimes informs Frye's writing (see also McGann 1984, Peckham 1985, Privateer 1991). Frye does appear sometimes to embrace the hermeneutic quest in Coleridge's terms, for unity in multiplicity, but not as the New Critics did in individual poems, but in the poem of poems, literature itself (see Norris 1988: xii). Although Frye recognizes the limits of Romanticism and, more specifically, of Blake, he builds his theory of literature out of his reading of Blake and displays visionary and Romantic traits in his works. His emphasis on irony and satire balances this side. Frye seeks the recreation of primitive modes of thought through metaphor and myth, which implies distance, but perhaps not as much as the early de Man. Frye asserts that language constructs reality and is arbitrary, but he still holds before him the hope for the poet's and reader's reconstruction of a world without subject-object split through metaphor. The early de Man renounces the dream of language that reconciles subject and object, mind and nature in a moment of access to truth through poetic imagination. Instead, he renounces this belief and views authentic reading as facing the contingency of language and the pedestrian figures, like metonymy, behind the privileged tropes, like metaphor and symbol. Only from *Allegories of Reading* onwards does de Man say that our predicament as humans means that we seek moments of transcendence and vision, which is not possible in language, and thereby misinterpret texts. De Man unties the connection between language and the human will (Norris 1988: xv-xvi; see also Minae Mizumura in Brooks et al. 1985: 92). In opposition to most interpreters of Romanticism, as Christopher Norris argues, de Man sees in the language of metaphor and symbol dead and arbitrary signs (Norris 1988: xviii). Frye is not so willing to give up this Romantic aesthetic ideology. De Man prefers metonymy, Frye metaphor to face existence and mortality.

In 1960 de Man considers metaphor to be at the centre of the shift from eighteenth-century poetics to Romantic poetics:

> in accordance with a dialectic that is more paradoxical than may appear at first sight, the structure of the language becomes increasingly metaphorical and the image – be it under the name of symbol or even of myth – comes to be considered as the most prominent dimension of the style. This tendency is still prevalent today, among poets as well as among critics. We find it quite natural that theoretical studies such as, for example, those of Gaston Bachelard in France, of Northrop Frye in America, or of William Empson in England should take the metaphor as their starting point for an investigation of literature in general – an approach that would have been inconceivable for Boileau, for Pope, and even still for Diderot.
>
> (1984: 2)

De Man finds in the 'Romantic' imagination, as exemplified in writers like Rousseau and Wordsworth, an independence from the outside world, a questioning of the ontological priority of the sensory object. In examining this 'oscillation in the status of the image' de Man wants to see how it is connected with the crisis that threatens to make poetry extinct although poetry 'remains the depository of hopes that no other activity of the mind seems able to offer' (1984: 16–17). The early de Man, like Frye, finds hope in poetry and also shows an interest in allegory, although he disagrees with Frye on intention (de Man 1983: 25–6, 268–9).

None the less, as Norris points out, de Man addresses Romantic ideology, giving artistic creation, especially as expressed through metaphor and symbol, a high value. De Man resists this ideology, which allows that metaphor and symbol transcend everyday perception and language and provide access to visionary or intuitive insight that overcomes time, change and contingency. Especially in the last decade of his life, de Man resists the mystification of genius and the aesthetic. Romantic theorists, like Coleridge, claim poetry as a source of secular salvation that arises from imaginative vision. De Man deconstructs the rhetorical mystification of tropes like symbol and metaphor. He is sceptical that the imagination, as in Schiller's aesthetic education, disguises in its idealizing, formalizing, utopian movement totalization, autocratic power and potential violence (Norris 1988: 28–30, 62–4; see also de Man 1979: 249, 1984: 263–90). Frye himself is ironic, comic and satiric: his wit will not allow his visionary imagination to soar or dominate, but he does end many of his works with visions. De Man thinks that Frye makes some of the same mistakes Wimsatt did in regard to intention because he 'reifies the literary entity into a natural object: with the added danger, moreover, that put in less ironic hands than his own, his theory could cause much more extensive damage' (1983: 26). Frye would counter that he is not, in Blake's terms, turning poetry into an idol. He himself recognizes something similar to de Man's apt criticism of the aesthetic impulse. The danger is there, and I shall later turn to Frye to see whether any aesthetic or poetic autonomy can work without creating social and political damage and whether by abolishing the aesthetic we give in to dominant ideologies as much as by unselfconsciously accepting an aesthetic ideology (see Frye 1986a for his views on de Man).

I want to turn briefly to three theorists from a later generation who discuss Frye in terms of ideology: Catherine Belsey, Fredric Jameson and Terry Eagleton. Belsey's discussion of Frye in *Critical Practice* (1980) is exemplary (1980: 21–9; for a discussion of these and other critics in relation to the ideological contexts of Frye's work, see Hart 1993b). She acknowledges his attempt to make literature into an autonomous and systematic discipline and thereby to oppose the unsystematic and elitist view of literature as a mystery of good taste. Although Belsey praises Frye's project and his range, she does not think his project succeeds. Even if Frye sees himself as at least in part being like a latter-day Aristotle, Belsey thinks that he is Neoplatonic because he sees 'literature as realizing a potential golden world rather than imitating a brazen one' (Belsey 1980: 22). Belsey calls attention to Frye's view of the autonomy of culture, which I think lies at the centre of Frye's desire to defend literature against political and social ideologies (Frye 1957: 127; see also Belsey 1980: 22). She points to Frye's use of anagogy, in which nature is in the mind of an infinite human, the 'imaginative limit of desire, which is infinite, eternal, and hence apocalyptic', and is not reality (Frye 1957: 119, Belsey 23–4). In Belsey's reading of Frye, he admits, like the New Critics, that human nature is essential and unchanging and that literature transcends ideology and history (Belsey 1980: 24). Belsey sees that Frye catches glimpses of the conventional nature of meaning, which is more than a glimpse, especially in his later work (1980: 26). She proposes a break with the empiricist-idealist tradition of Anglo-American criticism, a radical position which, in her view, Frye glimpses when speaking about the plurality of meaning, and does away with implicit intention and the tyranny of the author (26–7; see also Frye 1957: 17–18, 87). Frye contains pluralism, according to Belsey, with a 'repressive pluralism' that does not allow for progress through the conflict of points of view and that is accommodating and breaks down barriers between approaches (Belsey 1980: 28). Belsey prefers dialectical materialism to Frye's classless society in the imagination (Belsey 1980: 28, Frye 1957: 347–8; see also Fekete 1977: 107–31). She wants human action in society and thinks that criticism cannot be detached from society and has ideological and social implications. Arguments over meaning and language are by definition, for Belsey, ideological: there can be no independent world or autonomy for literature and for criticism (1980: 29). This is the crux between Belsey and Frye, between Frye and his critics from the 'left'.

This is a crucial difference and cannot be wished away. It really comes down to belief and metaphysics. Which came first, matter or ideas? Which is prior, ideology or mythology? Is liberal humanist imagination or Marxist ideology the best means of approaching literature and criticism? I have always been sceptical about premises or assumptions, even my own, because they are conscious or unconscious conclusions masquerading as provenance or origin or a foundational truth. I am interested in both sides of the argument, Frye's and the critics' who have implicitly and explicitly brought him to trial or engaged him, because together they tell us something about literature and ideology. One of my goals is to see whether the late Frye has elaborated a position on ideology beyond that in *Anatomy*, which Belsey and others examine because of the fame and centrality of the book to criticism in English.

Fredric Jameson is interested in 'the problem of the proper uses of such critical gestures as demystification and ideological unmasking', but he says that his focus on narrative analysis will not allow him to ignore its 'great pioneers', like Frye, whose contributions are fundamental to that study (Jameson 1981: 12). Like Belsey, Jameson obviously admires Frye while he differs from him.

In *The Political Unconscious* (1981) Jameson argues that Frye's archetypal criticism valorizes desire as Freud's hermeneutic does and that it is valuable because it conceives of the function of culture in explicit social terms. Jameson contrasts myth criticism with Marxism: the one 'proposes an unbroken continuity between the social relations and narrative forms of primitive society and the cultural objects of our own', whereas the other stresses 'the radical break between the two social formations' (1981: 68–9). The break demonstrates how effectively capitalism has dissolved older forms of collective relations, so that their cultural productions, like their myths, appear to us as dead languages and codices, so that, for Jameson, Frye's 'virtual contemporary reinvention of the four-fold hermeneutic' of the theological tradition becomes a nexus for testing the Marxist argument for rupture (1981: 69). What is so engaging about Jameson's engagement of Frye is that he is not parochial or hostile about, or ashamed of, religion. Frye is not far from Voltaire in calling Christianity to task for its grim historical record, but he does use the structures, if not always the content, of a Christian hermeneutic (Frye 1991a). According to Jameson, 'for any contemporary re-evaluation of the problem of interpretation, the most vital exchange of energies inevitably takes place between the two poles of the psychoanalytic and the theological' (1981: 69). Jameson sees Frye's greatness in his willingness to discuss community and to draw social interpretative consequences from 'religion as collective representation' (69). Religious figuration becomes a symbolic space in which the collectivity figures itself and celebrates its unity. Literature is, in Jameson's interpretation of Frye, a weaker form of myth and 'must be informed by what we have called a political unconscious, that all literature must be read as a symbolic meditation on the destiny of community' (70). Jameson wonders why Frye sees this point and then retreats. In Frye's apocalyptic vision of desire, of the great human body, which also fascinated Belsey, Jameson finds that Frye moves from the left Freudian individuality to a figure of social revolution (see Frye 1957: 119).

Jameson is aware that Marxism cannot simply practise a negative dialectic, in which ideology is false consciousness or structural limitation, which overshadows the Marxian tradition that includes equivalents to Paul Ricœur's positive hermeneutic or doctrine of meaning. For Jameson, Ernst Bloch's ideal of hope, Bakhtin's idea of the dialogic as a rupture in the one-dimensional bourgeois narrative and as a carnivalesque dispersal of the dominant culture's hegemonic order, and the Frankfurt school's notion of strong memory as the trace of gratification and of the revolutionary power of that promise of happiness inscribed in the aesthetic text all 'hint at a variety of options for articulating a properly Marxian version of meaning beyond the purely ideological' (1981: 285). The desire to get beyond the 'purely' ideological, if anything human can be pure, is something that Frye and Jameson share with many others. How possible that goal is, is open to question, especially when there is probably no such thing as an essence of ideology. Jameson values Frye's system, especially as it allows for the distinction of the moral (the level of the individual soul or, in Jameson's words, 'the libidinal Utopia of the individual body') from the anagogical, which rewrites individual visions of utopian transfiguration in terms of the collective, the destiny of humanity. This distinction depends on the relation of Frye's scheme to the medieval system of four levels. Frye's system helps Jameson set out a Marxist positive hermeneutic based on social class, which also informs the Marxist negative hermeneutic of class character and ideology (Jameson 1981: 286). Jameson does not want to see the Marxist negative hermeneutic practised in isolation because it dwindles into an instrumental approach to culture, but warns that Frye's positive hermeneutic can relax into the religious and theological, the edifying and moralistic if class dynamics and cultural production do not inform it (291–2). Jameson's project is a 'simultaneous recognition of the ideological and Utopian meaning of cultural artifacts' that allows Marxist cultural study to play its role in political praxis, the *raison d'être* of Marxism (299). Like Frye, Jameson gravitates to double recognition, perhaps a two-eyed version of the Aristotelian *anagnorisis* or the modernist individual insight (Freud's reconstruction of the Oedipal 'all comes clear now', Joyce's Epiphanies, and Henry James' moments of illumination) socialized.

With some irony, Terry Eagleton says that 'we shall soon see Marxist criticism comfortably wedged between Freudian and mythological approaches to literature, as yet one more stimulating academic "approach"', but reminds his readers that 'Marxism is a scientific theory of human societies and of the practice of transforming them' and that its narrative is the story of 'the struggles of men and women to free themselves from certain forms of exploitation and oppression', hardly, in Eagleton's view, an academic exercise (1976b: vii). Marxist criticism is part of the theoretical analysis that attempts to understand ideologies, which Eagleton defines as 'the ideas, values and feelings . . . available to us only in literature' (viii). Eagleton thinks that to understand ideologies allows us to understand the past and the present better, which in turn contributes to human liberation (viii, 76). More specifically, Eagleton's critique of Frye's ideological position is also helpful and perceptive. His summary of Frye's position in *Anatomy* is instructive, if not sympathetic:

> Literature is not a way of knowing reality but a kind of collective utopian dreaming which has gone on throughout history, an expression of those fundamental human desires which have given rise to civilization itself, but which are never fully satisfied there. It is not to be seen as the self-expression of the individual authors, who are no more than functions of this universal system: it springs from the collective subject of the human race itself, which is how it comes to embody 'archetypes' or figures of universal significance.
>
> (Eagleton 1983b: 93)

In Frye's work Eagleton finds an emphasis on the utopian root of literature that results from 'a deep fear of the actual social world, a distaste for history itself' (1983b: 93). Eagleton also says that Frye thinks of literature as a spiritual home free of this society and of referential language (words that refer to the world), represents his *mythoi* in pre-urban natural images in a way that shows a nostalgia for a history before industrialism, considers history to be determinism and bondage, and combines beautifully extreme aestheticism and scientific classification. Paradoxically, in Eagleton's view, Frye 'maintains literature as an imaginary alternative to modern society while rendering criticism respectable in that society's terms' (93). In Frye's work Eagleton sees iconoclasm and Romantic yearning, an anti-humanist decentring of the human subject and a centring on the collective literary system and a Christian humanism in which the desire that drives literature and civilization will be fulfilled in the kingdom of God. Frye's theory of literature treats it as a displaced version of religion or, in Eagleton's view, 'an essential palliative for the failure of religious ideology' that gives us various myths that are relevant to social life

(93). Here, Eagleton is referring to Frye's *The Critical Path* (1971), which balances conservative myths of concern, which tend towards authoritarianism, with liberal myths of freedom, which tend towards social irresponsibility.

More recently, Eagleton has argued for the positive heritage of liberal humanism for critics on the left. This argument does not mean that we should approach only the bourgeois, liberal humanist, like Frye, for intellectual leadership, but that this heritage, a major part of our history, should not be cast aside. Eagleton's attempt to link aesthetics and political ideologies is an interesting and necessary project. As much of the energy in critical theory has come from the left and from feminism in the past ten years or more, it is important to be critical of, as well as enabled by, these positions, however much they may or may not be part of our own work. Eagleton's assessment is perceptive:

> But I must confess that I also have in my sights those on the political left for whom the aesthetic is simply 'bourgeois ideology', to be worsted and ousted by alternative forms of cultural politics. The aesthetic is indeed ... a bourgeois concept in the most literal historical sense, hatched and nurtured in the Enlightenment; but only for the drastically undialectical thought of a vulgar Marxist or 'post-Marxist' trend of thought could this fact cue an automatic condemnation. It is left moralism, not historical materialism, which having established the bourgeois provenance of a particular concept, practice or institution, then disowns it in an access of ideological purity.
>
> (1990: 8)

Eagleton's radical critique suggests that we use what we can from the past and dispose, without nostalgia, of what we cannot. While I agree with this approach, I do so only up to a point: the past reads us as we read the past. Like Eagleton, I do not think that we can deny bourgeois liberal humanism in our past, or, for that matter, in our present. There is room for these categories yet because we still live and read them. Eagleton then says:

> From the *Communist Manifesto* onwards, Marxism has never ceased to sing the praises of the bourgeoisie – to cherish and recollect that in its great revolutionary heritage from which radicals must either enduringly learn, or face the prospect of a closed, illiberal socialist order in the future. Those who have now been correctly programmed to reach for their decentred subjectivities at the very mention of the dread phrase 'liberal humanist' repressively disavow the very history

which constitutes them, which is by no means uniformly negative or oppressive. We forget at our political peril the heroic struggles of earlier 'liberal humanists' against the brutal autocracies of feudalist absolutism. If we can and must be severe critics of Enlightenment, it is Enlightenment which has empowered us to be so. Here, as always, the most intractable process of emancipation is that which involves freeing ourselves from ourselves.

(1990: 8)

Here, in Eagleton's recent work, as in Frye's later books, there is a desire for change and social transformation. Frye, and the other 'liberal humanists' who have written or write on behalf of political prisoners under the aegis of Amnesty International, are still helping in the struggle for human freedom and are not merely romantic figures or footnotes from the past. Frye understood the difficulties of getting beyond ideology. He took a critical path that shares some of the same terrain as Eagleton's. For us all, and Paul de Man is instructive in this regard, to free ourselves from ourselves is the most critical and difficult task at hand. And ideology is at the centre of this problem.

A convergence between Eagleton and the later de Man has been noted by Eagleton and others (Eagleton 1990: 9–10; see also Anderson 1979: ch. 4). This example of seemingly divergent theorists agreeing on important points might be an example of the critical conversation Frye thought lies beneath surface differences (Frye 1982b, 1986a, 1990e). Whether this underlying unity exists and whether the universal may be a reconstructed myth that fascinated Frye but that has no status as 'fact' is open to question. Eagleton's description of this convergence with de Man is significant because it shakes up easy stereotypes in recent critical debate and calls attention to the power and the dangers of naturalizing the aesthetic:

De Man's later writing represents a bracing, deeply intricate de-mystification of the idea of the aesthetic which, it could be claimed, was present in his thought throughout; and there is much that he has to say on this score with which I find myself in entire agreement. For de Man, aesthetic ideology involves a phenomenalist reduction of the linguistic to the sensuously empirical, a confusing of mind and world, sign and thing, cognition and percept, which is consecrated in the Hegelian symbol and resisted by Kant's rigorous demarcation of aesthetic judgement from the cognitive, ethical and political realms.

(Eagleton 1990: 10)

This confusion of word for world is a kind of linguistic imperialism in which all things are seen in terms of language. There is no denying the importance of language and the difficulty of getting through it to the world, but to equate the two is dangerous and serious because language is so much a part of our daily lives. If painters were to say the equivalent of what literary critics do – that the world is paint – we might not take the doctrine so seriously. Eagleton then says:

> Such aesthetic ideology, by repressing the contingent, aporetic relation which holds between the spheres of language and the real, naturalizes or phenomenalizes the former, and is thus in danger of converting the accidents of meaning to organic natural process in the characteristic manner of ideological thought. A valuable, resourceful politics is undoubtedly at work here, *pace* those left-wing critics for whom de Man is merely an unregenerate 'formalist'. But it is a politics bought at an enormous cost. In what one might see as an excessive reaction to his own earlier involvements with organicist ideologies of an extreme right-wing kind, de Man is led to suppress the potentially positive dimensions of the aesthetic in a way which perpetuates, if now in a wholly new style, his earlier hostility to an emancipatory politics.
>
> (10)

This negation of the politics of liberation is what Eagleton also objected to in Frye. (For a feminist critique of deconstruction and myth criticism – including Frye and McLuhan – as displaced theology, see Humm 1986: 7–8, 89–90; see also Hart 1993e). Frye would be glad to hear Eagleton speak about the positive nature of the aesthetic and shares with Eagleton, and perhaps the later de Man, an abhorrence of the fascist ideologies, including that of the organic society. From the outbreak of the Second World War, as we have seen, Frye wrote against fascism and, throughout his career, objects to the naivete of Eliot, Pound and Yeats in sympathizing with the fascist cause.

II

Northrop Frye's theory of literature gives priority to mythology over ideology, but acknowledges the importance and pervasiveness of the ideological (for other views, see Todd 1988: 86–7, Kavanagh 1991: 306–20, Bhabha 1990a, Perry 1987). It admits the historicity of the structural principles that literature translates from mythology but allows for their transhistorical, not transcendental, communication. Frye's thoughts on belief and ideology are central to the debate on the politics of interpretation that continues but that was particularly evident in the volume with that same name which W. J. T. Mitchell edited in 1983 (see Mitchell, Eagleton 1983a and Hogan 1990: 4–11). Another aspect of Frye's ideology or theoretical assumptions arises from his interest and participation in Romanticism, which Frye himself admits, especially in relation to the unity of mental elements in creation and the autonomy of the creative person (Frye 1986a: 51; Siskin 1988: 6–7; see also McGann 1983: 3–12). Frye is a visionary and a mythopoeic critic: he participates in the politics of vision, if not in the politics of imagination and apocalypse. Romanticism concerns itself with politics as well as vision, imagination and apocalypse. Like other Romantic poets, Wordsworth, according to M. H. Abrams, involved himself with political and social commentary but also transposed into the metaphors of mind in his poetry the political theories of the Enlightenment and the events and ideals of the French Revolution, particularly that of liberty (Abrams 1971: 357; see also 327–72). Abrams' view on metaphor is in keeping with Frye's, except that, like Gerard Manley Hopkins, Frye emphasizes metaphor as underthought that can run counter to or well up to the surface argument of a poem or a philosophical system. While calling attention to the Romantic aspect of Frye's views on ideology, which would be hardly surprising as he wrote his first book on Blake, I do not want to reduce his consideration of the ideological to just another voice of Romanticism. Instead, it is better to let Frye speak for himself as much as possible, particularly in *Words with Power*, his most sustained work on ideology, which contains his critique of ideology and his fascination with it.

Near the beginning of *Words with Power* Frye summarizes his argument:

> every human society possesses a mythology which is inherited, transmitted and diversified by literature. Comparative mythology is a fascinating subject, but it is quickly exhausted as a scholarly study if it remains simply a configuration of patterns. It is generally understood that it needs to be grounded in psychology or anthropology: it is much less understood that its central and most important extension is into literature (along with the criticism of literature) which incarnates a mythology in a historical context. In the opposite direction, a literary criticism that cuts off its own cultural and historical roots in mythology becomes sterile even more quickly. Some forms of it stop with an analytic disintegrating of texts as an end in itself; others study literature as a historical or ideological phenomenon, and its works as documents illustrating something outside literature. But this leaves out the central structural principles

that literature derives from myth, the principles that give literature its communicating power across the centuries through all ideological changes. Such structural principles are certainly conditioned by social and historical factors and do not transcend them, but they retain a continuity of form that points to an identity of the literary organism distinct from all its adaptations to its social environment.

(1990e: xiii)

Frye stresses mythology as the historical root of literature that passes structures on to it that are translated in a historical context but maintain a continuity of form. He is claiming different origins from some of his critics. He also insists that literature, despite its participation in ideological and historical changes, has a certain integrity. In an interview with David Cayley at Massey College in Toronto in December 1989, Frye also insists on the integrity of criticism and in some ways regrets having used the word 'autonomy' in *Anatomy* in 1957 because those who wanted to construed Frye's use of the word as meaning that he thought that criticism 'was a retreat from the world' (Cayley 1991: 26). Frye is not saying that we can turn from the world, with its history and ideology, but that because of the continuous forms that literature translates from mythology we can communicate as writers and critics despite historical and ideological change. This claim seems to be for an inessential essence or a transhistorical historicity. Frye differs from other recent theorists, some of whom we have discussed, especially those who proclaim the post-modern condition, because he stresses the possibility of communication over time and they do not.

The condition of subordinating literature and criticism to ideology, politics and other discourses represents, in Frye's view, the way things have always been and not a revolutionary or post-modern position. Western literature and the Bible have been given a putative but not an actual pre-eminence. Other discourses or linguistic forms are the sources of authority in society, so that the Bible's pre-eminence

is a close parallel to the traditional role of literature in relation to the ideologies that surround it in every age, where the very different linguistic structures of ideology and dialectic are normally regarded as superior and more trustworthy approaches to whatever words are supposed to do for us. The tendency to subordinate literary to other forms of language, though it has had its questioners, is essentially unchanged.

(Frye 1990e: xiv)

Frye thinks that literary critics have long been part of the problem. Ever since Plato, he argues, most of them have linked the word 'thought' with concepts and dialectic and have ignored poetic and imaginative thought (xvi). In *Anatomy* Frye's heuristic assumption was that, as the word *theoria* implies, criticism is not parasitical on literature and 'is a coherent but not exhaustible subject' (xvii). Part of Frye's stance, as he explains it, is a defence of the creativity of criticism, although he now wonders whether the situation has so reversed itself that the integrity of literature and other traditional verbal uses need to be defended. Beneath 'some temporary vogue or ideological illusion', Frye observes critical insight and wisdom, particularly in relation to single authors and historical periods (xix).

In *Words with Power* not surprisingly Frye is interested in the relation between words and power (1990e: 9). He is not an adherent of logical positivism, which shares with post-modernism a scepticism about metaphysics. In the earlier part of the twentieth century, Frye says, logical positivists said

> that metaphysics was a gigantic verbal illusion based on a mis-understanding of what language can do. One who has read, say, Aristotle's *Metaphysics* to the great enlargement and refreshment of his mind is not likely to take this very seriously, whatever his own philosophical qualifications.
>
> (10)

Frye does not agree with the logical positivists' integration of the conceptual and descriptive modes of language. For him, metaphysical systems are impressive structures that attempt 'to present the world to the conscious mind' (10). Frye astutely quotes Whitehead to make his case: 'Every philosophy is tinged with the coloring of some secret imaginative background, which never emerges explicitly into trains of reasoning'(12). He warns us about the excluded and that the logic of an argument leads us away from the realization that 'the argument is what the person constructing the argument wants to be true' (12). Moreover, Frye calls on the existentialism that stressed conceptual writers like Augustine, Pascal and Kierkegaard who emphasized the inseparability of the personal and the conceptual in writing (13). A discussion of 'power', which has become a central term in new historicism, arises in the debate on justice in the first book of Plato's *Republic*. Frye thinks of Socrates as a more agile and generous sophist than his opponent Thrasymachus, even though the one engages in dialectic and wants to define the good while the other practises rhetoric and thinks that good and evil are relative terms. Whereas Socrates talks about good words, Thrasymachus is speaking for the wordless world of power. He is a forerunner of Machiavelli and Hobbes and Marx and the late Nietzsche, who tell us about a world where material or other forces of power are effective and words are not, and where the use of such a word as justice means chiefly that someone who holds power is rationalizing the fact that he is going to go on holding it.

(14)

The *Republic* becomes, for Frye, 'a personal vision from the mind of Socrates' (15). Frye himself provides his own vision of ideology, in which he sets out the relation between dialectic, or argument, and rhetoric, or persuasion.

He associates rhetoric and ideology. In Christian ideology it is not possible or desirable to have a disinterested dialectic and 'to distinguish what we believe from what we believe we believe' (Frye 1990e: 16; see also Frye 1982b: 229). Our actions manifest our beliefs. Frye defines ideologies as 'the great frameworks of accepted (and by the great majority unexamined) assumptions', which are generally 'structures of authority, so far as verbal structures can articulate and rationalize authority' (1990e: 15). For him, ideology proceeds with some regard to dialogue with those outside it, but when the established social authority insists on given ideological postulates as essential, then dialectic is subordinated to the persuasion of rhetoric, or oratory, in order to establish conviction (16–17). Frye looks at the worst cases of rhetoric, when occasion narrows from the historical to the immediate, in order to clarify the relation between rhetoric and ideology. If dialectics can lead to endless argument, rhetoric can shut it down. The rhetorical use of *ad hominem* attack, of language as a personal weapon, stops debate because, for instance, one can be told that one is saying something because one has or lacks certain beliefs or is a woman, or whatever (18). But Frye does not think that all ideology is so active. There is a passive side to the ideological, 'where every verbal structure, simply by being conditioned by its social and historical environment, reflects that conditioning' (18).

Frye says that philosophers often present their metaphysical systems spacially, as if the schemas were above time, but time goes on and they are all too temporal. A thinker's work is more apt to be regarded as an ideological document the longer its author has been dead. For Frye, all verbal structures reach ideology, which is like a delta, an image that implies divergence and convergence, relation, multiplicity, branches, an end before language pours out into the oceanic, and perhaps even fertility. None the less, Frye qualifies this image: the most insistent reason is 'the constant tendency for any ideology to collapse into tyranny or mob rule' (1990e: 19). He does not deny the complexity and even the positive sides of ideology:

An ideology is most beneficial when it has the least power, when its assumptions can be most freely challenged by others, when the terrible claws of ideological authority, inquisitions and secret police and the like, are not simply pared but removed altogether.

(19)

It is important to ensure the independence of descriptive and conceptual modes by maintaining their standards of verbal authority. He notes that at any time, a new historical or scientific study may undermine an ideology. Frye appeals to reason as an arbiter but does so with qualifications and by making a distinction between the rational and the reasonable. To be reasonable, in Frye's scheme, is to be aware that all rational arguments are half-truths and that the other half needs to be included in a flexible and tolerant compromise.

The current ideological debate interests Frye. As opposed to the two extremes now at work in the debate, he concludes that 'Fact and concept can never be divided from ideology, but they can usually be distinguished' (Frye 1990e: 19). The extremes, according to Frye, are that our period represents an explosion in information, a time when none of us is free from assumptions or commitments, and that complete detachment is impossible. In Frye's view, the first position denies the ideological containers the information comes in and the second ignores the different degrees of detachment and considers to be futile the effort to be intellectually honest with people of different commitments (19–20). Frye is teleological and advocates ideal goals: although they can never be reached in human life, they represent important directions in which people can turn. Ideologies are mortal and, like the humans that construct them, are born, decay and die. Alternatively, they can metamorphose just as Christian ideology has in response to the rise of science and secular philosophy (20).

Mythology is prior to ideology in Frye's scheme, but in *Words with Power*, he discusses ideology first in order to establish mythology as an 'excluded initiative', as something even more inclusive than ideology (1990e: 20). What interests Frye is what first creates ideology and why social authority rationalizes its power in words rather than, as Thrasymachus suggested, asserting it. He thinks that the ideological unity of a speaker, speech and listener is human and social and that ideologies develop in proportion to the human realization of humanity's dominance over nature, which a primitive sense of helplessness and alienation precedes (20–1). For Frye, the ideological world 'tends to become a world of the human and the non-human, with nothing that is personal in it outside the human' (21). He argues that humans still feel alienation in a non-human environment. There are, for Frye, mysteries of birth and death, the arbitrariness of life, the awe and wonder before nature and the universe that make us unsatisfied with description, concept and ideology. The imaginative is open-ended and anti-dogmatic and so meets these needs for something other than the ideological (22). The imaginative, which occupies the realm of the putative and of possible worlds, descends from the Romantics:

> An imaginative response is one in which the distinction between the emotional and the intellectual has disappeared, and in which ordinary consciousness is only one of many possible psychic elements, the fantastic and the dreamlike having conventionally an equal status. The criterion of the imaginative is the conceivable, not the real, and it expresses the hypothetical or assumed, not the actual. It is clear that such a criterion takes us into the verbal area we call literature.
>
> (22)

Frye views literature as a fictional world (Hart 1988). But literature is not mythology, even if it descends historically from it. Narratives in literature arise from mythology, or the aggregate of myths (Frye 1990e: 22). Philip Sidney's influence is apparent when Frye says that poets need not assert the reality of anything they are representing. Frye admits that this stance deprives them of social usefulness and influence. Ideology excludes but assumes an initiative: myth. These myths express human bewilderment about the reason we are here and the direction in which we are going (23).

Frye's view that literature is a critique of ideology is a counterbalance for all the theorists today who assert that literature is ideology. But his idea that ideology is prevalent and finds its expression through a dominant class is not much different from that of Marx or of Althusser. Frye suggests that literature is a subversive means of opposing the dominant ideology and the class structure that supports it, so that he takes a different tack from those who proclaim the powerlessness of literature and the ineffectiveness of the imagination before the material forces in the world. Here is Frye's genealogy of ideology:

> An ideology starts by providing its own version of whatever in its traditional mythology it considers relevant, and uses this version to form and enforce a social contract. An ideology is thus an applied mythology, and its adaptations of myths are the ones that, when we

are inside an ideological structure, we must believe, or say we believe. Belief, in its usual sense, does not go beyond a declaration of adherence to an ideology (GC [*Great Code*] 229).

(1990e: 23–4)

Frye sets out what he thinks is the normal course for ideology and creates a context for his study of mythology that makes it subversive. He is attempting to beat ideological critics at their own game by portraying his cause as subversive:

> An ideology normally conveys something of this kind: 'Your social order is not always the way you would have it, but it is the best you can hope for at present, as well as the one the gods have decreed for you. Obey and work.' Persecution and intolerance result from an ideology's determination, as expressed through its priesthood, or whatever corresponds to a priesthood, backed up by its ascendant class in general, to make its mythological canon the only possible one to commit oneself to, all others being denounced as heretical, morbid, unreal or evil. This means that there is a strong resistance within an ideology to placing its excluded initiative, the myth it lives by, into focus and examining it in a broader perspective.
>
> (24)

Frye considers the assertionless nature of literature, which asks for the suspension of judgement and a variety of reactions, to be more corrosive of ideologies than rational scepticism is. Reason may be necessary in the face of a hysterical society, but, Frye says, it acts as a conscious filter of fantasy or dream, which function in literature. Every social contract gives the poet a pretend realm, not to be taken seriously, unless the poet returns to an ideological mode (Frye 1990e: 24). Frye admits that in an age of clashing ideologies, a suspicion exists that myth inspires bad ideology. For him, mythology precedes ideology and both can be good or bad. The word 'mythology' should not be regarded simply as trivial or bad ideology, other peoples' ideology, or sick mythology. Frye calls on Coleridge's idea that we must often distinguish where we cannot divide, thereby preserving the whole and the distinctive parts. For instance, Frye defines criticism as 'the theory of words and of verbal meaning' and distinguishes it from dialectics, rhetoric and the other forms of verbal practice that he mentions (26). He reformulates a critical position, which he consolidated in *Anatomy*, that many critics are unwilling to get past ideology in discussing literature because they are more interested in the relation of literature to some ideological interest – religious, radical, feminist, historical or whatever. Frye thinks that some critics should be interested in literature in terms of its own metaphorical and mythical language, which is primary to literature. He does not wish to deny or belittle the ideological relations of literature, but he wants 'to ascertain more clearly what it is that is being related' (27). In Frye's scheme 'criticism is language that expresses the awareness of language' and its expository prose is meant to relate poetry to its wider verbal contexts (27). As literary works communicate in mythical wholes, form and content are inextricably related (27). Language is a means of intensifying consciousness: criticism separates science from superstition, philosophy and politics from propaganda, history from rumour and legend and so on. Although criticism plays a similar role in literature, it is not built into the structure of literature and thus is more elusive. An individual produces the creative structure of literature, while criticism forms a social consensus around it. Intensified language turns metaphorical, a quality that often marks literature, so that one has only to look at literature to intensify consciousness. Frye sets out Dante's Virgil as his emblem of 'literature in its Arnoldian function of criticism as a "criticism of life", the vision of existence, detached but not withdrawn from it' (28). But Frye, who owes much to Dante and medieval theory, says that Beatrice represents a higher awareness or criticism of the Virgilian vision, that limits are often open doors.

The open door that Frye chooses is the contrast between two forms of rhetorical language, the rhetorical and the ideological, in other words, the imaginative and the persuasive (Frye 1990e: 29). He sees the trial of Socrates as a trial of a revolution in verbal culture in which *logos* superseded *mythos*, dialectic or argument, storytelling or narrative. Here, Frye has shown a constant position in defending the mythical and metaphorical language of poetry and has prefigured Derrida and others who have questioned the propositions of philosophy with the metaphors of poetry. In *La Dissemination* (1972) Derrida looks at the 'literary', or the effects of language that are not conceptual, and the first essay, 'La Pharmacie de Platon', is an examination of writing in Plato. Frye reiterates his defence of literature and poetics, a position that he takes from the beginning of his career and has made, most notably, in *Fearful Symmetry* and *Anatomy*:

> From Plato and Aristotle to the Hellenistic philosophies, from them to Christian theology and scholasticism, and from there to the secular ideologies of our own time, democratic or Marxist or whatever, the ascendancy of dialectician over poet has been relatively constant.
>
> (1990e: 33)

Myths that the *logos* adapts for a social function are ideological; those that are no longer believed or part of ritual are literary (33). What keeps Frye's criticism representing an ideological translation of the mythology of the literature it discusses? Even though Frye uses myth and metaphor in his criticism, can he escape argument as readily as a lyric poet? Would this choice of genre, of criticism, make literary criticism an inferior kind of writing? Possibly, Frye does not get around this problem as much as he would like to think. By proclaiming that mythology as it is translated into literature is a critique of ideology is he not making that into a concept that supports an ideology? Would it not be better to see argument and myth co-existing in Plato's *Phaedrus*, Shakespeare's *Troilus and Cressida* and *Othello* and Thomas Mann's *The Magic Mountain*? Frye admired the modernists and their myth-making. Perhaps he preferred Eliot's *The Waste Land*, Woolf's *To the Lighthouse* and Joyce's *Finnegans Wake* because they were metaphorical and mythical stream-of-consciousness and affirm little. One can argue that Frye's prose is aphoristic and creates a tension with his system, that he tells and retells stories and that he builds up his own 'fictional' or metaphysical system, but he must also seem, as a critic, to have an argument. None the less, Frye, Derrida, Kristeva and others have challenged this notion of argumentation and criticism. Perhaps they all move along a sliding and fluid scale between the mythological and the ideological. The tension and close relation between Othello's mythological storytelling and Iago's ideological argumentation help to give Shakespeare's play dramatic power. Perhaps this kind of relational tension provides the critical work of Frye and others with a similar power.

Ideology attempts to make mythology secondary and subservient. Using Frye's analysis of Hegel, which I outline briefly below, we can observe that Frye is in danger of reversing the opposite and thus making the work of ideological critics secondary. He tries hard not to reverse the binary opposition of traditional Western values. Perhaps because of the recent relative neglect of mythology, Frye has to overstate his case just as ideological critics probably had to when his theory of literature was at its height. Frye agrees with post-structuralists about the importation of the 'transcendental signified' into Christian institutional religion. He thinks that the opening of John's Gospel attempts to identify *logos* and *mythos*. But Calvin, Trotsky and other ideologues have made words the servants of acts (Frye 1990e: 34). Even though Frye shares with Sidney the view that the poet 'never affirmeth', he distances himself from Sidney's assumptions that poetry must serve or cannot compete with dialectic because it is primitive, childish and imaginative and it supplies a rhetorical analogue to the ascendant ideology of its time (35–6). Allegory and realism are the displacements of myth in the service of ideology (36–7). Frye asserts, as the new historicists do, that 'ideological language supports the anxieties of social authority' (37).

Dialectic supports ideology but is limited because it has to assert a truth whose opposite must be false. Frye appeals to Hegel's insight – his 'dialectic'. Frye omits Hegel's term, but its silent resonance can make Frye's use of the earlier form of the word confusing when it is applied transhistorically. Hegel demonstrated that every affirmation is partial and contains its own opposite, which is attached to the affirmation. This Hegelian dialectic, which Marx incorporated into historical or dialectical materialism, informs Frye and the post-structuralist writers, like Derrida, who show the limitations and one-sidedness of binary oppositions. Frye says that the most effective ideologies now are those which have become flexible and tolerant and have thus taken into consideration Hegel's insight that a statement contains its opposite (38). Liberalism may be the unnamed example that Frye would cite as such an ideology.

Writers are uncertain about their status, their authority, because of the ideological pressures on them and persecutions against them (Frye 1990e: 39). In the popular mind discursive prose is more serious than poetry because the playfulness and pleasure of poems throw into question the work ethic (41). Frye returns to the myths of concern, which, along with the myths of freedom, he first sets out in detail in *The Critical Path* (1971) but which he is exploring as early as *The Modern Century* (1967b: 105–6; see also 'Ideas' 1990: 24; Cayley 1991: 33–4). In *The Critical Path*, as we have seen, Frye says that there are two related opposites – as in a Hegelian dialectic – two opposing myths in Western culture: the myth of freedom and the myth of concern. The myth of freedom is liberal, detached and individual and emphasizes tolerance, correspondence and objectivity, whereas the myth of concern is conservative and communal and stresses belief, coherence and authority. These two myths unite and produce the social context of literature. But in *Words with Power*, Frye is interested in the conservative myths of concern. He declares, keeping in mind Coleridge's principle of the distinguishable indivisible, 'I should distinguish primary and secondary concern, even though there is no real boundary line between them' (Frye 1990e: 42). Primary concerns are made up of four areas: food and drink, sex, property and liberty of movement. Secondary concerns grow out of the social contract, such as patriotism, religion and class attitudes, and 'develop from the ideological aspect of myth, and consequently tend to be directly expressed in ideological prose language' (42). Frye does not deny the ideological nature of mythology, as some of his critics have proposed, but he limits the effect of ideology to secondary concerns, more specifically by calling them rationalizations of these concerns (43). He says that the longer one looks at storytelling patterns, or myths, the more clearly their connections to primary concerns, especially the anxiety of not having these concerns fulfilled, appear. Anxiety and desire, which are the concerns of new historicism and psychoanalytical criticism respectively, lie at the centre of Frye's view of the social role of literature. Any fiction written in the past two centuries, Frye says, will show primary and secondary concerns, survival and basic needs as well as ideological questions. Frye remains hopeful that no matter how ridden with anxiety and how ironic this fiction is, it also possesses an underlying positive impulse, the one 'to express a concern for more abundant life . . . a *gaya scienza*, a form of play or self-contained energy' (43). Throughout history, as Frye repeats in *The Double Vision* (1991), in part a kind of public redaction of *Words with Power* just as *The Educated Imagination* (1963) is of *Anatomy*, secondary concerns have been given priority over primary ones (1990e: 43; see also 1991a: 6). For many writers who are victims of a hostile ideology, truth becomes a dedication to primary concerns (44).

Ideological principles, according to Frye, are metonymic because they are substituted for the ideals that primary concern envisages. In other words, we cannot have a perfect society, so what we have is the best available, and the primary goals are postponed indefinitely (Frye 1990e: 44). Frye contrasts the ideals of Marxism and democracy with their actualities:

> Marx owes his status as a prophetic thinker to the incisiveness with which he analyzed the ideology of capitalism in relation to the primary needs and anxieties of an alienated working class. But the tactical adaptations of Marxism, when it comes to power, turn it into another defensive ideology, in contrast to the original Marxist ideal of a world without classes or states. Similarly, the dynamic of democracy rests on its primary concern for what the American Constitution calls life, liberty, and the pursuit of happiness. But democratic ideology is mainly the camouflage of an oligarchy or of various pressure groups within the society.
>
> (44)

Frye sees the second half of the twentieth century as one in which there is a growing revolt against ideologies and an attempt to emphasize primary concerns of body and mind, of peace, freedom and dignity (45). He takes the title of his book from Luke 4: 32 to suggest a power of words, rather than of guns, that is consistent with human survival. The ideological conflicts of the early twentieth century made Frye suspicious of the benefits of ideology and its promise in the life-and-death questions that face humanity (45–6).

Frye looks at the relation between vision and ideology, which is a central concern of my study, and uses Gibbon's *Decline and Fall* as an illustration. His comments on Gibbon's book might suggest how Frye thinks his own work might be remembered:

> It soon dates as the definitive authority on the subject, but it continues to be read because of its great conceptual power, its vision of the ancient world gradually taking on the outlines of the modern one. Whether the details of this vision are right or wrong is not relevant just here: they are expressed in a coherent and eloquent narrative, and such things are always right, so far as they go. Eventually the book enters the rhetorical area (GC [*The Great Code*] 92) and becomes a typical example of one aspect of eighteenth-century ideology. Not that it was ever out of this area, of course: I am speaking of the order in which its readers normally discover its qualities.
>
> (1990e: 46)

The difference is that Frye is writing on literature, which translates myth and metaphor, and Gibbon is describing Roman history as a meditation on the ruins of Rome. Frye thinks that a descriptive text, perhaps any text, has an ideological dimension that is forgettable but inescapable. Many theorists and critics today might also begin by reading against, rather than with, the text, so that they might discover the ideological dimension of the text first and then, if they were to believe that it could be anything other than ideological, they would move on to that area. Often, critics now begin from opposite poles, those who read texts as ideology and those who do not. It seems to me that texts are and are not ideology. Paradoxically, the assumption that a text is not ideological may be ideological and the assumption that a text is only ideological might be an aestheticizing of ideology as a text. We occupy the space, process or energy between.

Whereas in *Anatomy* Frye traced a historical sequence of modes in literature, beginning with the mythical and descending through the Romantic and mimetic to the contemporary ironic modes, in *Words* he outlines a series of verbal modes in the opposite direction, in a counter-historical pattern, starting with descriptive writing arising out of modern technology and concluding with the mythology from which literature descends (1990e: 47). From the beginning of his career, Frye has argued for a literary history that takes genre and convention into account, so that we could consider why comic plots and characters, for instance, those from Aristophanes, have incurred so few changes to the present. Here, the influence of the synchronic aspects of Francis Cornford's theory of comedy on Frye is apparent (see Cornford 1934). Frye may place too much emphasis on the continuities in comedy. Although Harry Levin remarks on the recurring devices of comedy, he notes the changes in comedy, considers it as a social institution and wonders whether comedy has had it (Levin 1986: esp. 19–20, 50–60, 85–90, 119–32; see also Hart 1989b). Frye resists literary history, manifested as a chronological survey, as a particular department of history and suggests in its stead a history of genres and conventions. The synchronicity or transhistorical nature of literary history is something that Frye often stresses. He considers the poet to be at the middle of a cross, or plus sign, in which the horizontal bar represents the ideological and social conditioning that allowed him or her to be intelligible to his or her contemporaries and to himself or herself and in which the vertical bar is the mythological line of descent from the earliest poets to our time (Frye 1990e: 47):

> It is because of this vertical line of literary descent that we are able to understand poets remote from us in time and culture, and can even admire them for many reasons that they themselves, to say nothing of their original audiences, would have found unintelligible.
>
> (1990e: 47–8)

This passage is reminiscent of the one in the 'Polemical Introduction' to the *Anatomy* where Frye says that critics of Shakespeare are supposed to be ridiculed by the suggestion that if Shakespeare came back from the dead he would not understand or appreciate their criticism, but that Shakespeare did not care too much about criticism, and if he did, his interpretation or direction of *Hamlet* would not be definitive (Frye 1957: 5–6).

Frye modifies Harold Bloom's notion of the anxiety of influence, which he admits has been particularly prevalent since the copyright law, by reorientating it from the individual poet's relation to earlier poets to his or her 'ambiguous relation to the ideology around him' (1990e: 48; see also Bloom 1973). Frye also sees literary descent, not through personalities, as Bloom does, but through conventions and genres (48). He also qualifies the position of historicist critics. While Frye admits the historical dimension of ideology, which, he says, surrounds the writer the way a womb does an embryo, he does not consider this historicity to make up the whole of criticism. He takes this position because

> the ideology surrounding every great writer in a past at all remote from us is, so to speak, a great deal deader than he is, and it seems clear that one cannot understand the communicating power of such a writer without a study of the place in the history of literature itself that he inherits and transmits, and the conventions and genres that he found it natural to use.
>
> (48)

In Frye's view, literature participates in history but has its own history, the centre of which is the conventions and genres that are modified to adapt to and oppose different social conditions. He asserts that normal historical methods cannot always account for sources and influences only when they are proven to exist because these often go underground and resurface unpredictably. The primary way to establish a writer's context is a comparative generic study. Many critics today do not want to hear Frye's position that the reading of poets is elusive for literary history:

> the prejudices inherited from the ascendancy of *logos*-language are still so strong that any suggestion that literature, like science, might have a structure of its own, and be something more than simply a reflection of social influences or an inorganic aggregate of imaginative efforts, stirs up the same anxieties that the 'art for art's sake' paradoxes of a century ago did.
>
> (Frye 1990e: 49; see also Cayley 1991: 26)

But this element of art for art's sake in Frye is one of the things that drew Bloom to Frye. They both believe in an art with integrity, though Frye is probably more interested in the social and the historical, and both admire the other's work but are ambivalent towards it. Bloom says of Frye: 'He is certainly the largest and most crucial literary critic in the English language since the divine Walter and the divine Oscar: he really is that good' (Salusinszky 1987: 62). Wilde and Pater do inform aspects of Frye's criticism as well as Bloom's, but Bloom is more willing to part company with Arnold and Eliot than Frye is. There may be something to Bloom's caustic observation in *A Map of Misreading* that 'Frye's "myth of concern" is a sort of Low Church version of Eliot's High Church myth of "tradition and the individual talent"' (Salusinszky 1987: 62–3; see also Donoghue 1992: 26). Bloom admits that Frye is a precursor, but the anxiety of influence cuts both ways: the predecessor worries about what the successor will do with his or her earlier work.

Frye modifies Bloom's anxiety of influence but uses it, none the less. Bloom does not like it when Frye turns towards the social and the historical, and is not enough like Wilde and Pater, but this is the very turn that attracts Marxists, like Jameson, to Frye's theory. Frye observes that the ideology of Western society has tended to place *logos* above *mythos*. He suggests that Jean-Jacques Rousseau's society of nature and reason buried beneath exploitation and luxury has something to do with this ascendancy, although it is not, Rousseau implies, necessarily desirable and unchangeable (Frye 1990e: 50). In his examination of logocentrism Derrida concentrates a good deal of attention on Rousseau, looking, for instance, at his *Essai sur l'origine des langues* in *De la grammatologie* (1967, trans. 1976). In fact Derrida borrows Rousseau's phrase the 'logic of the supplement' to discuss the relations between speech and writing. But Derrida sees in speech a momentary fusing of form (sound) and meaning, which might be akin to Frye's view of metaphor: they both seem to unite subject and object, inside and outside and to give immediacy and self-presence. But in regard to Rousseau and others, Derrida argues that if writing is as our metaphysical tradition says it is, then speech is a form of writing (see Culler 1982: 102–6, 183–4, 217–18). Derrida's critique of logocentrism reveals the contradictions of this system but can never get beyond it. Frye's critique of the *logos* may never get beyond the logocentric, but it is also possible to say, with Frye, that poets work in a mythological universe and never get beyond *mythos* or to *logos*. Whether Frye's criticism can be so poetic that it could escape argument and the *logos* is something I have raised and that remains more problematic because Frye has recourse to arguments no matter how much he wishes to subordinate them to myth and metaphor and a general poetic language or a high valuation of poetry. But then, as Derrida suggests, in pointing out the problems of presence, we do not escape it.

In his *Defence of Poetry* Shelley also attempted to place *mythos* before *logos*. Such a reversal, Frye says, has been accepted by few, but work on the unconscious and myth, especially that of Freud, put to rest the idea that the primitive meant historically outmoded (1990e: 50). Freud's point that in childhood we re-enact major myths, like those of Narcissus and Oedipus, makes, in Frye's view, all ancient and exotic literatures accessible. Similarly, Freud's complication of our understanding of the psyche shows that reason is not the sole part of our minds and that the imagination, which produces and responds to literature, is multifold (50). Frye agrees with the poets that consciousness is not enough, that poetic creation expands beyond the controlling will (51–2). He says that we appear to come up against a gap between poetic and ideological language. This assertion brings Frye to the visionary and the prophetic in literature. He connects the prophetic with the poet's authority and relates it to social context (53). None the less Frye can sound very Derridean when he distinguishes between prophetic writers inside and outside literature: 'This troublesome apparatus of inside and outside will not go away even when so many aspects of it vanish under examination' (54). Frye does not think there is an original mythology that contains all its descendants (55). Some biblical scholars, Frye says, tried to demythologize the Bible by taking out the primitive aspects, and as myth develops through literature, it tends 'to dehistoricize whatever is historical in its structure' (56). This tendency, Frye argues, explains the charge that critics interested in myth are antihistorical because it involves a displaced epithet of the subject matter to the scholar.

Frye uses Gerard Manley Hopkins' terminology of underthought and overthought as a means of explaining and criticizing ideology. Overthought is the surface meaning of the poem, what the contemporary audience and, for the most part, the poet took to be its significance, the conscious, syntactical meaning of the poem. Underthought is made up of the progression of metaphor and images that affords an 'emotional counterpoint' to the overthought, which it supplements and often contradicts. Frye cites Shakespeare's *Henry V* as a good example (1990e: 57–9; see also Hart 1992d). In this debate Frye concludes that the critical principle involved is the relation between the poetic and the ideological or rhetorical: in this play the audience receives as history 'what it is prepared to accept as history' (59). Frye equates overthought and ideological content. He sees the relation between overthought and underthought as including 'the whole spectrum from total agreement to total disagreement' (59). There is a certain wiliness in using terms from Hopkins, a difficult and highly aesthetic and religious poet, and applying them to poetry, which, especially in its lyric form, is supposed to be beyond ideology. If there was any doubt in what Frye is up to, he amplifies this strategy with the influence of Poe on the *symboliste* movement from 1850 to 1950 and refers specifically to Eliot and Paul Verlaine. Now Frye is at the heart of the aesthetic movement that leads to high modernism. Instead of accepting the received wisdom of art for art's sake or the tenets of New Criticism, that the poem is some kind of Grecian urn, Frye moves from Poe and his French followers to Eliot and back again to Verlaine, to show that it is not possible to separate poetry from rhetoric or to purge the rhetorical from the poetic. This aesthetic ideology, this purification of poetry, including Verlaine's rhetorical comment that poets should take rhetoric and wring its neck, which, as

Frye observes, is also an ideological remark, could only be temporary: 'However, a cult of separating poetry and rhetoric could never have been much more than a temporary change of emphasis: what is interesting is the awareness that two distinguishable verbal modes are involved' (59). While Frye is prepared to say that poetry and rhetoric cannot be separate, he is not willing to go as far as saying that poetry is rhetoric. He actually equates myth and vision with poetry as opposed to ideology or allegory. The division between vision and allegory he takes from Blake. Frye cites John Bunyan's *The Pilgrim's Progress*, which represents the Christian ideology of the forgiveness of sins through Christ's atonement, as an example of a work that could not survive the waning of Christian ideology in British middle-class homes (59). None the less, Frye tries to recuperate Bunyan's poem as a story that people can still read from a non-Christian point of view. Narrative flexibility becomes the saving grace of literature. Frye paraphrases D. H. Lawrence: 'we should trust no writer's beliefs or attitudes, but concentrate on his myth, which is infinitely wiser than he is, and is the only element that can survive when the ideology attached to it fades' (60). To paraphrase Yeats, however, is to ask how we know the dancer from the dance, how we separate myth from ideology. Are we not experiencing Frye's beliefs posing as myth or the structure of narrative? Why has Frye apparently circled back to the position of Verlaine and Eliot? There is a difference. Frye is not a synchronic formalist as the two poets are: they think that they can separate poetry from rhetoric, whereas Frye thinks time or history does. The difference is even more complex because Frye asks the reader and critic to concentrate on myth and not on the writer's ideology but does not say that the ideological aspect is not in the text. We can never deny history, that Bunyan's time is not ours. The time of the writer and the time of the reader are always present in reading and criticism.

Frye then shifts to the state of criticism at the present time. He compares the burden of Christian's sins in Bunyan's poem with the burden of tradition for the contemporary critic. Although Frye will reiterate his position in *The Double Vision*, it is worth quoting it here at length, because it is a central twist in his argument on, and myth of, ideology:

Continuing with the image of the burden, critics caught up in a new ideological trend may feel oppressed by the burden of the past, and wonder why we should feel obliged to keep maintaining a cultural tradition that practically ignores the interests of the trend. The next step is to set up a value system that gives priority to whatever seems to illustrate the trend and devalues the rest, or else to devalue the whole cultural tradition of the past in favor of a more satisfying culture to be set up in the future.

(Frye 1990e: 60)

In my last chapter, 'The Power of Words', I shall address this question of tradition further, so that I want to say here only that Frye is returning to Eliot's 'tradition', a word without much allure for those interested in a radical remaking of literature, critical theory and society, but he does so with a more Romantic cast than does Eliot, who is more interested, for historical and personal reasons, in returning to the classics. Both Eliot and Frye take a long pit stop in medieval poetics, especially in the work of Dante. What Frye is arguing against is 'topiary criticism', the vulgar Marxist, Christian, humanist, feminist and other forms of criticism that clip literature into a distorted shape to buttress their distinct positions. 'Here', Frye concludes, 'it is the ideological trend that becomes the real burden, and the cultural tradition that delivers us from it' (60). But I wonder how any of us, including Frye, escapes supporting our ideological positions. If myth does survive belief over time, then it may be the myth of what Frye is setting out and not his belief in the defence of myth that will endure. The big question in studying his work is: is myth a belief or the foundation of the verbal universe? In other words, has Frye stumbled on to the great mystery, the beginning of words, or is he taking, consciously or unconsciously, an ideological conclusion and making it appear as a natural assumption? Does Frye confront the myth of ideology with the ideology of myth?

But there are many twists to Frye's argument. He is as slippery as the eiron. Like Socrates, however, Frye has a position, no matter how elusive and subtle it is. In another twist Frye confronts another historicism, not the older one he responded to in *Anatomy* but a newer one. After showing the historical falling away of ideology in history, Frye is going to give priority to mythology over history. Although I have argued that he is in one sense a historical critic, in another he is not because he does not make history primary. In fact, for him the newer kinds of historicism, which speak of 'historicity', are a kind of topiary criticism. He defends the dehistoricizing tendency of myth and does not think that it indicates a corruption of the critical process or a kind of static idealism. Frye states his position:

> To me myth is not simply an effect of the historical process, but a social vision that looks toward a transcending of history, which explains how it is able to hold two periods of history together, the author's and ours, in direct communication. It is very difficult,

perhaps impossible, to suggest a social vision of this kind, even within ideology, without invoking some kind of pastoral myth, past or future.

(1990e: 60–1)

He cites Marx's *Communist Manifesto* as a work that says that the historical process will deliver humanity from its class struggles in history and will restore some pre-bourgeois human relations. Frye argues that the mythical features of Marx's social vision help to clarify the function of history and not to demean it. Another example is the crucifixion, which is mythical as well as historical but which derives its power to be at the centre of human vision from the fact that it speaks in the mythical present to those who suffer today. Frye is bold in his assertion that history falsifies primary concerns and is 'the continuous record of what ascendant ideologies do' (61). Surprisingly, he speaks about going beyond myth and history in the realm of the personal (62).

In discussing identity and metaphor, a recurrent theme throughout his career, Frye concentrates on language. He calls literature 'an art of words' and then proceeds to split the art from the words as a matter of emphasis for those who study the field. If students emphasize words, they find it increasingly difficult to separate the traditional disciplines, but if they stress the art, they have no such trouble. What is said in literature is the ideological and rhetorical; how it is said is poetics. Words are arbitrary or conventional, but poetics makes a function of the accidents of sound, a kind of magical means to minimize the sense of arbitrariness (Frye 1990e: 63–5). According to Frye, the critical study of poetry depends on holism, the heuristic assumption that every detail of a poem can be related to its unity, just as criticism depends on the premise of coherence (66). Frye's poetics, like New Criticism but unlike deconstruction, assumes that we should read with the text and regard it like a well-wrought urn. For him, the reader encounters a series of well-wrought urns that reflect one another in an unfinished room with spaces for future urns. Frye distinguishes between poetry and rhetoric through a comparison of the poet and the orator. While admitting that the poet borrows from the rhetorician, Frye says that the poet as poet has nothing to say and does not have the kinetic and immediate cause-and-effect relation with his or her audience that the orator has. To make his point clear, Frye elides two situations. First, we have written rhetorical texts such as speeches, like those of Lincoln and Churchill, whose immediate audience is remembered but cannot be live and kinetic, that are often poetic. Second, we have poetry performed orally before a live audience. The search for a pure rhetoric and poetry is definitional and heuristic because although Frye says that his interest in language is primary, it is his insistence on art, even for its own sake, that underlies his interest in literature as an integral discipline and in its genres. Still, Frye says that rhetorical speeches and poems focus on community, but whereas the one demands uniformity, the other fosters variety (66–7). Poetry uses sound the way music does (68). In discussing the oral and the written, Frye alludes to Derrida, the critic who most fascinated Frye in his last decade. He does not discount Derrida's view but says that he has metaphysical texts in mind more than poetry, which, in Frye's view, most often begins orally in the body of the writer but which is freed through writing. The forms of written poetry, like the epigraph, Frye readily admits, although he implies that the oral and magical types of poems are more central and prevalent than the visual and the disjunctive kinds. He says that there are two successive operations in reading, the pursuit of narrative and the simultaneous understanding, what others have called the diachronic and the synchronic, which he associates with the metaphors of listening and seeing respectively (68–70). This visualizing of the whole meaning represents Frye's distinction between reading and criticism and relates to his concern with vision and structure.

Structure is a central concept in Frye's work. It is both dynamic and static. He says that one can never see the total structure of the *Divine Comedy* or *King Lear*, but recalls his discussion in earlier books of a 'thematic stasis' of the simultaneous vision of a narrative in which he identified it with Aristotle's *dianoia*, or thought or meaning. Frye also considers image-clusters as units of structure, and characters as images who mediate between author and public. This is the observation that the gods in myths are ready-made metaphors that prefigure characters in literature, so that literature is polytheistic and metaphorical, echoing an animism that violates common sense and, one might add, the reasonable and ideological stance of normal science and criticism. Frye is also distancing literature from myth, admitting that some of Ovid's *Metamorphoses* involve stories about the breakdown of metaphor, while saying that the role of poetry is to keep metaphorical thought alive (1990e: 70–1).

Here I want to call attention to the ideological dimension of the metaphor. The longstanding debate between philosophy and poetry, found in Aristotle, Sidney, Fenellosa, Pound and others, centres on the relation between abstract and concrete language, form and content, concept and percept. The debate over unity and contradiction, between New Critics and structuralists on the one hand and deconstructionists on the other, is really a matter of coming down on the side of the mythical and magical identity or animism of the poet (even if this effect happens briefly and seldom) or on the sceptical, critical, ideological or systematic resistance to fiction and an identity with God, the gods or nature. Plato resisted the poet's magic: de Man saw the poet as someone whose poems resisted themselves and anticipated the deconstructive critic. Frye admits a distance between first and critical reading, but he favours the dream of poetics, that, even if for a moment, the poet and reader recognize their unity with the poem and nature. In the theatre of this world, however, Aristotle would have us pass from *anagnorisis* to *catharsis*, in which we purge ourselves of pity and terror through experiencing the experience of the characters. With ironic distance, we re-enter the world from our house of fictions. But Frye's comic tendencies – by which I always mean his identification of and admiration for the structure of comedy, for its happy ending, although he rarely shies away from irony and wit – often bring him to an emphasis of the conjunctive nature of the imagination rather than, as with his deconstructive counterparts, with the distinctive. None the less, he discusses and does not deny the distance between myth and literature and the role of distinction in the literary. Reading is experience; criticism is knowledge. The first is immediate, the second is distanced: 'Experience is of the particular and the unique, and takes place in time; knowledge is of the universal and the assimilated, and contains an element withdrawn from time' (Frye 1990e: 74). How the critical distance contributes to a recreation of the structure of a work while not qualifying or undercutting it becomes a pressing question in responding to Frye's poetics. Is ideology somebody else's ideas? Is the critic not already fallen or alienated from the poem when writing about it, even if he or she has experienced an epiphanic identification, a moment of unity? Distinctions need to be made. It is consistent with Frye's theory that the distinction between form and content, between the art and words in the art of words is heuristic and not something that will hold up to close scrutiny. By looking at difference, at the extremes of poetry and rhetoric, Frye sets up a hypothetical realm in which to separate the form, sound and indirection of poetry from the content, arbitrariness and direction of ideology. Although Frye distinguishes between experience and knowledge in reading, he sees an eventual assimilation of them both as aspects of the same thing. The extremes that Frye wants to avoid are the views that readers are detached and objective observers or are involved in narcissism in which their psyches are reflected in each text. Frye's reader is a participant. Writing is, for Frye, more than a creative craft, something that seems magical, an invocation or compulsion of an unauthorized and apparently objective presence that happens to the writer despite what the ideologies or doctrines of the time might say to the contrary (75–6).

Uniqueness occurs only in experience, but, Frye says, the contemplation of literary structure as an individual of the class poem unites experience and knowledge (1990e: 78). He explores identification or the existential metaphor, which Heidegger calls the ecstatic, a standing outside oneself in order to identify with something else, if only for a moment (79–82). Frye is moving from the visual to the visionary: 'The imaginative element in the poetic means that all the doors of perception in the psyche, the doors of dream and fantasy as well as of waking consciousness, are thrown open' (82–3). Here is the vision of poetry. I have already alluded to the close connection between metaphor and ideology in Frye's work, and he relates these terms to vision, which is the subject of my next chapter:

> Vision also suggests the fragmentary and the temporary, not necessarily something seen steadily and whole, to paraphrase Arnold, but more frequently providing only an elusive and vanishing glimpse. Glimpse of what? To try to answer this question is to remove it to a different category of experience. If we knew what it was, it would be an object perceived in time and space. And it is not an object, but something uniting the objective with ourselves.
>
> (83)

What the objective is Frye does not say. Here we have a vision for vision's sake, a process that can be identified but not named. How noumenal this visionary energy is can only be imagined, which suggests that the innocence of the post-critical is not always readily distinguished from the innocence of the pre-critical. Frye himself seems to realize the strain on the metaphors of seeing that he is using, so he looks for metaphorical reinforcements, and finds them in the metaphors of the reader being above and below a work (83–4).

Frye identifies three aspects of metaphorical experience – the imaginative, the erotic and the ecstatic – in all of which an alternation occurs between identity and difference. In the poem the reader joins or separates metaphors; in the erotic the lovers unite and separate; in the ecstatic people unite themselves in a presence that soon turns out to be an absence. Plato's image of the lover climbing the ladder of refining experience, discovering that identity is love and difference is beauty, represents, Frye says, a central image in the last three quarters of *Words with Power* (1990e: 85). The image of Plato's ladder becomes, for Frye, an upward journey of the imagination in which subject and object are at one (a kind of atonement) and which occurs in literature through an interchange of illusion and reality: 'Illusion, something created by human imagination, is what becomes real; reality, most of which in our experience is a fossilized former human creation from the past, becomes illusory' (85). As an illustration, Frye returns to one of his favourite texts, Shakespeare's *The Tempest*. Prospero tells us that what we call reality eventually disappears like other illusions. Miranda's discovery of a 'brave new world' will become another illusion, but, for the moment, is an epiphany, a vision of how things should be in the midst of how things are. Frye says that innocent or childlike vision, like Miranda's, is often associated with the garden of Eden, the pre-lapsarian state in which the human, animal and vegetable existed harmoniously (85–6).

These observations bring us to the relation between vision and ideology. The close connection between myth, metaphor and ideology in Frye's thought is reflected in the structure of my book because these topics occupy its centre. Frye opposes those in each of the major religions who stay in 'the ideological framework of its revelation' and observe its rituals and laws and those who try a more direct way through ecstatic metaphor. He tends away from ideology towards vision and mysticism and shares with mystics an interest in Platonism. Although in *Fearful Symmetry* Frye distinguishes between the mystic and the visionary, in *Words with Power* he elides the two. When listing mystics such as Dionysius the Areopagite and Erigena, he includes 'various medieval and later visionaries' like Meister Eckhart, Ruysbroeck and Boehme. Frye observes that their central axiom is 'One becomes what one beholds', which represents a disciplined and consistent vision that ends with a type of identification he associates with existential metaphor. While we tend to think of Jesus as the teacher who used parables to illustrate his doctrine, he can be and should be considered, in Frye's view, as the teller of parables, which are the teachings, the content or doctrine being their applications. The descent of the visionary ladder is a demonic parody or opposite that involves a world where subject and object grow further apart until the subject becomes its own object and indulges in a kind of narcissism (Frye 1990e: 86–7). The epiphany – in Frye as well as in Joyce – occurs when the perceiver transfigures objective things through identification with them. Frye summarizes his position: the more we approach literature with a personal commitment or involvement, the more one pole resembles 'the revelation of a paradisal state, a lunatic, loving, poetic world where all primary concerns are fulfilled' and the other pole looks like 'the imaginative hell explored in tragedy, irony and satire' (88). The paradisal puts the hell-world into perspective – psychosis occurs in all societies, but the culture of societies contains something that is congenial:

The sense of the congenial, of a genuine human communication through words, pictures, textiles, ceramics or whatever, comes from the innocent vision at the heart of all human creation and the response to it. Such a vision is a presence created by an absence, a life that remains alive because the death that was also in it has gone.

(88–9)

Frye's world of culture has two features. First, it alternates between two perspectives of existence, the oceanic sense of being submerged in a larger unity and the sense of individuality without ego, that is without fear and aggression. Second, it allows for an environment that presents a vision of the possibility of complete intelligibility, which the Bible symbolizes as creation through the Word. While telling of a vision of love, Frye's account becomes his own vision of love. He says that, for the New Testament, the Word clarifies while the Spirit unifies, so that together they make the genuine form of human society, 'the spiritual kingdom of Jesus, founded on the *caritas* or love' that is, for Paul, the only virtue (89). Criticism is like the Spirit that completes the Word, a kind of secular hermeneutics that involves knowledge fulfilling fallen experience. Frye discusses what he considers to be the central literary metaphor – the journey – which he traces to an image for life in the vision represented in the Book of Ecclesiastes and relates to the vision at the end of the narrative and quest (90–4). Jesus' remark in John 14 that 'I am the way' in response to his disciples and as an explanation of what awaits them in the afterlife 'explodes, or, perhaps, deconstructs, the whole metaphor of journey, of the effort to go there in order to arrive here' (94). The way is here and now. Frye returns implicitly to experience and knowledge in reading. For him, following a narrative is a journey that is metaphorically horizontal, from here to there, but coming to the end of the narrative means looking up and down, a vertical metaphor that represents the attempt to understand what has been read. Frye maintains that the second half of *Words with Power* examines the vertical metaphor of the journey of consciousness to higher and lower worlds, the *axis mundi*. Literature is a kind of meditation in Frye's scheme, but it leads him back to ideology (95–6).

In discussing spirit and symbol Frye begins by saying that he has been avoiding the word 'religion', which has mainly come up in the context of ideology. He says that religions are part of a larger group of ideologies and that most of them translate a mythological background into a conceptual doctrine to be believed, and these beliefs are manifested in the way of life and actions of the believer. Frye juxtaposes religion and Marxism as ideologies:

It is possible to have an ideology that substitutes concepts for divine personalities, such as we have in Marxism. But the absence of personal gods did not prevent Marxism from developing a parallel apparatus of inspired texts, saints, shrines and martyrs, a professional hierarchy corresponding to a priesthood, orthodox and heretical beliefs, and commitment to an accepted ideology.

(1990e: 97)

The preference that Frye expresses is for those who seek a religion that transcends ideological commitment, detailed rules for ordering one's life according to patterns of ritual and morality, and fixed doctrines rather than for fundamentalism in Western ideologies and religions. Language is one of Frye's primary interests: he says there are three 'serious' modes of verbal communication – the descriptive (perceptual), the dialectical (conceptual) and the rhetorical (ideological). The ideological, he notes, is the furthest we can go in this perspective. Frye also observes that traditionally dialectic was supposed to keep rhetoric or ideology in check, that the difference between religious and non-religious ideologies is that the religious ones attribute dialectic or effective conscious will to God and the non-religious ones to some analogue of Rousseau's general will in society. The fourth mode in Frye's scheme of language is the poetic or imaginative. For him, rhetoric lies between the dialectic and poetic and shares qualities with both (98–9).

Poetics is not an illusion of an aesthetic ideology, for Frye, but a necessary heuristic distinction or fiction. He measures the poetic nature of the Bible without seeing it as literature. The Bible is literary but not literature. This is one of Frye's central points in *Words with Power* and explains why, as in *The Great Code*, he insists on the phrase 'the Bible and Literature' in the subtitle:

> The poetic does not depend on the conscious will to the extent that the other modes do; it depends on a half-voluntary, half-involuntary, integration of the conscious will with other factors in the psyche, factors connected with fantasy, dreaming, let's pretend, and the like. It expresses itself in myth and metaphor, myth being a story which is not the same thing as a history, and metaphor being a verbal relation which is not that of logic. And while it would be an abuse of language to speak of the Bible as a work of literature, there is still the fact that most of it, including nearly all of its prophetic part, is written in the literary language of myth and metaphor.

(1990e: 99)

The distinction between the poetic and the rhetorical is difficult, and, he

observes, although the Bible often seems closer to the ideological than
to the literary, it is full of myth and metaphor and great poetry. That
being said, Frye wants to look at the poetic and literary nature of the
Bible, which is too often only regarded as a historical and doctrinal
construct. He is also concerned with *kerygma*, a term that he has
borrowed and adapted from the theologian Rudolf Bultmann, which is
proclamation, a kind of language that is rhetorical and poetic but is not
quite either and is like and unlike apocalypse and prophecy. Frye moves
through the literary to understand the language of the Bible but assumes
that he will arrive somewhere else. The Bible, according to Frye, has
become over the centuries, in terms of its historical reception, a unity,
despite its multiple authorship over time. Frye contends that this unity,
held together through the structure of myth and metaphor, is an opening
up of perspectives (99–102). One might say that Frye's critical assumptions or ideology are those of unity. Like theoretical physicists and
astronomers who assume that the universe is tending towards entropy or
is becoming more organized or unified, literary critics attempt to justify
their claims through evidence, which is what Frye does in the second
half of *Words with Power*. But, in Harry Levin's words, is literature an
exact science? Was the course at the University of Toronto in the mid-
1970s, the Poetry of Physics, a rumour or an entry in the calendar? The
nature of evidence in literary theory and criticism is a crucial if largely
ignored question at the present time. Like the astrophysicists, Frye is
interested in cosmology, and, like them, he believes in evidence, but,
unlike them, he cannot use an apparently purely formal language like
mathematics (or music in the case of symphonic and operatic cosmol-
ogers) to prove his point. Words may be less abstract and precise than
mathematics, although the latter contains many fictions, approximations, that approach something but are never quite there, such as an
asymptote, or the idea of a line itself.

In the fourth chapter of the Book of Revelation, Frye asserts, there is
a *tour de force* in which the author works out the whole *dianoia* or
metaphor-cluster, as well as its demonic parody, for the Bible. This turn
represents a point where rhetoric becomes literature, a vision of the
expanded present rather than anxieties about the future, where ideology
yields to poetry. Visions of the Expanded Present might have been the
title for my next chapter, because it is this world of the eternal now
which Frye turns to again and again (1990e: 102–3). The editorial work
in the Bible is not an infantile attempt to reduce poetry into plain prose,
which is an appeal to the 'infantalism' of popular religious and other
ideologies, but is 'an absorption of a poetic and mythical presentation
that takes us past myth to something else' (104). Frye does not say

explicitly what lies beyond myth, but he observes that John identifies *mythos*, narrative or story, with *logos*, consciousness, which is what Frye is also attempting to do (105). The relation between unity and monotheism interests Frye. He observes that many of the visions of God in the Bible represent what human passions and fantasies might wish God to be. The difference between unity, of oneness with variety, and uniformity, of likeness without variety, is something Frye emphasizes in the discussion of one God with many attributes. The visionary tradition stresses that God is not a thing because there is no such thing as God, that language represents its own inability to express God, often in ambiguity and paradox, saying that God is and is not. Frye's verbal modes place rhetoric between the conceptual and the poetic and the poetic between the rhetorical and the kerygmatic: here he is interested in 'the mysterious borderlands between the poetic and the kerygmatic' (111; see also 106–10). Frye uses an inductive method despite his claims that knowledge involves an overview of the flow or sequence of experience because he asks his readers to go along with him, to accept analogous terms like 'prophetic' and 'metaliterary' before having the definition of kerygmatic before them. This heuristic method makes sense, but it either qualifies Frye's insistence on criticism as an overview or it allows for an ironic gap between this critic and his readers, which destabilizes his rhetorical use of 'we' (111).

The critic to whom Frye turns is Longinus, the author of the *Peri Hypsous* or *On the Sublime*, because he understands ecstatic response and the difference between ideological rhetoric, which persuades, and proclamation, which takes one out of oneself. The allusion to Longinus allows Frye to return to the epiphanic, the oracular or discontinuous prophesy, 'the passage in the text where we suddenly break through into a different dimension of response' and to ground the sublime in the Bible because Longinus cites as an example the 'Let there be light' verse from Genesis (1990e: 111). Frye supplements his usual allusions to Vico and Joyce, especially *Finnegans Wake*, with those to William James, the 'Dies irae, dies illa' poem that is part of the Requiem Mass, the last of these as a reminder that terror cannot be separated from the prophetic or apocalyptic vision (112–13). The Frygian discussion of ideology tends towards the visionary. Frye's own vision is a movement in the Bible beyond Plato and Derrida, beyond speech and writing, through 'a *resurrection* of the original speaking presence in the reader', so that the duality of speaker and listener vanishes into a united verbal recognition (114). Frye moves from the *mimesis* Plato and Aristotle discuss to the creation of the word or *logos* that Longinus describes and

Coleridge develops. The point at which active speech and reception of speech unite is kerygmatic (118; see also 114–17).

In Frye's theory the descriptive, conceptual and rhetorical are languages of nature that relate the physical to its contexts in space and time, whereas the poetic or imaginative are spiritual. Discussing the poetic, he argues that traditionally the kerygmatic Word of the Bible has had a primary relation to spirit, the creative power of humanity, and a secondary one to nature. Spiritual aspects of the descriptive, conceptual and rhetorical language exist only as elements in a poetic structure. The spiritually descriptive is the *mythos*, fiction or narrative; the spiritually conceptual is the 'underthought', the metaphors underneath the ideological or explicit meaning; the spiritually rhetorical reverses the use of figurative language to address an audience directly that occurs in traditional or ordinary rhetoric. These three polysemous aspects of the poetic in Frye's schema 'make up a total descriptive narrative that I called elsewhere the loss and regaining of identity, a conceptual argument based on a pattern of imagery that separates a world of metaphorical unity from its demonic opposite, and a rhetoric based on example and illustration rather than direct assertion' (Frye 1990e: 121; see also 119–20). For Frye as for Blake, our world is a marriage of heaven and hell, the two real abodes of human life. Frye's fable of identity, of paradise lost and paradise regained, conceives of the Bible as a compressed and unified epitome of such a poetic universe and the proclamation of God's Word to humanity, the wildly paradoxical idea of an Infinite-I-am speaking to its finite counterpart. The distinction between soul and spirit, which Frye also later makes in *The Double Vision*, relies heavily on Paul's discussion of that relation. He also observes: 'The Greek conception of soul and body corresponds closely to our first three linguistic modes, the body's awareness of its environment being expressed in descriptive language, the soul's in the language of argument and ideology' (123). A helpful remark that Frye calls on is Yeats' that we make rhetoric out of quarrels with others, poetry, with ourselves. The New Testament identifies spirit with God and the understanding of God it advocates. At I Corinthians 15: 44, Paul differentiates the *soma psychikon*, the mortal soul-body, from the *soma pneumatikon*, the spiritual body (124). The spiritual body of the risen Christ is, Frye says, in everyone and everywhere: spiritual personality and love are inseparable. Frye says: 'The capacity to merge with another person's being without violating it seems to be at the center of love, just as the will to dominate one conscious soul-will externally by another is the center of all tyranny and hatred' (126). The spirit is often associated with the metaphor of breath or air, with the childlike, with the erotic and with the greatest intensity of consciousness (127–8). As I note in the next chapter, Frye asserts that in the New Testament faith is the *hypostasis* or substance of the *elenchos* of the unseen, or the hoped-for (Hebrews 11: 1). He paraphrases the verse in Hebrews as 'Faith is the reality of hope and of illusion' (129). This hope is in the future – potential – and relates to the open possibilities of literature (see Hart 1988). Illusion is also a large part of literature. Frye thinks little of religious orthodoxy with political power: 'we can hardly help noticing how often faiths of the type described as orthodox, fundamentalist, or what not, are pernicious in their social influence whenever they get into a position of secular power' (132; see also 130–1). He considers their false linguistic assumptions to be part of the problem. Biblical hermeneutics prefigures many of the questions in critical theory, and Frye considers the Bible to be the clearest illustration in explaining them. He resists the facile either–or in separating the religious from the secular. As an illustration of this resistance to separation, Frye relates Michel Foucault's secular observation in *The Order of Things* (II.v) that 'God is perhaps not so much a region beyond knowledge as something prior to the sentences we speak' to the sacred context of the opening of the Gospel of John, which relates the Word that begins all things to the power behind the beginning that Jesus represents through the metaphor of the Son and the Father (133).

An important question that Frye raises is why the New Testament, written in the language of myth and metaphor but proclaiming a truth that transcends myth, is so ready to proclaim as untrue and mere fiction all else expressed in that poetic language. Frye, the literary critic, opposes himself to the early Christians: 'What transcends myth is still myth in the terms of this book [*Words with Power*], but those who originally responded to the Gospel must have felt that they had got clear of something futile in the mythopoeic imagination and its undirected procedures' (1990e: 133). The biblical canon may have helped to define secular literature by opposing it. Frye follows Vico and Yeats in a similar vision of the ages in the history of culture. With Emily Dickinson, Frye thinks that in our age we have asked for the return of our gods and human creations from the God of the Bible, which Christianity made His domain. For critics as for poets, Frye invokes Vico's axiom *Verum factum*, 'Truth is the truth we have made', as an important principle. But Frye reads the Bible more hopefully and in a way more accommodating to metaphor, myth and literature:

The Bible begins by showing on its first page that the reality of God manifests itself in creation, and on its last page that the same reality is manifested in a new creation in which man is a participant. He becomes a participant by being redeemed, or separated from the predatory and destructive element acquired from his origin in nature. In between these visions of creation comes the Incarnation, which presents God and man as indissolubly locked together in a common enterprise.

(135)

Frye points out the comic structure of the Bible. Here is his hope and redemption. In this vision of unity Frye hopes that in words and other media we can move towards a peace that passes all understanding, as the liturgy says, towards 'the proclaimed or mythological model of a peace infinite in both its source and its goal' (135). This is a religious if not mystical telos, a visionary and prophetic hope, kerygmatic in its desire to transcend the temporariness and temporality of ideology. To see with Frye is to say that to transcend myth leads us to myth, with metaphor, but to assume the priority of ideology is to see the transcendence of myth into myth as an ideological position because myth really becomes ideology in its attempt to transcend itself. If myth is form and ideology is content, it becomes a matter of emphasis to separate the inseparable, but on Frye's side and on the other, such possibilities are worth exploring because without heuristic distinctions, we discover nothing but the chaos or mass of prejudices that face us to begin with.

Briefly, as this book is more concerned with Frye's theory than with his practical criticism, I want to follow his vision into his examples in the last two-thirds of *Words with Power* as they relate only to ideology. In his Prefatory Note to Part Two of the book, 'Variations on a Theme', he returns to his myths of concern, which he formulated in the late 1960s and which first appear in full form in *The Critical Path* (1971). He organizes the four variations or chapters that follow according to the concern to make and create, the concern to love, the concern to sustain oneself and the concern to escape from constraint and slavery (139–42). Frye is concerned with vision in the Bible and literature. His hope is that coherent ways of life, connected with primary concerns and the kerygmatic mode, will arise from 'the infinite possibilities of myth' (143).

In 'First Variation: The Mountain', Frye gives us some evidence as to a contributing factor in his own position on the creativity in, and the integrity of, criticism and the arts: 'In Romantic times a contrast in critical theory between "allegory" and "symbol", in which the latter was generally preferred to the former, marked the beginning of a sense that literature creates and lives within its own cosmos, and advances into or retreats from other verbal modes' on its own terms (1990e: 148). Another motive might have been Frye's desire well into adulthood if not middle age to write fiction and, in the absence of the publication of a large number of stories or a novel, to consider his criticism as creative as fiction (see my Chapter 9). This suggestion is not meant to detract from the idea of the integrity and creativity of criticism and theory – I agree with Frye that at a high level it can be cosmology and as imaginative as theology, philosophy, mathematics and physics – but only to draw out a possible genealogy from Frye's assumptions or ideology. Frye also borrows from Freud the concepts of displacement and condensation, but translates them from the context of dream to that of literature. In a literary context displacement means making a mythical structure more plausible and accommodating to ordinary experience, whereas condensation involves the transformation of the similarities and associations of ordinary experience into metaphorical identities (148–9). The extreme examples of displacement and condensation are the Stalinist ideology that attempted 'to make all literature into an allegory of its own obsessions' and *Finnegans Wake*, which transforms a day in a life into a vast interlocking and mutually reflective verbal structure fraught with symbolism' (149). Frye will reiterate his comments on vision and cosmology in *The Double Vision*, subjects I shall discuss in the next chapter (150–63). The *axis mundi* or vertical image is of primary importance for Frye's analysis: 'The feature that particularly concerns us here about this chain of being is that it represents the primary ideological adapting of the ladder metaphor to a rationalizing of authority' (167). From the 1950s onwards, and recently with great intensity, Renaissance scholars have questioned E. M. W. Tillyard's view in the 1940s, which adapts Arthur Lovejoy's work in the 1930s, that writers like Shakespeare celebrated the chain of being or Ptolemaic system in approval of the reigning social order. Frye's observation about rationalizing would, for some recent critics, apply more to Tillyard than to Shakespeare (see Dollimore 1984 and 1985, *Shakespeare and the Question of Theory* (1985), Greenblatt 1988). The chain of being was made up of four levels: heaven, the order of nature or unfallen nature, physical nature and the demonic world (168–9).

Frye is acutely aware that much tyranny has occurred in the name of God and nature – what is natural depends on what level of nature one is talking about – and that cosmologies, such as the chain of being, are often used as rationalizations for the ideologies of social authority (1990e: 170). With Romanticism, Frye says, the hero of literature became the poet and helped to question such ideologies as those derived from the P creation myth or Priestly account, the structurally first but historically later account of creation in the two creation myths in Genesis (see Genesis 1:1–2:3). This account allows for a limited place for human creativity in a cosmos where God made nature as a work of art (173; see also 156). Frye cites Spenser's *Mutabilitie Cantos*, which are attached at the end of the *Faerie Queene*, as 'perhaps the greatest single vision of the four-level universe and the ideology that accompanies it' (181). These cantos are a secular apocalypse and contain a visionary realm: 'The vision of being beyond change is a Sabbath vision, a human glimpse of creation corresponding to the contemplation of it by God himself on its seventh day. It is also a vision of hosts or multitudes (*tzabaoth*) that the divine creation has made into an order' (182). In discussing Spenser's secular apocalypse, his representation of the mountain-top Transfiguration, Frye relates vision and ideology. Frye says that in each of the four variations he discusses in separate chapters, there is an authentic myth, an ideological adaptation of the myth to a structure of social ascendancy and a demonic parody (184). The ideological adaptation is the acceptance of the false authority of rulers, whereas the authentic myth is the authority we learn through science, dialectic and poetry that emancipates rather than subordinates the person who accepts it (184–5). This view, as discussed in my sixth chapter, is the foundation of Frye's idea of a liberal education that is found, potentially at least, in the university. A study of the structure of great poetry, including its image patterns, is emancipatory. Poetry expresses freedom of movement, one of Frye's myths of concern, through music, dance and play. He ends this variation with a vision of identity in which all is in all, which suggests the interpenetration of centre and circumference 'and a unity which is no longer thought of either as an absorbing of identity into a larger uniformity or as a mosaic of metaphors' (186). Frye's vision includes Yeats and invites the reader:

> In the spiritual vision we recover the sense of energy to the extent that we identify with the creating power, and have come from Yeats' polluted heart where all ladders are planted to the place where all ladders end. But where the ladder of progressive steps ends the dance of liberated movement begins.

> (187)

We are now not supposed to know the dancer from the dance.

In 'Second Variation: The Garden' Frye shifts from the P account of creation, which is a vision of nature as *natura naturata* – nature as a system or order – to the Jahwist or J creation myth, beginning in

Genesis 2: 4, which is a vision of *natura naturans*, the nature of vitality and growth (1990e: 189–90). Frye discusses the ideology of prudery or sexual repression as it relates to sex in the J account. This ideology transforms the poetic and metaphorical, primary concern of sex into a form of ideological authority (197–8). One of Frye's interests here is the nature of male–female imagery in the New Testament, of which there are two aspects, one concerned with the virgin mother and with Jesus as a son and the other with the images of bridegroom and bride. The one is associated with the first coming and the Incarnation, the other with the second coming and the apocalypse. Frye implies that the church exacts much more ideological control over the interpretation of the male figures of the Trinity than of the female figures (202–3). He is ironic about this neglect of the female: 'Mother, bride, virgin: no Council ever decided that these were different persons of the same substance, and that anyone who confounded the persons or divided the substance was, etc. They are only female figures after all' (203). The mythical and metaphorical relations of the female symbols of the Bible that Frye discusses are woman as one of the human sexes, as the representative of human community and as symbol of the idea that humanity cannot be redeemed without nature (203–4). He is also concerned with the sexual imagery of the Bible, in which the symbolically female is the community and the circumference and the symbolically male is the individual and the centre (208). The historical context of Genesis, Frye says, should be considered if the assumption is correct that it is partly a patriarchal reaction against the cults of the earth-goddess that most likely preceded it (210). Another example of the ideology of gender occurs in the story of Ruth, whose Moabite nationality seems 'to be making a very subversive point, although after the book became canonical, the inevitable commentators arose to explain that the Deuteronomic law did not apply to women' (213). The position of women in the Bible, like leverate marriages and miraculously late births, 'have a dimension in which woman expands into a kind of proletariat, enduring, continuous, exploited humanity, awaiting emancipation in a hostile world: in short, an Israel eventually to be delivered from Egypt' (215; see also 238). Frye's view of the gender of ideology takes its cue from Marx's notion of ideology based on class.

The first variation on the mountain is about the myth of wisdom; the second on the garden is about the myth of love, which also has three elements. The first element is demonic parody. Here, when men write the poems, women tyrannize men and the cycle of jealousy is dramatized in the conventions of the cruel mistress or *femme fatale*. The second element is the ideological adaptation of the myth. This adaptation often takes the form of a social institution dominated by incest-taboo imagery and metaphors of paternal and maternal authority. This ideological transformation takes as much spirituality as possible out of sex. The third element is the authentic myth that the hierogamy or sacred marriage symbolizes (Frye 1990e: 223–4). In this chapter Frye concentrates on the oasis-paradise of gardens and fountains that comes from the biblical Eden and the Song of Songs (225). Frye says that contact with supposedly primitive societies has shown that our traditional ideology is skewed in relation to the earth when compared to theirs. The bride-garden in the Bible moves in the opposite direction of connected love with nature, so that, he observes, it is no accident that feminism and ecology have come into the foreground at the same time. To complicate matters, Frye reminds us that we derive from Western Semitic mythology, which is opposite to Egyptian mythology with its female sky and male earth. One wonders what is the mythological ground of ecology in Egypt. Frye reminds us that another aspect of hierogamy is the identification of Eros as the creator of all the arts and of the association of creation with procreation. Ideological pressures, he says, surround the term 'beauty', and can be seen in a wider perspective, as in Kant's *Critique of Judgement*, which connects the experience of beauty with the teleological, with the intuition of a purpose in creation. A hierogamy where the bridegroom is love and the bride beauty leads to a discovery of reality in beauty (225–7). In this perception, as with other myths, there is soon an expansion 'from the Bible to the great recognition scene of myth that lies behind the totality of creation' (227). This is the *anagnorisis* that lies behind all of Frye's works. In this vision Frye speaks of the gods, first of human creations who were both natural forces and personalities, and how their survival in the arts allows them to return to extend 'the expression of our energies and vision' (228).

From the two higher worlds of the variations of the mountain and the garden we move to the lower worlds of the cave and the furnace. In 'Third Variation: The Cave' Frye says that from the New Testament to the eighteenth century, ideological derivations like the chain of being hamper the full metaphorical exploitation of descent themes in literature and provide little place for a creative descent. He argues that hell is here and now on earth, a state where there are people without community, solitude without individual space (Frye 1990e: 230). Israel is a kind of proletariat that has been repressed and will return from its exclusion: the exploration of repressed worlds has made Marx and Freud portentous figures in the contemporary world. In the Old Testament the emancipating revolt is the Exodus, whereas in the New Testament it is the Resurrection, Christ's escape from death and hell

(238). In the eighteenth century the old four-level authoritarian mythology began to disappear. There are, according to Frye, no new myths, but a new ideology can be created when a new stress on a complementary myth occurs and replaces an ideology that is losing its imaginative ascendancy (239–40). Frye says that in terms of his argument Rousseau, who anticipates Marx and Freud, heralds the collapse of the four-level structure or the ideological adaptation of the emblematics of a world up there and the beginning of a revolutionary realm in which the energy comes from below, from the repressed aspects of human nature (241–2). Moreover, Frye states his debt to Blake, who he says was the first to realize that the old mythical universe was dead and that a new mythical shape or emphasis was required for the revolution in response to the old ideological rationalizing of traditional authority (243). In Blake the childhood vision of innocence is driven underground into the unconscious, into a furnace of desire, so that human life 'takes the form of a force of experience, that is, of compromise with "reality" (ascendant ideology, sitting on top of a human desire that has no real outlet' or Urizen and Orc (244). The inversion of the traditional four-level cosmos is found most fully in Blake and Shelley (248–9). Frye's buried-world theme, as explored in the Romantic movement, leads to an archaeology of civilizations, primary concerns and the primitive world in which no distinction exists between subject and object (250). Knowing thyself, as the motto of Delphi suggests, constitutes a unity of Word and Spirit: the only book Frye thinks that is devoted wholly to 'this hidden intercommunion' is *Finnegans Wake* (250). He argues that the Romantic mythological revolution deserves more study because of its impact on history (251).

The ideological implications of this revolution involve 'a new kind of alliance with nature, cemented two centuries ago' that 'has shifted the conception of man from a primitive reasoning or conscious being, who creates in imitation of God's creation, to a primarily willing being whose creations are allied to natural energies like the mutations of evolution' (Frye 1990e: 252). The Romantic myth re-emphasizes the myth of death, disappearance and return and has a concern for food and drink (252–3). This myth also tends towards the cyclical, which, for most ideologies and religions, is pessimistic and needs the supplement of hope, so that, in Frye's view, the unending cycle is a demonic parody. The continuity of the vegetable cycle is the foundation of the ideological adaptation of the myth because the anxiety over the disappearance of food and drink and the desire to keep them in supply expands into a similar anxiety and desire to maintain social institutions and ideological causes (255). In the Old Testament an ideology occurs in which the king is the Lord's anointed just as in the Tudor myth of kingship that Shakespeare represents, although the figure of Christ the king complicates the king's two bodies in medieval and Renaissance Europe (259–60; see also Hart 1992c). Frye says there are two organizing patterns in the Bible and in literature: the natural cycle and the apocalypse or the final separation of life from death, a hope for the future in history or in an afterlife, the hope in a revolution that will reverse but not revolve (260–2). We return to vision. Christ descends to the lower world in his death and burial, surfaces in his Resurrection, ascends in the ascension and descends at the apocalypse, so that, Frye concludes, the whole '*axis mundi* is traversed in this quest, and any second coming after that can be only an enlarged vision in ourselves of what is there now' (262). Frye associates the image of excretion with the apocalypse as well as two other motifs, amnesia and doubles or twins (262–6).

In the eighth and last chapter of *Words with Power*, 'Fourth Variation: The Furnace', Frye looks at the fall in the light of the P account, the story of the rebel angels, the war in heaven and their expulsion (1990e: 272f.). The three elements of this fourth variation are like those of the preceding three. The demonic parody is the descent into nothingness for an individual or society. That power always corrupts and nothing can be done about its ascendancy is the ideological adaptation. The authentic myth is the ascent after the creative descent to wisdom and to the genuine sources of human power (293). It is possible that the figure of Prometheus is the centre of this chapter and of Frye's book. For Frye, there are four main aspects of Prometheus, which he relates to Robert Frost's west-running brook, which, like the river of Eden, divides into four parts and suggests the theme of creative ascent: the tormented champion of mankind (the purgatorial stream), the bringer of fire to humanity (the technological stream), the god of forethought (the educational stream) and the ultimate creator of humankind (the Utopian stream) (294). In discussing technological imagery Frye says that the image of the furnace can be used for positive and negative aspects of the lower world, the purgatorial crucible from which the redeemed emerge purified and the hell of heat without light (296). These images become vehicles for vision:

> The goal of the creative ascent is the transcending of time and space as we know them, and the attaining of a present and a presence in another dimension altogether. The present is the expanded moment of awareness that is as long as recorded human history; the presence is the love that moves the sun and the other stars.

(303)

This situation applies to Dante as he reaches the top of the *axis mundi* and is in God's presence at the end of the *Paradisio*, but the vision of the eternal now, even if temporarily before history reasserts itself, haunts Frye's work. Literature, for Frye, is like prayer, because it is not addressed to anyone directly in this world and is overheard. The primary concern of the variation of the furnace is property, to make something proper to oneself (303–6). As in *The Double Vision*, Frye says here that humanity now needs to interest itself in primary and not in secondary or ideological concerns in order to achieve 'a renewed integration of humanity with nature' (307). He argues that the technical, purgatorial and educational elements of the Promethean vision contribute to a social vision. Ultimately, Frye is concerned with power. The title of his book, *Words with Power*, is from Luke 4: 32 and refers to Jesus' many references to power. Frye distinguishes demonic power from creative power. He laments the path of power without words in our century, with the barbarity which, since the 1930s, he has so often associated with the Nazis:

> The degenerating of society begins with the sacrifice of primary concerns to the secondary concerns of an ideology. Once a society is at this point it finds that it cannot maintain a consistent ideology either, but breaks down into simple brutality and barbarism. The final stage is a genocide that eventually turns on itself.
>
> (309)

For Frye, the opposite of dystopia is a sense of a social norm. On the lower level of the norm there is a vision of fulfilled secondary concerns, a political idea that has some connection with what is going on in the society. On the higher level a vision of fulfilled primary concerns occurs. If this vision of freedom, health, happiness, equality and love disappears or gives way to an ideological one, however admirable the ideology, Frye says that it will become obsessive and slip downwards. Primary vision needs to remain for creativity to survive (310). In the Bible primary concern reminds us of the Book of Job. God and Job return us to questions of vision of personal and social restoration. Job's great speech at the end of Chapter 31 expresses primary concern. It is here and now on earth that we make heaven or hell. Frye ends the book in which he is most concerned with ideology with a paradox. When we are most oppressed by the mystery of existence and the apparent impotence of God to care about human suffering, we hear the rhetoric of the ideologues until, perhaps, 'the terrifying and welcome voice may begin, annihilating everything we thought we knew, and restoring everything we have never lost' (313; see also 311–12 and p. 260 below).

Frye ends his discussion of mythology and ideology, as mediated through metaphor, with a paradoxical vision, strangely oral and aural. Is he proclaiming that proclamation is ideology, although the author of the Book of Job and Frye himself are given to prophecy and apocalypse? This remains a difficult question for the ironic medium of criticism from the metaphorical identification of poetry. Criticism may be one kind of writing, but can this genre recreate the epiphanic union of subject and object, of a timeless now, as well as the more concrete and apparently more direct images of poetry? Are 'vision' and 'mythology' just other words for ideology? There is a great human desire to get beyond ideology, but such a quest may be impossible. Politics does get in the way of feeding starving children, but perhaps another kind of politics mobilizes people to find a way to feed them. Nature may breed greed as much as sharing, just as politics can. But there are nagging doubts about ideology, especially when it has lost touch with the basic needs of people. Frye raises these necessary psychological and social questions. He meets power without words with words with power.

8   A visionary criticism

So all their praises are but prophecies
Of this our time, all you prefiguring,
And for they looked but with divining eyes,
They had not still enough your worth to sing.

(Shakespeare, Sonnet 106)

The subject, as it so frequently was, is God.

(Margaret Atwood, *Vic Report* ['A Tribute to Northrop Frye'], 1991)

In 'General Note: Blake's Mysticism' near the end of *Fearful Symmetry*
(1947), Northrop Frye clarifies the relation between vision and mysticism as it pertains to William Blake, the inspiration for so much of
Frye's work. Frye characterizes Blake's art as a spiritual discipline and
says that for visionaries like Blake the true God is not the orthodox
Creator but an unattached creative Word who is free from an eternal
substance and an eternal nothingness. Only an effort of vision that
rejects the duality of subject and object and attacks the antithesis of
being and non-being can attain unity with God. The effort of vision is
the realization in complete experience of the identity of God and the
human in which both disappear. Frye says that 'Blake's conception of
art as creation designed to destroy *the* Creation is the most readily
comprehensible expression of this effort of vision I know' (1947a: 431).
This effort of vision is, according to Frye, at the foundation of Zen
Buddhism and of the great speculative Western school that forms a
well-integrated tradition – the mystical. Blake is not a mystic if
mysticism means a contemplative quietism or a spiritual illumination
expressed in a practical and unspeculative piety, but, Frye asserts, 'if
mysticism means primarily the vision of the prodigious and unthinkable
metamorphosis of the human mind [Frye's description of which I have
outlined above] . . . then Blake is one of the mystics' (432). It is in this
last sense that I call Frye a mystic: he is one of the visionary company

244 *Northrop Frye*

(for reviews of Frye's work that include comments on vision, see, for instance, Becker 1982, Bloom 1957, Breslin 1982, Cahill 1983, Dudek 1982, Duffy 1968, Gillespie 1986, Globe 1983, Kenner 1982, Kermode 1982, Keynes 1947, Kirss 1983, Mandel 1982, Poland 1984, Schwab 1983, Speirs 1983, Wellek 1949 and Wheeler 1984).

It may be a little perverse to yoke 'mysticism' and 'vision', although Frye suggests that a specific meaning for this connection is possible in his 'General Note', but it is because there is some slippage between the two terms. Having admitted specifically that Frye is only a mystic in so far as he is a visionary, I shall mention in passing that he is, in these terms, a mystic-visionary and then call him a visionary henceforth, though the word 'mystic' may slip in from time to time. At the beginning of his study of Blake, Frye is more interested in making a sharp distinction between the mystic and visionary than he is at the end in his supplementary note. Frye thinks that mystical poets are rare and says that

> most of the poets generally called mystics might better be called visionaries, which is not quite the same thing. This *is* a word that Blake uses, and uses constantly. A visionary creates, or dwells in, a higher spiritual world in which the objects of perception in this one have been transfigured and charged with a new intensity of symbolism. This is quite consistent with art, because it never relinquishes the visualization which no artist can do without. It is a perceptive rather than a contemplative attitude of mind; but most of the greatest mystics, St. John of the Cross and Plotinus for example, find the symbolism of visionary experience not only unnecessary but a positive hindrance to the highest mystical contemplation. This suggests that mysticism and art are in the long run mutually exclusive, but that the visionary and the artist are allied.
>
> (1947a: 8)

Frye then admits that the distinction between mysticism and vision cannot be absolute, but he stands by its spirit (8). He also admits the visionary aspect of mysticism in his 'General Note' but might have mentioned in this early passage in *Fearful Symmetry* that there are mystical and visionary critics because criticism is an art as well as a science (or social science) and that writing is writing. In what follows, I want to expand on the view of Northrop Frye as a visionary critic, by tracing his use and vision of vision from his early work to his last words. Frye's metaphor of vision connects Blake's interest in the Bible and in art with his own. It is this visionary dimension that allows us to understand Frye's parallel interests in the Bible and literature, in keeping their analogical relation alive while maintaining their independence. The Bible is more than a work of art; literature is more than a secular scripture. But the Bible is the code of art, and literature displaces and translates biblical metaphors and myths into secular society. Contemporary critical theory derives from biblical hermeneutics, but it translates that debate in a different context. Frye connects these axioms through vision.

The visionary is the person who passes from sight into vision, and the artist is visionary. He or she struggles to develop perception into creation, to realize, through the mind's ordering of sense experience, a higher reality than experience or memory. In his discussion of Blake, Frye outlines three worlds: of memory, sight and vision. The world of memory is an egocentric, unreal world of abstract ideas and reflection, where we see nothing. The world of sight is an ordinary and potentially real world of subjects and objects, where we see what we have to see. The world of vision is a world of creators and creatures, where we see what we want to see. Frye equates the world of vision with that of art: this realm is one of 'fulfilled desire and unbounded freedom' (1947a: 26; see also 25). As works of art are more unified and concentrated than sense experience, it follows that the unlimited use of the imagination is not chaotic. Any antithesis between desire and reason, energy and order is fallacious. Although Frye distances himself from Blake by aligning himself with the sensible reader through the use of 'we', he is close to Blake because he realizes that the visionary, like the child, engages in the metaphorical or magical thinking that if we imagine something to be so, it will be (26–7). Frye reminds us that 'The Greek word for revelation is "apocalypse", and the climax of Christian teaching is in the "Revelation" or Apocalypse at the end of the Bible which tells us that there is an end to time as well as a beginning and a middle, a resurrection as well as a birth and a death; and that in this final revelation of the unfallen world all mystery will vanish' (44). John's symbol, Frye says, is the burning of the Great Whore, or Mystery. Frye's examination of Blake cannot be separated from a discussion of religion:

> Vision is the end of religion, and the destruction of the physical universe is the clearing of our own eyesight. Art, because it affords a systematic training in this kind of vision, is the medium through which religion is revealed. The Bible is the vehicle of revealed religion because it is a unified vision of human life and therefore, as Blake says, 'the Great Code of Art'. And if all art is visionary, it must be apocalyptic and revelatory too: the artist does not wait

to die before he lives in the spiritual world into which John was caught up.

(1947a: 45)

Although Frye does not say so here, criticism is an imaginative act that has a spiritual and visionary dimension that helps to defeat the chaos of time. To Frye's death, as I shall argue, especially in the light of what he says from *Fearful Symmetry* to *The Double Vision* (1991), one can apply his explanation of eternity and salvation in Blake: 'The man survives the death of the natural part of him as a total form of his imaginative acts, as the human creation out of nature which he has made' (47).

Frye's vision of Blake brings out the visionary in Frye. In speaking about Blake, Frye speaks about an important aspect of his imaginative life. Frye's *Anatomy*, which begins with the theoretical apparatus that surrounded the study of Blake, is an imaginative framework and not a rationalist's homage to reason and mania for rational classifications. It is a work that is more like Robert Burton's *Anatomy of Melancholy*, Blake's poetry, and W. B. Yeats' *A Vision*. But to return to Frye's discussion of the visionary in *Fearful Symmetry* reminds us that Atwood's comment, which I have made one of the epigraphs for this chapter, has more than a little truth in it. Frye says: 'The visionary sees, as the final revelation of the Word which God speaks to his mind, that the whole "outside" universe is a shadow of an eclipsed Man' (1947a: 48). The twofold vision that Blake mentions in a poem in a letter to Butts on 22 November 1802 means, according to Frye, the ability to see an unfallen and a fallen world at once (50). This double vision in this context provides the title for Frye's last and posthumous book. Although Blake associates the visionary with art, with a full imagination, and represents prophecy as that imaginative activity, it seems that by presenting an imaginative recreation of Blake's poetry, Frye is implying that criticism is a creative and imaginative act, a vision. Frye often makes statements without attribution to Blake or reference to him. He often speaks in his own voice in the larger context of his discussion of Blake, but without notation or a reminder that he is speaking about Blake. There is more here, I think, than wanting to avoid the aural white noise of interpolated phrases of attribution. Frye as subject and Blake as object frequently seem to meet in the 'eternal' relation of the metaphor. By a prophet, Blake means an honest person with great imaginative powers and not a seer who is predicting the future (59). Frye's later works bear out that he thinks that criticism is creative: the poet and the critic are visionary – they do not separate desire and reason. In Blake's scheme, all visionaries speak with the voice of God (78).

To separate Blake and Frye is, then, not an easy task. But before proceeding through Frye's study of Blake as a means of finding the groundwork for Frye's own visionary tendencies and then briefly discussing Frye's œuvre from that starting point, I want to take a step back and examine a visionary moment that Frye thinks is critical for Blake. Although there are obvious differences between Blake and Frye (for instance, one is a poet born in England in 1757; the other is a critic born in Canada in 1912), an important historical period that enabled Blake's vision is, by extension, important for Frye's vision.

In *Fearful Symmetry* Frye traces a crucial antecedent to Blake's 'thought'. He provides a general context for Blake's thought, and especially focuses on humanists and Renaissance writers who pertain most to Blake's vision. Frye argues that to comprehend Blake's thought historically, we should be aware of the relation between three Renaissance traditions: Italian Platonism (the imaginative approach to God through beauty and love); left-wing Protestantism (the doctrine of inner inspiration); and occultism (the theory of creative imagination) (1947a: 155). Frye returns to the cosmopolitan humanist culture between the Renaissance and Reformation, whose representatives are Erasmus, More, Rabelais, Cornelius Agrippa, Reuchlin, Paracelsus, Ficino, Pico della Mirandola and others. These writers emerge 'into a kind of visionary Christianity' (150). In Frye's view they envisage a greater reform than the Reformation or Counter-Reformation achieves, but they also wish to maintain the central vision of Christianity. For the most part, Frye says, in religion and literature, these scholars and writers defend Plato's visions against Aristotle's logic, imaginative interpretation against argument and God's Word against human reason.

The primary influences on Blake's vision are visionaries, such as Agrippa, Paracelsus, Jakob Boehme, Plotinus and Ficino. Citing Agrippa's *Vanity of the Arts and Sciences*, Frye calls attention to its argument against reason to the point of madness and its support for a true theology that consists of interpretation and prophecy. Agrippa bases his concept of interpretation on the four levels of allegory that descend from Dante. Here, Frye is using shorthand because the fourfold interpretative system derives from Aquinas, who inherits this tradition of interpretation from Philo Judaeus and early Christians like Origen, Clement, Jerome, Augustine and Gregory, and because Boccaccio takes it up after Dante (see Dante 1304–8, 1318). In the tenth article of the *Summa*, Aquinas answers the objection that it is not possible for a word in the Bible to have the following four senses: historical or literal, allegorical, tropological or moral, and anagogical. Dante extends these principles of interpretation to secular writing in his letter to Can Grande della Scala, and this extension probably makes Frye think of him in connection with Blake, who connected the Bible and poetry intimately. Frye himself adapts the terms 'literal', 'allegorical', and 'anagogic' in his theory of symbols in *Anatomy* (see also *Il Convivio (The Banquet)*). Agrippa equates prophecy with vision. *Vanity* ends with a panegyric on the Word of God, which, Frye reminds us, is not the tree of knowledge but the tree of life. Agrippa's argument (he uses one even though he prefers imaginative interpretation) is that the only source of authority in religion is the Word of God, but imagination is the authority for interpreting the Word of God. For Agrippa, the Word of God must be understood symbolically and not literally. Frye thinks that the humanists' interest in biblical scholarship and translation as well as in the occult derives from the doctrine of the Word of God (see Vickers 1984).

Cabbalism and alchemy, as Frye says, contribute means towards a better understanding of 'the central form of Christianity as a vision rather than as a doctrine or ritual' (1947a: 151). Frye thinks that these visionary Christians, including Thomas Vaughan, one of Agrippa's disciples, seek a *via media* of vision and theosophy, a conception the Reformation curtails. Nevertheless, the Anabaptists keep, as part of their faith, apocalyptic vision and their belief that the only authority is the 'inner light' of the scriptures, which Frye says is close to Blake's theory of imagination. Frye traces the connection between the Anabaptists and Blake through Jakob Boehme and the Quakers. The 'inner light' of the Anabaptists and Blake's vision also converge through occultism, from which the humanists take a theory of imagination. In particular they are drawn to the idea of the microcosm.

Paracelsus, apocalyptic philosophy, Boehme and Plotinus are also proleptic for Blake's vision. For Paracelsus, 'man' epitomizes the universe and, with imagination, relates the corresponding universe to himself. Whereas Paracelsus speaks about vision for doctors, Blake does so for artists. To some extent, Frye distances Paracelsus from Blake and from himself because he thinks that Paracelsus tends towards superstition in the view that there is a latent correspondence between the human and natural orders. Frye links apocalyptic philosophy and Blake because the alchemical process occupies a similar position to art in Blake: through transformation, they attempt to restore or resurrect humankind (1947a: 152–3). Boehme combines the occult and left-wing inner-light Protestant traditions. His visionary poetry represents biblical accounts of creation, fall, redemption and apocalypse. Frye suggests that Boehme's idea of creation and fall most influences Blake (153). But this visionary tradition is old and complex. Here are a few of the connections Frye discusses. In addition to likening the lower half of the mystical system of Plotinus to that of Blake, Frye connects Plotinus to Ficino, who combines Eros and Venus with the Plotinian idea that humans are mental units in a world-spirit (154). This vision of love, Frye says, also appears as the climax of the courtier's education in Castiglione and enters English literature through Spenser (155). Frye looks at the seventeenth- and eighteenth-century contexts of Blake's thought, but these rarely touch directly on the question of vision (155–86). He builds his vision on Blake's and on those to whom both visionaries owe a debt: the church fathers; Aquinas, Dante and Boccaccio; and the Renaissance, humanism and the Reformation as I have just discussed. I want now to return to tracing the changes to Blake's own vision and to Frye's.

The view of Frye as a visionary does not discount his use of critical distance, which he would recognize in Aristotle, but calls attention to the idea of the sublime he found in Longinus and, most of all, the centrality of vision in the Bible and Blake. My emphasis on the visionary Frye is polemical in so far as I realize that Frye's work has many facets, but the central aspect of vision has been relatively neglected among literary critics. Two sources, the Bible and Blake, are formative for Frye. He connects Blake with the Bible, whose myths and metaphors the poet recreates in all his poems. And the question of vision recurs in this context:

> Jesus is the Logos or Word of God, the totality of creative power, the universal visionary in whose mind we perceive the particular. But the phrase 'Word of God' is obviously appropriate also to all works of art which reveal the same perspective, these latter being recreations of the divine vision which is Jesus. The archetypal Word of God, so to speak, sees this world of time and space as a single creature in eternity and infinity, fallen and redeemed. This is the vision of God (subjective genitive: the vision which God in us has). In this world the Word of God is the aggregate of works of inspired art, the Scripture written by the Holy Spirit which spoke by the prophets. Properly interpreted, all works of art are phases of that archetypal vision. The vision of the Last Judgment, said Blake, 'is seen by the Imaginative Eye of Every one according to the situation he holds'. And the greater the work of art, the more completely it reveals the gigantic myth which is the vision of this world as God sees it, the outlines of that vision being creation, fall, redemption and apocalypse.
>
> (108)

The word 'vision' comes up over and over again in this passage. It is the centre of Blake's art as well as the Bible. From the beginning, it is also at the core of Frye's theory, of his career. He begins with the Bible and ends there. That is not to underestimate Frye's contribution to genre theory. His work on comedy and romance is ground-breaking. Nor is it to neglect the contributions he makes to the study of Shakespeare and Milton. Frye's writing in the fields of education and the social function of criticism also expands our vision. As encyclopedic as Frye is, he returns us to the Bible, to its metaphors, images, narratives and typologies. In the paragraph following the passage I have just quoted, Frye declares:

> The Bible is the world's greatest work of art and therefore has primary claim to the title of God's word. It takes in, in one immense sweep, the entire world of experience from the creation to the final vision of the City of God, embracing heroic saga, prophetic vision, legend, symbolism, the Gospel of Jesus, poetry and oratory on the way. It bridges the gap between a lost Golden Age and the time that the Word became flesh and dwelt among us, and it alone gives us the vision of the life of Jesus in this world.
>
> (108)

And the Bible, for Blake, is the great code of art. Blake calls his work visionary and uses the word 'vision' repeatedly. Frye uses the word again and again, but does not call attention to the visionary element in his criticism.

Frye discusses Blake's notion of art in terms of vision. He represents Blake's distinction between allegory and vision in *Vision of the Last Judgment*. Here, Blake says that allegory depends on memory and possesses some visionary aspect, whereas vision is imagination, a representation of what exists, eternally, really, and unchangeably. He also declares: 'The Hebrew Bible & the Gospel of Jesus are not Allegory, but Eternal Vision or Imagination of All that Exists' (quoted in Frye 1947a: 116). The role of art in Blake's poetic world is to humanize nature, to make it into a human form. The most concentrated vision of an animal, for instance, a lion, has an archetypal human creature in it (Frye 1947a: 123–4). At the heart of Blake's vision is the notion of a central form, within whose huge framework, Frye says, 'certain states of the human mind that created it inevitably appear and take on human lineaments, just as a pantheon crystallizes from a religious vision' (124). The larger unit of Blake's imaginative state is a larger human body or being: Jesus and Albion are eternals (127).

In his poems Blake keeps imagination before him. Blake often represents Orc, whom Frye describes as 'human imagination trying to burst out of the body', as a serpent bound or nailed to the tree of mystery, which is a prototype of the crucifixion, or in Frye's words, 'the image of divine visionary power bound to a natural world symbolized by a tree of mystery', which 'is the central symbol of the fallen world' (1947a: 136–7; see also 223; for other descriptions of Orc, see, for instance, 206–8, 218–20, 227–30). In discussing the view of life as an Orc cycle in Blake, Frye says:

> The real man . . . is the total form of the creative acts and visions which he evolves in the course of his 'Becoming' life. The latter exists in time and space, but his 'Being' or real existence is a work of art, and exists, like the work of art, in that unity of time and space which is infinite or eternal. The imagination or Being, then, is immortal, a form constructed out of time but existing in what Paul calls the 'fullness of time'. We arrive at the conception of immortality as soon as we grasp the idea of a reality which is not merely part of an indefinite persistence of an indefinitely extensive physical world. But for that very reason immortality cannot mean the indefinite survival of a 'Becoming' life arrested at some point in its development . . . as in most conceptions of an immortal personality. What is immortal about the man is the total form of his creative acts, and these total forms are the characters, or 'identities', as Blake calls them, of the men who made them, the isolating of what is eternally humane in them from the accidents of Becoming.
>
> (247–8)

Immortality, for Blake, is like a work of art, a kind of synchronic, unified and humane act of imagination drawn from the diachronic realm of becoming. The eternal now derives from but transforms the sequential world of experience. It is vision that enables us to see ourselves and our lives whole. In *The Double Vision* Frye reveals that he shares Blake's idea of immortality, which he describes in *Fearful Symmetry*:

> There is no revelation except that which unites the human with the divine through human channels, and our moral acts owe their value, not to faith in what we do not see, but to the form of what we do see, the vision of the world as fallen, redeemed and proceeding to apocalypse. This vision is the framework or larger form of all good acts, and the more consciously the good act is related to this vision the better it is.
>
> (1947a: 250)

Like Blake, Frye seems to think that the real artist is the total form of his creation, his vision of life, a part of the Word of God, the archetypal vision (250). The unification of humans and God occurs in the whole form of God's creation, which is Jesus (251). In art is Blake's redemption.

Some of Blake's poems show the restorative power of vision. In *The Four Zoas*, for instance, Blake represents the loss of identity between human and divine natures, the struggle to regain this identity (which Jesus completes), and the apocalypse (Frye 1947a: 270). In the ninth Night of *The Four Zoas*, Blake ventures where no English poet has gone – the *Dies Irae* – because Blake represents the city of God, in Frye's words, as 'a phoenix arising in the human mind from the ashes of the burned mysterious universe' (305). In this ninth Night, Frye argues, Blake appears 'to have found his way back to the very headwaters of Western imagination, to the crystalline purity of vision of the *Völuspa* or the *Muspilli*, where the end of time is perceived, not as a vague hope, an allegory or an indigestible dogma, but as a physical fact as literal as a battle and as imminent as death' (305–6). Frye discusses how Blake chooses his apocalyptic images. *The Four Zoas* does not give us an imaginatively coherent view of how we get from Blake's time to the Last Judgement, or a definitive or total vision of the city of God, but it represents tremendous creative power (306–9). Frye's relation to Blake is similar to Blake's to Milton. Blake's *Milton* 'attempts to recreate the central vision of life, based on the Bible, which made Milton a great Christian poet' (346). This poem is a prelude to *Jerusalem* (355). The latter poem shows that the vision of the city of God, as clarified through art, presses down on Albion's retina, and with consciousness, he will perform an act of vision until the image assumes its proper form. By extension, 'we become what we behold' because the image of God, the form of human life, is the reality of ourselves (401). Frye says that a Blakean epic is 'a "divine vision" of a whole life' (405).

In the twelfth and final chapter of *Fearful Symmetry*, appropriately called 'The Burden of the Valley of Vision', Frye assesses what Blake can teach the modern critic. He can teach us about the delight of art from which instruction is inseparable. The work of art that is most complete in itself suggests something beyond itself: or, as Frye says in explaining Blake, 'its integrity is an image or form of the universal integration which is the body of a divine Man' (1947a: 418). Blake's art attempts to achieve 'absolute clarity of vision', but we cannot understand Blake without comprehending all the texts important to him, if we believe in an archetypal vision, which great art reveals to us (418). Frye believes in archetypal vision. He also discusses how Blake's vision is distant from us (including a critique of Blake's Prophecies and a recognition of Blake's historical difference) and how it can restore a mythopoeic or archetypal criticism, a grammar of imaginative iconography (419–21).

Blake's recognition of 'a total form of vision' is a return to critical principles found among the Renaissance humanists and Elizabethans and attempts to complete the humanist revolution, which points out how the classical in art and the scriptural in religion approximate each other and make each other healthier while providing the authority for humane letters (420). Frye has a vision of Blake's vision:

> Such a cultural revolution would absorb not only the Classical but all other cultures into a single visionary synthesis, deepen and broaden the public response to art, deliver the artist from the bondage of a dingy and nervous naturalism called, in a term which is a little masterpiece of question-begging, 'realism', and restore to him the catholicity of outlook that Montaigne and Shakespeare possessed. And though the one religion would be, as far as Blake is concerned, Christianity, it would be a Christianity equated with the broadest possible vision of life.
>
> (420–1)

Here, we have Frye finding identity in Blake and, even in historical distancing, a beginning to a larger project, which, of course, is composed of the articles leading up to *Anatomy*, the great book itself, and many of Frye's works that owe something to it. Frye distinguishes Blake's vision from the Romantics' and our own but advocates our use of Blake to recover and fulfil the humanist moment in the Renaissance (421). Like Frye, Foucault also thinks the Enlightenment took a wrong turn towards rationalism, so that one must hearken to the Renaissance to find a better way (Foucault 1961; Frye 1947a: 413–14).

Frye's work echoes and plays variations on a theme from Blake's visionary poetry. In 'The Burden of the Valley of Vision' Frye says that Blake wanted to teach England that empire is a descent from art and how to use its vast imaginative reservoirs, found especially in its great poets (406–7). Blake's vision informs Frye's. Of Blake, Frye says:

> The only legitimate compulsion on the artist is the compulsion to clarify the form of his work, and in accepting other compulsions he is at once trapped in compromise. . . . Cockney cheek and Nonconformist conscience, two of the most resolute and persistent saboteurs of the dark Satanic mills in English life, combine in Blake to establish an incorruptible mental court without appeal to which all apologies for the traditional and conventional are referred. The public's contemptuous neglect of Blake was as wrong and foolish as it could be, but nevertheless Blake owes much of his integrity to his isolation.
>
> (412–13)

Frye is not Blake and is too sane to think he is, but his visionary side shares some of Blake's search for clarity of form through repetition, nonconformism and isolation. In 'Expanding Eyes', perhaps the central essay in *Spiritus Mundi* (1976) and one that takes its title from Blake's *The Four Zoas*, Frye describes himself and his unbudging position in terms that sound like his description of Blake:

> The sense of being something of a loner has always been in any case rather exceptionally true of me, with my introverted temperament, indolent habits and Canadian nationality. . . . My work since then [*Anatomy*] has assumed the shape of what Professor Jerome Bruner would call a spiral curriculum, circling around the same issues, though trying to keep them open-ended. This may be only a rationalization for not having budged an inch in eighteen years, but the most serious adverse criticisms of me seem to me to be based on assumptions too remote from mine for revision to meet them.
>
> (1976c: 99–100)

Frye's criticism and Blake's poetry attempt to recover or recreate the mythological universe. They are not the same but show an identity. It is no wonder that in the same place in *Fearful Symmetry* from which I just quoted, Frye says: 'Blake's great value as a personal influence in English literature is that he is so outstanding an example of a precious quality of mental independence' (1947a: 413). Frye traces Blake's movement after *Jerusalem* from poetry to painting and prose criticism. Blake's theory of art lies at the foundation of Frye's, and at the centre of the poet's theory is his idea of 'the recreation of the archetype, the process which unites a sequence of visions, first into a tradition, then into a Scripture' (415). Moreover, Blake illustrates the visions of other poets in order for their readers to understand better their archetypal significance. Frye contends that Blake found a way to combine his role as creator and teacher, mythopoeic art and instruction in how to read it. Blake's movement from poet to critic makes him more like Frye, who had, in fact, also begun as a writer as much as critic (Frye 1947a: 415, Ayre 1989: 147, 167–8).

   To return to the very end of *Fearful Symmetry*, one can hear Frye's vision of order, as set out in *Anatomy*, arising from his discussion of Blake as visionary: 'It is with criticism as with so many other aspects of contemporary life: for better or worse the reign of *laissez faire* is over, and the problem of achieving order without regimentation is before us' (1947a: 423). Frye says that critical theory will follow the great mythopoeic literature of modernism, especially *Finnegans Wake*. Frye has not wavered from his vision of unity and identity, which is not the same as conformity and sameness, and much of the impetus or analogy for that vision was found in Blake:

> Blake's doctrine of a single original language and religion implies that the similarities in ritual, myth and doctrine among all religions are more significant than their differences. It implies that a study of comparative religion, a morphology of myths, rituals and theologies, will lead us to a single visionary conception which the mind of man is trying to express, a vision of a created and fallen world which has been redeemed by a divine sacrifice and is proceeding to regeneration.
>
> (424)

Frye sees criticism doing what anthropology and psychology can only suggest because a comparative study of rituals and dreams can give an intuitive sense of the unity of the human mind, but a comparative study of art – anagogy – should demonstrate it. He seeks the missing link in the whole pattern of contemporary thought, a fitting together of theories, all of which seem to find resemblances to aspects of Blake's work (424–5). But Frye is also ironic. He cautions his reader that Blake is a typical great poet because he possesses a scale and an imaginative unity, not because he is a 'spiritual preceptor', like the figure in Blake's sketch 'Visionary Head' (426). But Frye's observation probably occurred to readers when first looking at the title of this chapter: 'Even Blake's favorite words "imagination" and "vision" are now rather tarnished, because so long used for the sentimental vagueness associated with them by vague and sentimental people' (427). This feeling about these words may have changed a little after their revival in the 1960s. In Frye's schema, as in Blake's, the author provides words, and the reader meaning. Frye cannot help speak of Blake's vision in terms of his own: to pursue the meaning of a word in poetry is to pursue the Word, 'the unit of meaning, the Scripture, and the Son of God and Man' (428). Here, Frye says, we arrive at the gate, where Blake identifies word with a single comprehensible form, yet Frye ends *Fearful Symmetry* with a vision that is Blake's and his own:

> But the gates are to be opened, and there is still much to be seen by the light of the vision Blake saw – perhaps the same light that broke in on the dying Falstaff when he babbled of green fields and played with flowers, and on his hostess when she told how he had gone into 'Arthur's' bosom, and how he had talked of the Whore of Babylon.
>
> (428)

The critic makes his gigantic form of unified insight from words that come down to him, but not without humour.

It is obvious from my comments on vision in *Fearful Symmetry*, which are not exhaustive, that the question of vision in Frye's canon is central and pervasive. Except for more detailed discussion of *The Double Vision*, my argument will be brief, in the spirit that an essay is an attempt but is not exhaustive. Although it is not sufficient, the aspect I want to concentrate on in Frye's intervening works is visionary or apocalyptic endings to his essays and books, which are in keeping with his fascination with comic and romance endings in literature, which are derived, in part, from the U-shaped narrative of the Bible. All contain a movement towards a happy ending or positive vision (see Frye 1948, 1978). I have selected representative works of Frye from the 1950s, 1960s, 1970s, 1980s and 1990s with which to look at this phenomenon.

At the end of *Anatomy*, Frye returns to the vision of literature, of the author and reader, as mediated through the critic. He reminds us that literature, like mathematics, is a language that is not true but that provides means for expressing innumerable truths. For Frye, after providing a great anatomy of literature, the objective world only gives a provisional way of unifying experience, so that it makes sense 'to infer a higher unity, a sort of beatification of common sense' (1957: 354). All verbal constructs, including law, metaphysics, history and theology, lead us to their metaphorical and mythical outlines and to the story of the Tower of Babel: when we construct a system to unite earth and heaven, we discover we can't make it and are amid a plurality of languages. But Frye returns to *Finnegans Wake*, which he invoked at the end of *Fearful Symmetry*, in which the dreamer awakens after spending the night in communion with a gigantic body of metaphorical identifications, and forgets what he has learned. Frye says that the recovery or recreation of the keys to dreamland is left to the ideal reader, or the critic. And this leads Frye, at the end of his great schema, which too many have attributed to sterile reason, to hearken to a Blakean imagination. In a low-key vision (who says that sight is the only function of vision?), Frye concludes *Anatomy*:

> Some such activity as this of reforging the broken links between creation and knowledge, art and science, myth and concept, is what I envisage for criticism. Once more, I am not speaking of a change of direction or activity in criticism: I mean only that if critics go on with their own business, this will appear to be, with increasing obviousness, the social and practical result of their labors.

(1957: 354)

When Frye enters into the local and political debate over Canada and participates in the celebration of the Canadian centennial in 1967 with some ironic detachment, it is because he believes in a higher reality or identity than the everyday world of experience. He also has a social and political vision, which, as he implies in the last phrase in *Anatomy*, arises out of the critic's relation to literature. At the very end of *The Modern Century*, Frye provides another example of his 'utopian' vision:

> One of the derivations proposed for the word Canada is a Portuguese phrase meaning 'nobody here'. The etymology of the word Utopia is very similar, and perhaps the real Canada is an ideal with nobody in it. The Canada to which we really do owe loyalty is the Canada that we have failed to create. In a year bound to be full of discussions of our identity, I should like to suggest that our identity, like the real identity of all nations, is the one that we have failed to achieve. It is expressed in our culture, but not attained in our life, just as Blake's new Jerusalem to be built in England's green and pleasant land is no less a genuine ideal for not having been built there. What there is left of the Canadian nation may well be destroyed by the kind of sectarian bickering which is so much more interesting to many people than genuine human life. But, as we enter a second century contemplating a world where power and success express themselves so much in stentorian lying, hypnotized leadership, and panic-stricken suppression of freedom and criticism, the uncreated identity of Canada may be after all not so bad a heritage to take with us.
>
> (1967b: 122–3)

Although at the end of 'Expanding Eyes', the central essay in *Spiritus Mundi*, Frye discusses the descending side of 'our world-picture', he ends the essay with the ascending side, or 'the power of creation, directed toward the goal of creating a genuinely human community' (1976c: 122). This recreation of a genuine human community sounds very much like the endings of the books we have discussed, in particular, *The Modern Century*. It hearkens to Frye's ideal of humanism before the Reformation and Counter-Reformation closed much of the window of hope. But Frye, here and in his theory of the structure of comedy and romance as well as in his discussions of biblical typology, realizes the chaos, darkness, desert and alienation that occur before our regaining of order or paradise. Once again, at the end of 'Expanding Eyes', after evoking Blake, Frye gives us our recreation of the divine comedy:

> On the ascending side there is a reversal of metamorphosis, a disenchanting journey back to our original identity that ends when the

human creator recovers his creations from his Muses, and lives again, like Job, with the daughters of his memory transformed into a renewed presence.

(1976c: 122)

At the end of the last essay in *Spiritus Mundi*, 'Wallace Stevens and the Variation Form', Frye also speaks of imagination, *Finnegans Wake* and vision, thereby echoing the endings of *Fearful Symmetry* and *Anatomy*. With Stevens, and in the shadow of Blake, Frye supposes 'we see the world as total process, extending over both death and life, always new, always just beginning, always full of hope, and possessed by the innocence of an uncreated world which is unreal only because it has never been fixed in death' (1976c: 294). With Stevens' own lines, Frye expands and amplifies this point.

As an aside, I want to break my pattern, backtrack to the 1960s and mention some of Frye's other works besides the ones I have selected to represent each decade of his writing career. The end of *Fables of Identity* (1963) appeals once more to vision in Blake and *Finnegans Wake*. The final passage in *The Return to Eden* (1965), which is a study of Milton, returns to Frye's central theme and conclusion, with which he seems to end the variations on the one book he is writing and rewriting throughout his career:

> the central myth of mankind is the myth of lost identity: the goal of all reason, courage and vision is the regaining of identity. The recovery of identity is not the feeling that I am myself and not another, but the realization that there is only one man, one mind, and one world, and that all walls of partition have been broken down forever.

(1965c: 143)

Frye ends *A Natural Perspective* (1965), a discussion of Shakespeare's comedy and romance, with *The Tempest* and an appeal to vision: 'When Prospero's work is done, and there is nothing left to see, the vision of the brave new world becomes the world itself, and the dance of the vanishing spirits a revel that has no end' (1965b: 159).

These works are from the central decade of Frye's working life, the 1960s, but even as late as 1986, Frye and his editor, Robert Sandler, use *The Tempest* to end the collection of Frye's undergraduate lectures, *Northrop Frye on Shakespeare*. Frye echoes the ending of *A Natural Perspective*, and plays a variation on his familiar coda:

> perhaps our children can sow the seeds in the sea and bring forth again the island that the world has been searching for since the dawn of history, the island that is both nature and human society restored to

their original form, where there is no sovereignty and yet where we all of us are kings.

(1986b: 186)

Frye gives his students and readers another fable of identity, another vision of recreation where the fall brings us back a renovated Atlantis, or Eden, a greater fulfilment of what was lost in the first place. Frye's return to the Bible in *The Great Code* (1982) and *Words with Power* (1990) reinforces Frye's comic vision. His last sentences in *The Great Code* personify the Bible, partly to take advantage of an Old English riddle whose answer is a book, or Bible codex, but mainly to speak of the resurrection of the Bible as the Word:

> The normal human reaction to a great cultural achievement like the Bible is to do with it what the Philistines did to Samson: reduce it to impotence, then lock it in a mill to grind our aggressions and prejudices. But perhaps its hair, like Samson's, could grow again even there.
>
> (1982b: 233)

Here, then, the Bible plays the hero, pulling down the figurative temple on cultural Philistines, so that they might rediscover the imaginative power of the Bible, rather than bind it to their envy and ignorance. Even in the Babel of contemporary critical theory, perhaps with its share of Philistines, Frye hopes, in the Introduction to *Words with Power*, for a common underlying vision. This hope recalls Blake's doctrine of a single original language that Frye had noted near the end of *Fearful Symmetry* (1947a: 424). Productive scholars, not merely those who publish to show their competence, may operate in a variety of 'schools', but they seem to Frye

> to have, for all their surface disagreements, an underlying consensus of attitude, out of which a progress toward some unified comprehension of the subject could emerge, and lead to a construction far more significant than any deconstruction of it could possibly be. This corresponds to the situation of literature itself, where 'original' writers form a core within a larger group that follows fashionable conventions and *idées reçues*.
>
> (1990e: xviii)

Frye has kept alive his earlier vision for literary criticism, especially as it is expressed at the end of *Anatomy*. And he ends his career as he began it, which is not surprising for someone who prized Blake's repetition, and his own, as a sign of steadfastness in dignity and someone who often returned to Eliot's words in *Four Quartets*, that in our end is our beginning. Frye ends *Words with Power*, as he began it:

> When we become intolerably oppressed by the mystery of human existence and by what seems the utter impotence of God to do or even care anything about human suffering, we enter the stage of Eliot's 'word in the desert', and hear all the rhetoric of ideologues, expurgating, revising, setting straight, rationalizing, proclaiming the time of renovation. After that, perhaps, the terrifying and welcome voice may begin, annihilating everything we thought we knew, and restoring everything we have never lost.
>
> (1990e: 313)

At the end of Frye's last book published during his life, in an apocalyptic vision, he expresses hope for the restoration of an implied Word, the underlying unity of our creative imagination, which, paradoxically, was never lost. It was, however, forgotten, or obscured, or displaced in a hostile cultural climate. This vision at the end of things is the vision we need to begin anew. With characteristic allusion, Frye invites us to break through illusion.

The Double Vision was published posthumously in 1991: it is Frye's last book (for a more detailed discussion, see Hart 1992a). The first chapter looks at the double vision of language. In Frye's discussion of alienation, he suggests that spirituality may be a way to undo alienation and complete the person. He appeals to the rebirth or resurrection of the individual in the New Testament (Frye 1991a: 13–14). Frye contrasts the dismal history of Christianity to its ideal spirituality, to its vision:

> As the New Testament begins with the myth of the Messiah, so it ends, in the Book of Revelation, with the metaphor of the Messiah, the vision of all things in their infinite variety united in the body of Christ. And just as myth is not anti-historical but counter-historical, so the metaphor, the statement or implication that two things are identical though different, is neither logical nor illogical, but counter-logical. It presents the continuous paradox of experience, in which whatever one meets both is and is not oneself. . . . Metaphors are paradoxical, and again we suspect that perhaps only in paradox are words doing the best they can for us. The genuine Christianity that has survived its appalling historical record was founded on charity, and charity is invariably linked to an imaginative conception of language, whether consciously or unconsciously. Paul makes it clear

that the language of charity is spiritual language, and that spiritual language is metaphorical, founded on the metaphorical paradox that we live in Christ and Christ lives in us.

(17)

This emphasis on myth and metaphor occurs throughout Frye's writings. The spiritual body of Christ, like one of Blake's giant forms and like Finnegan, appears in many of Frye's works, especially in his endings. In a way *The Double Vision* is Frye's textual ending, which he seemed to sense, when he describes the opinions in the book not as those of final conviction but as those at a rest stop in a pilgrimage, 'however near the pilgrimage may now be to its close' (1991a: xviii). Frye contrasts literary and biblical myths because the vision of the spiritual life represented in the New Testament represents myths to live by and metaphors to live in, the transforming power of *kerygma* or proclamation (17–18).

Frye returns to a poem in Blake's letter to Thomas Butts on 22 November 1802 for the title of his book:

For double the vision my eyes do see,
And a double vision is always with me:
With my inward eye 'tis an old man grey;
With my outward a thistle across my way.
(quoted in Frye 1991a: 22)

Following Blake, Frye implies that sense perception is not enough, and that a subject recognizes itself as part of what it perceives. Like Blake, Frye advocates the humanizing of the world (22–3). The human consciousness of being in nature but apart from it represents a sabbatical vision (30–1). Frye says that to survive we must love ourselves and nature: because of the threat of nuclear war and ecological catastrophe this generation has no choice but to be wise (34). He is calling for the redemption of nature. Frye is indebted to Paul and Hegel in his appeal to idealism. The vision of an ideal, the spiritual kingdom that Jesus reveals in the Gospel, must be present and realizable. Paul's *soma pneumatikon*, the spiritual body or genuine human being, can only understand and realize this ideal. Moreover, Frye appeals to Hegel, who argues that we are aware of the division between the conscious subject and the unconscious object and that, by bridging the gap and abolishing the difference, we progress in knowledge and consciousness. For Frye, truth is a kind of spiritual body, but in religion people must maintain a sceptical attitude or they end up with self-idolatry. A spiritual vision depends on a creating God, not a Nobodaddy (38–9).

From the double vision of nature, Frye proceeds to the double nature of time. In Christianity, a spiritual vision means that everything is always everywhere, and time is a cross, where Christ descends and ascends through the horizontal axis of history (Frye 1991a: 41, 46). The story the Bible tells, from creation to apocalypse, moves from one creation to another that renews and restores humankind and expands its experience (49). Frye refers to the Preacher in Ecclesiastes, who sees wisdom as a double movement: it begins with present experience disappearing into past knowledge but becomes past knowledge illuminating and inhering in present experience (53). Our hope lies not in abstract constructs of history, which the nineteenth century passed on to us, but a social concern, a vision that emphasizes our individuality and our primary needs for survival, including ecological awareness (56–8).

In the final chapter, 'The Double Vision of God', Frye speaks of his design. He has tried to contrast the natural (physical) to the spiritual vision with regard to language, space and time. Single or natural vision must give way to double or spiritual vision (see Frye 1991a: 78). He also notes that only through human elements in the world can we come to the spiritual God (59), although the 'metaphorical vision may see the reflection of God from his works in nature'. As in *Fearful Symmetry*, here Frye advocates 'metaphorical literalism' and returns to Dante's view of language and interpretation as polysemous (69). He advocates a double vision, which includes spiritual vision, and glosses it with the line Shakespeare gave to Duke Orsino when he sees the twins, Viola and Sebastian, on stage together at the end of the play, 'A natural perspective, that is and is not' (71; see also Frye 1965b). Paradox is a central aspect of double vision (72). The polysemous levels of the Bible interest Frye. At these levels, 'the biblical stories form a myth to live by, transformed from the kind of story we can construct ourselves to a spiritual story of what has created and continues to re-create us' (76–7). The stories in the Bible may exhibit three levels: demonic parody, redemptive power and apocalyptic power (79). In his discussion of biblical narratives, Frye provides the keys to his vision of love:

> The virtues of faith and hope are purgatorial virtues, and culminate in the paradisal vision of love. Love in the New Testament is agape or caritas, God's love for humanity reflected in the human love for God and for one's neighbour. The sexual basis of love is subordinated, because the primary emphasis is on the individual and the community, but erotic love is clearly a part of the total vision. Such love, it seems to me, has to begin with the human recognition that it is only human beings who have put evil and suffering into human life, and

that no other entity than ourselves, certainly not God, is responsible for its persistence. I have expressed this elsewhere by suggesting that love or charity begins by asking the question, 'Why do *we* permit so much evil and suffering?'

(81)

Human love brings us to identity with God (81). Frye also asks whether our growing awareness of the limitations that our social conditioning imposes on us is connected with a process of cleaning up our vision of God (82).

Frye tells us that the single vision of God sees in Him human panic, rage, cruelty and domination and leads to a human appeal for Him to maintain these negatives in human life, whereas the double vision sees God as being close to human life when that is purged of human evil (1991a: 83). The double vision of language is the purifying of language to plain speech, aphorism, parable, to 'a power that re-creates the mind . . . as though there really were a Logos uniting mind and nature that really does mean "Word"' (83). Frye speaks of Blake's double vision as 'one in which the vision of gods comes back in the form of a sense of identity with nature, where nature is not merely to be studied and lived in but loved and cherished, where place becomes home' (83–4). Frye takes up Blake's cause: if the concept of nature grew from a mani-festation of intellectual coherence and of order into an object of love, that change would effect the harmony of spirit and nature that, Frye says, has been the central theme of his last book (84). He suggests that perhaps in a world of higher energies than the matter we inhabit, in a spiritual nature, 'we should be gods or numinous presences ourselves' (84). Then the spirit of humanity and the spirit of God would inhabit the same world. Frye challenges us with a vision that seems mystical within the limits of our senses and our knowledge. He tells a Blakean or biblical fable, as if to recall that for the metaphorical–literal imagination, a thistle is and is not a thistle. His is a visionary love, not concerned with theological doctrine, and in it Frye tries to overcome the future tense of tomorrow and the afterlife. Instead, he gives us a vision of the eternal now:

In the double vision of a spiritual and a physical world simul-taneously present, every moment we have lived through we have also died out of into another order. Our life in the resurrection, then, is already here, and waiting to be recognized.

(85)

Here, in Frye's very last words in his last book, we recognize his familiar movement to recognition, either as *anagnorisis* or epiphany, which, as he explains at the end of *The Return of Eden*, is its theological equivalent. God's metaphorical generation of Christ is such an epiphany, which manifests the Son in His divine capacity to others. This manifestation also recurs in the Incarnation (1965c: 142). It doesn't take too much of a surmise to see that in Frye's view a like epiphany occurs at the Resurrection. Frye's recurring fable of identity is something that raises us from the dead now into a life that tries to purge itself from an evil that we have made in the world. This is a divine comedy that begins with words but must be made flesh in the world.

Frye is a paradoxical visionary. His first and last books are on vision, the one on Blake's, the other on Frye's. But even in *The Double Vision* he summons Blake for his title and epigraph, if not for more. Frye found identity in Blake's texts. Still, Frye's first articles (1942–4), as opposed to reviews, are on music, the genre of the anatomy (Menippean satire), satire and Canadian poetry. They all indicate many of the critical concerns he discussed for the rest of his life. In 1945 he also writes brief articles on education, another of his lifelong fundamental interests. There are three strands to Frye's writing: the visionary, the anatomy, and the social and educational. The last two are more secular but are informed by the visionary. Why do I call Frye a paradoxical visionary? Obviously, he wanted to speak to a greater audience than could be reached from the pulpit of the United Church of Canada, and, like Dante, he was not content to interpret the meaning of the Bible on many levels and not literature. Here is the connection between the visionary works that relate the Bible and literature – *Fearful Symmetry*, *The Great Code*, *Words with Power* and *The Double Vision* – and *Anatomy of Criticism*. Frye goes back to the early church and to the Middle Ages to find terms for his symbolic modes at the heart of *Anatomy*, which was to revolutionize modern criticism in the English-speaking world. In the 'Prefatory Statements and Acknowledgements' to *Anatomy*, Frye traces the genesis of this book from what Blake had taught him about literary symbolism and biblical typology through work on Spenser, which led to a theory of allegory, and so on to Frye's *magnum opus* (1957: vii).

But, as Frye says in relation to Spenser, who learned from the literary theory of his day, in *Anatomy* Frye himself is interested more directly in critical theory. Frye's theory does grow out of his work on Blake and the Bible and represents a Dantean extension, but it is also an anatomy, ironic and satirical in places and certainly devoted to a discussion of irony and satire, genres that are conducive to the modern temperament. Frye refers to Aristotle as much as to the Bible because

Aristotle is the beginning of literary criticism in the West. In *Anatomy* Frye doesn't forget Plato, who also has a claim to be at the beginnings of criticism, but Frye cannot share the Renaissance humanist view that one had to prefer Plato's visions to Aristotle's logic. More to the point, in *Anatomy* Frye could not ignore Aristotle's perceptive and influential remarks on *mimesis*, catharsis and genre (especially tragedy). *Anatomy* is largely about genre. At the height and heart of Frye's career is his most famous book, the one that made him an international figure, and it is a study that began with Blake and the Bible but that could not ignore the secular, ironic and satirical spirit of the age in which it was written. Thus, if Frye's *Anatomy* is not a kind of latter-day version of Aristotle's *Poetics*, it is close enough.

The beginnings of Frye's career allow us to see this dual interest in anatomy and vision, both of which affect all his other topics. At the heart of his vision is the anatomy of literature, which is and is not a secular scripture, but at the heart of *Anatomy* is the trace of its visionary beginning and end. Frye knows more Aristotelian distance than Blake did, but with the poet he shares ironic and satiric distance. Frye is and is not a visionary. By definition a literary critic or theorist has to have more distance from the text than does a reader, but throughout his career, and especially in *Fearful Symmetry* and *The Double Vision*, his first and last books, Frye tends towards the great comic ending, the recreation and redemption of the author in the great imaginative body. His last words at Emmanuel College, University of Toronto are about religion, which is like but is not literature, and in particular about double vision, of this world and the world of the imagination. First and last, Frye's vision is the wholeness and atonement that imagination allows in literature and religion, here and now in the eternal.

9 The critic as writer

Art never expresses anything but itself. It has an independent life, just as
Thought has, and develops purely on its own lines. It is not necessarily
realistic in an age of realism, nor spiritual in an age of faith. So far from
being the creation of its time, it is usually in direct opposition to it, and the
only history that it preserves for us is the history of its own progress.
                              Vivian, in Oscar Wilde's 'The Decay of Lying'

The relation of art and thought, the fiction of criticism and the criticism
of fiction, holds a central place in Northrop Frye's work. He advocated
the creativity and integrity of criticism as well as of literature. This
Romantic position may also be a personal and historical one. Frye
himself stressed the creative aspects of myth and metaphor both in his
criticism and the fiction that he published in his twenties and continued
to plan well into middle age. The post-war age has become an age of
critical and scholarly output that is unmatched in 'Western' history. A
view, like Frye's, that elevated criticism to the level of literature and
justified the ways of departments of literature to humankind found
favour in a field that had so many doubts about whether it existed or if
it did, whether it should. The rise of English studies as a successor to
classics was a relatively new phenomenon (see Eagleton 1983b, Graff
1987, Murray 1991). These insecurities in the discipline are understandable. When examining the relation between Frye as a critic and a
fiction writer, I am not interested in psychoanalysing him. Instead, my
wish is to see whether his fiction can tell us something about his views
of creativity and writing in general. He didn't realize as early on as he
says in his interviews and critical works that he had no vocation for
writing literature. His hopes for his literary writing occur at the time he
is working out his commentary on Blake. Was writing about metaphor
as satisfying and as creative as creating it? Perhaps Frye realized where
his true talents lay and made the most of them; perhaps not. In an age
when Derrida, Kristeva, Cixous and many others are treating all writing

as writing, whether it is fiction or criticism or ficto-theory, Frye's proclamation that criticism is creative seems enlightened if different. His criticism tells stories, although stories that often retell those from literature or from class, but is set out in the language of argument and follows the conventions of scholarly or critical prose. His criticism is not constructed ostensibly as a fiction, although it may be a supreme fiction, like a cosmology. The fiction is different from the criticism. The two share properties but are generically distinct. This chapter will concentrate on Frye's fiction but, whenever possible, will relate it to his criticism and theory. For the most part, it will circle back to Frye's youth in order to try to illuminate the criticism that followed, to see whether he is a writer who chose criticism or a critic who wrote. Writing well was good enough for Auden in praising Yeats, but for Frye it was Yeats' vision that made him a major poet. It may be Frye's vision that makes him a major critic, but that still leaves us with the problem of whether criticism can be visionary in the same way and with the same effect that poetry can be. Is it the concrete nature of metaphor that resists the philosopher's abstract descriptions of it? Was Frye breaking new ground or was he like Wilde's liar seeking the impossible with spectacular success? Is it necessary to create a world of fiction to make a fictional world (see Hart 1988)? In this chapter I want to work backwards from the notebooks, journals and correspondence to Frye's stories in the 1930s and 1940s.

In Frye's papers at Victoria College in the University of Toronto there is much about his desire to write fiction. In Robert Denham's view Frye's plan to write a novel stayed with him a long time, although, as yet, because of the vastness of the papers, which occupy about 30 to 40 metres of shelf-space, and the difficulty in reading his handwriting, it is not possible to say how long. According to Denham, whatever Frye completed of his novel *Quiet Consummation* has been lost or may be the beginnings of a novel about the Reverend Kennedy and a woman called Megill, which runs to about fifteen pages in one of the files. In one journal that has the title *Quiet Consummation* and the subtitle *A Novel in Sonata Form*, and includes an accompanying 'musical', most of the notebook contains notes on the history of music. In a letter of 14 July 1935 Frye tells Roy Daniells that he has made substantial headway on *Quiet Consummation*, which is based on the sonata form:

I come up blushing shyly to confess that I am taking advantage of my unaccustomed freedom to start working a bit on a novel. It[s] provisional title is Quiet Consummation. It's not much of a novel, but I want to get it out of my system. No plot or theme or thesis or anything, just yet. It's laid out in sonata form. Amusing, I think, if it comes off at all. I am beginning to realize that, while I may and probably will turn out some fairly decent things on Blake and Shakespeare and Augustine and the rest critically, that the larger problem they refer back to, the relation of religion and art in symbolism, will require fictional and dramatic treatment. I have drawn up prospectuses of a magnum opus on purely speculative lines, but, while I could write about it, it wouldn't carry conviction to anybody.

He also tells Daniells that this novel is a secret, except to Helen Kemp, his future wife. One reason for this chapter is that I agree with Frye that fictional and dramatic treatments extend our understanding of critical problems. Although Frye's fiction is not extensive and was not published when he was at the height of his powers, it clarifies and extends some of his critical ideas. Narrative can always do some things that argument cannot. Denham also discovered two unpublished stories, 'Interpreter's Parlour' and 'Incident from the Golden Bough', which may be the second and fourth dialogues along with the two published ones, 'The Ghost' and 'Face to Face' (Denham 1992).

In Notebook 28 (transcribed by Denham in June 1992) Frye reveals his thoughts on why he wants to write. As this material is revealing and unpublished, it deserves extensive quotation as well as commentary:

All my life I've had an ambition to write fiction, either as a series of novels, or as one big novel. Some of the motivation is dubious: I want to prove to myself and to others that I can be 'creative' in the conventionally creative genres. The idea of a series of novels has gradually faded or has left me with the desire to leave, like Santayana, a single work of fiction behind me.

Frye qualifies his desire to write fiction because of his wish to prove himself to those who think that literature is the only creative written medium. This desire casts doubt on the creativity in his criticism as a means to win the approval of such people. The very success of such a putative novel could detract from the success of his criticism. He seems to be looking back here, perhaps in his old age, on his life, settling in the end for a wish to write a single novel as Santayana did with *The Last Puritan* (1935), seventeen years before his death in his eighty-ninth year. This work is not the one for which Santayana is most remembered, and it may not lead many to think of his creativity. Nor does Frye mention Santayana's poetry. Frye does not seem to have been driven to write poetry.

In this recollection Frye recalls that his first efforts were in realistic and representational form, which was out of fashion when he was writing this undated note and not, in his view, suited to his temperament because he had not experienced enough or did not think in those terms. Frye considers the success of Tolkien and the rise of science fiction. Since that time, Frye has been attracted to 'philosophical romance': 'It would have to be entirely "software", as I don't know anything about hardware, and I notice that most of the hardware is used to transpose the characters to a remote spot in some other galaxy that turns out to be a category of something on earth. So why not stay on earth?' This reference to 'software' implies a metaphor from computing and probably points to the late 1970s onwards as a source for the passage, because the discussion of word-processing enters Frye's work in the 1980s.

Frye outlines his themes and expectations. His starting point would be 'the relativity of what the sane waking consciousness sees to other perspectives' such as 'those of (a) dream (b) madness (c) mythopoeic imagination (d) existence following physical death'. Psychology, myth and apocalypse, or the separation of life from death, are recurrent interests in his criticism. If he never writes such a novel, he says, collecting notes for it could loosen up 'the imaginative faculties'. But he has reservations about fiction: 'The idea is to write what I myself would be most interested in reading. And I find great difficulty in finishing most works of fiction: they don't tell me enough.' This observation indicates his ambivalence if not defensiveness in the face of fiction. On the one hand, he thinks that 'A great writer could achieve tremendous effect by localizing what science fiction (or some form of it) projects into distant space (or, in Tolkien, distant time) as different aspects of here and now'. He praises Tolkien but will not imitate his success, which is unique. On the other hand, he implies that he would not follow the model of John Fowles' *The Magus* (1966, revised version 1977), which he began 'with the highest expectations, but finished it thinking he didn't know what the hell he was doing'. Because of the reference to Fowles' novel, we can assume that Frye was at least 54 when he made these comments in which he outlines his desire to write fiction. These plans are hardly the scribblings of youth that he liked to say he had abandoned when he realized he did not have any vocation in the field.

As early as 18 February 1949, Frye could say in one of his diaries that for years he had been pondering the possibility of a new formula in prose fiction. Although he admits he has considered a novel on the life of Christ, he raises the possibility of writing a Bardo novel:

I wonder what would come of a Bardo novel. Huxley appears to be one of the few who have tried the story of the persistence of consciousness after death, & I gather it's a bad novel (Time Must Have a Stop). Yet here might be a formula to handle my interest in fantasy & the tale of terror in that novel way I've been looking for. Let's say a man dies. His personality splits into a ghost that hangs around the body & another focus of consciousness. He realizes that he's 'saved', whatever that means, because he's committed his consciousness to the latter. Those who commit themselves to the former are demonic. He becomes the centre of a world, or rather its circumference: the world is apparently in dream space. He's a *Lare*, a fixed point, no longer a living body rolling from place to place, but a watcher, & things come to him – a psychoanalytic analysis of his past first, a pure vision of his 'damned' self (on my principle that the mouth of hell is the previous moment), other perspectives of the world, & so on. There isn't anything that couldn't fit a scheme like that. (Re extrasensory perception of books: Sawyer shoved Williams' *All Hallows' Eve* through my door today & I didn't open it until I'd written the above as far as 'looking for'. The rest was thought out independently.)

(This and the other transcriptions are by Robert Denham, 1992)

Frye's anxiety of influence, declaration of independence or fear of rivals is apparent in this passage. He also shows how he begins with a theoretical idea as dramatic fiction in framing his plans for a fiction. Vision and perspective concern him in his fiction as much as they do in his criticism. On 19 February 1949, Frye says that he is still reading *All Hallow's Eve* and observes: 'It's a measure of our civilization that a type done in clinical disbelief by Godwin and with detachment by Bulwer Lytton should now be taken so seriously.' Frye also says that the Bardo novel is not popular but will be. Williams' novel is, in Frye's view, a purer example of a Bardo novel than *Portrait of Jennie* and Henry James' *Sense of the Past*. Another paragraph from the entry of 19 February shows the close relation between Frye's conceptual framework for fiction and for criticism:

[203] *All Hallows Eve* was exactly the book I was looking for: I have temporarily lost my ambition to write a Bardo novel myself, & consolidated my impulse to write an article, perhaps for that *Trollopian* magazine, on the occult novels of Bulwer Lytton. After fifty pages of Williams' book, one has to pass a special critical Order-in-Council to keep oneself from dismissing it as a lot of blithering nonsense. That kept me reading it, but it's still as crude & tasteless a performance as the genre supplies. His public is too

sophisticated to worry about the factual basis of magic, so there's none of Lytton's naive & detached curiosity, & Lytton's normal Victorian prejudices are replaced by a fetid, miasmic, oppressive & appallingly obtrusive priestly morality. The ingenuity & intelligence with which he gears his fantasy to Christian doctrine makes the book positively bad instead of negatively inept, but reveals how completely ritual, the physical transmission & recreation of the divine community in time, is white magic, & exists & has influence only insofar as the forces of evil are conceived as black magic. I can't help feeling that the Christian drama of heaven & hell is one thing & Bardo another; that Bardo is essentially bound up with Karma & reincarnation, & though purgatory is the point of contact, it still wouldn't come together even if one didn't feel that the purgatory idea was alien to Christianity. I'm not clear on this point yet. In terms of my four forms, *All Hallows Eve* is a romance-anatomy, a Gothic horror tale in which the villain is (as he is occasionally in the cruder examples) the devil, & in which the anima moves in Bardo, as Lilian does in *A Strange Story*, which also ends with a magician destroyed within his own magic circle. This Gothic horror romance is linked to an auctorius theory of Bardo: someone like Yeats who didn't feel a compulsion to make Bardo rationalize priestcraft might have brought it off.

The Bardo novel might serve as a vehicle for Frye's interest in the overview and in the suspension of time, in his desire to bring together the intellectual and the spiritual without surrendering literature to religion, criticism to priestcraft. Although Frye seems to have given up the task of writing a Bardo novel, he thinks that a Bardo novel is not a different drama from the Christian drama of heaven and hell. But the wish to write a Bardo novel resurfaces for Frye and may do so more often and later than the evidence we now have suggests (it will take Denham and others years to go through and transcribe or publish Frye's unpublished diaries and papers).

In another notebook (brown cover, 7557 stamped on the recto of the front flyleaf) Frye has eighteen leaves with writing, the first sixteen of which are in ink and are material for a novel, and the last two of which are in pencil, seem to be written later and concern a Bardo novel (transcribed by Denham). Robertson Davies' *Murther and Walking Spirits* (1991) begins with a similar premise about a character who narrates moments after his death, although Frye's scheme is different because his character does not know he is dead. In April 1962, three months before Frye's fiftieth birthday, he is planning this novel: 'How

the hell would one write a *good* Bardo novel. It would have to be short,
or get laborious.' Frye wants to be as concrete as Dante but not to
depend on traditional church fables. He thinks of the work in terms of
original sin or karma and advises himself: 'The trick is to make a logical
sequence of experiences without preaching, and yet implying a complete
theory of Bardo.' His fiction would be theoretical, though he wants to be
concrete, a novel of ideas without seeming so. The ideas Frye sets out
for the novel 'are, first, the old Swedenborgian notion that the newly
deceased doesn't know he's dead' and, second, 'the Paracelsian idea
that the things [not?] seen are really there, like stars in daytime'. Frye's
interest in Swedenborg relates to Blake's, and his familiarity with
Paracelsus would derive from a study of Renaissance alchemy that
might arise in the reading of Ben Jonson's *The Alchemist*, of the
Rosicrucians (see Yates 1972), of Pope's *The Rape of the Lock* or
Browning's *Paracelsus*. The desire to write a powerful and popular
novel is palpable and urgent, even as Frye approaches 50: 'Oh, hell, I'd
want to do something versatile and with a light touch, like the Sword in
the Stone, yet packing a terrific wallop and making monkeys out of the
persons [?].' Frye debates whether the novel should be 'a continuous
philosophical narrative' or whether 'that's an easy way out' and that
'The ideal job would be a sequence of scenes on the pattern of the first
one, constituting a sequence of dramatic metamorphoses.' The problem,
it seems, was that Frye did not doubt that he could write a good novel
but wasn't sure whether he knew how to write it. He notes that the shape
of the Bardo novel would be purgatorial, perhaps ending with reincarnation, which is implicit in his scheme, a kind of satiric resolution.
The narrator, Frye explains, prepared for death with reading and
meditation, but death or the 'swoon' caught him unawares, so that he
awakened in Bardo without realizing that he had died: this is the Tibetan
formula. Frye says that reincarnation is a second swoon and that 'the
climax would come at the upper limit of Beulah, whatever that involves
me in: a vision of the liberated world *beyond* all conventional heavens'.
Frye returns to Blake's Beulah, which, for the poet, is the lower
paradise, taken from Isaiah and meaning 'marriage', and 'the relation of
the land to its people', 'the garden of Genesis in which the gods walk in
the cool of day' (Frye 1947a: 49–50). On this vision, Frye adds: 'I'm
vague here, of course, but so's everybody.' The celebrated author of
Anatomy muses in this notebook, about five years later, that in writing
about Bardo he doesn't want it to be a breaking of 'a priest's racket' or
simply 'supernatural materialism'. Instead, the novel's 'ideology would
be a Bardo projection of my own: perhaps the deadee would regret not
having developed my kind of outlook and would go back to get it'. Frye

is carrying on a dialogue with himself that reveals his desires and doubts about his writing of fiction, a genre in which he has not established himself, let alone in which he is renowned internationally. He then says: 'It wouldn't be quite as bald as that in presentation, but it would be in essential theory. God damn it. This kind of mooning isn't fiction-writing.'

The second possibility for the opening scene that Frye describes is similar to Swedenborg, an influence on Blake, like the beginning of *Outward Bound*. Frye criticizes the opening of that play for not being a Bardo experience but one of detachment from the world, a 'crossing of the bar', to allude to Tennyson's poem of that name whose speaker at the end wants to see his Pilot face to face when he has crossed the bar. None the less, Frye wishes he 'could get away with stealing it'. He also notes (in parentheses) that

> (One curious feature of all my fictional reveries is the prophetic: several times a notion I've had actually turns up in some professional writer. Thus Katherine Anne Porter's *Ship of Fools* has just (April 1962) appeared. This is one of the many reasons why I suspected my Bardo novel is not something to write, but a *koan* to think about and exercise the mind. If I write it I might be snatching the bread out of the mouth of somebody who otherwise would have done it better.)

Frye brings his critical ideas and concerns to his plans for fiction – liberation, vision and prophecy – and takes what he wrote in *Fearful Symmetry* even closer to mysticism and a religious quest for the afterlife. The notebooks reveal the private Frye who speaks the same language as his public persona but does so with even greater intensity and edging into the occult. In fiction as in criticism he is fond of puzzles like the *koan*, the riddle in Zen to show the inadequacy of reasoning. Only in *The Double Vision* do we witness a Frye who is nearly as public about religion and his vision as in this entry addressed to himself, perhaps with the expectation that, as he was a famous person, it would be overheard, years later, by others. Frye ends the entry with a blend of mysticism and technical literary terms: 'The crisis of a Bardo plot is almost necessarily a threshold scene, a plunge into another order of being.' He ends with an observation about recognition, one of the central notions in his poetics, which carries a freight from Aristotle onwards (see Cave 1988: 190–9). Seeing things in and beyond time as we know it is at the centre of Frye's writing. It is to Frye's youth – although Robert Denham has told me that he thinks that Frye may have been talking about plans for fiction in 1985 and later (conversation, 18

August 1992) – to the published and unpublished fiction of his twenties that I would now like to turn.

The fiction Northrop Frye published between April 1936 and September 1941 in the Victoria College magazine, *Acta Victoriana*, and in *Canadian Forum*, with which he was affiliated, is really of two types, the fable and the religious or spiritual story. These stories show Frye's interest in the moral and mythical borderlands between life and death, something similar to his proposed Bardo novel years later. Two of these stories, 'The Ghost' and 'Face to Face', are probably part of what he called in manuscript 'Four Dialogues'. I want to consider the four dialogues together, including the unpublished stories or dialogues, the second and fourth in the series, 'Interpreter's Parlour' and 'Incident from the Golden Bough'. It is also possible that 'Affable Angel' and 'Prelude' are closely related to these stories, especially in their technique and emphasis on dialogue, and formed part of a larger plan. 'Fable . . . in the Nineteenth Century Idiom' stands apart as a kind of latter-day Victorian reworking of the medieval fable or of John Gower's moral poetry or of the morality play into narrative, which Tennyson, William Morris and others had sometimes done. 'Prelude' is the most overtly classical and mythological of the stories.

Under the pseudonym Richard Poor, which the editor of *Canadian Forum*, Eleanor Godfrey, gave Frye, perhaps with a glance towards Benjamin Franklin's *Poor Richard's Almanac* (1733–58), his second published story, 'Fable . . . in the Nineteenth Century Idiom', appeared in that magazine in June 1936, only three months after 'The Ghost' came out in *Acta Victoriana*. The nineteenth-century idiom is Romanticism, as if Franklin had got a hold of Shelley. This brief story is about a young man who wishes to become a great writer seeking the 'counsel of his daimon' (15; all references to the same page). The daimon gives a promise to call forth the seven spirits that know the 'seven great secrets of writing'. Marlowe's and Goethe's Faustus may be present behind the scenes. It is soon apparent that the fable is a slightly veiled manifesto of what it is to be a great writer, the hope, it seems, or at least one of the hopes, of the young Northrop Frye. But Frye in his youth is also a maker of ironies, so that the end of the story makes the moral ambivalent and complicates the stark declarations on what it takes to be a great writer by juxtaposing the values of the writer and the world. Through a procession of seven figures, Frye represents the seven secrets of writing: genius, savage indignation, reflection, power to record, imitation, varied experience, and the reality of sexual life. For instance, the first figure, 'the daimon', summons forth a purple figure who is a bit given to purple prose:

'I give you', said this figure, 'confidence in your own genius. All artists must have in them the spirit of Prometheus, ready to defy anything to associate form with fire. I give you independence and revolt, refusal to compromise with the world, the dignity of the creator.'

The daimon, genius, Prometheus, defiance, revolt and the poet as creator are all the stuff of Romanticism. A poet as an independent creator is the kind of integrity and dignity that Frye soon sought for the critic. The young Frye has learned his Blake and Shelley well.

'The Resurgent', which appeared in *Canadian Forum* in February 1940 under the name H. N. Frye, seems to be an allegory of the way official and heroic propagandistic state art, as practised by the Nazis in Germany, literally tears the artist apart in a kind of totalitarian sacrifice. The narrator, Hortense Larrabin, the sister of the great artist Andrew Larrabin, is an apologist for such heroic state art, which was also a characteristic of Stalin's state, whose official policy was Soviet realism. Frye's technique is to move from Hortense's analysis of her brother's death, a kind of critical mediation, through entries from his diary, which are interspersed with her commentary, to her concluding interpretation of his life and death as an artist and critic.

Frye contrasts the public world of the National Emblem, which Andrew Larrabin designed, with the private world of his diary and makes his sister Hortense the mediator and a kind of executor who is bent on preserving reputation and serving the interest of state power. She suppresses evidence: 'My reluctance to publish any of this material will be understood when my account of it is read, but the pressure of inquiries has forced me to give a large public some indication of its nature' (Frye 1940b: 357, here and below). Hortense admits that her 'brother was a thinker and critic as well as a painter' and that much of the diary and some of the letters deserve publication, like 'the literary efforts of Gauguin and Cezanne', but that the sensational events surrounding his death make it likely that this material would be misunderstood. Andrew's sister condemns his teacher, Walter Lomat, who once taught painting at what is now the School of Insular Art, because, it seems, he was a figurative or abstract painter with a sense of humour that she doesn't like. 'That so egregious a charlatan', Hortense says, 'was one of the most prominent artists of his time will give some idea of the state of our culture before the Resurgence.' To infer from the story and from Frye's position on the arts elsewhere, Hortense is blind to the avant-garde and subject to the insularity of government-controlled and nationalistic or propagandistic art. This position is not to deny the social function of art, but Frye appears interested in opposing an art to which the state dictates. Lomat's definition of painting is playful, 'the adventures of the mind among pattern and color'. Hortense's interpretation of it, in a relative clause that modifies and responds to the definition, is less charitable, for she sees it as a summary of 'the whole morbid, egotistic, precious mentality of his age'.

Six months later, in 'War on the Cultural Front', Frye observes:

> But art under dictatorship seldom dares to be anything but mediocre and obvious. . . . But crude, gaudy realism of painting and pompous brokendown classicism of architecture in both countries had been foreshadowing the Soviet-Nazi pact for years.
>
> (1940b: 146)

The fiction and the criticism converge here. This cultural critique illuminates the content of the short story, although it cannot account for its form and the ambiguities that arise from the expression, rather than analysis, of metaphor and generic structure.

'The Resurgent' can also be considered as a satirical parable. Hortense Larrabin appears too strident and lacks irony. Her response to Lomat's revolutionary words about art is to say that it is not surprising that the Resurgence came in the same year. There is a chill in her observation: 'Lomat was proved to have been, largely on the evidence of my brother's diary, quite revolutionary and devious enough to be dragged away to parts unknown.' This is the voice of totalitarianism, the kind of tone a Nazi might take, expressing a view matter-of-factly, a view that Frye fought early in his letters and articles and continued to fight to the end (see 1940c, 1945a and b). As early as a letter of 10 May 1934 to Helen Kemp, who later became his wife, Frye outlines his first sermon in Saskatchewan, in which he denounced the idolatry and evil of tyranny in general and the Nazis in particular: 'The present trend to dictatorships is therefore idolatry, and there is nothing to save us from the same progression toward the evil, which is why Hitler and Co. appeal to the worst and cruelest instincts of mankind' (quoted in Ayre 1990: 100). In 'War on the Cultural Front' (1940) Frye speaks about Nazism and 'the delirious absurdity of its race theory' (1940c: 144). Hortense wants to protect (her brother's notorious diary) in order to maintain her reputation, and her brother's. This is a voice without humour, wit or irony as she justifies the atrocities against those who created or defended decadent art. Her brother saw all too well, perhaps, and not with 'the modesty of genius', that he was a dwarf in a desert, yet she declares: 'But there was nothing dwarflike about the painter who gave us "Hard Work", that sensitive study of the strength of horses, the unconscious nobility of the peasant, and the dignity of honest labor' (1940a: 357). Frye's irony may be a bit heavy here, but it probably stems from a contempt for this kind of Soviet or Nazi realism. Orwell was a great satirist of totalitarianism, and it is in a similar spirit that Frye wrote. Hortense's very defence of her brother confirms the criticisms of Lomat's circle, that Andrew was maudlin, mediocre and obvious. As evidence of her brother's genius, she also cites

the portrait of our leader, in which the modelling of the features shows in its very sharpness and precision that a deep personal love and loyalty can be directed toward an impersonal will. 'Art is power, and a work of art is a study of power', is my brother's triumphant comment on this portrait.

(1940a: 357)

'Führer' means 'leader' in German, and 'impersonal will' might be an allusion to Schopenhauer's immanent will and Nietzsche's will to power, which the Nazis translated into propaganda. This kind of adulation, in this case the love of the leader, is, as Frye will later suggest in *The Great Code, Words with Power, The Double Vision* and elsewhere, idolatry or a demonic parody of love for God, who so loved the world that He gave His only begotten Son. Nor from Hortense's description of another of Andrew's paintings, *Holy Trinity*, does his painting seem anything more than official art, although occasionally some works in this category can, in spite of themselves, maintain aesthetic interest. Andrew's *Holy Trinity* represents the holy family as now a soldier instead of a father with mother and child, not to mention the unfortunate allusion to God as Father, Son and Holy Ghost. The painter's parody turns unwittingly against itself. On the day he finishes this unfortunate painting, which his sister says 'can never become hackneyed', he reports in his diary: 'I have just heard that Lomat, egocentric to the last, succeeded in killing himself a month ago with a broken bottle in his cell' (357–8). Like his sister, Andrew feels no remorse, even as he completes a monstrous work of propaganda the day he finds out the terrible results of his betrayal of his teacher. But the guilt, remorse or, more precisely, obsession begins. This is the turning point. As his sister notes, 'After this entry there is hardly a page of the diary on which Lomat's name does not occur' (358). Here, Andrew and Hortense Larrabin diverge. He is haunted by Lomat; she takes his old view of Lomat.

Hortense destroys *Insanity*, her brother's last painting, and preserves what she takes to be the National Emblem, which the country adopts. Instead, she gives her interpretation of her brother's death, which is sometimes wooden and sometimes vapid and sometimes slips from satire to caricature. Is Frye being savage or heavy here? She defends her brother, and herself, when she says his madness wasn't degenerate and a failure to live up to the heroic ideal. The question of genius once again arises in Frye's fiction, as if it could be positive or a demonic parody of itself. Is Hortense's mind not as deformed as anyone else's? Here is a sample of her peroration, a kind of strange eulogy, in which she first speaks of her brother's 'affliction':

> Rather I take it to be a proof of the objective, impersonal quality of patriotic duty, and it was as patriotic duty my brother conceived his art. Our leader, as he has repeatedly said, does not guide the country for his pleasure any more than for ours; he has become, through relentless self-discipline and obedience to the national genius, an incarnation of that genius, which is a force achieving its fulfillment regardless of the hopes or desires of the individuals on whom it acts. My brother was a vehicle of the national genius in its artistic aspect, and it seemed to him a malignant spirit, destroying him in the act of creating itself. That may seem inexplicable but it is really not so. The history of great men frequently shows genius tearing itself out of them with a purpose and direction of its own, not only independent of but often against their wills.

This is a funeral oration in which her brother becomes a hero and genius for the state in spite of himself. The general or immanent will governs the destiny of the nation. This view becomes more sinister when Hortense then says that the national destiny will be as it will even if it means the destruction of all who read her apology. She also says that any sort of calamity, including death, if it entails 'heroic loyalty', represents a renewal of the state and, she implies, is therefore worth the sacrifice. Hortense could not have written her account if she did not believe that her brother's ordeal and death were the call of a hero to duty to his country. Frye ends this story with this voice of totalitarianism, which he opposes the rest of his life, and which, from the late 1960s onwards, he sees as an ideological means of depriving citizens of their primary concerns, life, liberty and the pursuit of happiness, or, in other words, food, sex, freedom of movement or any other basic need that allows for survival and dignity. As a writer and as a critic, Frye did not waver, as Yeats, Eliot, Pound and others did, and give in to the dreams of an organic society and the voice of the folk or people or of a high art purified from cosmopolitanism. His private papers are vast, so that it will take years to sort them out, but from evidence like this story, Frye did not pander to the prejudices of

English Canadians, so many of whom were of British and Irish descent, and did not chase after strange gods.

The last of the stories in *Canadian Forum*, a magazine founded in 1920 that addressed a socialist and liberal audience, is 'Prelude' (September 1941), Frye's last published story and the only one where he drops the H. N. Frye (perhaps echoing the British tendency to use initials, as in the names of W. B. Yeats and T. S. Eliot) for the name he chooses for publication for the rest of his life (the H. for Herman left behind). In one way, then, the 'Prelude' is a preface to his public life as a critic, Northrop Frye. This is a mythological story by a writer whose criticism will focus increasingly on mythology.

The story begins in Frye's characteristic way, with dialogue that brings us to the heart or midst of things, *in medias res*:

> 'I NEVER WANTED to see you naked', said Paris sullenly, 'I suppose you're going to turn me into a stag, or something, but it isn't my fault. If you're so much stronger than I you ought to be fair about it, and for the same reason you don't need to be modest.'
>
> (Frye 1941: 185 here and below)

Frye has a good ear for dialogue and knows it. He dives into his stories and has none of the stilted Victorian or colonial pseudo-medieval or Shakespearian cadence or diction that Eliot, Pound and others opposed with their own version of making the medieval and Renaissance inheritance new.

'Prelude' is a story about the Judgement of Paris, which is well known as the prelude to the Trojan war in the *Iliad*. The best-known account of this judgement occurs in Euripides' *Trojan Women*, but may be found in a partial or new form in Apollodorus' prose tale on Oenone and in George Peele's play *The Araygnement of Paris* (1584). Frye turns the story into an engaging philosophical dialogue in which Paris asks questions and Minerva (Athena), Venus (Aphrodite) and Juno (Hera) answer with wit and subtlety about which of the three he should declare the most beautiful. This ironic dialogue debates the consequences of choosing as the beautiful either wisdom, beauty or power.

The remaining published stories by H. N. Frye appeared in the magazine of Victoria College, *Acta Victoriana*: 'The Ghost' (1936), 'Face to Face' (1938) and 'Affable Angel' (1940). In typescript the first two stories are the first and third stories of 'Four Dialogues'. 'Interpreter's Parlour' is certainly the second of these dialogues, and 'Incident from the Golden Bough' is probably the fourth as it is located in the same place in the typescripts, although there is a chance that 'Affable Angel' is the fourth because Frye publishes it in the same magazine, perhaps as a series. There may have been two versions of 'Four Dialogues' or the idea may have begun to make less sense to, or have less of a hold on, Frye. He never published the stories as part of 'Four Dialogues'.

The published form of 'The Ghost' is shorter and more direct than the typescript version in E. J. Pratt Library at Victoria College. After interpreting the tale, I will make a few comments on the unpublished version. Frye divides the story into three parts, and begins it with his characteristic use of dialogue to get to the heart of the matter: '"At the moment of death", said the ghost, "I was aware of two things only. I hated you, and I loved Margaret"' (1936a: 14). The ghost's speech provides the rest of the premise. He says that a priest bent over him, that his mystical eyes first unnerved him and then gave him courage and that they appeared to say that they had come back from 'there', presumably the dead. The ghost's enemy answers in ironic fashion, mocking his adversary's 'portentous style of speech', which he assumes was learned among the living rather than among the dead. The ghost proposes to drive the enemy insane. In this part the ghost and the enemy show their hatred for each other and debate whether the enemy can shut out the ghost from his world and therefore prevent his revenge, in other words the status of belief and incredulity. The ghost cannot move against his enemy and peters out. In the second part the ghost returns to the girl he loves and whom he thinks his enemy has deceived. Here his impotence arises from his lover saying that he couldn't possibly be who he said he was because the man who loved her said he would rather kill himself than get in the way when she fell in love with someone else. In the first part he lost the debate to hate and in the second he loses it to love. The third part represents the ghost's return to the priest and includes the ghost's complaint that he can no longer love or hate. The priest disclaims that he encouraged the ghost to return from beyond the grave but only wanted to encourage him to go further on the other side. For the priest, the ghost has returned out of self-importance. When the ghost proposes he is an avenger (the revengers' tragedies of the Renaissance, including *Hamlet*, need a ghost), the priest says wryly that while it would be fun to be Mephistopheles, the ghost is a fool and not an evil spirit. Here Frye's satire on folly has a long history, including the tradition of the fool in Christ that Erasmus develops in the *Praise of Folly* and Lucian's dialogues of the dead, in which he places famous historical figures in foolish or ironic situations. Frye is showing how the dignity and importance of the man has been shown to his ghost to be much less than he thought it was, not to mention his power as a ghost. The priest says: 'And I am afraid your enemy was quite right. For him, and for people on his level, you do not exist' (16). But Frye's satire is not one-sided because the priest is, as the ghost says, given to sermons and the author seems to be implying that an imitation of Christ means in part an imitation of the holy fool. While the priest is one word into yet another sentence, the ghost says 'Excuse me' and then 'Could you get me a drink? I am very thirsty' (16). In this abrupt way the story or dialogue ends. This is where the typescript version in Pratt Library is especially illuminating because it includes a footnote to the last line that says 'Luke xi, 24; Luke xvi, 24'. This simple note opens up the religious interpretation of the dialogue beyond what appears in the body of the story.

There are enough changes to 'The Ghost' from the typescript version to the one in *Acta Victoriana* for the difference to be more than a matter of a change of name from Northrop Frye (typescript) to H. N. Frye or vice versa. My guess is that the typescript preceded the publication because the published version is tighter. The story in both versions is substantially the same, for instance, in the way they begin and end and in the fundamental structure (although the typescript does not formally demarcate the three parts with roman numerals). Interesting differences occur in each part. In the first section, the ghost knows that his hatred and love would live on after his death and speaks about his body as a burden, but in the published version, he says: 'After that I knew nothing until I appeared here' (Frye 1936a: 14). The ghost in the typescript seems to know that he doesn't know much about the spirit world but thinks that there must be better places for the ghost in that world than on earth. The ghost is also less direct about the insanity he will cause in his enemy. Frye emphasizes the body more in the typescript, for instance, when the enemy says, 'I never realized before how much my dislike of you was disgust at your body.' Both versions of the story reflect Frye's interest in his criticism and fiction in the borderlands between life and death and his early preoccupation with moral and religious themes. The plan for the Bardo novel and his emphasis on vision in *Words with Power* and *The Double Vision* illustrate this concern.

'Interpreter's Parlour' is an unpublished fictionalized *explication de texte* or New Critical reading (avant la lettre?) of a poem, ARX, which Frye has devised for his main character, the poet. The dialogue is a reversal of a Socratic dialogue because the naive person is the one asking the questions here of the teacher figure, the poet, who pontificates a defence of modern poetry and then elaborates and explicates the poem in an ingenious close reading on one of Frye's favourite themes in his criticism: comparative mythology or religion. The poet thinks that it is too easy to criticize modern poetry for being deliberately obscure and unintelligible. Anyone who can see anything intelligible in the contemporary scene is to be congratulated, and poets struggle to achieve synthesis, order, creative form. And a synthesis of contemporary life, to be authentic, has to reflect the difficulty of making one at all at such a time. So any poetry really attuned to the beat of the world today must be difficult.

This opening argues for modern poetry's fascination with what's difficult and a possible imitative fallacy in modernism that to reflect the complexity of the modern world is a complex art. It may be true that the world is becoming increasingly complex, or more correctly, human understanding and transformation of it are more intricate, but why then do simple lyrics still move people? If primary concerns are the basis of poetry, as Frye implies from the late 1960s onwards, then there is another equally good argument for a simple but not simplistic poetry that awakens in us our basic needs in life. There may also be a touch of satire in Frye's portrait of the poet because he allows him a little vanity: 'In my own poetry, I admit I have never shirked the necessity of being difficult, and I daresay that the terrific concentration has been a bit too much for you. Isn't that so?'

The poem in 'Interpreter's Parlour' is a riddle, a descendant of the Anglo-Saxon riddles. The poet is also equally at home with interpretation and criticism and with experimental poetry. Whatever one thinks of the poem Frye has given him, whether it is being satirized as over-ingenious or held up as an example, the author gives this character an intricate interpretation of the poem. The poet is astute in his description of the poem: 'Nothing there but a few crabbed words, seemingly, yet it's an entire essay on comparative religion.' According to the poet/critic, heaven and earth are the leading ideas of each great religion, the first representing light, the second life, so that 'every god worshipped as a supreme being is connected both with the sun and with the coming of rain to a waste land'.

In 'Face to Face' Frye combines an interest in anthropology and religion that occurs in his criticism. He uses the slang and tough-talking tone that were popular in the 1930s and 1940s, especially in Hollywood movies, and some of it seems jarring in this age, such as the use of the word 'nigger' in the narrator's report of the tales of the 'chap' who had 'spent years in the South Seas' (Frye 1938: 10). But in this report where the chap uses that word, the narrator uses some irony to caricature him: 'then he changed his tune and started to go all Boy's Own Annual on me' (10). The representation of the hierarchy on the whisky bottle is also telling and may be one of the reasons the narrator is bored: trading vessels and rubber plantations at the top, palm-trees and surf in the middle and 'island paradises and brown-eyed mistresses nearer the bottom' (10). The chap describes an island, which falls in the utopian tradition beginning with Thomas More, in which there is no colour for the colour-blind inhabitants. In this dialogue Frye represents a parable of extremism, of people who do not think in black and white but in grey in a world stripped of the distraction of colour. The narrator thinks that the chap has gone off the deep end after implying that the 'savages' who live in 'an easy-going sort of patriarchal society' that is full of justice and wisdom are more happy and free than 'our supposedly more "civilized" races' and have been able to get 'rid of all their taboos and superstitions' (10). The dialogue occurs between the chap who thinks he has discovered paradise or the golden age and the narrator who thinks that this view is an indication of a troubled mind or the disease of lying. It is not clear whether the first sentence of the dialogue or story, 'I suppose they must have a disease for lies, as they have kleptomania for stealing', refers to liars like the chap. The narrator may view himself as a sceptic who resists the tall tales of island paradises and innocent new lands, a tradition in Western literature and especially travel literature. When speaking of the natives, the chap sounds, however, a little like Hegel and Heidegger, two philosophers whom Frye takes seriously in his criticism: 'Well, God to them was a pure Being or form in which all opposites and antitheses were reconciled. They thought of all movement and life as something uncompleted – as Becoming.' Even more than in 'Interpreter's Parlour', in this dialogue the issue of which speaker's view the reader is to adopt becomes primary. That is not to rule out ambiguity and a tension or disjunction between the two speakers, but often in dialogues from Plato through Dryden to Thomas Love Peacock (who mixes the Socratic dialogue with the anatomy or Menippean satire) and beyond, one speaker's point of view prevails. Perhaps like Peacock, Frye writes dialogues that represent visionary or extreme points of view. The chap speaks about a glimpse of something we have lost, a kind of paradise perhaps, the 'amazing synthesis they had' (10). Frye's dialogues are usually two or three printed pages, so that he glimpses at positions, including the visionary, but does not develop them.

The published version of the story is much the same as the unpublished version. Some differences occur in the typescript. In this version the narrator does not report the chap's claim that in religion the inhabitants of the island had rid themselves of taboos and superstitions and he does not say that the chap is 'going off the deep end' (10). It doesn't contain the part that brings the two speakers into conflict: 'You see – I don't know where to approach it, as it's such a perfect whole, but you were asking about their religion.' (I wasn't)' (10). The inhabitants' ethical system is 'absolutely consistent' in the typescript but only 'consistent' in the publication (10). The typescript says that black and white were (as part of being and not simply as symbols) for the inhabitants and that grey 'was opposed to everything based on tension or contradiction', whereas the published version does not. The last change is the beginning of the chap's final speech in the typescript: 'It took a while to sink in, of course, but when I finally understood the secret of their strength I began to understand the secret of our weakness. Everyone knows part of that, of course'. This passage is more explicit about Western weakness, while admitting that everyone, or by implication every Westerner, knows about this vulnerability. Both versions centre on seeing things, the question of vision. Whether the chap is a visionary or a fool, even a visionary fool, is the central concern of the dialogue.

The fourth and final dialogue, 'Incident from the Golden Bough', which is in the form of a typescript with revisions in Frye's hand, seems to take Attis, whom James Frazer discusses in *The Golden Bough*, and make him the focus of the dialogue in a version that is quite different from Frazer's and the traditional accounts. Frazer implies a parallel between Christ, Adonis and Attis. Nana was Attis' mother, and a virgin like Mary. At the beginning of Chapter 34, 'The Myth and Ritual of Attis', Frazer says:

> Another of those gods whose supposed death and resurrection struck such deep roots into the faith and ritual of Western Asia is Attis. He was to Phrygia what Adonis was to Syria. Like Adonis, he appears to have been a god of vegetation, and his death and resurrection were annually mourned and rejoiced over at a festival in spring.

In Frazer's account Attis is said to have died after being killed by a boar as Adonis was or by castrating himself under a pine tree, where he bled to death. Some thought that Cybele, the mother of the gods and the Asiatic goddess of fertility, was Attis' mother. They were lovers. Those who became the priests of Attis emasculated themselves in a religious frenzy. Frye's story is about Attis visiting a mortal woman of great beauty to engender a new breed of demi-gods. His story or dialogue is about fertility, but has a different focus. In Frye's dialogue Attis visits virgins before their mortal husbands can, so that these women live through the ritual act and are not sacrificed, but their husbands and the community come to resent the strangers who stand in for him, if not the god himself.

Frye divides the dialogue or story into three parts. 'Incident from the

Golden Bough' concentrates on one of Frye's central critical interests: comparative mythology. His theme is human disagreement over religious custom. The dialogue and the first part begin with the meeting and conversation of a Phrygian, who wants a stranger to sleep with his daughter before her wedding in order to please Attis and the Phrygian gods, and a Greek, who is either reluctant to oblige or uses his reluctance as a means of securing virgins in his travels through this country because he has already slept with eight to oblige their fathers. Apparently, according to the father, Attis' appearances have become 'irregular in this degenerate age'. The second part of 'Incident from the Golden Bough' represents the next morning. The Greek or Athenian and the bridegroom are having a discussion about the necessity and foolishness of customs. Whereas the one thinks that the custom demonstrates devotion or cowardice and violates one of the deepest human instincts, the other is bitter and thinks that his wife 'will be poisoned in both body and mind for the rest of her life'. In the final part the Athenian stays to watch the revolt even though the groom had warned him to leave. He watches as the groom harangues a large crowd in front of the temple, where the night-before-marriage custom had occurred. The groom concludes the story with the observation: 'There is nothing to be on our guard about: neither of us need fear the jealousy of the gods.' By this statement, he seems to mean that Attis has slept with his wife while neither the Athenian nor he has and that the god controlled the situation and put the revolt down to establish a regime in which humans have little place except to show their pious devotion. The Promethean impulse is contained, and there is a nagging doubt about how much the forces of establishment have helped to reassert the forms of traditional piety. This is Frye's longest story: it runs to just over seven typescript pages, and pursues religious, social and mythological questions that concerned him from the 1930s onwards. Here Eros and Prometheus, recurrent figures in Frye's criticism, find themselves in conflict.

'Affable Angel', which appeared in *Acta Victoriana* in 1940, uses similar techniques to 'Four Dialogues'. The story is set in West India Dock Road in London, and its characters Harry and Augustus might have come out of Samuel Beckett, perhaps from *Murphy* (1938), his novel about London. But Frye's story returns to the spirit world of brownies, benevolent goblins with shaggy appearances, and nixies, water-nymphs or female water-elves. An angel appears to Harry and Augustus, but is not what Augustus had in mind when he wanted to see someone from the spirit world: he is more disturbing, like a devil. The men proceed to have a debate with the angel about the nature of the world and which is more likely to exist, angels or devils. The debate and encounter are humorous, partly because Frye makes the angel and heaven all too human. Harry has read about angels and corroborates the angel's question about whether they can read his thoughts and his claim that he can't read theirs. The angel becomes an ironic character Harry, Augustus and the reader can feel superior to in some respects, but he comes up with some ideas that are suggestive. For instance, the angel says: 'If it weren't for that soot covering you couldn't see me at all' (Frye 1940a: 3). If there were a comma after 'covering', then we could say that the angel means the smog covering him, which is probably the intended meaning, but the soot may also be covering 'you' or Harry and Augustus. I am not suggesting a full-blown allegory on sin, but only possible glances at or jokes about such matters. The angel denies Augustus' view that heaven is dry and tells the story of an 'old girl' (the angel speaks in the slang of 1940), obviously one given to temperance, who showed up in heaven and tried to convert the angels:

> We asked her if she'd ever heard the Dives and Lazarus story. She said yes, she had, and the moral of it was that one should always give one's scraps and crumbs to the poor if there are any left over. We said no, the moral of it was that there's nothing to drink in hell. So off she beetled for hell and we haven't seen her since.
>
> (3)

The story is full of gags. For instance, Harry asks the angel a technical question in a drunken stutter about what kind of angel he is, and when Augustus asks him to mind his step, the angel replies, 'Woops! Unnerstan' now about the fallen angels?' (4). A running gag for over half of this brief story is the appearance of a policeman who thinks that he is breaking up a fight between Harry and Augustus when they are responding to the angel.

The story is well constructed. It begins with Harry talking about the universe being a 'big gyroscope' and how the brain is also like a wonderful gyroscope because it also spins and keeps balance (Frye 1940a: 2). Frye's humorous look at cosmology, perhaps the dearest of all subjects to him, is like a morality play in which hell and evil fall on hard and dry times. The story seems to anticipate London during the blitz in 1940. They hear a bomber overhead:

> 'One of them Nazis', said Harry. 'Not bad chaps, Nazis. I was in Munich last summer. Always givin' seats to women on trams. But could I get them to drink? Not them. Wonderful beer they got in Munich. Wonderful. But would they drink it? Not them.'
>
> (4)

Like the woman for temperance, the Nazis are destined to a dry place in hell, perhaps because they have repressed the waters of life, have replaced morality with moralism. This is a symbolic and not a sociological observation, one meant to shore up the spirits of a people at war, a kind of defensive propaganda, a more understated version of what occurs in Olivier's film of *Henry V*, the stoic and humorous few embattled but triumphant before an overwhelming enemy. The plane plunges into the Thames and they hear a whoop 'far up in the air'. The story ends with a serious joke, the juxtaposition of a providential act and a gag:

> 'NICE WORK, ANGEL'! yelled Augustus at the top of his voice. 'Break it up, boys; break it up', said the policeman, reappearing.

> (4)

This last sentence is almost the same as the one when the policeman made his first of two appearances and helps to invoke closure as much as to temper the possible sentimentality about angels that Augustus mentions earlier (see 2). Frye lends his fiction as well as his criticism, as in 'War on the Cultural Front' (1940), to bolster the forces of democracy and to fight tyranny. In 1940 it was less easy to take democracy for granted than it seems to be today: for all its flaws, Frye wrote in its service, with passion and with humour. The ironic distance might have been harder to achieve on the banks of the Thames awaiting the bombs, but Frye had been there a few years before and could have been there under other circumstances. This onslaught on London later gripped the memories and imaginations of a generation, figuring, for instance, in the opening of Thomas Pynchon's *Gravity's Rainbow* (1973).

The apparent fragment that centres on the Reverend Lyman Kennedy and Sarah Megill was never published and exists in typescript with some handwritten revisions. It is fifteen pages long and is divided into four parts and is probably, judging from the brevity of Frye's other short stories, part of a novel rather than a long story, although this hypothesis cannot be proved, and only with extensive study of Frye's unpublished papers may we know its status. Perhaps it is *Quiet Consummation*, perhaps not. I am calling it the Kennedy-Megill fragment. This fragment is more domestic and seemingly autobiographical than Frye's other stories. It concentrates on religion and education, youth and age, and although unfinished and perhaps not entirely revised, it offers, as Frye's writings always do, something of interest and something pleasurable.

I want to concentrate on the strengths of the story and the ways in which it elaborates themes and concerns that recur in Frye's theory and criticism. The first part is satirical in its physical descriptions and in the introduction of Kennedy's family and the parishioners' response to his sermon. The opening sentence of the fragment shows Frye's penchant for satire: 'The only building in Pilkey, a loutish, shambling church, owed its distinction to a wooden dunce-cap on its head, covered with green shingles.' The church is a synecdoche for the town or a metonymy for its congregation, for the loutish collection of dunces. The central panes of the row of windows on each side wall 'were frosted, to aid in concentration'. The children think that the stained-glass, rounded windows and 'dunce-cap' spire were all vestigial, implying that they were a remnant or useless leftover from an earlier age. Even the title of Kennedy's sermon, 'A Christian Rebels', is ironic. His congregation rebels against his sermon as it rebels against them. Even Kennedy's son, Horace, dreams and day-dreams during the service. Frye has his narrator record the boy's reaction to the ribald possibilities of the name of Horace Howell Kennedy, perhaps in keeping with Frye's view that a major satirist has a scatological vision. The narrator introduces us to other characters such as Lauder, Miss Peace (the school teacher who also suffered for her name), John Goremont and others. Miss Peace is, predictably, a bluestocking who produces aureate poetry. Frye, who had wondered why preaching was a course at Emmanuel College, where he was a theology student (Ayre 1989: 90), gives his narrator an ironic view of how much the congregation pays attention to sermons: 'John Goremont had built up a powerful sermon resistance early in life, and now found a church service, so far from disturbing him, a stimulus to free association.' He also thinks about Vanya, Reverend Kennedy's 17-year-old daughter. The narrator characterizes Kennedy as a man with two degrees who deserved 'a cultivated urban community' rather than a small one like Pilkey and as a preacher who describes the historical context of a biblical passage and then applies it to the present:

> This Sunday his text was from Paul. He reminded his hearers that in the later Roman Empire conditions were very much what they are today: recurrent wars, imperialism, crowds of unemployed and discontented poor in the cities, farmers impoverished, and the people indifferent to religion. There were, then as now, those who thought everything could be cured by a revolution: there had been slave uprisings and Jewish rebellions, but they had ended in failure. The message of Christianity to the poor and downtrodden was, not to try to amend their lot through violence and hate, but to make their hearts and minds pure. And Christianity had been right, for it had converted the Roman Empire and erected a new civilization . . .

One of Frye's positions in opposing the student rebellions of the late

1960s was to argue for a rebellion of the spirit or imagination and not a political revolt among the students because it lacked deep roots like that of the civil rights movement and, he added later, feminism. Like Tolstoy, Thoreau and Gandhi (who also appealed to Hindu doctrines or *ahimsa* or non-violence), Martin Luther King had just cause and took the position of pacifism that might approach Frye's 'Christian' ideal. The narrator says that the congregation was flattered with 'a highbrow sermon'. Frye's biographer reports that when Frye preached one summer in the early 1930s in south-western Saskatchewan to 'a congregation which was usually poorly educated, culturally isolated and beleaguered by drought and plague, he preached to them like Emmanuel College graduates' (Ayre 1989: 100). Whether Frye's congregation was as uneducated and isolated as Ayre says – Saskatchewan was not Toronto, but Toronto was not London – it may have appeared so to Frye, although he is more generous and wry about it in his fiction. Apparently, Kennedy was not fooled by the ploy of any member of the congregation who would advise not talking over the heads of those not quite up to that member's intelligence. In more satiric fashion, the narrator says how Kennedy hated prayers and how Helen Grodenus had to settle for a piano although she was called the organist. Frye gives his narrator a good knowledge of music, one of Frye's fortes, when he says that Helen's 'left hand was always a grace-note's length ahead of her right one, and she beat time with her right foot on the damper pedal'. More satirical details occur at the conclusion of the first part. For instance, the narrator observes wryly: 'Mr. Kennedy raised his hand in benediction, thinking, as usual, that some day he really must work his nerve up to raise both. The congregation formed gossiping knots in the back of the church, and were slowly pumped out the door by Kennedy's handshake.' The death of Sarah Megill is announced at the end of this section.

In the second part, Kennedy, a native of Western Canada, returns home from Eastern Canada and sees the landscape of his youth with a new clarity. To a certain extent, he sees it in a way that is similar to Frye's accounts in letters to Helen, his future wife, and to friends and relatives from whom Ayre quotes in his biography. In a letter of 19 May 1934 to Helen, Frye says: 'God Himself seems to fade away on these grim prairies: not that He is far away – I never feel that; but He seems curiously impersonal' (quoted in Ayre 1989: 99–100). The narrator expresses Kennedy's view of the prairies on his return: 'The village did not "nestle", as villages elsewhere are said to do: it sprawled rigidly along the two roads to its distant markets, ignoring its natural surroundings as though it were itself supernatural.' Frye spent the summer in the

Bench, a dry upland, which is part of the badlands: Kennedy's appoint-
ment had been in a hamlet called Bad Land (see Ayre 1989: 96). A
character is not an author, but a creator of fictional worlds may translate
experience and reading into character. Perhaps Frye's experience in
Saskatchewan informs Kennedy's thoughts, which rise to consciousness,
address him and provide him with a recognition: 'these people could do
[get along] without any religion at all: there may be a reason why they
should have your kind of religion, but you don't really know what it is'.
Kennedy also thinks that his wife doesn't believe in God but takes out
insurance against His existence, especially through her 'energetic dislike
of the less important vices, such as drinking and smoking'. Old
Jurgensson, the best farmer in the area, was similarly sceptical.

The story is about immigration, displacement and survival, a tale
familiar to Canadian literature, a kind of roughing it in the bush garden
that Frye describes in his writings about that literature and that
Margaret Atwood develops in *Survival* (1972) (see Frye 1971a). Other
settler or immigrant cultures, whether of Australia, New Zealand, the
United States, Brazil, Mexico, Argentina or elsewhere, represent
similar themes in their pioneer days. The indigenous peoples have also
recorded their struggles to survive their displacement and suffering in
the face of the settlers and immigrants. Sarah Megill, born Sarah
Goremont, is one of the main characters, who is presented by report but
dies at the end of the first part; she came from England 'and for many
years was wretchedly homesick on the prairie'. Frye himself felt so
homesick for Toronto that about two weeks after he arrived in
Saskatchewan, he told Helen that he knew that he would commit suicide
if he had to spend the rest of his life on the prairies (19 May 1934, cited
in Ayre 1989: 99). His description of lack of privacy is similar to
Sarah's. The narrator says of Sarah: 'She loved walking alone, for one
thing, and found herself in a country which had concession lines instead
of lanes, and where she was an object of close scrutiny, sometimes with
field-glasses, from all the neighbouring farmhouses.' In his biography
John Ayre states that Frye felt foolish and self-conscious riding on the
prairies: 'In later years, he joked that across the flat areas of the parish,
he felt he couldn't even relieve himself because he was convinced that
the ladies of the parish – one especially – continually kept the preacher
boy under view with binoculars' (1989: 99). This feeling had occurred
to Frye much before the joke he would tell later in life. Authors
generally 'identify' or split their experiences among their characters
and do not favour one. This experience is mediated and refracted, so
that I can suggest a relation between Sarah, Kennedy and Frye but not
reduce these characters to autobiographical manifestations. Another

aspect of Sarah and Kennedy that the narrator discusses is that she seemed a mystic to Kennedy, who claimed to be anything but. In *Fearful Symmetry*, as well as in later works like *Words with Power* and *The Double Vision*, Frye talks about mysticism at length and opposes it to vision. This distinction, as I have argued, is not always so clear, and from these works and from his notebooks, it seems that Frye had many visionary, if not mystical schemes, in his criticism, even if, like Kennedy, in public he claimed or believed that he wasn't mystical or visionary. For some critics, *Anatomy* is a vision (see Levin 1967: 22–4). In reporting Kennedy's feelings about Sarah, the narrator says: 'she seemed to understand his own religion so much better than he did that her presence made sense of his job in a way that nothing else he had experienced did'. Like all good authors, Frye also tries to distance himself from his characters. Frye was 22 when he experienced the prairies, whereas Kennedy is 46 as he remembers.

Like the first part, the third represents life in Pilkey, a town in Eastern Canada, whereas the second part gives a view of Bad Land in the West. Sarah Megill was the link between the West and East, had probably arranged for Kennedy to be called back (he went to the university at Champlain, which sounds like Victoria College, where Frye studied), and joined her daughter there. The third part looks at the reaction to Sarah's death as a result of cancer. This develops the psychological aspect of Frye's fiction. John Goremont, who earlier is called Sarah's 'alleged grandson', for instance, 'was rather distressed that, though genuinely fond of his grandmother, and in contact with death for the first time, all his emotions were floating on a current of what was unmistakably exhilaration'. Kennedy, John and Mr and Mrs Lauder (Sarah's daughter) all speak of Sarah, and Kennedy witnesses their idealization of her. This response does not trouble him, and he observes: 'Her life had been released from all the accidents that made her appear domineering or imposing, selfish or virtuous; and what was now upon them like a spell was the sense, not of the goodness of her character, but simply of its reality.' This observation leads to a sense of timelessness or eternity that one finds in Blake and that Frye seems to have contemplated in his criticism and in his notes. Similarly, the narrator says of Sarah: 'She had finally completed her personality now that she had become timeless.' The narrative qualifies this state with some irony or an apologia that 'the doctrine of immortality filtered into Kennedy's mind' and the weak answers he gives in support of that doctrine.

The fourth part moves to Champlain, the home of the university, where Kennedy was trained and where Sarah wanted John to study. This part focuses on the family of Sarah Megill's son, especially on the piano playing of his daughter Ada and on her audience, which includes her brother Jack, a youth from the Conservatory and Harvey Oclose, 'more or less Ada's fiance'. She plays the Brahms rhapsody not terribly well but plays a Scarlatti sonata admirably, which she justifies with her theory of music, that 'something organic had gone out of music after Mozart's time, to reappear with Debussy and a few other moderns, everything between being a little suspect in its taste'. The narrator sets out the thoughts of Harvey and Ada's father, who are opposites, but who share ideas about her. Harvey strikes up a conversation about journalism with Jack, and they banter about quality, which seems to have to do more with the political affiliation of the newspaper than with anything else. The satire serves as an interlude to the music, but cannot often be separated, as in Oclose's conventional and limited but 'well-meaning' responses to a new recording of a Mozart quintet. When the guests leave, the phone rings, and Megill reports to the children that it was their Aunt Agnes Lauder in Pilkey and that their grandmother has died. After the family's reaction, the son, a lawyer, introduces a romance motif: John is actually a foundling who was left on Sarah's doorstep. He doesn't know that his parents were Boeschler, a man with the British Army of Occupation, and a woman from Cologne, who died on the way to Canada. Boeschler abandoned the child for a life in journalism, which became a life of alcoholism, so that the subject of newspaper reporting recurs in the story. The tone of the story is relaxed and almost jocular here. The narrative shifts from the death of Sarah Megill and her relation with her family to, after Jack's departure, whether Ada should marry 'that Oclose boy'. There is then a debate on the nature of love and the Canadian character between father and daughter. The discussion of love is almost Shavian. Ada asks Megill: 'But is it really so silly to think I might make a perfectly good marriage out of a not very passionate affection? I'm not a passionate female; if I have a passion for anything it's for music.' Comic writers have always understood the need for inversion, often the conventional inversion of conventionality, and this is why when Frye represents a father who defends passion in marriage and a daughter who opposes it, he inverts the usual roles of the generations. Theseus in Shakespeare's *A Midsummer Night's Dream*, a favourite example of Frye's in his discussion of comic structure, is more typical of the senex, the old father blocking the wishes of the younger generation in marriage. But the discussion between father and daughter over money, character, love and marriage is also modern because of the willingness and openness of the father to discuss these matters with his daughter and not to impose his will. Megill discusses Harvey Ociose's mother and father, her cultural pretensions and his financial success, her ability to give dinners as a key to their social and economic well-being. The fragment ends after this discussion of conventional society and returns to the character that holds the four parts together structurally and thematically, Sarah Megill. The final sentence turns to her: 'Ada looked thoughtful, but seemed anxious to drop the subject, and they went back to discussing her grandmother's death.' Although apparently unfinished, the Kennedy-Megill fragment has the materials for a longer story. None the less, it stands on its own.

I have found three poems of Frye's, two brief ones published in *Acta Victoriana* in December 1931 when he was 19 – a limerick called 'Our Monthly Current' and a four-line poem with the same rhyme, 'To My Beloved's Shoes' – and a sonnet in his letter of 14 July 1935 in a letter to his friend Roy Daniells. The first two are satirical trifles or conceits on love and women, while the third poem is a sonnet on his twenty-third birthday, which parodies Milton's and distinguishes Frye from Milton with the hope and confidence, if not conceit, that Frye will be great like and unlike Milton:

Milton considered his declining spring
And realized the possibility
That while he mused on Horton scenery
Genius might join his youth in taking wing;
Yet thought this not too serious a thing
Because god's well-known propensity
To take and re-absorb inscrutably
The lives of men, whatever gifts they bring.
Of course I have a different heritage;
I've worked hard not to be young at all,
With fair results; at least my blood is cooled,
And I am safe in saying, at Milton's age,
That if Time pays me an informal call
And tries to steal my youth, Time will get fooled.

Frye calls this sonnet 'horrible doggerel, like all my alleged poetry'. Time is no subtle thief of youth to Frye's persona, who has stolen his own youth to fool time. Perhaps this is Frye's Blakean, Christian and comic desire to find eternity or timelessness, to fool time rather than to be a tragic fool of time. In sonnet 7 Milton's syntax is notoriously complex, and one way of rendering the end of his sonnet is to see that time is, if he has the grace to use it so, eternal in God's view. Milton and Frye seek eternity, but Frye does so with satire, without quite the same theological intensity. In this same letter Frye says that he thinks his work on Blake is going to be 'a minor masterpiece' and notes that he has begun the novel *Quiet Consummation*. Here is a writer who is working out his ideas and images in fiction, poetry and criticism at the same time with the hope and confidence of youth and with a promise that we, with retrospection, can say was no idle boast.

There is probably more of Frye's fiction and poetry to be discovered. It is not my wish to dredge up unpublished work that Northrop Frye never intended or did not get round to publish in order to diminish his accomplishment. Instead, it is a means of showing a road not taken, a way to give a fuller view of a great writer. It is doubtful that any of the fiction and certainly any of the poems were written past the age of 29. Unless the voluminous unpublished papers yield novels or stories or poems that are from a more mature period and of the quality of Frye's criticism from his thirties to his seventies, we can only imagine what might have been. Frye, according to Ayre, was disappointed with his fiction and asked the advice of his senior colleague and distinguished Canadian poet E. J. Pratt, who advised him to establish a reputation in criticism and then return to fiction (Ayre 1989: 166–9). Frye never returned to fiction as a way to establish himself as a writer in the world. I think Pratt in his good will was mistaken, though the advice was good if Bernard Shaw served as a model. Late in life, it seems from Robert Denham's discoveries, Frye still wanted to write a masterpiece in fiction, partly to show those who thought conventionally that he could be creative in a conventional way. But I suggest that there were other unresolved tensions and motives here. He proclaimed that criticism was creative and recreative and that literature was a subject that stood on its own merits. There is truth to what he says. None the less, it is always dangerous for us to do what is natural: to build a system on our strengths. Perhaps Frye, while raising criticism another notch, made his strengths and those of the age he helped to shape – prose and criticism – the centre of literary studies. Near his death he wondered whether literature was now under siege from criticism, whereas in his youth it was the other way round. Perhaps Frye wished he were a poetic genius like Blake, but in a time warp or an eternal grain of sand, Blake might wish that he were a critical genius like Frye. But much as Frye did to advance an understanding of creativity, it still needs to be better understood. The word 'genius' is now generally met with embarrassment in departments of literature, but it is a concern for Frye. He had great admiration for and anxiety over Blake. The general public, in so far as it reads, and poets, playwrights and novelists, who have a vested interest, still think of criticism as second words even in this age of criticism. But Frye is one of the leading writers in English since the Second World War. He achieved that status mostly with criticism, developing it into metacriticism and theory as a supplement to close reading, interpretation or hermeneutics, but his fiction suggests that we might have gained had he published literature and criticism throughout his life. For Frye, these were different but equal parts of the same imaginative enterprise, augmenting each other through complementary labours rather than detracting from each other through internecine squabbles. Frye had style, image and idea enough to write in even more modes than he did. Until the 1960s in Canada, it was very difficult to be heard at home or internationally as a writer, but Canada had produced a disproportionate number of well-known literary scholars and critics. It was a struggle that writers like Irving Layton and Robertson Davies had to contend with. In 1941 the surge in Canadian literature was something almost never expected if not dreamt of. Frye made his choice, but not without regrets or new hopes, as his notebooks reveal. Perhaps it was a matter of time. Paradoxically, perhaps the idea of *écriture* or writing that Derrida proposes or the *écriture feminine* of the French feminists, which he thought about but did not always agree with, might bring theory and literature closer together and make younger readers more attentive to the stories and anecdotes Frye tells in his criticism and to these writings that I have tried to resurrect from their neglect.

10 The power of words

Words, words, words.

(Hamlet)

All writers are destined for literary history. Critics cannot avoid the inevitable. But literary history means different things to different people. For some, it is the dustbin of history. In this view a critic has performed his or her function and has been superseded in the comic plot of the progress of criticism. For others, the critic becomes part of the history of the criticism of a genre, author, period or a kind of theory or problem. Few critics, as well as few poets, dramatists and novelists, are made part of a myth of the fall, given a place of honour in the golden age, looked upon as giants in time immune to the tragic stumble into disintegration and decline. Aristotle and Plato have sometimes occupied a place in this pastoral – in name if not always in practice – but all too often critics in our age have been willing to discredit or to devalue their predecessors or apparent rivals. This is a wearisome ritual better suited to cockfights than to a criticism that has a social dimension. Nevertheless, there seems in recent years to be a division between theory and criticism, and Frye, the theorist, now seems more read by those who wish to apply his work to specific texts. With characteristic irony, Frye said in an interview that he was no further down skid row than the deconstructionists were. Depending on the myth, the time for general theories, as opposed to the variety of specific theories today, will return or will never rise again. This book would place Frye neither on the scrapheap nor in a prelapsarian critical paradise. Instead, it argues that Frye has made important contributions to the theory of genres, especially to satire, comedy and romance; to the study of authors like Spenser, Shakespeare, Milton, Blake and Eliot; to the discussion of language, mythology and ideology; to literary history as a history of genres; to the defence of literature and criticism; to poetics; to education; and to the dignity and independence of the critic as a creative writer and a member of a discipline. In Frye's literary history he would be a central figure in the genre of criticism, as an essay writer, and as something separate, a theorist of literature. The theoretical imagination for Frye was as much a part of the critic as of the physicist. Criticism, according to Frye, is the theory of literature. For polemical reasons, he did not necessarily want to combine his defence of the imaginative and creative aspects of criticism with his declaration that criticism was its own field because at the time he wrote, in his view at least, too many critics thought of themselves as failed writers or parasites on literature who were doomed to spout second words.

Frye's work in the period from about 1936 to 1957 involves an attempt to find a critical path between the determinism of Marxism and the aesthetic isolationism of New Criticism. In finding his middle way, or at least his own way, Frye had to contend with perhaps the most influential English-speaking poet and critic of his generation: T. S. Eliot. Although Frye had his differences with Eliot, who did not warmly receive Frye's book on his work (Ayre 1989: 280–3, 290), he was very much taken with Eliot's notion of tradition and the individual talent. He looked beyond Eliot's preference for classicism and his own preference for Romanticism. Frye's argument in *T. S. Eliot* (1963) can be applied to Frye's writing. In the book Frye distinguishes between Eliot's polemical criticism and his 'genuine' criticism, between the practice and study of literature and the historical myth, like Spengler's (with an echo of Gibbon's), of the decline of the modern world and of Christianity. Frye is a polemical and 'studied' critic who, like Eliot, is drawn to the myth of decline and fall as well as that of the divine comedy and to the view that literature possesses a simultaneous existence and order. Like Eliot, Frye's work displays a structure of images and icons that conveys an imaginative world, that mixes satire and polemics with vision, especially in his later works. *Four Quartets* is visionary, and so too are *Words with Power* and *The Double Vision*. But, as Frye points out, criticism is creative like literature, but it is also a separate discipline that is not a minor genre of literature. Frye's cosmology takes us back to the medieval as Eliot's does. Frye is poetic and critical just as Eliot is. But, as I have suggested, Frye never really seems to have resolved his assertion that a critic is as creative as a poet and his desire to separate poetry from poetics, the poet from criticism. Frye's desire to be a writer of fiction, which lingers longer than he seems to have remembered, may be an indication that his system could not escape a social dimension, a desire to be popular, a desire to be heard. Frye admits as much, but he makes his decision not to write fiction sound earlier than it was and easier than it was. This is not to detract from the magnitude of Frye's work – critics still have doubts about the nature and value of their work. It is possible that the very likeness between Eliot and Frye explains Frye's ambivalence in *T. S. Eliot* and elsewhere and made him turn to the real political differences between them. Frye may have 'identified' with Eliot, but no such identification or identity can be complete and enduring, especially between two accomplished writers.

Eliot was someone Frye had to face while he was making his decisions on what kind of a writer and critic he was going to become. Frye chose not to become a Marxist or a New Critic. I do not want to labour Frye's critique of New Criticism for not looking at the connection between texts, although he shares with the New Critics an interest in poetics and, in his practical criticism, analyses individual texts in analogous ways. This is ground we have covered, and so we should move from the gates of ivory to the gates of horn. Another distinguished critic and contemporary of Frye, Harry Levin, who takes up the Homeric metaphor of Odysseus' choice of gates, also sought in the same period to reconcile formalism and historicism. Eliot's tenure as the Charles Eliot Norton Professor of Poetry at Harvard made a lasting impression on Levin and others. Although Frye and Levin came under the influence of Eliot, they both rejected his conservative social views and sought their own critical paths. Levin's theory balances formalism and historicism in literature as an institution (1946; see also 1963 and Hart 1989b). Frye's theory in this period accepts the visionary and seeks history in the history of literary forms. Much later, in *Words with Power* (1990), Frye was able to compare the situation his generation faced with the new generation that he faced in his last years. Because of the relative neglect of poetics or of formalism among these younger theorists, Frye came to concentrate more on the extremes of ideological criticism as opposed to those of aesthetic hermeticism. He says that critics propounding 'a new ideological trend' may feel the weight of the past, and so set up a value system that devalues cultural tradition and emphasizes their own propensities as part of a utopian and teleological project:

> The Marxist criticism of a generation ago carried these tendencies to such an extreme that knowledgeable Marxist critics now speak of 'vulgar Marxism'. But there is also a vulgar Christian, a vulgar humanist, a vulgar feminist, and many other forms of what may be called topiary criticism, an art of clipping literature in order to distort it into a different shape. Here it is the ideological trend that becomes the real burden, and the cultural tradition that delivers us from it.

(1990e: 60)

Did Frye feel this way at the height of his fame? Behind the differences, which only the topiary critics who vulgarize their positions insist on at the expense of others, Frye implies a field theory. He often shies away from a 'loose' pluralism and instead insists on identity, diversity in unity. This difference between identity and pluralism may be a matter of perspective and emphasis.

Frye shares with Levin a desire to find a middle way that recognises the historically unique processes of conditioning and the technical matters unique to literature, although Frye tends to stress content less than Levin does. Perhaps Frye was responding too much to topiary critics of his own day, who emphasized content too much. Since Aristotle, the interdependence of form and content has, quite sensibly, been advocated by many. Frye is not dismissing content but asserts that form distinguishes literature from other types of writing. In the current theoretical climate genre is often neglected and formalism considered to be antithetical to political criticism. It would be blind to go back to a notion of structure that refuses to take into consideration the post-structuralist critique of structure (Derrida 1967: 4, 59; 1980, see Hart 1992c: 221–3, 237–8). Frye admits that literature is a self-referential universe that is therefore not like descriptive prose and that genres are human constructions within the construct of culture. It is, according to Frye, only when one confuses literary form with a structure in the world or reality that formalism goes astray.

Nevertheless, to say that we do not know the provenance of something is to admit that we begin arbitrarily in most areas of human knowledge and culture, but it is not to say that there need not be any beginning, middle and end, or whatever form, to our stories and arguments and that those forms will not recur over time. We have to begin somewhere and get on with our poetry and criticism. No human product, system or interpretation is perfect, and by saying so we are performing necessary critiques of one another's work. A negative hermeneutic is useful, but a positive hermeneutic is desirable. If there is no play, pleasure, wit, laughter, hope in our criticism, then why bother? We can pull the thread on any argument, even one that argues for the impossibility or necessary failure of argument, but perhaps it is a thread that will lead us, even if momentarily, out of the maze. Frye is playful, witty and hopeful. His muse is often comic and romantic, and not only when he is making a joke or plotting his next move into another structure. For Frye, literature has forms that distinguish it from other verbal worlds, although those distinctions are more heuristic than provable in practice. This is a flexible poetics.

Frye is interested in the question 'What is literature?', but also sees the desirability of the application and testing of theory through an empirical study of literature (Salusinszky 1987: 32). While in the 1940s and 1950s he set out to put some theoretical rigour into Anglo-American criticism and to give criticism a place of greater independence and self-sufficiency, in the years before his death he lamented that critical theory was now threatening other disciplines and that literature now needed its defenders. This view is the flip-side of his desire to see criticism as a discipline with its own integrity and not a second order that depends on other fields. He wants these disciplines to continue their own independence. There should be separate disciplines so that we can begin from a strong position when we seek to be inter-disciplinary. Each field also has its own practice with its own rules and moves (see Chambers 1992). Frye said that he wanted to write another volume of practical criticism as an application of the theory in *Anatomy*, but he never wrote such a book. His own empirical or practical criticism occurs particularly in particular essays on individual authors like Castiglione, Spenser, William Morris, Joyce and others and in his first and last books published during his life, *Fearful Symmetry* and *Words with Power*.

Why is Frye still one of the most cited and, presumably, read critics, but is not in the theoretical allusions of our time? The reputations of writers – poets and critics – seem to come and go in and through the ages. Frye himself began by defending Blake, who he thought deserved a better reputation and a fair and careful reading, and then he followed Sidney, Shelley and others in defending poetry from the charges of immorality, uselessness and ornamentality that have, since at least Plato, been laid against it and any variation of fiction and fabrication like the theatre and the novel (see Barish 1981). Having written this book I obviously think that Frye is worth reading and rereading, and that there is much pleasure and learning to be garnered from his many books and articles. He also tells good stories: his best-known tales occur in his criticism. Today, speaking to other poets and critics, I am not sure that defensiveness is entirely avoidable. Our culture has conditioned all of us to justify poetry, to feed it with praise in the abstract and to starve it in practice. We fund criticism better because it is supposed to be non-fiction and therefore closer to truth and reality. But Frye and post-modern critics, which include post-structuralists, feminists, new historicists and cultural materialists to name a few, see creativity, fictionality and contingency in criticism. Will criticism be funded less, the more fictional it is or the more it calls attention to its fictionality? Perhaps critical fictions will go unnoticed by governments and the public, as legal fictions generally have. This is a long way of saying that for a long time defensiveness has been a part of literary criticism. With Frye, I share the attitude that we need to scrutinize one another's work but that if the walls are really burning around us as it sometimes seems (all paranoia aside), then what are we doing standing on the wall arguing over our lesser differences rather than looking at how our multiplicitous views converge? That is not to wish for conformity and an erasure or deflection of difference. Within interpretation and theory there is a politics, but to ignore its relation to the larger political order can range from benign foolishness to dangerous neglect.

Still I return to defend one critic to defend us all when we are defensible. Why is Frye's name not in the thick of many current theoretical allusions and debates? Here are a few of the possible reasons. The turn away from his work is relatively recent, and the major critics have turned away from structure, form and system as a sin of their fathers or of their youth. Younger theorists underestimate his interest in politics and ideology, which is perhaps the central concern of this theoretical moment. Too many critics have locked Frye in 1957, which is understandable, though not desirable, considering the impact of *Anatomy of Criticism.* They have neglected many of his books and have not had time to assimilate his later work. In a climate where the possibility of literary language and of literature is doubted, except as an ideological weapon or as a tool of the established social and economic powers, Frye's defence of literature and criticism as independent but correlative disciplines in respect to each other and to other disciplines often proves unpopular. In a rebellion against grand narratives and vast metaphysical systems, many post-modernist or oppositional critics point to the negative historical consequences of such grand designs. One of those systems is Christianity, and some critics might displace the authoritarian and political abuses of Christianity on to the Bible, in spite of its ambiguous stories, like that of Job, and parables, like those of Jesus. Frye was quite happy with the separation of church and state and seemed to think that worldly power had been a dismal and corrupting influence on Christianity. The post-modern position against vast schemes and narratives is a necessary corrective to the great celebrations of order, harmony and intellectual power that the West has used to blind itself to other cultures and to its own inhumanity, its tolerance of slavery, racism, sexism and other intolerant and systemic wrongs. But this is not an altogether new stance. The pre-Socratics and Nietzsche have opposed systematic metaphysics, and social reformers have taken liberal positions against civil wrongs for over two centuries. I am not saying that these arguments do not still need to be made. They do – unfortunately, over and over. One only has to read Franz Fanon and C. L. R. James to realize that the universal rights proclaimed by

European revolutionaries did not apply to people of colour in the Napoleonic era and too often do not in our century. Frye admits that, and would agree with Edward Said, but where he differs from many of the following generation of critics is that a system can be positive and heuristic and not necessarily negative and imperialistic. But there are other debates in literature that also have to be made. Frye hopes that his system is suggestive and not prescriptive and closed. To be liberal or aware of social problems does not, in Frye's view, mean that one abandons the study of what makes literature unique – genre, form or structure – for politics, history and other social disciplines. Frye's political track record is one of tolerance and democracy. There is a fallacy that words and action necessarily correspond. It is easier to talk revolution than to create one. Although Frye maintains that words have their own power of action, he is dubious about the possibility of political revolutions changing life and proposes a transformation of individuals through the ambiguities and complexities of literature. The poetic language and structure of literature, its metaphor and myth, resist being marshalled for evidence as if literature were descriptive prose. The very intensity of literature resists its capture for any ideological position, including, I assume, liberalism or humanism. In any case, as Frye points out, he may call others and himself humanists, but outside classics departments there has not been a large body of scholars trained in the classics of ancient Greece and Rome for a very long time now. Schools and universities have largely turned their backs on classical languages and literatures. The word 'liberal', even though Frye liked to quote John Stuart Mill, has also changed over time. Literature is an ambivalent production that enters into these ever-changing contexts. It can be read into these ideological and cultural changes, but its form refracts and resists being treated as content in the service of ideology. Such is Frye's view.

There are some continuities with Frye's work in the past decade. It is not for me to say how posterity will judge him: this would bring us back to stock marketism. Some theorists, especially in Britain, Germany and Israel, are continuing Frye's philosophical or systematic method and his counterbalancing interest in poets. Although different from Frye, the proponents of the Polysystem Theory and the Empirical Study of Literature advocate a systematic approach to literature (see Dimić and Garstin 1988, Tötösy: 1992). When Polysystem theorists say their system is open, they are partly responding to the implicit criticism that Frye faced, that today many critics think that a system is by definition closed and restrictive and not heuristic and enabling. Theorists of the Empirical Study of Literature would benefit from a consideration of Frye, the creator of one of the great literary systems of this century if not over the whole of Western literature, even if they have a different definition of empirical and a vastly different system (see Schmidt 1983, 1985, 1992). To ignore Frye's system does little to clarify the distinctions of the new empiricism from the old, how positivism has been superseded and the influence of the British empirical tradition (see Weimann 1965, 1973, 1974). The English-speaking tradition is also too selective in its reading and theoretical allusions. Whereas earlier in the century our theorists drew their influences from English-speaking critics, they now look elsewhere. There is a long tradition of borrowing. Sidney borrowed from Italy; Coleridge from Germany; now many theorists look to France. It is possible that nostalgia for the pastoral, the dream of the agrarian, the fears of Luddites, are reasons for an aversion to the systematic as much now as in 1959, when C. P. Snow spoke about these attitudes among 'humanists' in his discussion of the two cultures in the Rede Lecture. It can also be said that Marxists like Jameson and Eagleton can admire the systematic nature of Frye's thought, but they also think that he hangs too much on the pre-industrial images of earlier literature and the Bible rather than moving his recurring images or archetypes into the industrial age. Like Frye, Jameson is especially interested in the relation of narrative and politics but has recently been drawn to the debate on postmodernism (Jameson 1984, 1990). Although Derrida, Kristeva and Cixous are different critics from Frye, they have taken his position that criticism is creative further by using the narrative techniques of poets and novelists much more widely and overtly than Frye did. Their cosmology is not only macroscopic, like his, but also microscopic, in the very syntax and arrangement of the words on the page. Frye blended the aphorism, where he began in his notebooks, into sentences and paragraphs, but these theorists are more like Nietzsche and McLuhan, not to mention Barthes, whose relation to McLuhan and the question of influence needs to be addressed, because in certain works they foreground the aphoristic, discontinuous and fictional. Paradoxically, Plato, even more than Longinus, may be smiling sublimely in the background.

There are some other affinities. Elsewhere, I have discussed Greenblatt's use of story-argument, a technique that gives him some affinity with Frye (Hart 1991b). Greenblatt foregrounds the fictional or storytelling aspect of his work more than Frye often does. Both are interested in anecdote and analogy. Greenblatt is like a metaphysical poet, a John Donne, creating bold and striking comparisons, to make the familiar wondrous and the wondrous familiar, to perform an out-of-the-way act with such virtuosity that readers will take it as natural. Frye liked metaphysical poets and their latter-day counterpart, Wallace Stevens, who wrote many variations on the bold metaphor, different versions of 'Anecdote on a Jar'. Frye also looked into metaphor and made what could have appeared to be a personal mnemonic system into a successful public performance in *Anatomy of Criticism*. Perhaps, as Frye said of Blake, there is no private mythology. Ross Chambers has made the study of narrative, to which Frye has contributed so much, more flexible and more responsive to rhetoric by discussing situation, seduction, manœuvrability, and other notions. Chambers' work moves away from structuralism, shows a close understanding of specific texts and is evolving a theory of reading literature and an informed awareness that the language of literature may, through mediation, help to constitute oppositional criticism. Others, like Patricia Parker and Terence Cave, continue necessary and suggestive work on the relation between poetics and rhetoric. Parker has extended these inquiries into the area of gender and Cave has examined recognition or *anagnorisis*, which is at the centre of Frye's vision of comedy and of literature. Terry Eagleton's discussion of aesthetics is also illuminating and shares with Frye's a distrust in illiberalism.

These affinities are not meant to deny historical changes or to erase differences between Frye and those theorists who have come after him. Rather, they suggest that theory and criticism are an archaeology in which new layers appear and reconfigure the other layers that never go away no matter how much they are forgotten or studied. The past does not go away conveniently. Whether the return is Viconian or Freudian or some other myth or surmise, its possibility makes us face our predecessors. Frye himself advocated a kind of eternal moment, as Nietzsche did in a different way. Sometimes Frye could be as visionary as a prophet and as utopian as any Marxist. The future of past dreams or logics can be embarrassing to the actual future, but we will cause similar embarrassment. The hopes, needs and anxieties of some periods in the future may call upon Frye more than on us.

But this is a book on Northrop Frye and should end with him. He was and is a member of a community of critics – he might say a tradition – but in some senses he must stand alone. In returning to Frye's work I found a critic with a corpus as complicated, varied and surprising as most of the great writers whom we study. Although we construct canons and reputations, it seems that to endure a writer or critic must have something to which subsequent generations need or want to return. There are moments when in emphasizing Frye's accomplishment I think I might be blinded by my own rationalizations, my own desire that critics do something we can admire and return to, but then I also wonder whether I am a member of a society that has conditioned itself to make criticism into secondary words about poetry or an administrative task, an explanation, translation and dissipation demanded by a society that finds fictions dangerous or incomprehensible, too much like its dreams or nightmares to admit to and to let into its heart. These are questions Frye wrestled with. I am not convinced that he resolved his desire to separate literature and criticism while giving each its own dignity. If it is the very structure of literary form and metaphor that resists ideology and celebrates our primary concerns for life, freedom, reproduction and happiness, then why write criticism and not poetry? Is poetry as dumb and criticism as eloquent as Frye maintained? His answer is that the literary is a hypothetical or 'ideal' category and that of course we need it as a way of desiring and working towards our goals and that descriptive language and literary language overlap. Criticism uses metaphor just as poetry does. They both build up worlds. He thinks that criticism creates a climate for literature but is also a theory of literature. Frye's separation of powers is heuristic and is necessary because those powers are not inseparable – like those set out in the constitution of the United States. He defends literature and the imagination as necessary to our humanity, as products of culture that are in but apart from nature. It may be that the imagination is an imaginary place, a kind of tautological dream, but it is the faculty that most makes us human. Reason is also necessary, so that Freud is not enough: we are forgetting some of the story when we swing from the time when humans were said to be distinguished from animals because of their reason to a time when all is supposed to be unreasonable, when we are the irrationals of our dreams. Frye sees that criticism must have some autonomy and distance from literature, must be a theory of it, so that critics must use their reason to make clear and coherent arguments and schemes and exercise their imaginations to meet the visions in literature with another vision. The history of criticism, perhaps the pseudo-history in Frye's view, is one of tensions among, and the self-interested rankings or hierarchies of, philosophy, poetry and history. Criticism is none of these but has something in common with them. Whatever criticism is, Northrop Frye is a critic of his time and for all times, even if such a claim is a fiction, an act of imagination, a recognition, a vision, with some ironic distance and scepticism, which Frye himself recognized as necessary for criticism.

Appendix

Northrop Frye's papers are housed at the E. J. Pratt Library of Victoria University [Victoria College] in the University of Toronto. These represent vast materials that will take years to catalogue, transcribe and digest. Unfortunately, I could not get hold of or find all the manuscripts and typescripts I would have liked, especially in regard to Frye's fiction. Some books arrived too late for my consideration: David Cayley, *Northrop Frye in Conversation*, Toronto: Anansi, 1992; Northrop Frye, *Reading the World: Selected Writings, 1935–1976*, ed. R. D. Denham, New York: Peter Lang, 1990 and *A World in a Grain of Sand: Twenty-Two Interviews with Northrop Frye*, ed. R. D. Denham, New York: Peter Lang, 1991; *Visionary Poetics: Essays on Northrop Frye's Criticism*, ed. R. D. Denham and T. Willard, New York: Peter Lang. I shall consider these books in review articles, one of which, 'Frye/About Frye', will appear in *CRCL/RCLC* 20 (1993). A large international conference, 'The Legacy of Northrop Frye', was held 29–31 October 1992 at Victoria College, University of Toronto, and a collection of essays is planned from that conference. The conference and the new works by and about Frye show that he continues to be of great interest and may experience a 'renaissance'. But any new materials will have to wait for future work.

References

An excellent bibliography of Frye's works through June 1987 is Robert D,
Denham, *Northrop Frye: An Annotated Bibliography of Primary and Secondary
Sources*, Toronto: University of Toronto Press, 1987. Since then, Denham has
been updating the bibliography in his *Northrop Frye Newsletter*. He has also
begun to reprint Frye's fiction.

Abrams, M. H. (1959) 'Anatomy of Criticism', *University of Toronto Quarterly*
28: 190–6.
—— (1971) *Natural Supernaturalism: Tradition and Revolution in Romantic
Literature*, New York: W. W. Norton.
Adams, H. (1959) 'Criticism: Whence and Whither?', *American Scholar* 28:
226, 238.
—— (ed.) (1971) *Critical Theory Since Plato*, San Diego: Harcourt Brace
Jovanovich.
Aitken, J. (1991) 'Northrop Frye: An Appreciation', in *The Double Vision:
Language and Meaning in Religion*, Toronto: University of Toronto Press,
xi–xvi.
Albert, J. C. and Albert, S. E. (eds) (1984) *The Port Huron Statement*, in *The
Sixties Papers: Documents of a Rebellious Decade*, New York: Praeger,
176–96.
Alighieri, D. (1904) 'Letter to Can Grande Della Scala', c. 1318, *Translations
of the Later Works of Dante*, trans. P. H. Wicksteed, London: J. M. Dent &
Sons.
—— (1909) *Il Convivio*, c. 1304–8, trans. W. W. Jackson, *Dante's Convivio*,
Oxford: Clarendon Press.
Althusser, L. (1971) *Lenin and Philosophy and Other Essays*, trans. Ben
Brewster, London: New Left Books.
Altieri, C. (1972) 'Northrop Frye and the Problem of Spiritual Authority',
PMLA 87: 64–75.
Anderson, P. (1979) *Considerations in Western Marxism*, London: NLB.
Aquinas, T. (1927) *Summa Theologica*, trans. Fathers of the Dominican
Province, London: Burns, Oates, and Washbourne.
Arac, J. (1986) *Postmodernism and Politics*, University of Minnesota Press.
Arnold, M. (1970) *The Function of Criticism at the Present Time*, in W. J. Bate
(ed.) *Criticism: The Major Texts*, enlarged edition, San Diego: Harcourt
Brace Jovanovich, 452–66.

308   *References*

Atwood, M. (1972) *Survival*, Toronto: Anansi.
—— (1979) 'Fifties Vic', *The CEA Critic* 42: 19–22.
—— (1991) *Vic Report*, 'A Tribute to Northrop Frye'.
Ayre, J. (1989) *Northrop Frye: A Biography*, Toronto: Random House.
Balfour, I. (1988) *Northrop Frye*, Boston: Twayne.
Barish, J. (1981) *The Antitheatrical Prejudice*, Berkeley: University of California Press.
Barth, H. (1976) *Truth and Ideology*, trans. F. Lilge, Berkeley: University of California Press.
Barthes, R. (1957) *Mythologies*, Paris: Editions du Seuil.
—— (1967) 'The Discourse of History', in *Comparative Criticism: A Yearbook*, trans. S. Bann, Vol. 3, French original, 'Le Discours de l'histoire', *Social Science Information* No. 4 (1967): 67–75.
Bates, R. (1971) *Northrop Frye*, Toronto: McClelland & Stewart.
Becker, J. E. (1982) 'The Word of God and the Work of Man', *Worldview* 25: 5–8 [review of *The Great Code* by Northrop Frye].
Belsey, C. (1980) *Critical Practice*, London: Methuen.
—— (1990) 'Agents of Utopia: Subjectivity in the Postmodern Condition', *CIEFL Bulletin* (New Series) 2: 15–23.
Belsey, C. and Moore, J. (eds) (1989) *The Feminist Reader: Essays in Gender and the Politics of Literary Criticism*, New York: Blackwell.
Bershady, J. H. (1982) 'Utopia Surmised', in S. Leventman (ed.) *Counter-culture and Social Transformation: Essays on Negativistic Themes in Sociological Theory*, Springfield, IL: Charles C. Thomas, 141–61.
Bhaba, H. (1990a) 'Articulating the Archaic: Notes on Colonial Nonsense', in *Literary Theory Today*, ed. P. Collier and Geyer-Ryan, Ithaca: Cornell University Press, 203–18.
—— (1990b) *Nation and Narration*, London: Routledge.
Blake, W. (1965) *Poetry and Prose*, ed. D. V. Erdman, Garden City: Doubleday.
Bloom, H. (1957) Review of *Anatomy of Criticism* by Northrop Frye, *Yale Review* 47: 130–3.
—— (1961) *The Visionary Company: A Reading of English Romantic Poetry*, Garden City: Doubleday.
—— (1973) *The Anxiety of Influence: A Theory of Poetry*, New York: Oxford University Press.
Boccaccio, G. (1901) *Vita di Dante*, 1364, pub. 1477, *The Earliest Lives of Dante*, trans. J. R. Smith, New York: Holt, Rinehart, & Winston.
Bradley, A. C. (1957) *Shakespearian Tragedy: Lectures on Hamlet, Othello, King Lear and Macbeth*, 1st edn 1904, 2nd edn 1905, London: Macmillan, rpt. 1966.
Brecht, B. (1964, rpt. 1965) *Brecht on Theatre: The Development of an Aesthetic*, trans. J. Willett, London: Methuen.
Breslin, J. B. (1982) 'The Gospel According to Frye', *Book World* 12 (16 May): 11, 14 [review of *The Great Code* by Northrop Frye].
Brooks, P., Felman, S. and Hillis Miller, J. (1985) *The Lesson of Paul de Man*, Yale French Studies 69. New Haven: Yale University Press.
Bruner, J. (1960) *The Process of Education*, Cambridge, MA: Harvard University Press.
Burke, K. (1958) 'The Encyclopedic, Two Kinds Of', *Poetry* 91: 320–8.
Cahill, J. P. (1983) 'Deciphering *The Great Code*', *Dalhousie Review* 63: 412–21.

Calvino, I. (1986) 'Literature as Projection of Desire/On Northrop Frye's *Anatomy of Criticism*', in *The Uses of Literature*, trans. Patrick Creagh, San Diego: Harcourt. Original, 'La letteratura come prolezione del desiderio', *Libri Nuovi* (August 1969), 5.

Cave, T. (1988) *Recognitions: A Study in Poetics*, Oxford: Clarendon Press.

Cayley, D. (1991) 'Inside Mythology: Northrop Frye talks with David Cayley', *The Idler* 35: 23–34.

—— (1992) *Northrop Frye in Conversation*, Toronto: Anansi.

Chambers, R. (1984) *Story and Situation*, Minneapolis: University of Minnesota Press.

—— (1991) *Room for Maneuver: Reading (the) Oppositional (in) Narrative*, Chicago: University of Chicago Press.

—— (1992) 'Rules and Moves', *CRCL/RCLC* 19: 95–100.

Cixous, H. (1967) 'Une science de la littérature', *Le Monde*, Supplement to no. 7086 (25 October: iv).

Colebrook, J. (1979) *Innocents of the West: Travels through the Sixties*, New York: Basic Books.

Cook, D. (1985) *Northrop Frye: A Vision of the New World*, New York: St Martin's Press.

Cook, E., Hosek, C., Macpherson, J., Parker, P. and Patrick, J. (eds) (1983) *Centre and Labyrinth: Essays in Honour of Northrop Frye*, Toronto: University of Toronto Press.

Cornford, F. (1934) *The Origin of Attic Comedy*, Cambridge: Cambridge University Press.

'Courses from Free University Catalogues' (1969), ed. J. Berke, *Counter Culture*, London: Peter Owen Ltd, 249–59.

Culler, J. (1979) 'Common Cause: Notes on Frye's View of Education', *CEA Critic* 42: 23–8.

—— (1982) *On Deconstruction: Theory and Criticism after Structuralism*, Ithaca: Cornell University Press.

—— (1984) 'A Critic against the Christians', *Times Literary Supplement* (23 November), 1327–8.

Daiches, D. (1958) Review of *Anatomy of Criticism* by Northrop Frye, *Modern Philology* 56: 69–72.

De Man, P. (1971) *Blindness and Insight: Essays in the Rhetoric of Contemporary Criticism*, New York: Oxford University Press.

—— (1979) *Allegories of Reading: Figurative Language in Rousseau, Nietzsche, Rilke, and Proust*, New Haven: Yale University Press.

—— (1983) *Blindness and Insight: Essays in the Rhetoric of Contemporary Criticism*, 2nd revised edn, Minneapolis: University of Minnesota Press.

—— (1984) 'Phenomenality and Materiality in Kant', in G. Shapiro and A. Sica (eds), *Hermeneutics: Questions and Prospects*, Amherst, MA: University of Massachusetts Press.

Denham, R. D. (1978) *Northrop Frye and Critical Method*, University Park: Pennsylvania State University Press.

—— (1987) *Northrop Frye: An Annotated Bibliography of Primary and Secondary Sources*, Toronto: University of Toronto Press.

—— (1990) Introduction to R. D. Denham (ed.) *Northrop Frye: Myth and Metaphor, Selected Essays 1974–1988*, Charlottesville and London: University Press of Virginia, xiii–xviii.

310   *References*

3Northrop

3Derrida, J. (1967) *De la Grammatologie*, Paris: Editions du Minuit; trans. C.
G. Spivak, *Of Grammatology*, Baltimore: Johns Hopkins University Press,
1976.

—— (1972) *La Dissemination*, Paris: Editions Seuil.

—— (1980) 'La Loi du Genre – The Law of Genre', trans. A Ronnell, *Glyph:
Textual Studies* 7: 176–232.

Dimić, M. V. and Garstin, M. K. (1988) 'The Polysystem Theory: A Brief
Introduction, with Bibliography', in E. D. Blodgett and A. G. Purdy (eds)
Problems of Literary Reception/Problèmes de réception littéraire, Edmonton:
Research Institute for Comparative Literature, University of Alberta, 177–96.

Dollimore, J. (1984) *Radical Tragedy: Religion, Ideology, and Power in the
Drama of Shakespeare and his Contemporaries*, Chicago: University of
Chicago Press.

—— (1985) 'Introduction: Shakespeare, Cultural Materialism and the New
Historicism', in *Political Shakespeare: New Essays in Cultural Materialism*,
ed. J. Dollimore and A. Sinfield, Ithaca: Cornell University Press, 2–17.

Dolzani, M. (1983) 'The Infernal Method: Northrop Frye and Contemporary
Criticism', in E. Cook et al. (eds) *Centre and Labyrinth: Essays in Honour of
Northrop Frye*, Toronto: University of Toronto Press, 59–68.

Donoghue, D. (1992) 'Mister Myth' *New York Review of Books* 39, 7: 25–8.

Dudek, L. (1982) 'The Bible as Fugue: Themes and Variations', *University of
Toronto Quarterly* 52: 128–35 [review of *The Great Code* by Northrop Frye].

Duffy, D. (1968) 'The Too-Well-Tempered Critic', *Tamarack Review* 46:
115–20 [review of *The Modern Century* by Northrop Frye].

Dyrkjob, J. U. (1979) *Northrop Fryes litteraturteori*, Copenhagen: Berlinske
Verlag.

Eagleton, T. (1976a) *Criticism and Ideology: A Study of Marxist Literary
Theory*, London: NLB.

—— (1976b) *Marxism and Literary Criticism*, London: Methuen.

—— (1983a) 'Ineluctable Options', in W. J. T. Mitchell (ed.) *The Politics of
Interpretation*, Chicago: University of Chicago Press, 373–80.

—— (1983b) *Literary Theory: An Introduction*, Oxford: Blackwell.

—— (1990) *The Ideology of the Aesthetic*, Oxford: Blackwell.

Ellmann, R. (1968) 'Dissent and the Academy', *New York Review of Books* 10
(15 February): 6, 8, 10.

Elzey, R. (1969) 'Founding an Anti-University', in J. Berke (ed.) *Counter
Culture*, London: Peter Owen Ltd, 229–48.

Fekete, J. (1977) *The Critical Twilight: Explorations in the Ideology of Anglo-
American Literary Theory from Eliot to McLuhan*, London: International
Library of Phenomenology and Moral Sciences.

Felperin, H. (1972) *Shakespearean Romance*, Princeton: Princeton University
Press, 314–16.

—— (1985) *Beyond Deconstruction: The Uses and Abuses of Literary Theory*,
Oxford: Clarendon Press.

—— (1992) 'Political Criticism at the Crossroads: Towards a Utopian Hermeneutics', Talk, University of Alberta (16 January).

Feuer, L. S. (1975) *Ideology and Ideologists*, Oxford: Blackwell.

Fish, S. (1980) *Is There a Text in This Class? The Authority of Interpretive Communities*, Cambridge, MA: Harvard University Press.

Fletcher, A. (1966) 'Utopian History and the Anatomy of Criticism', in M. Krieger (ed.) *Northrop Frye in Modern Criticism*, New York: Columbia University Press, 31–73.

Flynn, J. R. (1973) *Humanism and Ideology: An Aristotelian View*, London: RKP.

For Alma Mater: Theory and Practice in Feminist Scholarship (1985), ed. P. A. Treichler, C. Kramarae, and B. Staffard, Urbana: University of Illinois Press.

Foucault, M. (1961) *Histoire de la folie*, Paris; *Madness and Civilization: A History of Insanity in the Age of Reason*, trans. London: 1971.

—— (1978) *The History of Sexuality*, Vol. 1, trans. R. Hurley, New York: Pantheon Books. Originally published as *Histoire de la sexualité*. Vol.1 of *La volonté de savoir*, Paris: Gallimard, 1976.

Fowler, A. (1982) *Kinds of Literature: An Introduction to the Theory of Genres and Modes*, Cambridge, MA: Harvard University Press.

Fox-Genovese, E. (1989) 'Literary Criticism and the Politics of the New Historicism', in H. A. Veeser (ed.) *The New Historicism*, New York: Routledge, 213–24.

Franco, J. (1989) 'The Nation as Imagined Community', in H. A. Veeser (ed.) *The New Historicism*, New York: Routledge, 204–12.

Fraser, J. (1907–13) *The Golden Bough: A Study in Magic and Religion*, 3rd edn, London: Macmillan, 8 vols.

Frye, N. (1931) 'Our Monthly Current' and 'To My Beloved's Shoes', two poems by Norrie Frye, *Acta Victoriana* 56 (3):42.

—— (1935) Letter to Ray Daniells, University of British Columbia Archives (14 July).

—— (1936a) 'The Ghost', *Acta Victoriana* 60: 14–16 (April).

—— (1936b) 'Fable . . . in the Nineteenth-Century Idiom', *Canadian Forum* 16: 15 (June).

—— (1938) 'Face to Face', *Acta Victoriana* 62: 10–12 (March).

—— (1940a) 'Affable Angel', *Acta Victoriana* 64: 2–4 (January).

—— (1940b) 'The Resurgent', *Canadian Forum* 19: 357–9 (February).

—— (1940c) 'War on the Cultural Front', *Canadian Forum* 20: 144, 146 (August).

—— (1941) 'Prelude', *Canadian Forum* 21: 185–6.

—— (1944) 'The Nature of Satire', *University of Toronto Quarterly*: 75–89.

—— (1945a) 'A Liberal Education', *Canadian Forum* 25: 134–5.

—— (1945b) 'A Liberal Education Part II', *Canadian Forum* 25: 162–4.

—— (1947a) *Fearful Symmetry: A Study of William Blake*, Princeton: Princeton University Press, rpt. 1969 with Preface.

—— (1947b) 'Education and the Humanities', *The United Church Observer*, 5, 25 (1 August).

—— (1947c) 'Toynbee and Spengler', *Canadian Forum* 27: 111–13.

—— (1948) 'The Argument of Comedy', in D. A. Robertson Jr (ed.) *English Institute Essays: 1948*, New York: Columbia University Press, 58–73.

—— (1950a) 'The Four Forms of Prose Fiction', *Hudson Review* 2: 582–95.

—— (1950b) 'Levels of Meaning in Literature', *Kenyon Review* 12: 246–62.

—— (1950c) 'Tenets of Modern Culture', in *The Church and the Secular World*, Toronto: Board of Evangelism and Social Service, 13–14.

—— (1951a) 'The Archetypes of Literature', *Kenyon Review* 13: 92–110.

—— (1951b) 'A Conspectus of Dramatic Genres', *Kenyon Review* 13: 543–62.

—— (1952a) 'The Analogy of Democracy', *Bias* 1: 2–6.

—— (1952b) 'Comic Myth in Shakespeare', *Transactions of the Royal Society of Canada* 3: 47–58.

—— (1952c) 'Three Meanings of Symbolism', *Yale French Studies* 9: 11–19.

—— (1952d) 'Trends in Modern Culture', in R. C. Chalmers (ed.) *The Heritage of Western Culture: Essays on the Origin and Development of Modern Culture*, Toronto: Ryerson, 102–17.

—— (1953a) 'Characterization in Shakespearean Comedy', *Shakespeare Quarterly* 4: 271–7.

—— (1953b) 'Towards a Theory of Cultural History', *University of Toronto Quarterly* 22: 325–41.

—— (1954) 'Myth as Information', *Hudson Review* 7: 228–35.

—— (1955) 'The Language of Poetry', *Explorations: Studies in Culture and Communication* 4: 80–90.

—— (1956) 'Introduction: Lexis and Melos', in *Sound and Poetry: English Institute Essays, 1956*, ed. N. Frye, New York: Columbia University Press, ix–xxvii.

—— (1957) *Anatomy of Criticism: Four Essays*, Princeton: Princeton University Press, rpt. 1973.

—— (1958) 'The Study of English in Canada', *Dalhousie Review* 38: 1–7, rpt. in *On Education* (1988c), 22–8.

—— (1960) 'The Critical Discipline', in *Canadian Universities Today: Symposium Presented to the Royal Society of Canada*, ed. G. Stanley and G. Sylvestre, Toronto: University of Toronto Press, 30–7.

—— (1961a) 'Academy Without Walls', *Canadian Art* 18, rpt. in *On Education* (1988c), 38–45.

—— (1961b) 'The Critical Discipline', in *Canadian Universities Today: Symposium Presented to the Royal Society of Canada in 1960*, ed. G. Stanley and G. Sylvestre, Toronto: University of Toronto Press, rpt. in *On Education* (1988c): 29–37.

—— (1962a) Introduction to *Design for Learning: Reports Submitted to the Joint Committee of the Toronto Board of Education and the University of Toronto*, ed. N. Frye, Toronto: University of Toronto Press, 3–17, rpt. in *On Education* (1988c), 46–61.

—— (1962b) 'To the Class of '62', *Douglas Library Notes* 11: 5–6, 11–13.

—— (1963a) *The Changing Pace of Canadian Education*, Montreal: Alumni Association, Sir George Williams University, rpt. in *On Education* (1988c), 62–73.

—— (1963b) *The Educated Imagination*, Toronto: Canadian Broadcasting Corporation.

—— (1963c) *Fables of Identity: Studies in Poetic Mythology*, New York: Harcourt, Brace & World.

—— (1963d) *T. S. Eliot*, Edinburgh: Oliver & Boyd.

—— (1963e) *The Well-Tempered Critic*, Bloomington: Indiana University Press.

—— (1965a) 'Letter to the English Institute', in M. Krieger (ed.) *Northrop Frye in Modern Criticism*, New York: Columbia, 1966, 27–30.

—— (1965b) *A Natural Perspective: The Development of Shakespearian Comedy and Romance*, New York: Harcourt, Brace & World.

—— (1965c) *The Return of Eden: Five Essays on Milton's Epics*, Toronto: University of Toronto Press.

—— (1966) 'Reflections in a Mirror', in M. Krieger (ed.) *Northrop Frye in Modern Criticism*, New York: Columbia University Press, 133–46.

—— (1967a) *Fools of a Time: Studies in Shakespearian Tragedy*, Toronto: University of Toronto Press.

—— (1967b) *The Modern Century*, Toronto: Oxford University Press.

—— (1968a) 'Research and Graduate Education in the Humanities', in W. G. Whaley (ed.) *Journal of the Proceedings and Addresses of the Twentieth Annual Conference of the Association of Graduate Studies in the Association of American Universities*, Austin: University of Texas Press, 37–43, rpt. in *On Education* (1988c): 101–8.

—— (1968b) 'The Social Importance of Literature', *Educational Courier* 39: 19–23, rpt. in *On Education*, 74–82.

—— (1968c) *A Study in Romanticism*, New York: Random House.

—— (1968d) 'The University and the Heroic Vision', *Wascana Review* 3: 83–7.

—— (1969a) 'The Ethics of Change: The Role of the University', in *A Symposium: The Ethics of Change*, Toronto: Canadian Broadcasting Corporation, 44–55.

—— (1969b) 'The University and the Personal Life: Student Anarchism and the Educational Contract', in W. R. Niblett (ed.) *Higher Education: Demand and Response*, London: Tavistock, 35–59.

—— (1969c) *Convocation Address by Dr. H. Northrop Frye*, Downsview, ON: York University.

—— (1970a) 'Hart House Rededicated', *University of Toronto Graduate* 3: 11–14.

—— (1970b) *The Stubborn Structure: Essays on Criticism and Society*, Ithaca: Cornell University Press.

—— (1971a) *The Bush Garden: Essays on the Canadian Imagination*, Toronto: Anansi.

—— (1971b) *The Critical Path: An Essay on the Social Context of Literary Criticism*, Bloomington: Indiana University Press, rpt. 1973.

—— (1971c) 'The Definition of a University', in B. Rusk (ed.) *Alternatives in Education*, Toronto: General, 71–90.

—— (1971d) 'Education and the Rejection of Reality', *University of Toronto Graduate* 3: 49–55, rpt. in *On Education* (1988c), 93–100.

—— (1971e) 'The Quality of Life in the Seventies', *University of Toronto Graduate* 3: 38–48.

—— (1972a) 'The Definition of a University', in B. Rusk (ed.) *Alternatives in Education*, London: University of London Press, 41–59.

—— (1972b) 'Universities and the Deluge of Cant', *University of Waterloo Gazette* 12: 2.

—— (1976a) 'The Responsibilities of the Critic', *Modern Language Notes* 91: 797–813.

—— (1976b) *The Secular Scripture: A Study of the Structure of Romance*, Cambridge, MA: Harvard University Press.

—— (1976c) *Spiritus Mundi: Essays on Literature, Myth, and Society*, Bloomington: Indiana University Press.

—— (1978) *Northrop Frye on Culture and Literature: A Collection of Review Essays*, ed. R. D. Denham, Chicago: University of Chicago Press.

—— (1980a) *Creation and Recreation*, Toronto: University of Toronto Press.

—— (1980b) *The Stubborn Structure: Essays on Criticism and Society*, Ithaca: Cornell University Press. Includes the Conclusion to the *Literary History of Canada*.

—— (1982a) *Divisions of a Ground: Essays on Canadian Culture*, ed. J. Polk, Toronto: Anansi.

—— (1982b) *The Great Code: The Bible and Literature*, New York: Harcourt Brace Jovanovich.

—— (1982c) *Something Rich and Strange: Shakespeare's Approach to Romance*, Stratford, ON: Stratford Shakespearean Festival (lecture, 11 July 1982).

—— (1983) *The Myth of Deliverance: Reflections on Shakespeare's Problem Comedies*, Toronto: University of Toronto Press.

—— (1985) With S. Baker and G. W. Perkins, *The Harper Handbook to Literature*, New York: Harper & Row.

—— (1986) *Northrop Frye on Shakespeare*, ed. R. Sandler, Markham, ON: Fitzhenry and Whiteside.

—— (1988a) 'Academy Without Walls', *Canadian Art* 18 (1962): 296–8, rpt. in *On Education* (1988c), 38–45.

—— (1988b) 'The Day of Intellectual Battle', in *On Education*, Don Mills, ON: Fitzhenry and Whiteside, 83–7, Convocation Address, University of Western Ontario, 27 May 1969.

—— (1988c) *On Education*, Markham, ON: Fitzhenry and Whiteside.

—— (1988d) 'The Study of English in Canada', *Dalhousie Review* 38: 1–7, rpt. in *On Education* (1988c), 22–8.

—— (1990a) *The Cultural Development of Canada*, Toronto: Massey College and the Vice-President-Research, University of Toronto.

—— (1990b) 'Lacan and the Full Word', *Criticism and Lacan: Essays and Dialogue on Language, Structure, and the Unconscious*, ed. P. C. Hogan and L. Pandit, Athens: University of Georgia Press, 187–9.

—— (1990c) *Myth and Metaphor: Selected Essays, 1974–88*, ed. R. D. Denham, Charlottesville: University Press of Virginia.

—— (1990d) *Reading the World: Selected Writings, 1935–1976*, ed. R. D. Denham, New York: Peter Lang.

—— (1990e) *Words with Power: Being a Second Study of the Bible and Literature*, San Diego: Harcourt Brace Jovanovich.

—— (1990–1) 'Response', *Eighteenth-Century Studies* 24, 1: 253–9. A special issue, 'Northrop Frye and Eighteenth-Century Studies'.

—— (1991a) *The Double Vision: Language and Meaning in Religion*, Toronto: University of Toronto Press.

—— (1991b) *A World in a Grain of Sand: Twenty-Two Interviews with Northrop Frye*, ed. R. D. Denham, New York: Peter Lang.

—— (1992) 'Henry James and the Comedy of the Occult: *Genre–Trope–Gender*, ed. B. Rutland, Ottawa: Carleton University Press, 11–33 [the Munro Beattie Lecture, 1989].

—— (uncertain or no dates) Notebooks, transcribed by R. Denham 1992. These papers, which seem to span Frye's career, include the typescripts of the 'Four Dialogues' stories and two unpublished ones ('Interpreter's Parlour' and 'Incident from the Golden Bough'), and another fiction that I have called the Kennedy-Megill fragment. All these materials are in the E. J. Pratt Library at the University of Victoria (Toronto).

Gabin, R. J. (1983) 'Northrop Frye: Modern Utopian', *Classical and Modern Literature* 8: 4–64.

Gallagher, C. (1989) 'Marxism and the New Historicism', in H. A. Veeser (ed.) *The New Historicism*, New York: Routledge, 37–48.

Gay, P. and Webb, R. K. (1973) *Modern Europe*, New York: Harper & Row.

Gillespie, G. (1986) 'Bible Lessons: The Gospel According to Frye, Girard, Kermode, and Voeglin', *Comparative Literature* 38: 289–97.

Girard, R. (1973) 'Lévi-Strauss, Frye, Derrida and Shakespearean Criticism', *Diacritics* 3: 23–8.

Globe, A. (1983) 'Apocalypse Now', *Canadian Literature* 97: 182–91 [review of *The Great Code* by Northrop Frye].

Gorak, J. (1991) 'Northrop Frye and the Visionary Genre', in *The Making of the Modern Canon: Genesis and Crisis of a Literary Idea*, London: Athlone Press, 220–52.

Graff, G. (1970) 'Northrop Frye and the Visionary Imagination', in *Poetic Statement and Critical Dogma*, Evanston: Northwestern University Press, 73–8.

—— (1987) *Professing Literature: An Institutional History*, Chicago: University of Chicago Press.

Grant, G.(1965) *Lament for a Nation: The Defeat of Canadian Nationalism*, Toronto: McClelland & Stewart.

—— (1969) *Technology and Empire: Perspectives on North America*, Toronto: Anansi.

Greenblatt, S. (1976) 'Learning to Curse: Aspects of Linguistic Colonialism in the Sixteenth Century', in F. Chiappelli (ed.) *First Images of America: The Impact of the New World on the Old*, Berkeley: University of California Press, 561–80.

—— (1986) 'As They Like It', *The New Republic* 44–7 (10 November).

—— (1988) *Shakespearean Negotiations: The Circulation of Social Energy in Renaissance England*, Berkeley: University of California Press.

Hamilton, A. C. (1979) 'Northrop Frye: The Visionary Critic', *CEA Critic* 42: 2–6.

—— (1990) *Northrop Frye: The Anatomy of his Criticism*, Toronto: University of Toronto Press.

Hart, J. (1988) 'A Comparative Pluralism: The Heterogeneity of Methods and the Case of Fictional Worlds', *CRCL/RCLC* 15: 320–45.

—— (1989a) 'Alienation, Double Signs with a Difference: Conscious Knots in *Cymbeline* and *The Winter's Tale*', *CIEFL Bulletin* (New Series), (1989), 58–78.

—— (1989b) 'Playboys, Killjoys and a Career as Critic: The Accomplishment of Harry Levin', *CRCL/RCLC* 16: 118–35.

—— (1990) 'The Book of Judges: Views Among the Critics', *CRCL/RCLC* 17 1/2: 112–19.

—— (1991a) 'The New Historicism: Taking History into Account', *Ariel* 22: 93–107.

—— (1991b) 'Stephen Greenblatt, *Shakespearean Negotiations: The Circulation of Social Energy in Renaissance England*', *Textual Practice* 5: 429–48.

—— (1992a) 'Frye's Anatomizing and Anatomizing Frye', *CRCL/RCLC* 19:119–54.

—— (1992b) 'The Mystical-Visionary Criticism of Northrop Frye', *Christianity and Literature* 41: 227–98

—— (1992c) 'Narrational Strategies in *The Rape of Lucrece*', *Studies in English Literature* 19: 59–77.

—— (1992d) *Theater and World: The Problematics of Shakespeare's History*, Boston: Northeastern University Press.

—— (1993a) 'Frye/About Frye', *CRCL/RCLC* 20.

—— (1993b) 'Northrop Frye and the 1960s', ed. Eva-Marie Kröller, Toronto: University of Toronto Press.

—— (1993c) 'The Road Not Taken: The Fictions of Northrop Frye', forthcoming.

—— (1994) 'The Ends of Ideology' (forthcoming).

Hartman, G. (1966) 'Ghostlier Demarcations', in M. Krieger (ed.) *Northrop Frye in Modern Criticism*, New York: Columbia University Press, 109–31.

—— (1970) 'Toward Literary History', *Daedalus* 99: 355–62.

—— (1980) 'The Sacred Jungle 3: Frye, Burke, and Some Conclusions', *Criticism in the Wilderness: The Study of Literature Today*, New Haven: Yale University Press, 86–114.

—— (1984) 'The Culture of Criticism', *PMLA* 99: 371–97.

Hassan, I. (1964) 'Beyond a Theory of Literature: Intimations of Apocalypse?' *Comparative Literature Studies* 1: 261–71.

Hayim, G. J. (1982) 'The Sense Experience in the Legacy of Counterculture', in S. Leventman (ed.) *Counterculture and Social Transformation*, Springfield, IL: Charles C. Thomas, 101–24.

Hernadi, P. (1972) 'Northrop Frye', in *Beyond Genre: New Directions in Literary Classification*, Ithaca: Cornell University Press, 131–51.

Hoffman, A. (1984) *Revolution for the Hell of It* [1968], in J. C. Albert and S. E. Albert (eds) *The Sixties Papers: Documents of a Rebellious Decade*, New York: Praeger, 417–27.

Hogan, P. C. (1990) *The Politics of Interpretation: Ideology, Professionalism, and the Study of Literature*, New York: Oxford University Press.

Holland, N. (1968) *The Dynamics of Literary Response*, New York: Oxford University Press.

Holloway, J. (1964) 'The Critical Zodiac of Northrop Frye', in *Colours of Clarity: Essays on Contemporary Literature and Education*, London: Routledge & Kegan Paul, 153–60.

Hough, G. (1966) 'Myth and Archetype II', *An Essay on Criticism*, New York: Norton, 148–56.

Howard, B. (1968) 'Fancy, Imagination, and Northrop Frye', *Thoth* 9: 25–36.

Hughes, P. (1977) 'Vico and Literary History', *Yale Italian Studies* 1: 83–90.

Humm, M. (1986) *Feminist Criticism: Women as Contemporary Critics*, New York: St Martin's Press.

Hutcheon, L. (1988) *A Poetics of Postmodernism: History, Theory, Fiction*, London: Routledge.

Hyman, L. W. (1985) 'Literature and Politics', *PMLA* 100: 237–8.

'The Ideas of Northrop Frye' (1990), the transcript of the radio programme *The Ideas of Northrop Frye* of the Canadian Broadcasting Corporation, 19, 26 February, 5 March 1990. Lister Sinclair, host; David Cayley, writer and presenter; Northrop Frye, interviewee and participant, Montreal: CBC Transcripts, 1990.

Inglis, F. (1975) *Ideology and the Imagination*, Cambridge: Cambridge University Press.

Iser, W. (1990) 'Reader Response Theory in Perspective', *CIEFL Bulletin* (New Series) 2: 1–14.

Jackel, D. (1976) 'Northrop Frye and the Continentalist Traditions', *Dalhousie Review* 56: 221–39.

Jameson, F. (1971) *Marxism and Form: Twentieth-Century Dialectical Theories of Literature*, Princeton: Princeton University Press.

—— (1972) *The Prison-House of Language*, Princeton: Princeton University Press.

—— (1976) 'Criticism in History', in N. Rudick (ed.) *Weapons of Criticism: Marxism in America and the Literary Tradition*, Palo Alto: Ramparts, 38–40.

—— (1981) *The Political Unconscious: Narrative as a Socially Symbolic Act*, Ithaca: Cornell University Press.

—— (1984) 'Postmodernism, or the Cultural Logic of Late Capitalism', *New Left Review* 147: 53–92.

—— (1990) *Postmodernism, or, the Cultural Logic of Late Capitalism*, Durham: Duke University Press.

Jarrett, J. (1969) 'Response of Northrop Frye', in W. R. Niblett (ed.) *Higher Education Demand and Response*, London: Tavistock, 152–5.

Jauss, H. R. (1974) 'Levels of Identification of Hero and Audience', *New Literary History* 4: 283–317.

Jewkes, W. T. (1976) 'Mental Flight: Northrop Frye and the Teaching of Literature', *Journal of General Education* 27: 281–98.

Johnsen, W. A. (1980) 'The Sparagmos of Myth is the Naked Lunch of Mode: Modern Literature as the Age of Frye and Borges', *Boundary* 2: 297–311.

Jones, D. G. (1973) 'Myth, Frye and Canadian Writers', *Canadian Literature* 55: 7–22.

Kavanagh, J. H. (1991) 'Ideology', in *Critical Terms for Literary Study*, ed. F. Lentriccia and T. McLaughlin, Chicago: University of Chicago Press, 306–20.

Kenner, H. (1982) 'Imaginative Proclamation', *New York Times Book Review* 87: 10–11, 28 (11 April) [review of *The Great Code* by Northrop Frye].

Kermode, F. (1959) Review of *Anatomy of Criticism* by Northrop Frye, *Review of English Studies* 10: 317–23.

—— (1982) 'The Universe of Myth', *New Republic* 186: 30–3 (9 June) [review of *The Great Code* by Northrop Frye].

Keynes, G. (1947) 'The Poetic Vision', *Time and Tide* 28: 1394 (27 December) [review of *Fearful Symmetry* by Northrop Frye].

Kirss, T. (1983) 'The Great Code: A Review Article', *Crux: A Quarterly Journal of Thought and Opinion* 19: 18–26.

Klonsky, M. (1977) *William Blake: The Seer and his Visions*, New York: Harmony Books.

Kogan, P. (1969) *Northrop Frye: The High Priest of Clerical Obscurantism*, Montreal: Progressive Books and Periodicals.

Korpan, B. D. (1967) 'Literary Evolution as Style: The "Intrinsic Historicity" of Northrop Frye and Juri Tynianov', *Pacific Coast Philology* 2: 47–52.

Kostelanetz, R. (1978) 'The Literature Professors' Literature Professor', *Michigan Quarterly Review* 7: 425–42.

Krieger, M. (1966a) 'Northrop Frye and Contemporary Criticism: Ariel and the

Spirit of Gravity', in M. Krieger (ed.) *Northrop Frye in Modern Criticism: Selected Papers from the English Institute*, New York: Columbia University Press, 1–26.

—— (ed.) (1966b) *Northrop Frye in Modern Criticism: Selected Papers from the English Institute*, New York: Columbia University Press, 1966.

Kuhns, R. (1959) 'Professor Frye's Criticism', *Journal of Philosophy* 56: 47–52.

Kuipers, J. (1969) 'Pro and Contra Frye', *Collage* 3 (October): 5–8.

Lawrence, D. H. (1950) *The Plumed Serpent*, 1926, Harmondsworth: Penguin Books.

Lentricchia, F. (1978) 'The Historicity of Frye's Anatomy', *Salmagundi* 40: 97–121.

—— (1980) *After the New Criticism*, Chicago: University of Chicago Press.

Levin, H. (1946) 'Literature as an Institution' *Accent* 6: 159–68.

—— (1957) *Contexts of Criticism*, Cambridge, MA: Harvard University Press, 1957.

—— (1963) *The Gates of Horn: A Study in Five French Realists*, New York: Oxford University Press.

—— (1967) *Why Literary Criticism Is Not an Exact Science*, Cambridge, Heffers, rpt. in *Grounds of Comparison* (Harvard Studies in Comparative Literature, 32), Cambridge, MA: Harvard University Press, 1972, 40–6.

—— (1986) *Playboys and Killjoys: An Essay on the Theory and Practice of Comedy*, New York: Oxford University Press.

Lewis, C. S. (1936) *The Allegory of Love: A Study in Medieval Tradition*, London: Oxford University Press.

—— (1964) *The Discarded Image: An Introduction to Medieval and Renaissance Literature*, Cambridge: Cambridge University Press.

Lindrop, G. (1977) 'Generating the Universe through Analogy', *PN Review* 3: 41–5.

Lipking, L. I. (1972) 'Northrop Frye: Introduction', in L. I. Lipking and A. W. Litz (eds) *Modern Literary Criticism, 1900–1970*, New York: Atheneum, 180–8.

Litz, A. W. (1979) 'Literary Criticism', in D. Hoffman (ed.) *Harvard Guide to Contemporary American Writing*, Cambridge, MA: Belknap Press, 51–83.

Lombardo, A. (ed.) (1989) *Ritratto di Northrop Frye*, Rome: Bulzomo Editore.

Lovejoy, A. (1936) *The Great Chain of Being: A Study of the History of an Idea*, Cambridge, MA: Harvard University Press.

Lyotard, J.-F. (1984) *The Postmodern Condition: A Report on Knowledge*, trans. G. Bennington and B. Massumi, Minneapolis: University of Minnesota Press. French original, a report for the Government of Quebec.

MacAdam, A. J. (1979) 'Northrop Frye's Theory of Genres and the New Literature of Latin America', *Revista Canadianse de Estudios Hispanicos* 3: 287–90.

McConnell, F. (1984) 'Northrop Frye and *Anatomy of Criticism*', *Sewanee Review* 92: 622–9.

MacDonald, R. D. (1979) 'Frye's *Modern Century* Reconsidered', *Studies in Canadian Literature* 4: 95–108.

McFadden, G. (1982) 'Twentieth-Century Theorists: Maurron, Cornford, Frye', in *Discovering the Comic*, Princeton: Princeton University Press, 152–75.

McGann, J. (1983) *The Romantic Ideology: A Critical Investigation*, Chicago: University of Chicago Press.

Mackey, L. (1981) 'Anatomical Curiosities: Northrop Frye's Theory of Criticism', *Texas Studies in Language and Literature* 235: 442–69.

MacKinnon, F. (1960) *The Politics of Education*, Toronto: University of Toronto Press.

McLuhan, M. (1962) *The Gutenberg Galaxy: The Making of Typographical Man*, Toronto: University of Toronto Press.

Malraux, A. (1951) *Les Voix du silence*, Paris: NRF, trans. Stuart Gilbert, *The Voices of Silence*, New York: Doubleday, 1953.

Mandel, E. W. (1958) 'Frye's Anatomy of Criticism', *Canadian Forum* 38: 128–9.

—— (1959) 'Toward a Theory of Cultural Revolution: The Criticism of Northrop Frye', *Canadian Literature* 1: 58–67.

—— (1982) 'Tautology as Truth and Vision', *Canadian Forum* 62: 30–1 [review of *The Great Code* by Northrop Frye].

—— (1983) 'Northrop Frye and the Canadian Literary Tradition', in Eleanor Cook et al. (eds), *Centre and Labyrinth: Essays in Honor of Northrop Frye*, Toronto: University of Toronto Press: 284–97.

Marx, K. (1964) *Economic and Philosophic Manuscripts of 1844*, ed. J. U. Dyrkjob, New York: International Publishers.

—— (1977) *Selected Writings*, ed. D. McLellan, Oxford: Oxford University Press.

Meynell, H. (1981) 'Northrop Frye's Idea of a Science of Criticism', *British Journal of Aesthetics* 21: 118–29.

Mitchell, W. J. T. (1982) 'Dangerous Blake', *Studies in Romanticism* 21: 410–16.

—— (ed.) (1983) *The Politics of Interpretation*, Chicago: University of Chicago Press.

Mugerauer, R. (1979) 'The Form of Northrop Frye's Literary Universe: An Expanding Circle', *Mosaic* 12: 135–47.

Murray, H. (1991) 'English Studies in Canada to 1945: A Bibliographic Essay', *English Studies in Canada* 17: 437–67.

Newton, J. L. (1989) 'History as Usual? Feminism and the "New Historicism"', in H. A. Veeser (ed.) *The New Historicism*, New York: Routledge, 152–67.

Nixon, R. (1987) 'Caribbean and African Appropriations of *The Tempest*', in R. von Hallberg (ed.) *Politics and Poetic Value*, Chicago: University of Chicago Press, 185–206.

Norris, C. (1988) *Paul de Man: Deconstruction and the Critique of Aesthetic Ideology*, New York: Routledge.

'Northrop Frye: A Tribute' (1979), Vol. 1, *The CEA Critic* 42 (November).

'Northrop Frye: A Tribute' (1980), Vol. 2, *The CEA Critic* 42 (January).

Northrop Frye in Modern Criticism: Selected Papers from the English Institute (1966), ed. M. Krieger, New York: Columbia University Press.

Nuttall, J. (1968) *Bomb Culture*, New York: Delacorte Press.

O'Hara, D. (1985) 'Against Nature: On Northrop Frye and Critical Romance', in *The Romance of Interpretation: Visionary Criticism from Pater to de Man*, New York: Columbia University Press, 147–204.

Ohman, C. (1970) 'Northrop Frye and the MLA', *College English* 32: 291–300.

Ong, W. J. (1989) *Orality and Literacy: The Technologizing of the Word*, London: Methuen.

Ostendorf, B. (1971) *Northrop Frye, Der Mythos in der Neuen Welt: Eine*

Untersuchung zum Amerikanischen Myth Criticism, Frankfurt These Verlag, 140–1.

Palmer, D. J. (1965) *The Rise of English Studies*, London: Oxford University Press.

Parker, P. (1987) *Literary Fat Ladies*, New York: Methuen.

Parrinder, P. (1991) 'Northrop Frye', in *Authors and Authority: English and American Criticism, 1950–1990*, New York: Columbia University Press, 281–7.

Peckham, M. (1985) *Romanticism and Ideology*, Greenwood: Penkevill.

Perry, B. (1987) 'Problems in Colonial Discourse Theory', *Oxford Literary Review* 9.

Plamenatz, J. (1985) *Ideology*, London: Macmillan.

Poland, L. (1984) 'The Secret Gospel of Northrop Frye', *Journal of Religion* 64: 513–19 [review of *The Great Code* by Northrop Frye].

The Port Huron Statement, in J. C. Albert and S. E. Albert (eds), *The Sixties Papers: Documents of a Rebellious Decade*, New York: Praeger, 176–96.

'Post-Colonialism and Post-Modernism' (1989) (Special Issue), *ARIEL* 20/4: 203 pp.

Powe, B. (1984) 'Fear of Fryeing: Northrop Frye and the Theory of Myth Criticism', 'McLuhan and Frye, Either/Or', in *A Climate Charged*, Oakville: Mosaic Press, 34–54, 55–8.

Privateer, P. M. (1991) *Romantic Voices: Identity and Ideology in British Poetry, 1789–1850*, Athens: University of Georgia Press.

Propp, V. (1968) *The Morphology of the Folktale*, Austin: University of Texas Press.

Protest and Discontent (1970), ed. B. Crick and W. A. Robson, Harmondsworth: Penguin.

Rebhorn, W. A. (1979) 'After Frye: A Review-Article on the Interpretation of Shakespearean Comedy and Romance', *Texas Studies in Language and Literature* 21: 553–82.

Report: Royal Commission on National Development in the Arts, Letters and Sciences, 1949–1951 [Massey Report] (1951), Ottawa: Edmond Cloutier, 1951.

Riccomini, D. R. (1979) 'Northrop Frye and Structuralism: Identity and Difference', *University of Toronto Quarterly* 49: 33–47.

Ricœur, P. (1983) 'Anatomy of Criticism or the Order of Paradigms', in E. Cook et al. (eds) *Essays in Honour of Northrop Frye*, Toronto: University of Toronto Press, 1–13.

Robertson, P. J. M. (1983) 'Northrop Frye and Evaluation', *Queen's Quarterly* 90: 151–6.

—— (1985) 'Criticism and Creativity VI: George Orwell', *Queen's Quarterly* 92: 374–84.

Robinson, B. (1972) 'Northrop Frye: critique fameux, critique faillible', *Revue de l'Université d'Ottawa* 42: 608–14.

Rockas, L. (1967) 'The Structure of Frye's *Anatomy*' *College English* 28: 501–7.

Rodríguez, J. (1984) 'Preliminary Notes to Northrop Frye's Theory Concerning the Relationship of Myth to Literature', *Revista Canaria de Estudios Ingleses* 9: 123–8.

—— (1985) 'El estudio científico de la literatura a través del mito de la búsqueda según los críticos anglo-norteamericanos especialmente a Northrop Frye', *Anales de Filologia Inglesa* 1: 33–51.

Roszak, T. (1969) *The Making of a Counter Culture: Reflections on the Technocratic Society and its Youthful Opposition*, Garden City, NY: Doubleday.

Rubin, J. (1984) 'Do It!' [1970], in J. C. Albert and S. E. Albert (eds) *The Sixties Papers: Documents of a Rebellious Decade*, New York: Praeger, 439–48.

Rueckert, W. (1975) 'Literary Criticism and History: The Endless Dialectic', *New Literary History* 6: 491–512.

Russell, F. (1992) *Northrop Frye on Myth: An Introduction*, New York: Garland.

Rutter, P. V. (1981) 'Northrop Frye et la littérature', *Zabadnienia Rodzajów Literackich* 24: 61–80.

Said, E. (1974) *Beginnings*, New York: Basic Books, 375–7.

St Andrews, B. A. (1986) 'The Canadian Connection: Frye/Atwood', *World Literature Today* 60: 47–9.

Salusinszky, I. (1987) *Criticism in Society: Interviews with Jacques Derrida, Northrop Frye, Harold Bloom, Geoffrey Hartman, Frank Kermode, Edward Said, Barbara Johnson, Frank Lentricchia, and J. Hillis Miller*, New York: Methuen, interviews with Frye and Hartman, 27–42 and 75–96 respectively.

Schmidt, S. J. (1983) 'The Empirical Science of Literature ESL: A New Paradigm', *Poetics* 12: 19–34.

—— (1985) 'On Writing Histories of Literature: Some Remarks from a Constructivist Point of View', *Poetics* 14: 279–301.

—— (1992) 'The Logic of Observation: An Introduction to Constructivism', *CRCL/RCLC* 19: 295–311.

Scholes, R. (1968) 'Towards a Poetics of Fiction: An Approach through Genre', *Novel: A Forum in Fiction* 2: 101–11.

—— (1974) *Structuralism in Literature: An Introduction*, New Haven: Yale University Press, 118–27.

Schroeter, J. (1972) 'The Unseen Center: A Critique of Northrop Frye', *College English* 33: 543–57.

Schwab, G. B. (1983) Review of *The Great Code* by Northrop Frye, *Christianity and Literature* 33: 87–9.

Schwartz, D. R. (1986) 'Two Major Voices of the 1950s: Northrop Frye's *Anatomy of Criticism* and Eric Auerbach's *Mimesis*', in *The Humanistic Heritage: Critical Theories of the English Novel from James to Hillis Miller*, Philadelphia: University of Pennsylvania Press, 118–50.

Shaffer, E. S. (1983) 'Editor's Introduction: The "Great Code" Deciphered: Literary and Biblical Hermeneutics', *Comparative Criticism* 5: xix–xxiv.

Shakespeare and the Question of Theory (1985), ed. P. Parker and G. Hartman, New York: Methuen.

Shibles, W. (1971) 'Northrop Frye on Metaphor', in *An Analysis of Metaphor in Light of W. M. Urban's Theories*, The Hague: Mouton, 145–50.

Siskin, C. (1988) *The Historicity of Romantic Discourse*, New York: Oxford University Press.

Slan, J. (1972) 'Writing in Canada: Innis, McLuhan, and Frye: Frontiers of Canadian Criticism', *Canadian Dimension* 8: 43–6.

Smith, B. H. (1983) 'Contingencies of Value', *Critical Inquiry* 10: 1–35.

Snow, C. P. (1959) *The Two Cultures and the Scientific Revolution*, New York: Cambridge University Press.

322   *References*

Sparshott, F. (1963) *The Structure of Aesthetics*, Toronto: University of Toronto Press.
—— (1979) 'Frye in Place', *Canadian Literature* 83: 143–55.
Speirs, L. (1983) 'The Myths and Visions of Northrop Frye', *English Studies* 64: 518–23 [review of *The Myth of Deliverance* by Northrop Frye].
Spengler, O. (1926–8) *Decline of the West*, trans. C. F. Atkinson, New York: Knopf [original *Der Untergang des Abend-Landes*, 1918–22].
Spivak, G. C. (1989) 'The New Historicism: Political Commitment and the Postmodern Critic', in H. A. Veeser (ed.) *The New Historicism*, New York: Routledge, 277–92.
Stansill, P. (1969) 'New Experimental College', in J. Berke (ed.) *Counter Culture*, London: Peter Owen Ltd, 260–81.
Stobie, M. (1958) 'Mr. Frye Stands Well Back', *Winnipeg Free Press* 58 (26 July).
Sturrock, J. (1979) 'Roland Barthes', in J. Sturrock (ed.) *Structuralism and Since: From Lévi-Strauss to Derrida*, Oxford: Oxford University Press, 52–80.
Teeuwissen, W. J. (1980) '*The Anatomy of Criticism* as Parody of Science', *Southern Humanities Review* 14: 31–43.
Thomas, C. (1979) 'Towards Freedom: The Work of Northrop Frye', *CEA Critic* 42: 7–11.
Todd, J. (1988) *Feminist Literary History*, New York: Routledge.
Todorov, T. (1970) 'Critique de Frye' and 'Frye et les principes structuralistes', in *Introduction à la littérature fantastique*, Paris: Editions du Seuil, 13–27.
—— (1973) *The Fantastic: A Structural Approach to a Literary Genre*, trans. Richard Howard, Cleveland: Press of Case Western Reserve University, 8–23.
—— (1984) Preface to *Le Grand Code: La Bible et la littérature*, trans. Catherine Malamoud, Paris: Editions du Seuil, 5–20.
Tötösy de Zepetnek, S. (1992) 'Systemic Approaches to Literature – An Introduction with Selected Bibliographies', *CRCL/RCLC* 19: 21–93.
Trickett, R. (1982) 'The Rhetoric of Revelation', *TLS* 712 (2 July) [review of *The Great Code* by Northrop Frye].
Trilling, L. (1972) *Sincerity and Authenticity*, Cambridge, MA: Harvard University Press.
The University Game (1968), ed. H. Adelman and D. Lee, Toronto: Anansi.
Vickers, B. (1984) *Occult and Scientific Mentalities in the Renaissance*, Cambridge: Cambridge University Press.
Walley, G. (1958) 'Frye's Anatomy of Critics', *Tamarack Review* 8: 92–8, 100–1.
—— (1973) *Metahistory: The Historical Imagination in Nineteenth-Century Europe*, Baltimore: Johns Hopkins University Press.
—— (1989) 'New Historicism: A Comment', in H. A. Veeser (ed.) *The New Historicism*, New York: Routledge.
Waswo, R. (1987) *Language and Meaning in the Renaissance*, Princeton: Princeton University Press.
Watkins, E. (1981) 'Conflict and Consensus in the History of *Recent Criticism*', *New Literary History* 12: 345–64.
Weimann, R. (1965) 'Northrop Frye und das Ende des New Criticism', *Sinn und Form: Beiträge zur Literatur* 17: 621–30.
—— (1973) 'Literarische Wertung und historische Tradition: Zu ihrer Aporie

im Werk von Northrop Frye', *Zeitschrift für Anglistik und Amerikanistik* 21: 341–59.

—— (1974) 'Literaturkritik als historisch–mythologisches System: Northrop Frye und die Krise der Literaturgeschichte', 3rd edn, Berlin: Aufbau-Verlag, 342–63.

—— (1976) *Structure and Society in Literary History: Studies in History and Theory of Literary History*, Charlottesville: University Press of Virginia.

Wellek, R. (1949) Review of *Fearful Symmetry* by Northrop Frye, *MLN* 64: 62–3.

—— (1970) 'The Poet as Critic, The Critic as Poet', in *Discriminations: Further Concepts of Criticism*, New Haven: Yale University Press, 253–74.

Wellek, R. and Warren, A. (1949) *Theory of Literature*, New York and London: Harcourt Brace Jovanovich, rpt. 1977.

Wheeler, R. P. (1984) 'An Affirmation of Literary Faith', *Shakespeare Quarterly* 35: 365–8 [review of *The Myth of Deliverance* by Northrop Frye].

White, D. (1973) 'Northrop Frye: Value and System', *Criticism* 15: 189–211.

White, H. (1973) *Metahistory*, Baltimore: Johns Hopkins University Press.

—— (1987) *The Content of the Form: Narrative Discourse and Historical Representation*, Baltimore: Johns Hopkins University Press.

Whitehead, A. N. (1925) *Science and the Modern World*, New York: Macmillan.

Wiebe, D. (1985) 'The "Centripetal Theology" of *The Great Code*', Toronto: *Journal of Theology* 1: 122–7.

Williams, R. (1970) 'A Power to Fight', *Guardian*: 9 (12 November).

—— (1973) *The Country and the City*, Oxford: Oxford University Press.

—— (1977) *Marxism and Literature*, Oxford: Oxford University Press.

—— (n.d.) *Writing and Society*, London: Verso.

Williamson, E. (1985) 'Plato's *Eidos* and the Archetypes of Jung and Frye', *Interpretations* 16: 94–104.

Wilson, R. R. (1988) 'Shakespearean Narrative: *The Rape of Lucrece* Reconsidered', *Studies in English Literature* 28, 39–59.

—— (1990) *In Palamedes' Shadow: Explorations in Play, Game and Narrative Theory*, Boston: Northeastern University Press.

Wimsatt, W. K. (1966) 'Northrop Frye: Criticism and Myth', in M. Krieger (ed.) *Northrop Frye in Modern Criticism*, New York: Columbia University Press, 74–107.

Woodcock, G. (1983) 'Frye, Northrop', in W. Toye (gen. ed.) *Oxford Companion to Canadian Literature*, Toronto: Oxford University Press, 282–4.

Yates, F. (1972) *The Rosacrucian Enlightenment*, London: Routledge & Kegan Paul.

Yü, Anthony (1992) 'Literature and the Conflict of Desire in *The Story of the Stone*', Part 1, Lecture, University of Alberta (10 September).

Index

Abrams, M. H. 205
Acta Victoriana 274, 279, 281, 293
Addison, Joseph 173
aesthetic ideology 108, 196–7,
    203–4, 220, 229–30; aesthetics
    158, 304
'Affable Angel' 30, 48, 274, 279,
    285–7
Agrippa, Cornelius 247–8
allegorical criticism (textual
    commentary) 156, 247–8; allegory
    35, 39, 40, 48, 53–4, 71, 86, 91,
    98, 101, 106, 131, 159, 197, 214,
    235–6, 247–8, 250, 264, 285–7
Altamira caves (Spain) 97
Althusser, Louis 165, 171, 176, 193,
    195, 210
*anagnorisis/cogito/*recognition/
    discovery 13, 60, 67–8, 70, 76–7,
    84, 114, 128–9, 132, 155, 200,
    252, 262–4, 273, 304; *culbute
    générale* 129, 132
anagogy 27, 38–9, 55, 73–4, 198,
    247–8
analogy 49, 64, 68, 97, 101, 161,
    245, 304
Anatomy of Criticism 2, 4, 6–7, 10,
    14–16, 19, 23, 25, 35–6, 38–9,
    43–5, 54, 56–90, 92, 94, 109, 111,
    124, 138–9, 144–5, 152–64, 174,
    191, 206–7, 211, 216–17, 222,
    246, 253–4, 256–9, 272, 291,
    300–1, 304; anatomy 39, 43,
    84–5, 115, 256, 264–5
anti-Semitism 51
anxiety 99, 101, 103, 105, 136, 144,
    176, 187, 215, 304; of influence
    72, 217–19
apocalypse 30, 74, 110, 115, 132–4,
    139–40, 164, 198, 205, 236–42,
    245
Apollodorus 279
apologia (defences of poetry) 1, 111,
    120, 173
Apuleius 42, 79, 85
Aquinas, Thomas 40, 54, 73, 247,
    249; Thomism 59, 123
archetypal criticism 72–3, 88–90
    156, 161, 174, 249–54; archetypes
    88–90, 92, 104, 249–54, 303
Archimedes 96
Aristophanes 64–5, 67
Aristotle 13, 23, 39, 61–2, 66, 68,
    78, 80–1, 83, 86, 95, 124, 126,
    144, 158, 173, 176, 183, 192, 198,
    207, 212, 224, 247, 264–5, 273,
    296, 299
Arnold, Matthew 36, 46, 57, 60, 64,
    74, 89, 96, 98, 107, 150, 159,
    169–70, 173–4, 181, 183, 192,
    212; touchstone theory 64
Atwood, Margaret 189, 243, 290
Augustine, St 109, 207, 247
authority 4, 63, 98, 123, 138, 235,
    238–9, 248
autonomy of literature and criticism
    1, 15, 145–6, 197–8, 206–7
axis mundi 11, 228, 235, 240
Ayre, John 6, 11, 289–90, 294

Bach, Johann Sebastian 138
Bachelard, Gaston 196

Bacon, Francis 28, 42
Bakhtin, Mikhail 200
Balfour, Ian 5, 25
Barthes, Roland 102, 144, 165, 178, 193–4; *doxa* 194
Bate, W. Jackson 219
Bates, Ronald 5–6
Baudelaire, Charles 32
Beaumont, Francis 86
Belsey, Catherine 193, 197–200
Berkeley, George 28, 35, 41
Bible 2, 10–15, 18, 22–55, 61, 68, 75–9, 85–6, 88, 93, 95, 100–1, 109–42, 155, 178, 191, 193, 228–34, 244–63, 301, 303; Authorized Version (King James Bible) 110, 130, 133, 137– 8, 191; Vulgate 116, 130, 137, 197
biographical criticism 63, 91; biography 6
Blackmore, Richard 65
Blake, William 1–2, 5–6, 11, 13–15, 18, 24–58, 71, 74, 83, 92, 98, 103, 115, 134, 137–8, 164, 173–4, 183, 189–90, 196, 232, 239, 243–66, 272–3, 275, 291, 293–4, 300, 304
Bloch, Ernst 200
Bloom, Harold 72, 149, 217–19
Boccaccio, Giovanni 40, 54, 247–9
Boehme, Jakob 227, 247–8
Boileau, Nicolas 196
Bradley, A.C. 39
Brecht, Bertolt 158
Browning, Robert 82, 272
Bruner, Jerome 122, 254
Bruno, Giordano 116
Bryant, Jacob 41
Bultmann, Rudolf 230
Bunyon, John 221
Burke, Edmund 37
Burke, Kenneth 116
Bush Garden, The 146
Bush, George 189
Burton, Robert 43, 56, 85, 115, 246
Butler, Samuel 30
Butts, Thomas 34, 246, 263

Calvin, John 213
Calvino, Italo 13
Campbell, Joseph 144

Canada 144–9, 151, 166–90, 247, 254, 256–7, 292, 294
Canadian: Canadian Broadcasting Corporation (CBC) 7, 146, 172; Centennial 146, 184, 256; *Canadian Forum* 2, 110, 169, 274, 279; literature 4–6, 146, 174, 179, 189, 264, 290, 294–5; prairies 30, 289–90
Cassirer, Ernst 60
Castiglione, Baldassare 249, 300
Cave, Terence 304
Cayley, David 7, 206
Chambers, Ross 304
Chapman, George 42
Chatterton, Thomas 41
Chaucer, Geoffrey 43, 78, 85
Chesterfield, Lord (Philip Stanhope) 87
Christ, Jesus 22, 46, 48–9, 121, 131, 133–5, 138, 142, 227–8, 237; Christianity 21, 25–55, 85–6, 93–4, 108–92, 169, 187, 199, 201, 204–42, 250–2, 243–65, 271, 288–93, 297–8, 301
Cicero 120
civil rights movement 17, 166, 185, 289
Cixous, Hélène 178, 266, 303
class (social structure) 93, 107, 159–60, 198, 200, 210
classicism 68, 159, 178, 253, 297
Coleridge, Samuel Taylor 74, 114, 173, 195, 197, 211, 232, 303
Collins, William 41
Columbus, Christopher 151
comedy 6, 76–7, 124, 178, 217, 257–9, 262, 292, 296; New Comedy 67, 76; Old Comedy 67
Communism 3, 169, 171, 184–5
comparative mythology/religion 205, 281, 284
concern (also myth of concern) 93–108, 148–9, 183, 185, 202, 214–15, 241, 278
conservatism 5, 41, 95, 100, 169, 214
construction 179, 182, 192, 209
convention 1, 72, 76, 83–4, 89, 92,

96, 158, 198
Cook, David 5
Cook, Eleanor 6
Cornford, Francis 76, 144, 217
cosmology 96, 190, 286, 300–3
Critical Path, The 7, 22, 26, 87,
    90–109, 143, 148–9, 187–8, 190,
    202, 214, 234, 298
criticism: as creativity 71–3, 82–3,
    161, 173, 178–9, 235, 254, 266–7,
    294–305; as discipline 59; as
    publicity 58; as science 59; as
    unified study 91; contextual 179;
    documentary 91; ethical 65,
    68–74, 89, 160; *explication de
    texte* 123, 281; formalist 144,
    298–9; intertextuality 72; literal
    70, 247; practical 6, 132–3,
    234–42, 298, 300; psychological/
    psychoanalytical 1, 91, 215;
    public taste 60; topiary 222,
    298–9, tropical 64; tropological/
    moral 247;
critics 1–2, 6, 35, 82–3, 88–108,
    114, 153–4, 172–82, 188, 221,
    225, 256, 265–7, 270, 296–305
cultural: criticism or critique 164;
    materialism 47, 147, 156, 165;
    pluralism 123; revolution 53
culture 74, 89, 93, 96, 114, 157,
    159, 181, 198, 299; counterculture
    164–90; oral 104, 120

Daniells, Roy 267–8, 293
Dante 27, 38, 40, 50, 54, 69, 73,
    78–9, 96, 115, 138–9, 212, 222,
    224, 247, 249, 262, 264, 272
Darwin, Charles 97
Davies, Edward 41
Davies, Robertson 271, 295
deconstruction 33, 66, 88, 92–3,
    118, 149, 153–4, 161, 174, 195–7,
    224–5
Defoe, Daniel 84
Deism 32, 42, 46, 48, 50
de Man, Paul 14, 65, 88, 90, 165,
    193, 195–7, 203–4, 225;
    metonymy 196
democracy 3, 4, 9, 94, 99–100, 147,
    164–90, 215

Denham, Robert 5–6, 9, 25, 212,
    267–8, 273, 294
Derrida, Jacques 88, 117–20, 149,
    152–3, 157–8, 161, 165, 214,
    219–20, 224, 231, 266, 303
Descartes, René 44
desire 2, 73, 75, 144, 174, 187, 190,
    198–200, 215, 245; wish-
    fulfilment 176
Destutt (Destutt de Tracy) 195
determinism 59, 91, 93, 156, 297
dialectic as anatomy of poetry 39
dialectical materialism 65
dialectics 1, 65, 107, 125, 211, 214,
    229
dialogues 279–87
dianoia 68–70, 74–5, 80, 83, 224,
    230
Dickens, Charles 39
Dickinson, Emily 233
Diderot, Denis 196
Dies Irae 231, 252
Dionysius 67
Dionysius the Areopagite 227
Divisions on a Ground 146
Dollimore, Jonathan 149, 160, 165
Donne, John 42
Double Vision, The 7, 26, 38, 44, 85,
    109, 191, 215, 221, 232, 235, 240,
    246, 251, 256, 260–5, 273, 277,
    281, 297
Dryden, John 60, 283
dreaming body/dreamer 175,
    199–200, 256, 305; Incarnation
    134
Dyrkjob, Jan Ulrik 5

Eagleton, Terry 144, 148–9, 193,
    197, 200–4, 303
ecology movement 2, 261
Educated Imagination, The 172–82,
    184, 190–1, 215
education 6, 9–10, 58, 102–4, 154,
    157, 160, 164–90, 236, 249, 264,
    288–9, 296
Einstein, Albert 2, 118
Eliot, T. S. 6, 13–14, 37, 46, 57,
    63–4, 71, 86, 89, 96, 115, 204,
    213, 218, 220–2, 260, 278–9,
    288–9, 296–8

Empson, William 196
England 4, 49, 52, 174, 192, 247, 253, 256, 290
Enlightenment 21, 54, 253
Erasmus, Desiderius 98, 118, 133, 247, 280
Erigena, John Scotus 227
epos 81–3
essence/essentialism 158, 178
ethos 68–9, 80, 83
Euripides 279
evidence 100, 107, 187, 230
existentialism 59, 103
experience 58, 66, 92–3, 156, 178, 225–6, 262

'Fable . . . in the Nineteenth Century Idiom' 274
Fables of Identity 258
'Face to Face' 268, 274, 279, 282–5
fallacies: centrifugal and centripetal, 93; *see also* intention
Fanon, Frantz 302
fascism 2, 3, 14, 97, 169, 186, 204
Fearful Symmetry 5–7, 10, 14, 23, 25–56, 109, 145, 154, 187, 227, 243–65, 273, 291, 300
feminism 2, 150, 152, 165, 189, 211, 289, 295, 298, 300
Fenellosa, Ernest 224
Ficino, Marsilio 247–9
fictional/imaginative/possible worlds 71, 122, 175, 267
fictions 232, 301–4; of Frye 266–95; Bardo novel 269–74, 281
Fielding, Henry 43
Fish, Stanley 153
Fletcher, Angus 155
Fools of Time, The 150
Foucault, Michel 54, 150, 157, 160, 165, 178, 233, 253
'Four Dialogues' 42
fourfold interpretative system 40, 247–8
Fowles, John 269
France 165–6, 303; French Revolution 32, 43
Franklin, Benjamin 274
Frazer, James 12, 18, 39, 41, 60, 121, 284

freedom (also myth of freedom) 93–108, 120, 141, 148–9, 180–9, 201–4, 214–15, 273, 278
Freud, Sigmund 60, 103, 118, 147, 192, 199–200, 219, 239
Freudian criticism 91, 147, 199–201, 304
Frost, Robert 240

Gadamer Hans-Georg 114
Gandhi, M. 182, 289
Geertz, Clifford 157
genre 1, 6, 56–90, 92, 137, 172, 178, 250, 264, 296
Geoffrey of Monmouth 49
Germany 275, 302–3
'Ghost, The' 274, 279–81
Gibbon, Edward 216, 297
Ginsberg, Allen 164
Gnosticism 129
Godfrey, Eleanor 274
God-is-dead syndrome 114
Goethe, Johann Wolfgang 118, 274
golden age 40, 54, 57, 77, 198, 250
Gospel 131–2
grammar 87–8
Gray, Thomas 41
Great Code, The 7, 10, 26, 38, 45, 85, 109–42, 152–5, 259, 264, 277
Greenblatt, Stephen 150, 157, 159–60, 165, 303–4
Greene, Robert 76
Gregory, St 247
Gurdjieff, G. I. 104

hamartia 78
Hamilton, A. C. 5–6, 25, 66
Hardy, Thomas 30
Hartman, Geoffrey 149
Havelock, Eric 117
Hawthorne, Nathaniel 27
Hayley, William 47
Hazlitt, William 60
Hegel, G. W. F. 78, 89, 107, 115, 125, 139, 203, 213–14, 263, 283
Heidegger, Martin 44, 88, 283
Heilsgeschichte 122–3
hermeneutics 52, 123, 199–200, 232; of suspicion 150, 158; negative and positive 299

Herodotus 144
historical criticism 66–8, 72, 85,
    91–2, 99, 144–5, 149, 156,
    158–60, 222–3, 247, 298
history 1–2, 6, 46–9, 51, 53, 65,
    90–3, 99–100, 106, 119–30, 133,
    143–63, 181, 189–90, 192, 201,
    211, 222–3, 229, 240, 247, 252,
    262, 296, 305; as cycle 82; of
    genres 62, 92; Whig history 3, 41
Hitler, Adolf 51
Hobbes, Thomas 208
Hoffman, Abbie 168
Hogarth, William 43
Homer 42, 46, 85–6, 143, 158, 279
Hooker, Richard 74
Hopkins, Gerard Manley 95, 220
Horace 22
humanism 4, 54–5, 59, 95–9, 157,
    164, 179, 193, 198, 201–4, 247–9,
    252, 298, 302
Husserl, Edmund 88
Huxley, Aldous 95

'Ideas of Northrop Frye, The' 7
identity 30, 49–52, 92, 97, 106, 134,
    143, 146, 148, 153, 175–8, 184,
    223–65, 298; communion 256;
    epiphany 174, 227, 264
ideology 1–2, 5–6, 21, 63, 96–108,
    114, 118, 120–1, 133, 142, 144–5,
    147, 169, 171, 191–242, 296–305
imagination 1–24, 71–2, 75, 98–9,
    107, 114–15, 148, 157–60,
    172–82, 184, 187–90, 245–63, 297
'Incident from the Golden Bough'
    268, 274, 279, 284–5
intention/intentional fallacy 62, 73,
    159, 197
'Interpreter's Parlour' 268, 274,
    279, 281–2
irony/ironic literature 75, 78–9,
    101, 115, 265, 274–81, 287;
    Socratic irony 111
Israel 302
Italy 187, 303

Jakobson, Roman 117
James, C. L. R. 302
James, Henry 58

James, William 231
Jameson, Fredric 20, 140, 143, 145,
    147, 162–3, 197, 199–200, 219,
    303
Jefferson, Thomas 96, 187
Jerome, St 116, 247
Job 136, 241, 258, 301
Johnson, Samuel 87, 114–15, 144
Jonson, Ben 272
Joyce, James 6, 58, 93, 104, 152,
    162, 177, 213, 227, 231, 235, 239,
    254, 256, 258, 300
Judaeus, Philo 247
Jung, C. G. 60, 144

Kant, Immanuel 90–1, 203
katascopos 50, 57, 62
Keats, John 58, 176
Kemp, Helen (later Helen Frye) 3,
    268, 276, 289
Kennedy-Megill fragment 30,
    287–93
Kermode, Frank 244
kerygma 117, 120, 141, 230–2, 234,
    261
Kierkegaard, Søren 101, 103,
    105, 107, 126, 207
King, Martin Luther 289
Klonsky, Milton 189
Knight, G. Wilson 3
Knight, Jackson 3
koan 273
Kogan, Pauline 5
Koheleth 130
Krieger, Murray 6
Kristeva, Julia 165, 266, 303
Kuhn, Thomas 9

Lacan, Jacques 165
Lamb, Charles 60
Lampman, Archibald 146
Langland, William 27, 45
language 1–2, 119–20, 153, 175–6,
    181–2, 194, 196, 198, 201, 212,
    222–4, 256, 260–4, 296; imagery
    (lexis) 75, 132–6; of love 141,
    232–7; *langage/langue* 116–17;
    style 6, 146, 302
Lascaux caves (France) 97
law 129–30

Lawrence, D. H. 98, 174, 221
Layton, Irving 146
Leavis, F. R. 57, 64
Leibniz, Gottfried Wilhelm 71
Lentricchia, Frank 155
Levin, Harry 59, 217, 230, 298–9;
  literature as an institution 298
Lévi-Strauss, Claude 115, 165
Lewis, C. S. 11–12
lexis 80, 83
liberalism 3, 4, 5, 59, 89, 94–5, 106,
  180–1, 186, 193, 198, 200–4, 214,
  236, 302
Lincoln, Abraham 87, 96, 182, 187,
  223
literary history 6, 58, 62, 70, 137,
  144–5, 217–19
Literary History of Canada 148
literature 1–2, 4, 5, 35, 107, 161,
  172–82, 199, 210–11, 230, 302; as
  dream 176–7
Locke, John 26–8, 42, 50, 106,
  173, 182, 187
logic 87–8, 100, 107, 187, 229, 247
Logos/logos 37, 74, 117–18, 139,
  212–13, 218–19, 230–1, 249, 263
London 285–7, 289, 303
Longinus 68, 86, 231
Lovejoy, Arthur 143, 235
Lucian 280
Luther, Martin 115
Lyotard, Jean-François 178; *grands
  récits* 178; *petits récits* 164, 178
Lytton, Bulwer 270–1
Lyly, John 76

McCarthyism 72, 181
Machiavelli, Niccoló 118, 208
McLuhan, Marshall 91, 105, 148,
  158, 165, 168, 194, 303
Macpherson, Jay 73
Mann, Thomas 213
Mao, Zedong 96
Marlowe, Christopher 274
Marx, Karl 64, 89, 107, 115, 118,
  159, 171, 184, 191–2, 195, 208,
  210, 214–15, 223, 237, 239
Marxism 5, 89, 91, 94, 96, 100, 114,
  123, 125–6, 129, 145, 147–9, 156,
  157, 171, 182, 185, 193, 195,

198–204, 212, 215, 219, 228–9,
  297–8, 303–4
meaning 4, 70, 90, 95, 198, 211;
  polysemous 111, 116, 138–9, 198,
  262
Menander 67
Menippean satire (Varronian satire)
  42, 61, 84, 264, 282–3
metanoia 131
metaphor 1, 87–90, 95, 97, 118,
  123–5, 157, 195–7, 205, 212, 219,
  223–34, 246, 249, 256, 260–2, 305
metaphysics 207, 301–2; of presence
  138
Middle Ages 54, 74, 222, 264, 274,
  297
Mill, John Stuart 19, 58, 86, 89, 107,
  160, 173, 182–3, 302
Milton, John 1, 6, 14, 16, 24, 27, 31,
  41, 46, 55, 65, 86–7, 95–6, 109,
  116, 141, 160, 170–1, 252, 258,
  293
mimesis/representation 73, 231;
  realism 75, 79, 219; Soviet/Nazi
  realism 275–9
Mirandola, Pico della 247
Mitchell, W. J. T. 205
Modern Century, The 146, 148,
  182–4, 214, 257
modernism 6, 164, 220–1
Montaigne, Michel Eyquem de 253
More, Thomas 106, 187, 247, 283
Morris, William 52, 99, 274, 300
Mozart, Wolfgang Amadeus 138, 292
music 46, 72, 146, 264, 291–3;
  melos 80, 87
Mussolini, Benito 97
mystery 70–1; mysticism 242–4
myth: criticism 1–2, 69, 192; Frye's
  central 90–1; of progress 157
mythological conditioning 102, 114;
  figures: Apollo 67, Attis 284–5,
  Eros 238, 249, 285, Prometheus
  240, 275, 285, Venus 105, 249,
  279
mythology 1, 3, 73, 88–108, 115,
  147, 153–4, 177–8, 191–265,
  296; as ur-literature 1;
  displacement/displaced 67, 75;
  open and closed 99–108,

148, 187–8; social 180–3
mythos 67–70, 74–80, 83, 88, 67–70,
74–80, 83, 101, 120, 194–5, 201,
212, 219, 230

narrative 6, 73–6, 92, 101, 120, 132,
134–6, 152, 178, 199–200, 210,
220, 224, 268, 300–5; anecdote
295, 304
Nazism 14, 18, 51, 100, 241, 275–9,
285–7
Nelligan, Emile 146
Nero 132
New Criticism 2, 63, 69–70, 91–2,
144–5, 149, 153–6, 159, 174, 195,
220, 223–5, 281, 297–8
New Democratic Party (NDP) 2,
149; Commonwealth
Confederation Party (CCF) 1–2
new historicism 47, 150, 152, 156,
165, 185, 215, 300
Newman, John Henry 107, 169, 173
Newton, Isaac 28–9, 42, 58
Nietzsche, Friedrich 33, 37, 118,
126, 140, 159, 184, 208, 302–4
Norris, Christopher 196–7
Northrop Frye in Conversation 7,
306
Northrop Frye on Shakespeare 150,
258

Olivier, Laurence 287
Ong, Walter 114, 158
opsis 80, 87
order: of types 116, 128–32; of
words 62, 70, 72, 116–28
Origen 247
Orwell, George 95
Ossian 41
'Our Monthly Current' 293
Ovid 27, 224

Paine, Tom 106
Paracelsus 247–8, 272
Parker, Patricia 304
Parks, Rosa 166
pastoral 133, 180
Pascal, Blaise 207
Pater, Walter 179, 218–19
Paul, St 119, 138, 232, 261

Pavel, Thomas 122
Peacock, Thomas Love 98, 283
Peele, George 279
Perse, St John 180
Petronius 85
pharmakos/scapegoat 67, 75–6
philosophy 59–61, 68, 88–90, 130,
144, 181, 205, 212, 219, 305;
philosophus gloriosus 42, 84
Plato 21–3, 31, 36, 40, 59, 61,
68, 81, 90, 106, 111, 117, 120,
131, 159–62, 173, 187, 192, 198,
207–8, 212–13, 226–7, 231, 247,
265, 283, 296, 303
Plautus 76
Plotinus 244, 247, 249
pnematikos 119
Poe, Edgar Allan 10, 220
poetics 62–3, 68–9, 90, 150,
222–34, 296–305; poetic
universals 74
poetry/poets 1, 5, 21, 90–1, 95–8,
144, 179, 192, 197, 205, 213–14,
219, 222–34; Frye as poet 293–4
politics/political criticism 1, 147,
152, 156, 175, 301; political
correctness 189
Poor, Richard (N. Frye) 274
Pope, Alexander 41, 173, 196, 272
Popper, Karl 9
Porter, Katherine Anne 273
post-colonialism 150, 152, 165;
imperialism 97, 194, 302
post-modernism 93, 164, 178, 207,
300–1
post-structuralism 151, 153, 164,
178, 299–300; *see also*
deconstruction
Pound, Ezra 14, 97, 204, 224, 278–9
Pratt, E. J. 294
praxis 86, 124
'Prelude, The' 274, 279
propaganda 4, 102, 121, 175–9
prophecy 40, 96, 103, 130–1, 220,
234, 246, 252, 273; *vates* 41
Protestant tradition 1, 5, 40, 55,
247–8; Anabaptists 248; Puritans
48; Quakers 248; Reformation 40,
247, 249; United Church of
Canada 264

Proust, Marcel 179
psychological/psychoanalytical
    criticism 1, 91, 215; *see also*
    Freudian criticism, Jung
Ptolemy 235
Pushkin, Alexander 182
Pynchon, Thomas 287

Quiet Consummation 267, 294

Rabelais, François 42–3, 85
radicalism 4, 190, 211
reactionary, the 5, 171, 190
readers/reading 2, 6–7, 66, 79, 92,
    101, 132, 141, 153, 158, 176, 221,
    225, 231–2, 256, 265
Reagan, Ronald 186
reason 88, 245–6; *ratio* 88
recreation 132, 254, 257, 259
religion 4, 74, 93, 201, 204–65;
    belief (faith/doubt) 101, 140–1,
    175, 183, 222, 228, 233;
    Buddhism 115, 134, 136;
    Hinduism 115, 289; idolatry 142,
    277; Islam 116, 129, 136; Judaism
    21; religious freedom 4;
    supernatural materialism 272;
    Taoism 115; theology 147,
    204–42, 255, 264; Zen Buddhism
    243, 273
Renaissance 31, 40, 52, 55, 179–80,
    247, 249, 253
resurrection 126, 131, 231, 240
'Resurgent, The' 58, 275–9
Return to Eden 258
Reuchlin, Johann 247
revelation 115, 120, 128, 227, 245,
    251
revolution 2, 4, 18, 32, 43, 89, 93–5,
    114, 129, 160, 171, 185, 199–200,
    239, 275–9, 302
Reynolds, Joshua 28
rhetoric/rhetorical criticism 72,
    79–80, 86–92, 120–1, 132,
    136–41, 157, 180, 208, 212, 220–
    4, 231–4, 241, 304; *oratio* 88
romance 6, 77, 84–5, 178, 257–9,
    296
Romanticism 6, 11, 31, 52, 54, 58,
    68, 81, 96, 114, 120, 159, 174,

177, 194, 196–7, 205, 210, 222,
    235, 239, 253, 274–5, 297
Rosenberg, A. 14
Rosenberg, Julius and Ethel 166
Rousseau, Jean-Jacques 88, 90, 106,
    173, 187, 196–97, 219, 229, 239
Rubin, Jerry 165, 168
Ruskin, John 52, 60, 114
Russell, Bertrand 88
Ruysbroeck, Jan van 227

Sainte-Beuve, Charles Augustin 60
St John of the Cross 244
Said, Edward 157, 302
Salusinszky, Imre 7
Sandler, Robert 258
Santayana, George 268
Sartre, Jean Paul 130
satire 40, 48, 52, 78–9, 98, 181, 265,
    281, 287–8, 293, 296–7
Scala, Can Grande della 247–8
Schiller, Friedrich 67, 92, 197
science 1, 12, 72, 88, 100, 118, 181,
    230; mathematics 161
Shakespeare, William 6, 16, 55, 76,
    86, 101, 130, 138, 150, 155, 158,
    162, 182, 213, 217, 220, 224, 227,
    235, 240, 243, 253, 255, 258, 262,
    280, 292, 296
Shaw, George Bernard 30, 50, 64,
    292
Shelley, Percy Bysshe 1–2, 23, 96,
    98, 103, 120, 173, 192, 219, 239,
    274–5, 300
Showalter, Elaine 178
Sidney, Philip 1, 23, 59, 86, 95–6,
    173, 192, 210, 213–14, 300, 303
social 1, 6; contract 106, 187–8;
    criticism 4; mythology 106;
    science 1, 2; vision 5
Socrates 111, 207–8, 212, 281, 283;
    pre-Socratics 301
soma pneumatikon 232, 261; *see also*
    dreaming body
soma psychikon 232
Sophocles 55
sparmakos 77
Spengler, Oswald 12, 18, 75, 297
Spenser, Edmund 13, 27, 41, 54–6,
    77, 236, 249, 264, 296, 300

Spiritus Mundi 148–9, 254, 257–8
Spivak, Gayatri 157, 165–6;
subaltern studies 165
Sprat, Thomas 88
Stalin, Joseph 235, 275
Sterne, Laurence 41, 43
Stevens, Wallace 134, 174, 258, 304
structuralism 2, 153, 174; structure
42, 92, 115–16, 154, 177–8, 206,
224, 256, 296–305
Stubborn Structure, The 149
student movement (1960s) 2, 18,
149, 164–72, 184–8, 288–9;
Students for a Democratic Society
(SDS) 167, 186
subjectivity/objectivity 86, 92, 100,
118–20, 132, 159, 219, 226–8,
245–6, 251–2
Swedenborg, Immanuel 35, 272–3
Swift, Jonathan 43, 61, 85, 140–1
system/scheme 2, 6, 62, 192, 205,
208–9, 302–3; Empirical Science
of Literature 302–3; empirical
study of literature 300;
Polysystem Theory 302–3

teaching 109, 111–12, 115, 153,
179–80, 183, 189, 227
techne 68
technology, media 96–108, 164–90,
217
temenos 93
Tennyson, Alfred 82, 274
Theobald 55
theoretical imagination 1–24
theoria 80, 124, 154, 160
theory 1–2, 5–6, 35, 153–4;
morphology of symbolism 41;
symboliste poets 68, 220; of
symbols 37– 8, 54–6, 68–74, 86,
195–7, 234–5, 264; of unity 60;
vulgarized 298–9
Thomas, Dylan 96
Thoreau, Henry David 103, 187, 289
Tillyard, E. M. W. 143, 235
time 262–5, 293
Tolstoy, Leo 58, 289
'To My Beloved's Shoes' 293
Toronto 2, 109, 206, 289–90

totalitarianism 2, 3, 48, 58, 97, 128,
186, 188, 275–9, 285–7
Tower of Babel 90, 181–2, 256
Toynbee, Arnold 12
tradition/cultural tradition 86, 89,
93–5, 114, 221–2, 297–305
tragedy 77–9, 83, 124, 178; catharsis
76, 176; *pathos* 77
Trilling, Lionel 182
Trotsky, Leon 213
T. S. Eliot, 297–8
typological criticism 85–6
typology 13, 56, 60–1, 77, 85–6,
115–16, 125–6, 134–5, 171, 257,
264

USA 4, 101–3, 144, 148–9, 152,
165–90, 290, 305
universities: Berkeley 16, 104, 166,
168–9, 184, 186; Columbia 168;
Cornell 187; Duke 184; Harvard
13, 298; McMaster 146; Oxford 3,
11; Queen's 184, 187;
Saskatchewan 184; Toronto 104,
109, 168, 172, 206
university 2, 3, 5, 106–7, 164–90,
291–3
University of Toronto Quarterly
146
utopia 3, 106, 155, 160, 162, 169,
182, 184, 187–8, 200, 240, 257,
282–5, 298

value judgements 16, 63, 176
Vanzetti, Bartolomeo 87
Vaughan, Thomas 248
Vico, Giambattista 93, 114, 117,
119, 231, 233, 304
Vietnam 17, 102, 185
Virgil 46, 97, 212
vision 5, 25–55, 62, 68, 71–2, 84–6,
89, 101–2, 108, 114–15, 134, 138–41,
171, 180, 184, 188, 196, 212, 223,
226–65, 267, 270, 273, 291, 297,
305; of love 228, 249, 262–3
visionary criticism 51–2, 62, 71,
188, 196, 205, 243–65, 267
Voltaire 3, 199
'War on the Cultural Front' 276, 287
Well-Tempered Critic, The 146

Wells, H. G. 97
Weltgeschichte 122
White, Hayden 120, 144, 150, 152, 157
Whitehead, Alfred North 12, 207
Whitman, Walt 103, 187
Whore of Babylon 255
Wilde, Oscar 23, 179, 218–19,
  266–7; art for art's sake 58
Williams, Raymond 57, 149–50,
  158, 195
Williams, C. W. S. 270
Wimsatt, W. K. 149, 197
wisdom 130, 188, 240
women, representations of 49, 51,
  105–6, 133, 141, 237–8
Woolf, Virginia 59, 213

Words with Power 7–8, 10–11, 26,
  38, 44, 85, 109, 153–4, 190–1,
  193, 205–42, 259–60, 264, 277,
  281, 297–8, 300
Wordsworth, William 23, 25, 41,
  174, 196–7, 205
World War II 204, 285–7
writing 1, 6, 46–7, 59, 82–3, 88,
  120, 145–6, 158–9, 173, 214–15,
  219, 221, 225–6, 254, 264,
  266–95, 299; *écriture/écriture
  feminine* 295

Yeats, William Butler 6–7, 14, 174,
  204, 221, 232–3, 236, 246, 267,
  278–9